The City in the Roman West, c. 250 BC

The city is widely regarded as the most characteristic expression of the social, cultural and economic formations of the Roman Empire. This was especially true in the Latin-speaking West, where urbanism was much less deeply ingrained than in the Greek-speaking East but where networks of cities grew up during the centuries following conquest and occupation. This up-to-date and well-illustrated synthesis provides students and specialists alike with an overview of the development of the city in Italy, Gaul, Britain, Germany, Spain and North Africa, whether their interests lie in ancient history, Roman archaeology or the wider history of urbanism. It accounts not only for the city's geographical and temporal spread and its associated monuments (such as amphitheatres and baths), but also for its importance to the rulers of the Empire as well as the provincials and locals.

RAY LAURENCE is Professor of Roman History and Archaeology at the University of Kent. He has published widely on the history of Ancient Rome, including *Roman Pompeii: Space and Society* (2nd edition, 2007), *The Roman Empire: Rome and its Environs* (*The Traveller's Guide to the Ancient World*) (2008) and *Roman Passions: A History of Pleasure in Imperial Rome* (2009).

SIMON ESMONDE CLEARY is Reader in Archaeology at the University of Birmingham. His previous books include *The Ending of Roman Britain* (1989) and *Rome in the Pyrenees: Lugdunum and the* Convenae *from the First Century BC to the Seventh Century AD* (2007).

GARETH SEARS is Lecturer in Ancient History at the University of Birmingham. He is the author of *Late Roman African Urbanism* (2007).

The City in the Roman West
c. 250 BC – *c.* AD 250

RAY LAURENCE

SIMON ESMONDE CLEARY

GARETH SEARS

CAMBRIDGE
UNIVERSITY PRESS

CAMBRIDGE UNIVERSITY PRESS
Cambridge, New York, Melbourne, Madrid, Cape Town,
Singapore, São Paulo, Delhi, Mexico City

Cambridge University Press
The Edinburgh Building, Cambridge CB2 8RU, UK

Published in the United States of America by Cambridge University Press, New York

www.cambridge.org
Information on this title: www.cambridge.org/9780521701402

© Ray Laurence, Simon Esmonde Cleary and Gareth Sears 2011

This publication is in copyright. Subject to statutory exception
and to the provisions of relevant collective licensing agreements,
no reproduction of any part may take place without the written
permission of Cambridge University Press.

First published 2011
Reprinted 2012

Printed and bound by MPG Books Group, UK

A catalogue record for this publication is available from the British Library.

Library of Congress Cataloguing in Publication data
Laurence, Ray, 1963–
The city in the Roman West, c.250 BCc–c.AD 250 / Ray Laurence,
Simon Esmonde Cleary, Gareth Sears.
    p.   cm.
ISBN 978-0-521-70140-2 (pbk.)
1. Cities and towns – Rome.   2. Urbanization – Rome.   3. Sociology, Urban – Rome.
4. City planning – Rome.   I. Esmonde Cleary, A. S. (A. Simon)   II. Sears, Gareth,
1977–   III. Title.
DG70.A1L38   2011
307.760937–dc22
2010053225

ISBN 978-0-521-87750-3 Hardback
ISBN 978-0-521-70140-2 Paperback

Cambridge University Press has no responsibility for the persistence or
accuracy of URLs for external or third-party internet websites referred to
in this publication, and does not guarantee that any content on such
websites is, or will remain, accurate or appropriate.

Contents

Illustrations

Preface

The city is widely regarded as the most characteristic expression of the social, cultural and economic formations of the Roman empire, perhaps especially in the Latin-speaking areas of the empire where urbanism was much less deeply engrained than in the Greek East. Yet there is no textbook (or book for that matter) that provides students with an overview of the city in the western Roman Empire. There are numerous reasons for this, one being that most academics focus on the study of the city in a single province or within a limited geographical region. We took a step to overcome this limitation to our understanding of the Roman city and began a dialogue that shared our expertise on the Roman city in North Africa (Sears); in Italy (Laurence) and in the North-West provinces (Esmonde Cleary). This three-way discussion produced some unexpected results that altered the way we conceived of the Roman city: certainly all of us gained from the experience. What it showed was that any single region could not encapsulate the variation in form, time and space associated with the Roman city. The results of our discussion are presented here.

We have used standard conventions and abbreviations for referring to ancient authors; these can be found in *The Oxford Classical Dictionary* (2nd edition edited by S. Hornblower and A.J. Spawforth) and for abbreviations of journals see *L'Année Epigraphique*. Although we have included numerous plans and illustrations etc., we refer readers to *The Barrington Atlas of the Greek and Roman World* (edited by R.J.A. Talbert) for locations of cities mentioned in the text.

We wish to acknowledge the support of colleagues in the Institute of Archaeology and Antiquity at the University of Birmingham, in particular Henry Buglass and Graham Norrie who went beyond the call of duty in the production of the line drawings and photographs respectively and deserve our warmest thanks. Michael Sharp at Cambridge University Press has consistently provided support for this project. The comments of the five anonymous referees, three who reported on the original proposal and two who reported on the text, have our warmest thanks for raising a number of issues that we had not foreseen. Sections of the book have been read by students at Birmingham, who offered further comments on the ease of use of the volume from their perspective. It has not been possible to take account of publications appearing since May 2009.

Introduction

The city is a wonderfully complex entity; it can be defined as either a physical space of architecture, or as a people living in a single place, or as both of these. Within these definitions a myriad other elements emerge that make the city a very slippery object of analysis. This is as true of the multiple entities categorised as 'the Roman city' as it is of any other urban form. Indeed, the idea that there was a single category, 'the Roman city', in the western half of the Mediterranean basin throughout the period of almost half a millennium that is the subject of this book, does not stand up to more than a few seconds' scrutiny. Indeed, one of the central tenets of this book is that what we see across this huge area and long time-scale is the working out by numerous local communities of their relationship to Rome as expressed through the almost infinite variations on common themes of urban form and urban structures which were first generated in Italy and then adopted and adapted in the provinces. Moreover, analysis of the Roman city has been shaped by a series of explicit and often implicit theoretical positions rather than by any single agreed narrative or type of explanation. Some of these positions have been articulated with reference to social theory, although much that is written on the Roman city has relied on empiricism and reference to an undefined 'common sense'. The Roman city has also featured in debates among scholars of the Roman Empire over Romanisation (and resistance), imperialism, the economy, cultural identity, discrepant experience, and phenomenology, to name but a few.[1] We do not intend to rehearse these general debates here,[2] nor to summarise the views of other authors (references are provided and these can be read at first hand). Instead we wish here to explain our view of the Roman city in the light of these discussions in order to articulate the conceptual and theoretical positions which underpin the chapters that follow.

---

[1] See for example on Romanisation: Mattingly (2004) for the provinces needs to be read with Mouritsen (1998), pp. 69–86 on Romanisation in Italy; on imperialism: Mouritsen (1998); papers in Mattingly (1997); see also Laurence (2001a).

[2] It would in any case fill a whole book: see Hingley (2005).

THE CITY AND ROMANISATION

For the last century cities have been considered by scholars to be the backbone of the Roman Empire, and it is safe to say that a Roman Empire without cities was an historical impossibility. Archaeologically, Roman cities can be identified right across western Europe and North Africa because of common (which is certainly not to say uniform and universal) features of their layout and the provision of monumental buildings and the functions those buildings discharged (e.g. street-grids, fora, baths, theatres, temples). What is particularly interesting is that in some areas the city had not existed in the Roman form prior to their incorporation into the Roman Empire, and, even where the city had existed previously, as, for example, in Italy and North Africa, we find a complete transformation of the urban form during the two centuries after 200 BC.

Roman urbanism had a dynamic to it that can be understood in terms of change and development – whether in the city of Rome, in Pompeii, or in Colchester. A hundred years ago, Francis Haverfield (author of *Ancient Town Planning*) and his colleagues would have viewed these changes in the light of their own experience of the workings of contemporary European empires and their understanding of cultural change.[3] Haverfield viewed the Roman city as part of a natural evolution, in which the savage barbarians became more 'civilised' and adopted a pure form of urbanism based on small-scale settlements with planned straight streets and an architecture that engaged not only with taste in ancient Rome, but also with the taste for modern neo-classical architecture that dominated the major cities of Europe and the United States of America in the first decade of the twentieth century.[4] The ideas from the observation of the modern city underpinning this interpretation of the Roman city were also closely associated with the spread of the city and the development of a concept of cultural change called 'Romanisation' – a term that was to shape the way the spread of Roman material culture in the past was understood throughout the twentieth century. Much, or even too much, has been written on the subject of Romanisation; but, intriguingly, relatively little has been said about the role of the city in the process of cultural change.[5] When, however, we view the urban development of a particular geographical area over time, it is clear that, although towns were founded and new architectural forms may have appeared in the century following conquest by Rome, the process of

---

[3] Freeman (1997) and (2007).   [4] Laurence (1994).   [5] Although see now Revell (2009).

town-building and urban development seems to have ceased or slowed down over time. Moreover, not everywhere in the Roman Empire developed cities to the same extent or with the same speed. For example, in Africa cities continued to add new monuments right through the third century AD, whereas some areas of Gaul at this time were undergoing major transformations in urban form and functions. Even within a single province we can identify quite different trajectories of urban development. These patterns are set out in this book and lead us to conclude that urban development did not coincide with an inevitable process of evolution spreading out from the Mediterranean as conceived by Haverfield and others a century ago.

The last two decades have seen an unpicking of the very idea of Romanisation. It has changed from denoting a process of acculturation of an elite-led society, according to which both provincials and Romans (however defined) became different, towards representing a more dynamic vision of cultural expression within the Roman Empire, according to which individuals engaged or disengaged with the dominant culture of Romanness in quite different and even undefined ways to produce a physical manifestation of their identity.[6] This approach allows us to envisage a global idea of Roman culture that was viewed differently according to the perspective of the individual. This view of cultural change under the Roman Empire at the level of the individual works rather well, if read from an inscribed tombstone, but becomes more problematic when dealing with collective entities such as cities. A city was by its nature a co-operative venture that required not just monuments and cemeteries but also a population which ensured its survival over a longer period than the life-span of a single individual. A man or a woman could contribute to the development of a city by building a temple, a forum, a theatre, or an amphitheatre – an action that can be read in the light of the newly defined emphasis on individual identity within the discipline of Roman archaeology. What is more difficult to read, however, is the development of a collective ideology or local *mentalité* over a time span longer than a single generation, and that saw a city as a physical entity and/or *habitus* ('lived environment'), which should be attractive and desirable and through which the population's collective identity could be manifested and displayed to outsiders.[7] In the context of a recently created province, the Roman city may have been viewed as a novelty, perhaps already experienced by some provincial inhabitants as a result of travel to other parts of the Roman Empire. At the same time, the knowledge that

---

[6] Now fully discussed in Revell (2009).
[7] As posited recently by Creighton (2006) and Revell (2009).

cities were being developed by neighbouring social groups would have increased the speed with which Roman urban forms were adopted or adapted locally. The impulse to construct a city, in whatever form, need not have been connected to a conscious understanding of cultural difference or a conscious choice to become more Roman. Indeed, it may be that the cultural form of the city, with its charter and regulations, presented a new set of opportunities to create not just identity but a sense of place, and it was an urban way of life rather than Romanness that was desirable.

THE URBAN PRODUCTION OF ROMAN CITIZENS

Throughout this book we wish not only to describe the development of cities under Roman rule, but also to emphasise their role in the production of Roman citizens. The language used in discussing the creation and development of cities was a distinctly Roman phenomenon. At this point, we need to define what we mean by the term 'Roman'. This is quite difficult because the Romans never provided a definition and were themselves aware that the basis for a Roman identity was subject to change. The best understanding of 'Roman' would be as something distinctive from both Greek and barbarian cultures, and exemplified by the use of Latin in official documents, the presence of bathing facilities in cities, the wearing of togas by officials, and the use of a central place in the city, a forum, for public business. These features provided a distinctive set of symbols from which a Roman identity was articulated to a greater or lesser extent according to an individual's choice and the time and place of their existence.[8] In the language of the city people expressed their identity as citizens of the city, or *municipes*, and even in a colony we find colonists of that place rather than Romans, and an identity primarily based on a legal definition of citizenship. In the cities of the provinces, it was legally only those people who had been municipal magistrates or their descendants who were Roman citizens. It was only after contributing to the maintenance of the city through holding civic office that a person could become a Roman citizen; the rate in most cities was about four persons *per annum*. At first sight this seems a small rate of change, but cumulatively, over a large number of cities in a province and over a period of a generation, the process would have produced an elite group of Roman citizens. So the Roman city, which was apparently in itself a desirable cultural form for those who adopted it, also produced a Roman

---

[8] See Revell (2009).

elite across the provinces of the Roman West, most of which had in some way contributed to the maintenance and/or development of urbanism. It was these men who were also involved in the collection of taxes at the local level and who interacted directly with the representatives of the Roman state – governors, procurators and their entourages. In every case these interactions occurred between people who shared the same legal status of Roman citizenship, but whose social and political status was quite unequal. The impetus for the creation of Roman citizens within the cities seems to have come from Rome, with its ideal of government by means of cities which through their town charters would produce ex-magistrates who were Roman citizens. While the provincials may have regarded a city as an advantageous material form, the Romans saw it as a means to govern an empire and to create a local elite of Roman citizens, who would collect the taxes. Hence, within the *mentalité* of both governor and procurators on the one hand and the provincials on the other, urbanism was a material and geographical development that was viewed as desirable. These desires integrated the Roman city with an imperial project to dominate territory and to extract taxes from that territory in order to maintain an army and feed the population of the city of Rome. For the Roman Empire to reproduce itself over time, it needed to produce and maintain a network of central places or cities from which it might extract taxes and within which social and economic surpluses could be utilised for the expression of an urban way of life.

At the heart of this book lies an understanding of Roman culture based on the reproduction of that culture in an urban context over time and space from the middle of the third century BC through to the early to mid-third century AD (a conception drawn from the work of Henri Lefebvre). Roman culture for the most part reproduced itself in an urban context, whilst at the same time the city formed part of the reproduction of society over time and was the institution that gave a unity to the Roman Empire. Interestingly, in Europe the spread of the Roman-style city did not extend beyond the boundaries of the Roman Empire and was not spontaneously adopted by barbarians inhabiting the ancient territories equivalent to modern Scotland, Denmark, Poland and much of Germany. Roman society pro-duced cities, and was at the same time produced in cities, by which the countryside could be said to have been urbanised/Romanised to a lesser or greater degree according to the strength of its connection to the city. The symbiotic relationship between a people and the physical space termed a city or *polis* has been thoroughly interrogated by others and we can safely conclude that both the physical space, into which a person was born, and their own actions, or agency, will shape the form and identity of a place.[9] Within the period covered by this book we can identify urban environments in a state of becoming different and taking on new physical characteristics, whether at the point of foundation or through the development of new urban forms. These manifestations represented some of the stimulating effects of the urban habitat in the Roman West. They lay at the heart of what we may see as a culture of cities unevenly distributed across the Roman West.

Running in parallel with the concept of the urban reproduction of Roman society is a recognition that the city, however that concept may have been defined, was an object or social formation that recently conquered provincials could find attractive. New towns might then develop in areas where the population may have created nucleated settlements, but had not had experience of, or seen cause to reproduce, the aesthetics of Roman urbanism. The latter can be seen most clearly in the adoption of architectural types: fora, grids of streets, temples, theatres, and amphitheatres (Chapters 6, 7, 8, 9 and 10). These features of urbanism were not adopted uniformly, and variation in the adoption of the architecture of Roman urbanism in time and space provides us with a means to understand variation in the city phenomenon within the Empire in the West. What we find across Italy and the western provinces is unevenness in the distribution of monuments; which is in itself interesting, and points to a considerable degree of variation in the shape of the urban landscape, when we attempt to compare regions or even make comparisons between cities within the same region. This variation on a common theme of urban form should be regarded as an aspect of the cultural reproduction of cities in the Roman Empire, by which any one city might make itself remarkable through the development of additional monuments. These not only contributed to an urban way of life, but also developed a greater sense of Romanness as well. The uneven pattern of urban development across the Western Empire should not surprise us. Programmed into the Roman city was a sense of difference. This sometimes asserted itself in the view that a monument was needed because another city had one, or at other times in the view that a monument found in a neighbouring city or a city in Italy was simply undesirable. In part, the development of urban form in any one city reflected the relation of that city with elite networks of patronage that could release economic resources for expenditure in that particular city.

---

[9] Giddens (1984).

THE SUSTAINABILITY OF THE ROMAN CITY

We shall frequently draw attention to the sustainability of the city over time and consider the fragility of Roman urbanism. Some cities today are well known for having become settlements of intense poverty and community conflict, whereas others can be seen as centres for social, economic and political development. In observing the cities of the Roman Empire through archaeological remains, we are able to chart the manifestation of sustainability in terms of the rather unequal distribution of, and expenditure on, economic resources on public monuments. Yet in many (but not all) cities of the Roman West an urban population developed alongside the monuments of the elite; and we have to admit that people were attracted to the city as a place within which new opportunities could be found that were not available previously, or within the countryside. Sustainability, for the Roman city, depended on an elite with the finance to build and to maintain the physical fabric of monumental space, and a non-elite population that believed that living in proximity to the monuments of the elite improved their lives (or was at least not deleterious to them). What is perhaps remarkable about the cities of the Roman West is that in many cases (but not all) there were the resources and will to sustain urbanism over periods of between 100 and 300 or more years. One factor that may have been key to sustainability, often overlooked as a given within the Roman city, was the management of elite conflict by the development of a series of rules or a town charter that, intentionally or unintentionally, created a dynamic of elite competition while managing to prevent that competition from developing a dynamic of violence. Of course, a city could cease to be sustainable, if there was no longer an elite willing to take part in the competitive development of the city's urban fabric and monuments over time, or one which walked away from the idea of maintaining the city in the longer term (concepts that are developed fully in the final chapter of the book).

The sustainability of cities has an economic aspect, as does the building of public architecture, and not surprisingly this question has proved of great interest to ancient historians and archaeologists. Moses Finley did more than any scholar in the late twentieth century to shape the parameters of the debate. He reintroduced into ancient history the model of the consumer city: in which the ancient city, unlike the medieval city, did not produce wealth itself but instead consumed the wealth of the countryside.[10]

---

[10] Finley (1973) and (1977).

What underpins the model are the notions that surplus wealth was concentrated in the cities of the Empire and that these were the places where a surplus was disposed of; in contrast Finley conceived of the medieval city as a place of production for export. Rather crudely, Finley could state that the ancient world did not produce the architecture of guild buildings found in the medieval world. However, recent re-examination of both the role and types of medieval guilds and the collective activities of Roman *collegia* (guilds or clubs) suggests that these urban institutions had rather more in common than Finley had suggested.[11] Moreover, the distinction between ancient and medieval cities in terms of productivity has been questioned by Wim Jongman, who has demonstrated with reference to wool production in Italy that the network of cities may have been just as productive as the urban networks of the medieval period.[12] Part of the problem with the consumer city model is that it views the city and its hinterland in isolation, whereas in reality the city exists in a much wider system of economic relationships.[13] These are difficult to define, but we need to recognise that the construction or sustainability of a Roman city may have depended on economic factors at a global rather than a local level. For example, Pliny the Younger owned estates in several parts of Italy, but the key source of the substantial sums of money (which he donated to fund the construction and maintenance of buildings in his hometown of Como) was inheritances from friends, associates and relatives.[14] These indicate an alternative means for concentrating surplus wealth at a single location, which did not involve the city's rural hinterland in any way.

The realisation that the city and its hinterland are in some ways a distraction in the writing of economic history (in its widest Braudelian sense) led Peregrine Horden and Nicholas Purcell to regard the emphasis on writing a history of cities in antiquity as irrelevant.[15] What these authors have suggested is that the city existed as a stable location or address through which resources flowed and it was the connectivity between cities that was the determining factor in development. For example, Claudius' conquest of Britain was accompanied by elite finance which produced loans to the new provincials so that they might realise their aspirations for new forms of cultural consumption. Famously the loans were recalled in AD 60 and were a factor in triggering the revolt of Boudicca.[16] There is more to

---

[11] Epstein (1991), pp. 10–40; Black (1992); Susan Reynolds (*pers. comm.*).

[12] Jongman (2000).   [13] Whittaker (1995), p. 22.

[14] See the discussion in Duncan-Jones (1990), pp. 174–84 on the costs of building cities, to be read with Duncan-Jones (1982) on costs and finances of senators.

[15] Horden and Purcell (2000).   [16] See Laurence (2001b) for a discussion.

this, though. Cities were stable and continued to exist in antiquity because they were known places, which were fixed by geography and recognised as political entities (even if like a 'rotten borough' in early nineteenth-century England they lacked a population). However, their sustainability depended on a flow of resources through them, and their ability to extract those resources for the maintenance of urbanism and their public buildings. If a city was disconnected from the global flow of resources, it was likely to fail or shrink to a level of urbanism that could be sustained solely by the economic surplus derived from its immediate rural hinterland.[17] What needs to be recognised in this process is that the city was very effective in extracting a surplus from the flow of resources and, in so doing, created a concentration of resources (in terms of population, economic wealth, cultural capital, and so on), that underpinned a distinctive material form within which a particular 'way of life' was pursued that was markedly different from that found in the countryside.[18] Only once the city is established as a stable nucleation does this distinctive 'way of life' emerge, with the population engaging in politics, economics, religion, etc. with a greater intensity from that found at locations in the surrounding countryside.

A DISTINCTLY ROMAN CITY

This book is more concerned with the construction of the public city and its relationship to the city's inhabitants than with these matters. We nevertheless recognise that behind the construction of the architecture and spaces of the cities of the Roman West lie men, women and children. Some are named in inscriptions providing us with an indication of their lives that is far from objective.[19] These epigraphic indicators of the agency behind the construction of individual monuments will be referred to, but we need to accept at the outset that we do not know much, or even in some cases anything at all, about the persons who decided that a city should exist, that money should be spent on its maintenance, and that a city would be a form of *habitus* suitable for them and their dependents. Even with the best preservation, if not the fullest publication, a site such as Pompeii fails to elucidate the nature of gender divisions, female identities, the formation of identity in childhood, or answers to simple questions such as: was this

---

[17] See Patterson (2006b) for a discussion; also Horden and Purcell (2000); Laurence (2001b) and (1999).
[18] Wirth (1938).   [19] See Revell (2009) for further discussion.

house inhabited by a man and his dependents or a woman and her dependents? Their identities are formulated in the tombs outside the city with their inscriptions and images that were reminders of their achievements in life to be remembered by the community after their deaths.[20] We also need to be quite clear that most cities in the Roman West (apart from Rome, Ostia and Carthage) had relatively small populations ranging from a few thousand up to 25,000. By the standards of the modern world, these settlements were extremely small, representing populations of a similar range to those found in a small college and a large university (from Lampeter [University of Wales] to the University of Birmingham). Cohesive social relations within these population centres would have been maintained through informal and formal face-to-face contacts between acquaintances and ritualised formal contact with strangers, and where necessary were formalised by a set of rules or a town charter.

This book sets out to map the changes in a distinctly Roman, as opposed to Greek, urbanism that developed in the late third century BC at Rome and drew on Greek and Italian traditions of the city to produce new ideas of the city (chapters 1 to 4). Following this Introduction is a series of chapters which are concerned either with the mechanisms of foundation, and therefore with the actions of the elite, or with types of public monuments. We are also concerned, however, with the cultural production of citizens in urban space and the ways in which the public monuments and the activities associated with them create a *habitus* of Romanness that for some at least was complemented by Roman citizenship. We recognise that there is a corollary in private space: in housing, artisan activity and the use of material culture, but that is a different story of Roman urbanism that would require a volume of its own. The relationship of the urban forms under discussion to changes in the urban fabric of the city of Rome is discussed, but in a way that looks to Rome as a reference point or location of new ideas about what a city should look like or what monuments it should contain. Since it would take another volume to do justice to all the developments within the city of Rome, what we highlight are the important new developments within the capital that were of relevance to the shaping of the city in the rest of Italy and the provinces. Just as we cannot find space to examine Rome, we have also omitted the very distinct forms of urbanism found in Ostia and Portus – places that were fundamentally linked to the capital city and whose development was so entwined with that of the capital that their story is quite different from that of the cities under discussion in

---

[20] See also Mouritsen (2006).

this book. Equally, in a single volume, we cannot do justice to the development of the city in the Roman East – where the conception of Hellenism intersected with and sustained a rather different conception of Romanness. Our interest lies instead in the majority of cities spread across Italy and the western provinces that were much smaller, and with lower population densities. The intention is to break away from studies of cities within single provinces and also to move away from the use of a few examples that dominate the literature: Pompeii, Ostia, Rome, Sabratha, or Lepcis Magna. We seek to provide a spatial and temporal overview of change in the city across the Roman West down to the third century AD. What we find is a pattern of spatial and temporal change that is a far cry from a simple evolution of urban form derived from Rome; a pattern that gradually, through a process of conquest and osmosis, spread across what was to become western Europe (a pattern that is automatically jeopardised once the African provinces are included in the discussion). The cities of the Roman West developed in quite different ways, at different rates and at different times, perhaps reflecting changes in the concentration of wealth and in the desire to spend that wealth on urban building (for further discussion see Chapter 11). We conclude that the diverse pattern of change in cities is part of the overall pattern that can be described as Roman urbanism, and that the individual variation of a city from a perceived pattern of urbanism is a feature of Roman culture in the West.

1 | The creation of an urban culture

In trying to understand the Roman cities that appeared and developed in Italy and in the western provinces from 200 BC, we need to begin our discussion with an investigation of what the Romans thought urbanism was about, the forms it should take and what were they trying to make when they placed a new building in a city. To understand these concepts, we need to look at the developments within the city of Rome that were to alter the shape of that city, alongside a series of initiatives taken by the state in the *coloniae* (colonies) across Italy in the early second century BC, a period we see as crucial to the definition of a 'Roman' style of urban form and urban buildings (see fig.1.1). However, the developments in Rome and its *coloniae* did not occur in isolation. Contacts between Rome and the Hellenistic monarchies were intensifying from the late third century BC.[1] This contact between the world of Rome and that of the eastern Mediterranean would ultimately result in the conquest of Macedonia and the incorporation of the cities of Classical Greece into the Roman Empire in 167 BC. The attitude of the Roman aristocracy towards Hellenism was complex, but can be illustrated by the fact that we find a number of senators sporting knowledge of the Greek language but refusing to use it in an official capacity.[2] The Roman elite recognised that culturally the Hellenistic world had much to offer them and so drew on Hellenism and tended to absorb the culture, but deployed it selectively. Through diplomatic missions and warfare members of the Roman elite were exposed to a tradition of urbanism very different from that manifested at Rome, one marked by elements of formal planning, a range of public buildings and monuments and the use of elaborate architectural forms along with materials such as marble. This was particularly true of the leading political centres of the Hellenistic world such as Alexandria, Antioch and Pergamum, and of the great cultural centre of Athens, with all of which the Roman elite would have become progressively more familiar. The impact of contact with the East and Greek

---

[1] See the incisive summary of the relationship of the Roman elite to Greek culture in Gruen (1992), pp. 223–71.

[2] For further examples see: Gruen (1992), pp. 52–83 on Cato; Gruen (1992), p. 242 on Fabius Pictor; Reiter (1988), pp. 114–15 on Aemilius Paullus.

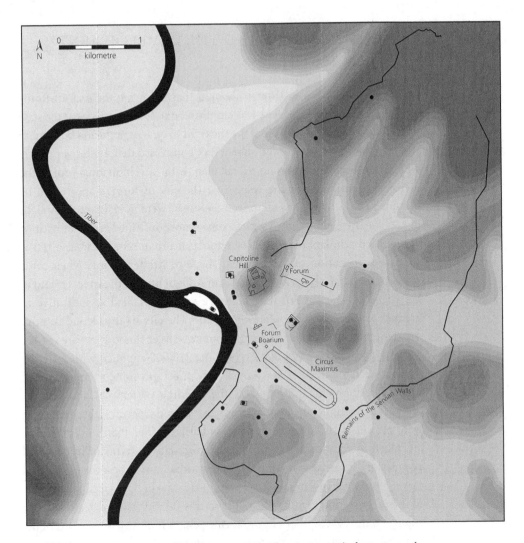

1.1 Mid-Republican Rome (late third century BC). The city centre is drawn towards the River Tiber. Its major monuments are found within this central area, temples (some indicated with black dots) have a wider distribution – often in prominent skyline positions.

culture can be seen in those independent cities of Italy such as Pompeii (see fig.1.2) that were themselves developing or adopting new building types and styles of architecture. These would have influenced Rome's view of the nature of urban life, whilst the acquisition of provinces, especially in the Iberian peninsula, provided new challenges to its definition. What we wish to examine in this first chapter is the development of an urban culture in the Roman West from about 200 BC down to the middle of the first century BC.

THE ROMAN STATE AND THE DEVELOPMENT OF URBANISM

There was a tradition in Roman thought that following the sack of Rome by the Gauls in 390 BC, the city was rapidly rebuilt. It is reported that the state provided tiles and granted everyone the right to quarry stone and cut timber wherever they liked, on condition that they completed their building projects within one year. There was no overall plan, with each individual project the focus of attention, with the result that the city of Rome appeared to be occupied rather than divided up, and the streets were not laid out in straight lines.[3] The truth behind the sack of Rome is not confirmed archaeologically, and has led scholars to see this statement of urban rebuilding as a retrospective explanation of the irregular shape of Rome's streets when compared to the carefully divided spaces and straight lines of the streets found in her *coloniae*. The pattern may be more easily explained as indicative of gradual or even rapid population growth.[4] The city by the second century may have had an irregular street grid, but its walls enclosed a vast area of 426 hectares containing a population of some 250,000 supplied with water by the hundred-year-old Aqua Appia. The most prominent monumental urban development at Rome was the building of temples and shrines. Some twenty-eight are known from the period 264–173 BC, but these were responses to vows made prior to battles rather than undertaken to embellish the city (fig.1.1). Although a mega-city in terms of its area and population, Rome was severely lacking in urban amenities: the public and private buildings of Rome were objects of ridicule in the Macedonian court of the early second century BC.[5] It is in this period that we begin to see a change in the development of urbanism as manifested by the actions of the censors, who were elected every five years and whose duties included the letting of contracts for state projects. These actions are represented in the surviving account of Livy covering the period 199–169 BC, and provide us with a snapshot of the thinking behind the development and embellishment not just of the city of Rome, but also of the *coloniae* of Rome within Italy.[6]

The five-yearly sequence begins in 199 BC with no public building works, but is followed in the next censorship (194 BC) with the rebuilding and enlargement of the Atrium Libertatis and Villa Publica.[7] The next censorship was involved in two major projects: the building of substructures to

---

[3] Livy, 5.55.3–5.   [4] Cornell (2000), p. 43.   [5] Livy, 40.5.7.
[6] Gros (1987), pp. 14–15.   [7] Livy, 32.7.1–3; 34.44.4–5.

expand the area of the Capitoline Hill and the paving of the Via Appia with basalt flagstones from the Porta Capena to the Temple of Mars outside the walls of the city.[8] The censorship of Cato the Elder and L. Valerius in 184 BC addressed the sorry state of the ever-expanding city: water-basins were now to be built from stone, the sewers were cleaned, new sewers were constructed on the Aventine Hill 'and elsewhere where none had been built', the Atrium Maenium, the Atrium Titium and the Basilica Porcia in the Forum were all constructed, as was a harbour mole at Aquae Neptunae, and a road was cut through the mountains at Formiae.[9] The language associated with these projects is of interest: *atrium* and *villa* were words synonymous with private architecture but were applied to public structures that, in the case of the Atrium Maenium and Atrium Titium, were later used for auctions,[10] whilst a *basilica* had an association with kingship and the Hellenistic East, but in Rome was utilised for courts of law, amongst other purposes. What was being constructed was a series of buildings for official business, legal business, and public meetings. Alongside the construction of these buildings, Livy describes the embellishment of the final section of the Via Appia into Rome, the artificial expansion of the Capitoline Hill, and improvements to the drainage and sanitation of the expanding city.

The next censorship (179 BC) saw further embellishment of the city and the development of an awareness of the aesthetics of architectural décor.[11] The Temple of Jupiter Optimus Maximus and its surrounding colonnades were cleaned and whitened, whilst the statues and captured weapons affixed to the columns were removed in an attempt to restore the view of the architecture of the space. A theatre, or at least a *proscaenium* (stage structure), was constructed on the future site of the Theatre of Marcellus. A basilica (an aisled hall) was constructed in the Forum behind the new shops of the moneylenders and silver-merchants, perhaps in association with the activities taking place in these shops. Adjacent to the Forum Romanum, a new forum for the sale of fish was constructed with shops placed around it, which were sold into private ownership.[12] This structure is an important development in the definition of a space for the sale of goods that could be called a forum, and contrasts with the gradual displacement of economic activities from the Forum Romanum itself. In the same censorship, the Tiber was developed as a river port and the construction of the piles for a bridge was undertaken. Close to this new harbour, a *porticus* (in this case a large colonnaded building) was constructed adjacent to the temples of Hercules

---

[8] Livy, 38.28.3.   [9] Livy, 39.44.5–9.   [10] Cic. *Leg. Agr.* 1.7.
[11] Livy, 40.51.   [12] Plaut. *Curc.* 466–82 for location.

and Spes and another was constructed downstream in the Emporium or harbour that had been constructed by M. Aemilius Lepidus, one of the censors, in his aedileship in 193 BC. The final project, though not realised, was the construction of a new aqueduct.

Five years later, in 174 BC, the city was enhanced further: the streets were paved with basalt stones and the roads outside the city were relaid with gravel and enhanced with the building of numerous bridges.[13] The Circus Maximus was redeveloped and a stage or *proscaenium* was constructed for the aediles' theatrical games. The road running from the Forum to the Capitol, the *clivus capitolinus*, was redeveloped as a paved street with colonnades. Meanwhile, the entire 487×60 metre-area of the Porticus Aemilia in the Emporium was paved and stairways were constructed from the colossal building down to the Tiber. The appearance of the city in these last two censorships was radically altered in order to impress visitors arriving by river or by land from the south (the route of those travelling to Rome from the Hellenistic East). There was now a theatre stage within the city, the streets were paved, there were adequate sewers, and overlooking it all was the whitened temple of Jupiter Optimus Maximus.[14]

However, the censors of 174 BC did not just content themselves with projects in Rome. Outside Rome, they constructed walls at Calatia and Auximum and built shops around the forum in each town – just as at Rome shops surrounded the Forum Piscatorium. It is an important fact that in these towns, and other *coloniae*, the fora were constructed with porticoes and shops surrounding them[15], and no mention is made of a temple in them. Elsewhere the censors also built a temple of Jupiter at Pisaurum, brought water to Potentia and extended the urban area of Sinuessa. These projects individually enhanced these particular towns, but can be taken together as a statement about the nature of urbanism: walls, a temple of Jupiter, good water, and a forum surrounded by shops were all essential features of what the leaders of the Roman state understood to be urbanism. The last feature, a forum surrounded by shops, was under review at Rome.

In the next censorship (169 BC), the last that is known in detail from Livy's surviving account, Ti. Sempronius Gracchus purchased the house of P. Scipio Africanus that adjoined the Forum Romanum and the old shops and butchers' *tabernae* (shops) adjacent to the Forum, so that a new basilica could be constructed, later called the Basilica Sempronia.[16] This further embellished and enhanced the Forum: a space that was surrounded by shops within which there also existed a number of ancient temples, the

---

[13] Livy, 41.27.   [14] Livy, 41.27.5–9.   [15] Livy, 41.27.11–12.   [16] Livy, 44.16.10–11.

curia (senate house) and the rostra (speakers' platform). The shops and the basilicas defined the rectilinear space of the Forum and created an ordered space.[17] What we see in Rome over a period of about thirty years is a total transformation of the city. The Forum Romanum was now lined with shops and adjoining basilicas creating a central space that was defined by buildings on all sides. In a move that anticipates the actions of Julius Caesar and Augustus, a Forum Piscatorium, also known as a *macellum*, was built on an area adjacent to the Forum Romanum (Vespasian's Temple of Peace was later built over it). These two fora defined a new architectural style that drew on the Greek *agora* but transformed it into a new structural format. Equally, the basilicas that were built can be interpreted as being related to the Greek *stoa*, but again the forms constructed in Rome were rather different. The river port had been thoroughly developed with the Porticus Aemilia marking the point of arrival in Rome, whilst at the same time the roads to and within the city had been paved to create a new experience of Rome for both visitors and inhabitants. Importantly, the Temple of Jupiter was restored and enhanced so that it dominated the skyline as a building that was white. The result of this thirty-year period of endeavour was to create a metropolitan architecture that would impress visitors to the city, whether ambassadors from Rome's allies and enemies, traders or migrants. Rome had become not just one of the largest centres of population, but also a city with architecture to match her ambition to be the dominant city in the Mediterranean. Importantly, the architecture that was constructed was not a direct copy of that found in the Greek East, but an adaptation that could also be found within the cities of the Italian peninsula.

URBANISM IN ITALY 200–80 BC

Pompeii was not a Roman city, but perhaps in its pre-Roman phase developed all the features that have come to exemplify what we regard as the trappings of Roman urbanism. The city walls enclosed an area of sixty-six hectares within which was a grid of streets mapped over the contours of the lava flow on which the city was built. There were two well-established temple complexes: that of Apollo near the forum, and that of Hercules close to the theatre (fig.1.2). An external sanctuary dedicated to Dionysus was placed at a distance from the city. The forum was a clearly delineated area to the west of the city, but architecturally it was something of a jumble of

[17] Plaut. *Curc.* 466–82.

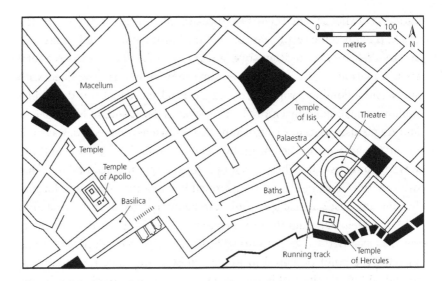

1.2 Central monumental area of pre-Roman Pompeii (second-first century BC). Monuments constructed in the period following the settlements of Sulla's veterans are marked in black including the Stabian Baths.

disconnected buildings: a basilica, administrative offices, shops, a market building or *macellum* and a temple of Jupiter(?) (fig. 7.1). In an attempt to create a form of architectural harmony, Vibius Popidius[18] constructed a tufa portico aligned with the front of the basilica and the Temple of Jupiter.[19] What we have in Pompeii, by 80 BC, is an example of a forum dominated by a temple with a basilica and shops: the very form of architecture that the censors in Rome were funding in their home city and in some of the *coloniae* in Italy. The actions of magistrates, inscribed in Oscan or Latin, strongly echoed those of the censors in Rome.[20] They were involved in laying out new roads, constructing porticoes within the city and reordering the existing Temple of Hercules to give it a greater impact when seen from a distance. But these magistrates also constructed *palaestrae* (courtyards for exercise and education) across the city, that would have been modelled on the Greek gymnasium – structures that the Romans, according to Plutarch, believed enfeebled the young.[21] It was also at this time that the Temples of Isis and Asclepius were constructed close to the theatre. The basic form of the Stabian Baths was remodelled in the second century BC to include heating by means of hypocausts and separate bath-suites for men and women. We

[18] Vetter (1953), no.13.   [19] Zanker (1998), p. 55.
[20] For relevant sources in translation see: Cooley and Cooley (2004), pp. 8–16.
[21] Plut. *Quaest. Rom.* 40.274D.

should also mention the presence of the so-called 'Republican Baths' close to the Temple of Hercules. By the end of the second century BC, therefore, Pompeii boasted most of the features or public buildings that characterised Roman urbanism. They were concentrated in two separate locations adjacent to the temples of Hercules and Apollo. Next to the latter, the forum with its basilica, shops, administrative offices and new temple of Jupiter(?) was constructed – all manifestations of *negotium* or public business. Adjacent to the former were the theatre, *palaestrae*, temples of Isis and Asclepius and baths – a series of features that would have been associated by the Romans with *otium*, or physical and intellectual pleasure.

It is difficult to establish what inspired the Pompeian magistrates and citizens to fund and build the types of structures mentioned above. In looking for archaeological parallels, scholars can identify similar structures in the cities of the Hellenistic East, for example in Priene. The culture of Greece could be found in nearby Naples, but it is interesting that the linguistic change from Oscan was not to Greek but to Latin. Similarly, the shape of the forum (fig. 7.1) is not the square of a Greek *agora* but a rectangle, a form seen to be distinctly Italian in the following century by the architect Vitruvius[22] and reproduced in Roman foundations elsewhere in Italy. The building projects mediated ideas about the city found in the East to a local context. These ideas fit into a wider pattern of cultural change that included the establishment of the elite of Rome in grandiose villas on the bay of Naples during the second century BC.[23] Indeed the links between the elite of Rome and the towns of the Bay of Naples may have been a catalyst for change both locally and in Rome. The ideas about urbanism were not a straight copy of the models from the East, but were adjusted to the Italian context, and it was these which were promoted by the censors in the *coloniae* across Italy.

The Temple of Hercules at Pompeii can also be understood as an urban sanctuary with its theatre for the performance of plays related to that cult, and as a destination for processions.[24] The open view across the Sarno river valley introduces echoes of sanctuaries constructed in other cities during the second century BC on a rather grander scale. Looking north from Campania, we come across cities whose skyline featured temples or sanctuaries. These were often associated with large piazzas artificially constructed to create a flat surface and using concrete barrel vaults to build out from the hillside.[25] These could be seen at the Temple of Jupiter Anxur outside Terracina. The result was that the city's skyline was dominated by

---

[22] Vitr. *De arch.* 5.1.   [23] D'Arms (1970).
[24] Coarelli (2001).   [25] See Coarelli (1987) for some examples.

the sanctuary, just as the Temple of Hercules at Pompeii provided a visual focus from the Sarno Valley. Perhaps the greatest articulation of the ability to enhance the hillside location of a sanctuary artificially is found at Palestrina. There a series of steps and ramps led the visitor to the sanctuary up the hillside and controlled their view of the final destination to be gradually revealed: a large piazza from which they could enter a small theatre and the shrine beyond. The association between a temple and a theatre in sanctuaries can also be found in, or adjacent to, the cities of Latium (for example at Gabii and Tivoli). It can also be found in locations that were not associated with urbanism. The excavations at Pietrabbondante have demonstrated the presence of a temple and theatre complex alongside another temple (see Chapter 9 and fig. 9.1).[26] The former was developed in the second century BC on a more monumental scale, but was certainly abandoned by the time of Augustus at the end of the first century BC. There were numerous finds of weaponry at the major temple, alongside inscriptions referring to the construction of the monuments, and it has been suggested that the theatre complex could have acted as a place for political meetings, and developed as a key place in the city at which the magistrates were commemorated in inscriptions and associated statuary.[27] Although there are few traces of other urban development at the site, it acted as a central place in a region that did not develop urban structures.[28] It is clear, however, that the presence of a sanctuary, even as central as this one, did not necessarily create the conditions for urbanism to develop.

Another strand of urban development needs to be explored: the forum. It has been argued by Filippo Coarelli that the forum found in the Latin colony at Fregellae (destroyed in the second century BC, fig. 1.3) corresponds in structure to the voting enclosure later to be constructed on the Campus Martius in Rome, known as the Saepta.[29] Both the Saepta and the fora of the cities of Italy have a very similar rectilinear shape. Coarelli has suggested that the lines of post-holes in the forum at Fregellae facilitated voting by supporting ropes that divided the voters into five groups. So this rectilinear urban form facilitated queuing and the division of people into the correct group. Another feature of government at Fregellae was the round *comitium* (assembly room) and its adjacent *curia* (senate or council house) at the northern end of the forum. Such structures have been found in other Latin *coloniae*, such as Alba Fucens, Cosa and Paestum (see figs. 2.1

---

[26] Coarelli and La Regina (1993), pp. 230–57.
[27] La Regina (1966) and (1975); Vetter (1953), nos 149–55.   [28] La Regina (1976), p. 247.
[29] Coarelli (1998), pp. 56–61.

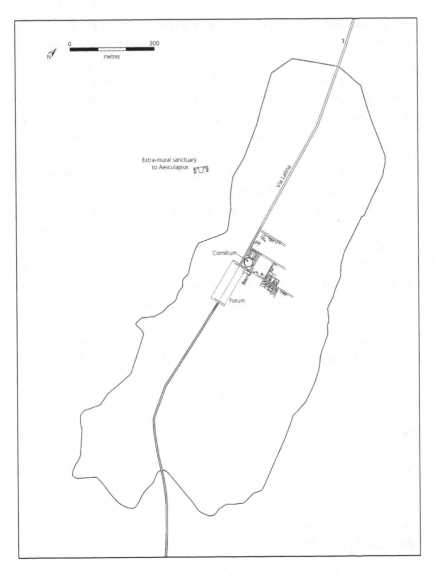

1.3 Fregellae (second century BC): showing the position of forum in relation to the Via Latina and walls of the city. Note the position of the *comitium* adjacent to the forum.

and 2.3). These structures owe much to the architecture of the Italian sanctuaries, with their temple fronted by the seating for a theatre, but at the same time replicate the position of the rostra and *curia* in Rome. What we are seeing is a fusion of ideas about the use of space for politics, which can draw on the Italian tradition of sanctuaries as central places and combine it with Rome's political structures that were founded on voting in groups, elected magistrates and a council. Interestingly, Fregellae had a major sanctuary to Asclepius located at a distance from the forum. This may indicate that the place of politics was considered by the Roman mind-set to be separated from the activities found at sanctuaries. These were two different types of urban space that characterised many Italian cities in the second century BC. Just as Rome had its forum as well as its sacred centre on the Capitol, Italian cities tended to develop a similar multi-centred form of urbanism with a forum and a separate sacred place. There were also other sacred sites that lay beyond the cities' walls.

A feature of the cities on the coast of Italy was the location of the harbour at a distance from the city itself. This is seen most clearly at Cosa, which was known to have had a separate harbour facility by the late third century BC.[30] Anna Marguerite McCann's team of researchers have investigated the archaeological features of the harbour of Cosa and dated the breakwater to the late third to early second century BC.[31] This can be compared to similar structures built in the second century, for example at Terracina in 184 BC, and is indicative of a general trend across Italy and at Rome itself: harbour installations were being constructed to enhance the facilities associated with concentrations of population both in cities and in the countryside, notably in the villas neighbouring the harbour at Cosa. Other cities, including Pompeii, had their port sited close by on a river estuary. These ports remain largely hidden from archaeologists by major alluvial deposits, but are considered to have enhanced their cities' importance as regional centres.[32] It is significant that across Italy many of these ports did not determine the position of the cities because these were mainly located on higher ground, as at Cosa or Pompeii. Perhaps this was to place the inhabitants in a more secure position, as a defence against both human incursions and mosquito-borne diseases associated with river estuaries.[33] Whatever the reasoning, the development of separate port facilities was a key feature of urbanism in the second century BC.

URBANISM BEYOND ITALY: SPAIN

Spain was the first province in the West to experience the presence of a Roman army over a number of years.[34] Almost continual warfare was waged in Spain throughout the second century, with the result that some native settlements were reduced in status by Roman military intervention from

---

[30] Livy, 22.11.6, 30.39.1–2.   [31] McCann (1987), p. 141.   [32] Strabo, 5.3.2.
[33] See Sallares (2000).   [34] App. *Hisp.* 38; Keay (1988), pp. 25–46.

poleis to villages.[35] At the same time, under the Roman Republic it was in Spain that scholars have seen the greatest development of the city in the West, apart perhaps from in Gallia Narbonensis.[36] The archaeology from these sites and those towns that appear in the Roman historical tradition is very patchy in the second century BC, which has caused some scholars to cast doubt over whether we should see the settlements as forms of urbanism[37] or featuring aspects of Romanness 'in the grandeur of their buildings'.[38] As we have seen, however, it was only in the early second century BC that Rome itself was beginning to develop the architecture of urbanism that we tend to associate with Roman towns from the first century AD. Indeed, as we will see in the next chapter, few towns in the second or even the first century BC utilised such architectural forms. This in itself is interesting, and for us, the Spanish cities which developed in the second century through to the mid-first century BC provide indications of Roman systems of thought about what urbanism was, the creation of urbanism, and also the challenges that these developments made to existing conceptions of urbanism. Many of these ideas are attested in the textual tradition and provide us with a means to understand and elucidate the nature and form of some of the settlements in Spain that might be described as cities.

Strabo reports Posidonius' criticism of Polybius for exaggerating the number of cities destroyed by Ti. Sempronius Gracchus, and for mentioning the appearance of cities in triumphal processions that were in fact defended towers or fortresses.[39] Hence in the second century, and even the first century BC, we should imagine a landscape in which there were cities as well as villages and defended towers, rather than accepting a tradition that there were at least a thousand cities in the Spanish provinces.[40] What the textual tradition reveals is a debate over the definition of urbanism. In the context of a Roman military triumph, villages and towers could be construed as urban because it was in the interests of the victorious general to emphasise his achievements, but in the context of geographical writing the remoteness of these settlements, the poverty of the soil and the population's mode of living caused even the larger settlements to be regarded as villages.[41] There was a different lifestyle for those inhabitants of the cities on the Mediterranean coast. These peoples were in contact with Italy through trade, and the places were regarded as the most developed[42] and subject

---

[35] Strabo, 3.3.5.   [36] Curchin (1990), p. 3.
[37] Fear (1996), pp. 14–15 lists what is expected of urbanism on the basis of later evidence.
[38] Richardson (1986), p. 172.   [39] Strabo, 3.4.13.
[40] Strabo, 3.4.13; for a discussion of *oppida* see Almagro-Gorbea (1995).   [41] Strabo, 3.4.13.
[42] Strabo, 3.2.4–10 with reference to Posidonius and Polybius.

to immigration from Italy.[43] The coast was seen to have had an urban tradition, which was in part nurtured by the governors and generals active in the area.[44]

This historical tradition of town foundation is incomplete, and in places simply misleading. For example, the foundation of Italica by Scipio Africanus was said to have occurred in 205 BC when he left his sick and wounded soldiers in the town. This action appears only in a single source, Appian, and may even be a foundation myth, as the association with Scipio increased the status of the city from which the emperors Trajan and Hadrian derived, thereby increasing their Roman credentials.[45] Despite this, there is little doubt that Italica existed prior to the second century BC and was involved in some form of monumental development; there was possibly a very early Italic temple.[46] We will return to foundation myths in Chapter 3. However, in the annalistic history of Livy, or at least the summaries of his work, we do find evidence for the foundation of towns in the region. In 179 BC, Ti. Sempronius Gracchus not only received the surrender of the Celtiberians, but also established the *oppidum* of Gracchuris 'as a monument to his deeds'.[47] We also have a later inscription referring to Gracchus' foundation of the town of Iliturgis.[48] The inscription (*Ti. Sempronio Graccho deductori populus Iliturgitanus*) needs to be treated with caution, since Iliturgis lay beyond Gracchus' *provincia*, but it is of interest in that the language and use of the verb *deduco*, in connection with a *populus* or people, suggest that the foundation refers to the formation of a body of people as much as a place in the landscape.

An earlier governor, L. Aemilius Paullus (191–190 BC), had organised the territory of the Hastenses to have both fields or land (*agri*), and an *oppidum* at *Turris Lascutana*.[49] The place-name is significant here – a tower was becoming an *oppidum* in the language of government – and the action of the governor was recorded on an inscription. As at Gracchuris, the *oppidum* was to become a monument to the deeds of the governor. In 138 BC, D. Iunius Brutus settled the followers of the general Viriathus in fields and an *oppidum* at Valentia,[50] as a reward for their surrender and to prevent them from returning to warfare. The governors' vision of a settled

[43] 3,000 Romans from Iberia were settled in Majorca, Strabo, 3.5.1; see Scheidel (2004) and Erdkamp (2008) on migration.
[44] Strabo, 3.3.5.   [45] App. *Hisp.* 38.
[46] Rodríguez Hidalgo and Keay (1995), pp. 396–9; *CIL* 1² 630; Knapp (1977), pp. 111–16; Mierse (1999), 3–10.
[47] Livy, *Epit. Per.* 41; Festus 86.5.   [48] La Chica Cassinello (1956–61), p. 61.
[49] *ILLRP* 514; Knapp (1977), p. 108; Reiter (1988), pp. 110–11.
[50] Livy. *Epit. Per.* 55; App. *Hisp.* 75; Diod. Sic. 33.1.3–4.

horreum

landscape was one in which there was an *oppidum* and agriculture. In the case of Valentia, an orthogonal street grid, baths and a *horreum* are evidence that the *oppidum* was rather more than a simple hillfort.[51] The tradition of governors reorganising native peoples into new settlements at the end of a period of warfare seems to have been a feature of Roman government in the second century BC.

definition

The landscape of cities, or at least *oppida* (proto-urban nucleated settlements, best described as something akin to a city, but without all the facilities of a city), seems to have been in place by the 170s BC. Embassies from several Spanish peoples arrived at the Senate in 171 BC to complain of the greed of the governors and their officials; it resulted in the trial of several former governors for extortion.[52] The Senate resolved that the governor could not impose prefects on the *oppida* for the collection of money, which would seem previously to have been collected by the local magistrates or officials. This implies that in many areas of Spain these allied peoples lived in cities or had a central place from which the Roman government sought to collect taxes. Some of these central places were established by the governors for the settlement of enemy soldiers or peoples who had surrendered to Rome. Another embassy to the Senate in 171 BC demonstrates the flexibility of Roman policy and the fluidity of settlement patterns in Spain. It came from a unique class of people, the sons of Roman soldiers and Spanish women. Under Roman law such persons had no right to marriage with Roman citizens (*conubium*), but they numbered four thousand men and asked for an *oppidum* in which to live, just as various Spanish peoples had. The Senate decreed that they should be settled at Carteia, and that the present inhabitants could be members of this *colonia*. Their existing home and lands would be redistributed, but they would receive land as other settlers would.[53] The colony would have Latin rights of marriage and be able to trade with Roman citizens. The descent from Roman soldiers would seem to have created a different status for Carteia from that of the other settlements previously discussed. The unique status of these sons of Romans and natives created a new type of citizenship – that of the Latin, a halfway stage between being a provincial and being a Roman citizen,[54] which was later to be applied to other cities in Spain.[55] What is clear from the actions of the Roman government, whether the Senate or the governor, is that the redistribution of land, whether to natives or to those of Roman descent, was

'Latin' citizens

---

[51] Keay (1995), p. 298 cites the evidence for Valentia.   [52] Livy, 43.2.   [53] Livy, 43.3.
[54] Knapp (1977), p. 118.   [55] E.g. Plin. *HN* 3.3.24 on Gracchuris.

allied to the gift of an *oppidum,* which the settlers would utilise as a central place or city.[56] The process cannot be seen as colonisation, since the settlers were not Roman citizens or Latins in most cases, but it utilises the mechanics of colonisation: the redistribution of land and the creation of a city or *oppidum.*

What were these new cities like? Córdoba illustrates the problems in reconstructing the nature of urbanism in the second century BC (fig. 1.4). The colony was seen as the *caput provinciae* or leading city by the middle of the first century BC.[57] According to Strabo it was founded as a colony of Romans and Iberians on the navigable section of the River Baetis.[58] The archaeology from the city reveals for the second century a forty-two-hectare site, surrounded by walls of ashlar masonry, and an orthogonal street grid of unpaved streets.[59] The houses were constructed with mud bricks or sun-dried bricks and there is absolutely no evidence for the use of tiled roofs, which was contemporary Italian practice. There is evidence for trade with the rest of the Mediterranean in the presence of imported pottery. In terms of the domestic structures, however, there is little to distinguish this site from other Iberian settlements in the region. What changes in the first century is the building material used in domestic properties: tiles are used for roofing and there is evidence of painted plaster and some peristyle courtyards. These are significant changes: the tiled roofs remind us of the clause in the town charter known as the *Lex Tarentina:* 'Whoever shall be a decurion of the *municipium* of Tarentum ... he is to have in the town or within the boundary of that *municipium* a building which is roofed with not less than 1500 tiles.' The elite at least needed to live under a tiled roof, and within a house of some magnitude, for urbanism to be present.[60] It is exactly this feature that we find in Córdoba in the first century BC, but not in the second century. We also know from texts that by the middle of the first century the city had a forum[61] and a basilica[62] and could even produce a few Latin poets,[63] all features synonymous with a process that Strabo would see later as the population of Turdetania and Baetica adopting a Roman way of life, 'so that they are not far from being all Romans'.[64] However, there is little of this in the second century BC. The city was defined as a place, and the land within and beyond the walls was divided up and assigned to the colonists. The walls and orthogonal grid of streets were the only real attributes of urbanism that can be identified in

---

[56] App. *Hisp.* 100.   [57] *BHisp.*3.1.   [58] Strabo, 3.1.2, 3.2.1.
[59] See the report of Ventura, León and Márquez (1998).   [60] *BHisp.*8.
[61] Cic. *Verr.* 4.56.   [62] *B Alex.* 52.   [63] Cic. *Arch.* 26.   [64] Strabo, 3.2.15.

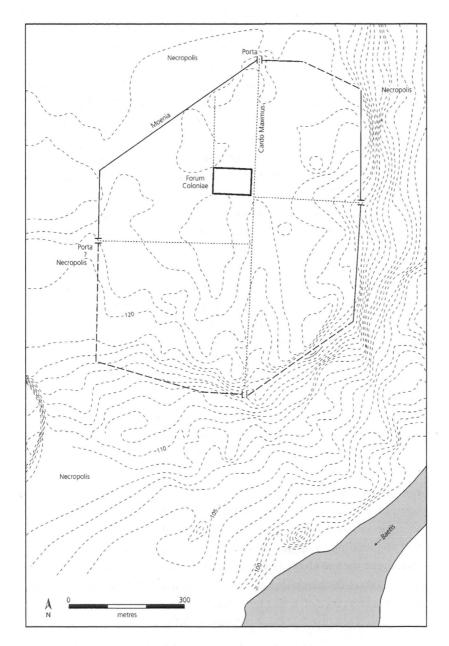

1.4 Córdoba (second century BC): showing the relationship between the internal layout of the city, the forum and the city's walls and gates.

the second century BC. Córdoba, however, was following a similar path of development to the contemporary *coloniae* of Italy: the establishment of the city as a place with walls, a forum and a street grid to which other features might be added (discussed further in Chapter 2).

Emporiae provides us with a settlement that by the end of the second century BC included features that could be termed urban. It was a double community: for the most part Iberian, but with a Greek or Massilian trading settlement established on the coast.[65] The settlements were involved in maritime trade and were at one end of a shipping-route between Narbonensis, or the Rhône, and Spain;[66] both were heavily defended sites.[67] The impact of Rome on this site was immense and can only be seen from the archaeology at the conclusion of the first century BC (fig. 1.5). An orthogonal grid of streets was built inland from the Greek city, with the earliest forum found in the provinces.[68] It has been suggested that the forum overlies the *praesidium* of a Roman *castrum* and, if this were the case, it would be the first urban forum to be built over a military camp in the provinces. It should be stated, however, that the complex with *insulae* (city-blocks) based around the measurement of a *iugerum*, an area of 35×70 metres, reveals little evidence of the reuse of military structures within the city.[69] The archaeological remains underlying the forum suggest that it overlies a fortified structure with large cisterns for the collection of rainwater.[70] This might represent an earlier phase of the town as much as a military structure. The Roman forum included shops and a temple, in many ways paralleling the contemporary development of Pompeii's forum,[71] and the conception, found in Rome during the second century BC, of a forum as a place surrounded by shops. It was a layout for the Iberian community, which would later become a *municipium* (a high-status city second only to a *colonia*) with both Roman settlers and native Iberians and would also incorporate the Greek community of Neapolis.[72] The adoption of Roman conceptions of the city is striking. There are Roman measurements of space based on the *iugerum*, as well as Roman conceptions of space: a forum with a temple and shops, and an orthogonal grid of streets. We should also note that the building techniques were those utilised in Italy rather than Spain. Looking at the site objectively without the textual traditions, we would say that this was a Roman rather than an Iberian city. Yet it was not a colony,[73] but an adaptation of a Roman space to the needs and conceptions of urbanism. It also marks a stark contrast with the conceptions and develop-

---

[65] Livy, 34.9.2; Strabo, 3.4.8.   [66] Livy, 21.60.

[67] See Richardson (1986), pp. 81–4 on the involvement of Rome in the subjection of the Iberian community.

[68] Mierse (1999), pp. 25–35.   [69] Kaiser (2000), p. 13; Sanmartí-Grego (1987).

[70] See Mar and Ruiz de Arbulo (1993), pp. 188–92 for a review of the evidence.

[71] Mierse (1999), p. 31.   [72] Mackie (1983), p. 231.   [73] Richardson (1995), pp. 346–7.

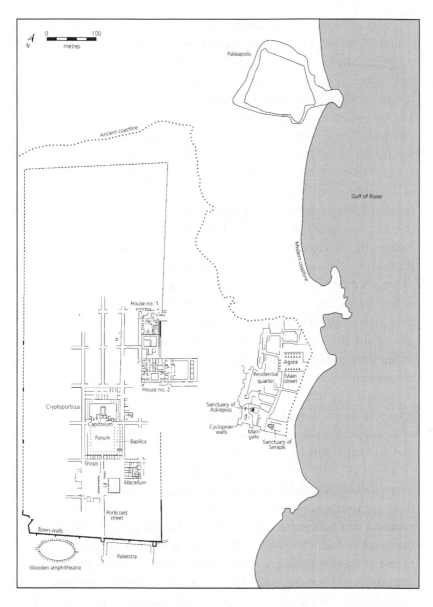

1.5 Emporiae: plan showing the relationship between the earlier city and the Roman transformation of this settlement.

ments of space within the Greek community of Neapolis on the coast.[74] Indeed, the new urban form may have been generated deliberately to contrast with the older Greek city of irregular streets, and this pattern is also found at the town of Valentia.

[74] See Kaiser (2000) for comparative spatial analysis with regard to Neapolis.

The number of cities in the Spanish provinces on the scale of Emporiae is difficult to estimate. Numerous Spanish *oppida* can be identified that might have had a temple or a set of baths, but it is at Baetulo that we see a fuller articulation of urbanism (fig. 1.6). The town was founded *ex novo* (i.e. there was no pre-existing settlement) by the late second century BC, and featured a set of walls enclosing an area of ten hectares, which was subdivided by an orthogonal grid of streets and very probably included a site for a forum. The excavation of the baths revealed parallels with the Stabian Baths of Pompeii (compare fig. 1.6 with fig. 8.1), pointing to the use of a sophisticated form of architecture and participation in Roman-style bathing. There are no texts to explain how this small but recognisably Roman style of town came into being. A number of explanations can be suggested. Perhaps the provincials did not have the capacity to develop urbanism and the town was instead founded by Italian settlers. Alternatively we might be seeing a Spanish response to, or understanding of, the nature of urbanism: a walled site, a forum, baths and a rectilinear grid of streets. Or the town may have been constructed by a governor holding *imperium* and represented his idea of the type of town that the provincials needed: small but with the architecture of Roman urbanism. The model for such an interpretation of urbanism did not entirely lie in Rome. Emporiae had developed a grid of streets and a forum, which, like the presence of a circuit of walls, had its origins in the *coloniae* of Italy. However, the presence of baths here and at other native sites points to the adoption of cultural practices from the East that had made their way into Italy from the late third and early second centuries BC. The provincials had adopted not just the architecture of urbanism but also the Roman notions of bodily cleanliness and appearance that were associated with their conceptions of urban life. This represented the adoption of a new technology to present the bodies of provincials as distinctly urban and synonymous with Romanness in this context. The combination at Baetulo of this new culture of a Roman body with an *ex novo* foundation with a variety of cultural traits has led modern scholars to resist the attribution of the site to the provincials. The coastal cities had quite simply become integrated with the nearby colony of Narbo, as well as the coastal *coloniae* of Italy.

The early cities of the Spanish provinces represent places of order from which tax might be collected and soldiers recruited, or where a governor might hold court. These functions of government were not dissimilar to those found in the towns that were developing in Italy at this time.[75] To

[75] Laurence (2002).

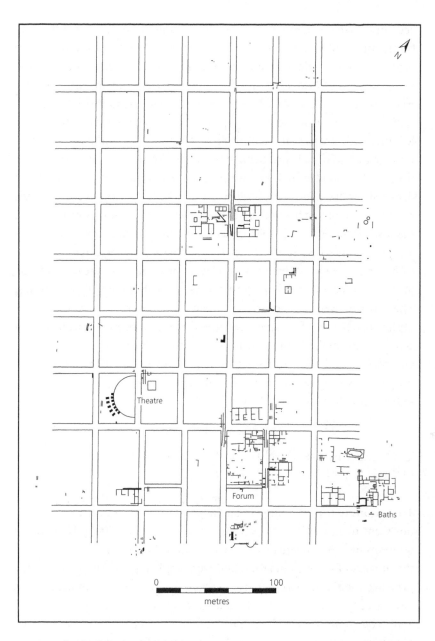

1.6 Baetulo: the fully developed Roman city.

accomplish them required a degree of centralisation or the existence of centres of population in which government might exert its authority. As we have seen, cities could be created as monuments to a governor's great deeds or for reasons of *Realpolitik* in relation to a defeated enemy army. People were displaced and replaced in the process that distributed land and an *oppidum* to the various peoples of Spain. These can be seen as central places, but they did not have the embellishments of basilicas, theatres and other features that were only just being built within Rome itself and were rare in the *coloniae* founded by Rome within Italy. Emporiae, Baetulo, and Italica demonstrate the adoption of Italian-style architecture with a focus on the establishment of temples and, in the case of Emporiae, a forum by the end of the first century BC. The development of public buildings appears haphazard, even more so as a result of the very variable archaeological record of this early period. We must, however, recognise the presence of the city in Spain in the second century BC in a form similar to that of the Italian peninsula. These places were categorised as urban, and governors saw themselves capturing cities and founding new cities that would be monuments to their achievements in the future. The impact of Rome during this early period of occupation was limited to a small number of towns and the resettlement of people in existing territories with an urban centre or *oppidum*. Elsewhere, settlement patterns displayed considerable continuity.[76]

THE DEVELOPMENT OF A CONCEPT OF URBANISM

The actions of town-building in Spain have been seen as rather odd and do not seem to fit the Roman patterns of colonisation in Italy. However, if we examine the individuals involved, we find that they had knowledge of the process of town-foundation and were applying that knowledge in the provincial setting as part of their *imperium* or capacity to command. As we have already seen, L. Aemilius Paullus, as governor of Spain, provided land and an *oppidum* at *Turris Lascutana* for a native people. The question arises as to how he formulated such an idea? If we look back at his career, we find that in 194 BC he served as one of the triumvirs for founding a colony at Croton.[77] Ti. Sempronius Gracchus, the founder of Gracchuris, was drawing on his experience as one of the triumvirs for the founding of the colony of Saturnia in the Ager Caletranus in Italy in 183 BC.[78] The governors were

[76] Carreté, Keay and Millett (1995).   [77] Livy, 34.45.3–5.   [78] Livy, 39.55.9.

applying their knowledge of resettlement in Italy to the native populations of the provinces. This may not have produced an official or legal *colonia*, but the process and effect was much the same: to (re)assign land and (re)define a city as a centre for the incoming and existing population. Other governors involved in the redistribution of *agros et oppidum* may have had similar experience of land-division in Italy, but the lacuna in Livy's text means this must remain an argument from silence. We see, though, a Roman approach to space and territory that is the same whether in the provinces of Spain or on the Italian mainland.

We still need to consider the question of where these ideas were coming from. Were they from contact with the Hellenistic world? Perhaps not directly. L. Aemilius Paullus does not appear to have had any contact with the Hellenistic world prior to his posting to Spain. However, his knowledge of the Greek language and a houseful of Greek tutors for his children points to a familiarity with the culture of the East.[79] Later, he would serve as a legate to assist the consul Manlius Vulso in the East.[80] He would then as proconsul (167 BC) reorganise the province of Macedonia, divide it into four regions, present the peoples of each of the four regions with a capital, permit the towns to use their own laws but to have elected magistrates rather than monarchs, and establish the payment of tax from the capital of each region to Rome.[81] He also travelled through Greece and admired the architecture of its cities, whose reputation he knew but which he had clearly not actually seen in person.[82] These included the cities of Athens, Corinth, Sicyon, Argos, Sparta and Olympia. This was a man seeing for the first time the culture of Greece and the marvels of its cities. In Spain what we may be finding is an idea of the city, influenced by Hellenism. This concept of urbanism was also being produced in the city of Rome.

The association between L. Aemilius Paullus and M. Aemilius Lepidus in 193 BC as curule aediles might be more revealing of where the concept of urbanism was coming from. Both had been involved in the construction of the Porticus Aemilia that became the focus of Rome's river-port and was subject to further development by the censors in 179 and 174 BC. Lepidus had seen for himself the cities of Greece, Macedonia, and the Ptolemaic kingdom of Egypt whilst acting as an ambassador in 201–200 BC.[83] His contact with the East may have led to his decision to build the Porticus Aemilia in 193 BC in order to create a focal point for arrival in the city. His

---

[79] Plut. *Aem.* 6.9–10, possibly confirmed by Plin. *HN* 35.135, see Reiter (1988), pp. 114–15.
[80] See Broughton (1951), p. 363 for the relevant sources.   [81] Livy, 45.16; 45.28–40.
[82] Livy, 45.27–8.   [83] Broughton (1951), pp. 321, 325.

actions as censor in 179 BC, discussed above, were to create a vision of Rome that was intended to impress those arriving in the city, just as the cities of the East may have impressed him. One of the two Aemilii had seen the culture of the cities in the East for himself, while the other had not. Yet both of them appear to have embraced a similar idea of the city and applied that concept in the provinces of the West.

Aemilius Lepidus' career in the early second century BC demonstrates a similar emphasis and trajectory to that of Aemilius Paullus with warfare, land-division and town-foundation at its heart. Between their aedileship in 193 and his censorship in 179, Lepidus had been praetor and propraetor in Sicily (191–190), then consul in 187, when he led an army against the Ligurians of north-west Italy, and he had also constructed the Via Aemilia. He would continue to be directly involved with north-west Italy. In 183 BC, he was one of the triumvirs (board of three magistrates) for the foundation of the *coloniae* of Mutina and Parma,[84] and in 177 BC he was a triumvir for the founding of the colony at Luni.[85] He was consul for the second time in 175 BC and led another army against the Ligurians. Finally in 173 BC he was one of the decemvirs for the settlement of non-occupied lands in Liguria and Gaul; ten *iugera* were granted to Roman citizens and three *iugera* to Latins.[86] The careers of the two Aemilii reveal very similar paths which permitted them literally to alter regions that they and other members of the Roman elite had conquered, by founding towns, redistributing lands, and of course leading armies against Rome's enemies.

At the same time the mobile elite was involved in the creation of a new architecture for the city of Rome that presented the capital to ambassadors and visitors as a city to surpass those of Campania and southern Italy and to rival the old cities of Greece and those of the kingdoms of the Greek East. The process by which Rome developed as a Hellenistic capital depended on the movement of resources from conquered territories to Rome itself, and at the same time on the development of a relationship between the aristocracy in Rome and the towns of the provinces. Q. Fulvius Flaccus had been governor of Hispania Citerior, where he captured and plundered the Spanish *oppidum* of Urbicana and fended off attacks from the Celtiberians in 182 BC, distributing the booty to his soldiers.[87] As consul a few years later in 179 BC, he insisted that a vow from this campaign had to be fulfilled: games were to be inaugurated for Jupiter Optimus Maximus and a temple of Fortuna Equestris was to be constructed, the money for which had been

---

[84] Livy, 39.55.7–8.   [85] Livy, 41.13.4–5.   [86] Livy, 42.4.3–4.   [87] Livy, 40.16.7–10.

collected in Spain for this purpose.[88] The connection between the governor
and the provincials did not end with the completion of the term of his
governorship. The relationship between former governors and the inhabitants of the Spanish provinces can be seen in the embassy of 171 BC, which
was mentioned above, when a complaint was made regarding the actions of
recent governors towards the provincials or Spanish allies that paid tribute
to Rome.[89] The Senate permitted the ambassadors from Spain to select
advocates in the first-ever trial of Roman governors. They chose M. Porcius
Cato, P. Cornelius Scipio, L. Aemilius Paullus, and C. Sulpicius Gallus to
represent them. All four were former governors of the provinces of Spain.
The Spanish allies of Rome seem to have maintained a link with their
former governors, who had been involved in the redistribution of land and
the protection of the cities of the Mediterranean littoral from Rome's
enemies in the interior. Just as Aemilius Lepidus was consistently involved
in the development of the region of Liguria and the foundation of towns in
that region, the governors of Spain maintained a connection with the
provinces. This implies links between the developing town-based provincial elite in Spain and the elite in Rome.

One of the attractions of wars in the West may have been the opportunity not just for battle and conquest but also to transform geography and
create monuments for the future in the form of towns. These included not
just the *coloniae*, but also a series of towns founded on the Via Aemilia such
as Rhegium Lepidum or Forum Lepidum.[90] The naming of places as simply
'Forum' with their founder's name points to the nature of these towns; they
were composed of a central space or a forum that was not dissimilar to the
fora being created within Rome, with shops and a central piazza. There was
a similar approach to urban form in the capital and in these new towns:
they were felt to require new formalised meeting-places for public meetings
and commerce. In founding the town of Gracchuris, Tiberius Gracchus saw
himself creating a monument or memorial for the future, just as the elite in
Rome were building monuments in the Forum Romanum, such as the
Basilica Aemilia or Basilica Sempronia, and along the river front, such as
the Porticus Aemilia.[91] One of the results of the process was that the names
of the Roman elite were given to geographical features in Rome, Italy and
the provinces. Their world was a new one in which physical geography was
altered by the building of roads, the division of lands, the establishment of
towns, the construction of fora, and the building of monuments in the

---

[88] Livy, 40.44.8–12.   [89] Livy, 43.2.   [90] Festus 332L; Livy, 39.2.10; Wiseman (1987), pp. 131–2.
[91] See Wiseman (1998), pp. 106–20 for the Aemilii.

capital. In this new geography, places could not be seen as Roman unless there was a town and, at the same time, Rome was developed as a capital city to which embassies might be sent from the cities of the provinces. By the middle of the second century BC, Rome had become one of the cities to see and the city to which more people were drawn than any other within the Mediterranean basin. It had, in short, become the reference point for the understanding of urban life and had eclipsed its rivals.

The link between the foundation of cities and Roman imperialism lay in the fact that some cities, those whose citizens were Roman citizens or who had Latin rights, secured territory on behalf of Rome by effectively establishing garrisons of citizens across a distinctly Roman landscape – not just in the immediate future, but into the longer term. For a city to perform its role as a garrison, it had to produce citizens in the next generation and the generations to come after that. The children of the first settlers were born into an urban *habitus* that created a sense of identity that was distinctly Roman (as well as urban). Over the course of their lives, these citizens were likely to have been recruited into the army, may have seen the monuments of distant Rome or at least heard tales of the great city, and were expected to return to their home city. These cities were reshaped through the addition of new monuments, often emulating those constructed in Rome, in order to develop further the sense of a distinctly urban *habitus*. The impetus for such new monuments may have come from the local elite, but often, as we shall see in subsequent chapters, the finance and delivery of new buildings depended on the patronage of outsiders – the political elite in Rome itself. This pattern of urban development developed as early as the second or even the third century BC. It is a phenomenon that we will see being reshaped under the new historical conditions that were to develop after the second century BC.

2 Colonisation and the development of Roman urbanism

municipium

The Romans of the Augustan Age identified the phenomenon of colonisation within their own history, according to which citizens or veteran soldiers were settled in captured cities or in cities established on new green-field sites. The legal status of a city as a colony or a *municipium* was important for the listing of cities by category.[1] The first emperor attached greater importance to the colony than to the *municipium*. Contemporary historians, such as Livy or Velleius Paterculus, could look back and see colonisation as part of a process of Roman imperial expansion and as a way of understanding the spread of the Roman people across the Italian peninsula – something that needed to be remembered rather than forgotten.[2] City foundation was a key aspect of Roman history and thus also of Roman identity.

Moving back from the Augustan Age to an understanding of what actually happened at these sites proves rather tricky. The later tradition does not necessarily map directly back on to the phenomenon of town foundation, even if it did prove to be a subject of considerable interest.[3] The historical tradition of these events, as preserved in the Augustan Age, leaves much out and provides only a sketch from which we may deduce an overall pattern of Roman colonisation in the earlier period and seek to set out a link between town foundation and imperial expansion from the late third to the first century BC.

For the early second century BC we have a record of the names of all those senators serving on special commissions for founding colonies, reinforcing the population of colonies with new settlers, or settling land disputes between colonies. In the period from 201–168 BC, eighty-six senators served on eighteen commissions. Most of those involved tended to be successful senators, who would serve, or had served, as praetors or consuls.[4] The actions of the senatorial commissions were to found twenty-one colonies, reinforce eight colonies with new settlers, decide one boundary dispute between the colonies of Luni and Pisa, and assign land across five regions to settlers,

[1] See Crawford (1995), p. 429 for the use of *municipatim* as an adverb by Augustus to refer to the cities of Italy; and compare the misunderstanding of the use of *municipes* in Gell. *NA*. 16.13.

[2] Vell. Pat.1.14. [3] Salmon (1969) remains the most comprehensive account of the subject.

[4] See Broughton (1951) for details of these individuals.

all within a period of thirty-three years. The areas affected were, for the most part, northern and southern Italy, in the recently conquered territories of the Gauls, Ligurians and other groups. What we are seeing here is the expansion or distribution of Roman settlers across conquered territories under the control of members of the Senate.

There was a symbiotic relationship here: Rome was protected by her colonies, while the personnel for those colonies came from Rome and her allies and ultimately enjoyed the protection of Rome. Livy makes this clear with reference to the small Roman colonies at Minturnae and Sinuessa – these were quite literally garrisons, with few political structures and no need for a forum, because these Roman citizens' forum was back in Rome.[5] Seen from an archaeological perspective, these were garrisons of Roman citizens in camps or forts.

An alternative explanation of this phenomenon takes account of changes in the distribution of the population across Italy. At their heart was the rapid growth in the population of the city of Rome, which may even have doubled every hundred years;[6] at the same time, people from Rome were wanted and were willing to sign up to be settled in colonies at a distance from the city. There is an assumption in the Augustan literary sources that the idle plebeians were siphoned off from Rome into colonies from an early date.[7] The land distributed to the settlers was seen as of equal importance as the foundation of a colonial town: if it was good or fertile land and was not at a considerable distance from Rome, the plebs signed up with enthusiasm to join the colony.[8] If it was poor land, they did not, or if it was at a distance from Rome, they might join and later desert the colony. The gift of land to each colonist came at a price; these settlements were regarded not so much as locations of urban life but as outposts on the frontiers of civilisation in locations that would protect Rome.[9] The reinforcement of colonies with new settlers is also a feature of the record of the early second century BC. The demographic shortfalls of citizens in the colonies may in part have been exacerbated by the continual warfare against Carthage, Macedonia, the Iberians and the Ligurians,[10] but it would seem that many of Rome's new colonies could not maintain a stable population, with many settlers leaving and perhaps even returning to Rome. To give one example, in 169 BC additional colonists were settled in Aquileia,[11] founded a mere fourteen years earlier.[12]

---

[5] Livy, 10.21.7–10.   [6] See Morley (1996) for a discussion of the population growth.
[7] Livy, 1.56.3.   [8] Livy, 5.24.4; 9.26.1–5.   [9] Cic. *Leg Agr.* 2.73.
[10] Hopkins (1978).   [11] Livy, 43.17.   [12] Livy, 40.29.2.

The historiographical tradition found in Livy and Velleius understands a certain relationship between colonisation and imperial expansion. Colonies were established to protect Rome's dominion, while providing land for her citizens and allies. It is only later that these places developed the infrastructure of urbanism. It is this end point that is reflected in an emerging ideology of urban life that gave the colony privileges over the *municipium*. What we will do in this chapter is set out the nature of colonial foundations from the third century BC onwards in order to see how these new settlements articulated an idea of urbanism or helped to develop a coherent notion of what was regarded as a Roman city.

COLONIES AT THE EDGE OF CIVILISATION: CREMONA AND PLACENTIA

The role of the colonies as urban nuclei and defensive centres, as well as their precarious nature, is revealed by the Latin colonies founded at Placentia and Cremona within the territory of the Boii. Placentia to the south of the River Po and Cremona to the north were fortified in 218 BC and 6,000 colonists were settled across the landscape in order to establish new towns.[13] The Boii and the Insubres revolted in the same year, and caused the agrarian population around these towns to flee, along with the senatorial land-commissioners, to the established town of Mutina, rather than to Placentia with its newly built walls.[14] Cremona and Placentia were to form the basis for the winter quarters of Scipio's army that year, attesting to their defensive or military functions.[15] The towns succeeded in holding out against Hannibal's and Hasdrubal's armies, yet after the conclusion of the war with Carthage, Placentia was captured in 200 BC by a Gallic and Ligurian coalition with as few as 2,000 of the colonists still there to be spared and held captive.[16] These captives were restored as colonists later in the year and returned to Placentia.[17] Cremona was also besieged in 200 BC but was relieved later in the year with the defeat of the Gallic army by Rome. Perhaps as a result of their perilous location, many of the original colonists fled, with the Senate being petitioned over this issue as early as 206 BC.[18] Little had been achieved however, and we find eight years later in 198 BC the consul Sextus Aelius spending his year in office ensuring that they returned to their place of residence as colonists.[19] The territory of

---

[13] Polyb. 3.40.   [14] Livy, 21.25.   [15] Livy, 21.56.8.   [16] Livy, 31.10.
[17] Livy, 31.21.18.   [18] Livy, 28.11.10.   [19] Livy, 32.26.1–3.

Placentia continued to be a place of danger, with the Ligurians laying waste the land up to the walls of the colony in 193 BC.[20] Peace was achieved with the Boii in 191 BC; half of their land was confiscated with Rome gaining the right to settle colonies in it if it so chose.[21] The two towns sent legates to the Senate in 190 BC to complain that there was a population shortage due to war, disease, and a desire not to live adjacent to the Gallic peoples. Both towns were reinforced with the addition of 6,000 families and a commission of three to establish these families in their new homes.[22] Other colonies were to be founded to reinforce and reestablish the strength of Rome in the region;[23] Bononia, for example, was founded in 189 BC with 3,000 colonists.[24] The twenty-eight years from the foundation of Cremona and Placentia to their refoundation coincided with the extreme conditions of the Hannibalic Wars, but the pattern portrayed is similar to the problems encountered in other colonies. Many colonies were abandoned by their populations, unbeknownst to those in the capital, and the fact was only discovered in the course of investigations into conspiracies such as that associated with the Bacchanalia in 186 BC; this also revealed that the colonies at Sipontum and Bruxentum had been abandoned, with the result that they were resettled by new colonists.[25] These examples of the problems of colonial foundations, described by the Augustan historian Livy, reveal the tenuous existence of these new towns in their early stages. In order to assess the nature of these colonies it is important to turn to the archaeological record and examine what it is within a colony that physically embodies a sense of Romanness.

A TALE OF TWO COLONIES: PAESTUM AND COSA

The two colonies founded in 273 BC at Paestum and Cosa provide us with archaeological testimony to their quite different histories.[26] The colonists sent to found Paestum were settled in the existing city of Poseidonia – originally a Greek colony founded in 600 BC, but taken over by the Lucanians some 200 years later (fig. 2.1). The colonists were settled around this city with its three monumental 'Greek' temples and external sanctuaries and city walls. The settlement of the colonists resulted in some modification: most notably the establishment of a forum on a different alignment to that of the Greek temples and the reoccupation or redevelopment of the

---

[20] Livy, 34.56.10.   [21] Livy, 36.39.3.   [22] Livy, 37.46.9–11.   [23] Livy, 37.47.1.
[24] Livy, 37.57.7.   [25] Livy, 39.23.3–4.   [26] Vell. Pat.1.14; Livy, *Epit. Per.* 14.

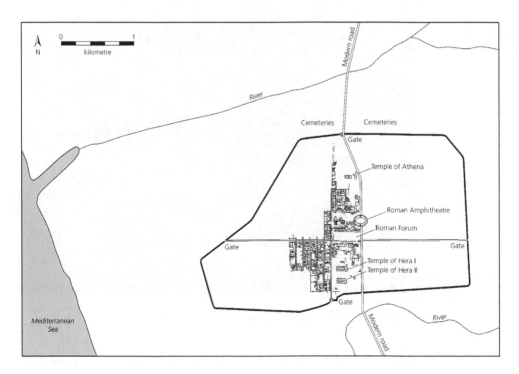

2.1 Paestum: showing the addition of Roman structures (forum and amphitheatre in particular) alongside the earlier temples constructed in the Greek colonial phase at this site.

domestic structures within the grid of streets.[27] The colonists sent to Cosa had a different experience (fig. 2.2). This was a settlement built on a barren site of 0.7 hectares, one twentieth of the area enclosed by the later walls of the city. What is clear from the archaeological investigation of this early city is that the century following colonisation saw little in the way of building on the site.[28] The population needed to be reinforced and in 193 BC 1,000 additional colonists were settled there.[29] Narnia provides another example of a city that was unable to sustain its level of population. Founded in 299 BC, it had to be reinforced a hundred years later.[30] It appears that even into the second century BC many colonies were lacking features that we would associate with Roman urbanism – most notably, monumental development and the ability to sustain a population. Both Paestum and Cosa might be regarded even at a later date as towns that failed. Paestum was described by Strabo at the end of the first century BC as a town ridden with pestilence

---

[27] See Pedley (1990) for details but also the discussion in Crawford (2006).
[28] Brown (1960), p. 2; Fentress (2000).   [29] Livy, 33.24.8–9.   [30] Livy, 32.2.7.

2.2 Cosa: the colony was founded on the summit of this promontory.

from its nearby marshes,[31] whereas Cosa, even in its final form, was more famous for its harbour.[32] It needs to be remembered that colonies were meant, in the words of Siculus Flaccus, writing under the Empire: 'either to coerce the local inhabitants [in the case of Paestum] or to repel enemy invasions', rather than to establish towns and urbanism.[33] Like other colonies, Paestum and Cosa were successful in repelling the enemy during the war with Hannibal at the end of the third century BC.[34]

The process of land-division within the colony can be seen most clearly from the results of excavations at Cosa during the 1990s (fig. 2.3).[35] The excavations on this site did not discover any domestic buildings from the original third-century BC colony. The original occupation associated with the colony consisted of a walled enclosure that incorporated some forms of governmental structure: the *curia* and some associated buildings and a sacred pit on the *Arx* (Citadel), where the Capitoline Temple would later be built. What the excavations revealed was that the colony, after its refoundation in 197 BC and the construction of its four temples, a basilica and a *comitium-curia* complex over the course of the second century, represented a different form of urbanism from that of the original colony. The domestic settlement of 1,000 new colonists in 197, drawn from allies who had fought

[31] Strabo, 5.4.13.   [32] Strabo, 5.2.8; Livy, 30.39.
[33] Translation from Campbell (2000), 103.20–8.   [34] Livy, 27.10.   [35] Fentress (2004).

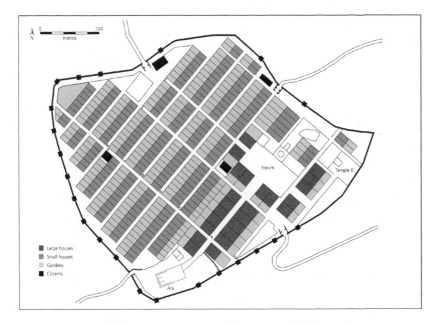

2.3 Cosa: plan of the second-century colony showing the distribution of property and location of monuments.

in the Hannibalic Wars, was not undertaken in a manner that emphasised equality. Instead, a hierarchy of plots was distributed, from the House of Diana, on a plot of 18 × 25 m with its *fauces* (entrance) opening on to the forum, down to much smaller plots for those of a lower status (fig. 2.4). As at other sites, the size of plot allocated reflected the colonists' military status and whether they were *equites* or *pedites*.[36] The mapping of this hierarchy created a zone of larger plots around a very small forum, comprising the area of a single *insula* block, and along the wider (nine metre-wide) processional route leading from the forum to the temples on the *Arx*, and smaller plots on the narrower (six-metre-wide) streets across the site (fig. 2.3).[37] The division of the site into these plots resulted in 24 larger houses and 224 smaller ones. This layout of the town ordered the landscape in the manner of the soldiers' camp described by Polybius.[38] As the team who excavated Cosa suggest, it is not a question of seeing the city derived from the camp or the camp from the city but instead of seeing these forms as an expression of Roman

[36] Livy, 35.9.7–8, 35.40.5–6, 40.34.2–4.
[37] See Sewell (2005) for discussion of the possibility of a larger forum in the original 273 BC foundation at Cosa, that was designed with a view to setting aside an area of land around the forum for the houses of the elite.
[38] Polyb. 6.27–30.

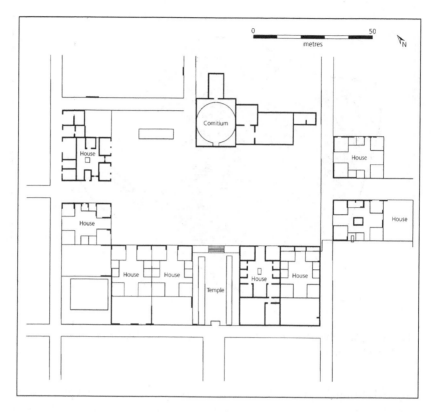

2.4 Cosa: the forum. It has been suggested that the forum was originally a much larger space, in which a number of large houses were constructed.

mentalité.[39] This mindset created a phenomenology of ordered hierarchy that was ultimately linked to wealth and the census declarations of Rome's citizens and her allies. At Cosa, this phenomenology was mapped on to an existing walled site to create a hierarchy and sense of order. Following on from the division of the site and the settlement of colonists, temples were added over the next fifty years.[40] A house in the forum was pulled down to build a temple opposite the *curia* (fig. 2.4). The eastern height was sculpted into a level area (30m by 23m) on to which another temple was constructed to form a sanctuary. In addition, a further temple was constructed on the *Arx* (fig. 2.3 for locations). Hence, on to the ordered landscape of a grid of streets and a hierarchy of houses were placed the liminal spaces or temples where communication with the supernatural was seen to take place by means of rituals such as sacrifice. The places chosen were significant: the

[39] Brown (1960) to be read with Fentress (2004).
[40] See the discussion of Bispham (2006) on the nature of the temples.

2.5 Cosa: temples were constructed so that priests might delineate the space within which to observe the flight of birds or other signs with reference to the peaks of mountains visible here.

centre of civic decision-making and the high points overlooking the city and its walls. These also formed ideal places from which to take the *auspices* that involved the observation of the flight of birds within a defined area (see fig. 2.5). The process of foundation and monument-building can be seen as rapid and occurring over a period of two generations.

LAND HUNGER AND THE ARMIES OF THE CIVIL WARS

During the later Republic there had been several initiatives to reorganise the population structure of Italy – the most famous being that of settling the *ager publicus* by Tiberius Gracchus in 133 BC.[41] However, the settlement of veterans by generals in the first century BC had an effect on the demographic structure of the cities in Italy.[42] Sulla, for example, settled

---

[41] App. *B Civ.* 1.7–8; Plut. *Ti. Gracch.* 8. [42] Brunt (1971), pp. 294–344.

former soldiers on confiscated property in the hostile city of Pompeii, which resulted in the transformation of the city's public monuments.[43] A *capitolium* was built in the forum, on the site of the existing temple, a new set of baths was built to the north of the forum, but maybe more impressively an amphitheatre was built as well as a covered theatre (fig. 1.2). Where we have evidence of the persons funding these monuments, we find that they tended to be not the locals but persons from outside the city. C. Quinctius Valgus, one of two men responsible for the building of the covered theatre and amphitheatre at Pompeii, was also a benefactor of the towns of Aeclanum, Casino and Frigento.[44] It needs to be noted here that the first appearance of amphitheatres in the early to mid-first century BC tended to be associated with veteran colonies.[45] It was money from outside these communities, in the form of wealthy patrons, that funded such structures, rather than money generated within the cities and their immediate territories. Without the wealthy patrons prepared to spend their spare cash on such buildings, we would not see the development of urbanism within these cities in the form of new public monument-types such as amphitheatres. Welch sees this change as directly related to the army reforms that introduced mass recruitment, loyalty to a general over Rome and training by those that trained the gladiators in Italy.[46] The experience of being a soldier remained with the colonists – after all they held their new land as a result of military service – and the presence of amphitheatres reinforced the connection with their service in the army. Their descendants appear to have maintained these values, with amphitheatres built across the cities of the Italian peninsula and beyond in the first centuries BC and AD (see Chapter 10).

The veterans' success in creating a stable or economically viable existence in their new city depended on numerous factors, but their failure appears in the literature from antiquity.[47] Equally, we find the dispossessed, whose ancestral lands had been handed over to the newcomers, holding grievances.[48] The process of founding colonies was inevitably divisive. We see an articulation of the opposition to such settlements in Cicero's three speeches against Rullus' agrarian law. The law would have redistributed land held by the Roman people (*ager publicus*) and also included the foundation of colonies in the *municipia* of Italy, as well as in the provinces.[49] Cicero's opposition to the agrarian law is expressed in two objections: first, that

---

[43] Cic. *Sull.* 60–2; Wiseman (1977); Zanker (1998).

[44] *CIL* 10.844, 10.852, 10.5282, 9.1140, *ILLRP* 598.

[45] Welch (2007), pp. 72–101; see original argument Welch (1994).   [46] Welch (2007), pp. 88–90.

[47] Sall. *Cat.* 11–12.   [48] Sall. *Cat.* 28.   [49] Cic. *Leg. Agr.* 1.16–17.

excellent lands would be given away and, second, that the lands given to individuals could be of very low quality and drought-ridden, for example at Sipontum, or else in a disease-ridden swamp, for example at Salapia.[50] Moreover, the refoundation of Capua would have created a rival to Rome itself,[51] and the colonies in any case were portrayed as garrisons as opposed to settlements of individuals.[52] The scale of the proposed undertaking was massive, with 200 surveyors drawn from the equestrian order with 20 attendants and a staff of architects, clerks, secretaries and other officials, as well as the logistical equipment of transport: animals, tents, furnishings and provisions.[53] What was envisaged was a redistribution of the population. It is, however, apparent that some cities, including Cosa, were suffering from desertion and general depopulation by the second half of the first century BC. Hence, the distribution of Sullan veterans across the towns of Italy can be seen as a form of repopulation and also as a form of redistribution of the veterans' booty. The historiography of the Catilinarian discontent reflects the settlement of veterans on abandoned land as well as a process of dispossession of those opposed to Sulla. Equally, the agrarian law of Rullus looked forward to the settlement of veterans across Italy by Julius Caesar and then the triumvirs during the next phase of civil war.

During the period 47–14 BC in Italy some 130,000 veterans were settled in 50 of the 400 or so towns across the Italian peninsula.[54] Given the total population of 4,000,000 persons in Italy, this represented a redistribution of 3 per cent of the population. However, the impact after each major campaign, culminating with the battles of Pharsalus, Philippi, Naulochus and Actium, would have been far greater at the local level where soldiers were settled. Keppie estimates that maximum numbers settled in the countryside around these 'new' colonies were in the thousands with the very high estimate made for Cremona of 9600 settlers.[55] The pattern in each individual town was unique and was a response to local conditions. This process should be seen in the context of the civil wars – many had been conscripted or recruited from the towns of Italy for long periods of service, and this had resulted in the depopulation of some towns and the possibility of founding new ones.[56] For example, the city of Rhegium suffered during the wars between Octavian and Sextus Pompeius and was repopulated by veterans after the period of conflict in order to reestablish the city.[57] At Cosa, by the time of Augustus much of the site had been abandoned, and we see the

---

[50] Cic. *Leg. Agr.* 2.71.   [51] Cic. *Leg. Agr.* 2.76.   [52] Cic. *Leg. Agr.* 1.16.   [53] Cic. *Leg. Agr.* 1.32.
[54] Keppie (1983) is fundamental to what follows and should be read with the update in Keppie (2000), pp. 249–62.
[55] Keppie (1983), p. 99.   [56] Hyg. *Const.*140–2 Campbell (2000).   [57] Strabo, 6.1.6.

renewal focussed on a mere nine *insulae* close to the forum and the restoration of the Capitoline Temple on the *Arx*. In the forum itself, over the next
fifty years the House of Diana was converted into a shrine to the goddess.
But still there are signs that the town could not maintain its public buildings: the basilica collapsed at some point between AD 15 and AD 37. The
curia appears to have been damaged and another temple was destroyed by
fire and renewed by imperial patronage.[58] Not all colonies were in regions
that were short of people. Many colonies of the Triumviral period utilised
lands expropriated from the proscribed, or confiscated from their occu-
piers for no other reason than that the veterans needed to be settled. The
process brought to Italy the brutality and injustices associated with the
foundation of Roman colonies in areas that had recently been conquered.

TWO AUGUSTAN TOWNS: AOSTA AND MÉRIDA

Rome not only founded colonies in Italy with a view to their development as
populous places but was also involved in the settlement of veterans outside
Italy in Africa, Macedonia, Sicily, Spain, Gallia Narbonensis, Achaea, Asia,
Syria and Pisidia.[59] The phenomenon of a colony outside Italy appeared for
the first time in 123 BC, with Gaius Gracchus proposing the founding of a
colony at Carthage. At that time, such a move was controversial, compli-
cated by the historical associations of the place of Carthage, and ended in
failure (Caesar would later refound not only Carthage, but also Corinth).[60]
Five years later, Saturninus founded the colony of Narbo in southern Gaul
in 118 BC and proposed colonies in Africa, Achaea, Sicily and Macedonia.[61]
Later, following Marius' army reforms, both he and Sulla founded colonies
in Corsica, and it is argued that Marius founded several towns in the
Medjerda valley in Africa, in which he settled veterans from the Jugurthan
War and also Gaetulian Allies.[62] From these tentative beginnings, colonial
settlement of veterans overseas had become acceptable by the end of the
civil wars between Octavian and Antony with, for example, some twenty-
six veteran colonies being established on the coast of the North African
provinces. Cassius Dio suggests that the process was terminated in 13 BC,
when the grant of land was replaced with a cash sum on completion of

---

[58] Fentress (2004).   [59] Augustus, *Res Gestae Divi Augusti*, 28.
[60] Livy, *Epit. Per.* 60; Vell. Pat.1.15, 2.7; App. *Pun.*136, *B Civ.* 1.24; Plut. *C. Gracch.* 10.
[61] Vell. Pat. 2.7; Aur.Vict. *Caes.* 73.
[62] Plin. *HN* 3.80; see Benabou (1976), pp. 35–6 for a summary of the debate.

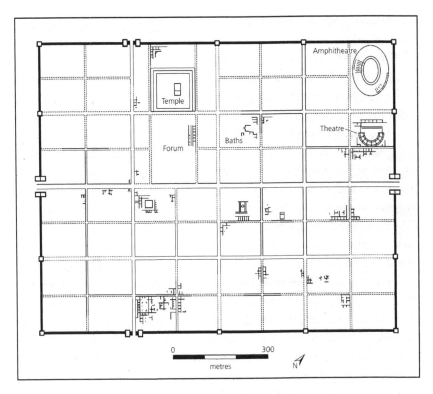

2.6 Aosta: plan of the Augustan colony: showing the relationship between the location of major monuments (forum, theatre, amphitheatre), the major route through the city and the city's walls.

service.[63] Nevertheless, we find numerous veteran colonies founded in the western provinces after this date and down to the early second century AD. The question remains whether these new settlements were significantly different from those traditionally founded in the Republic of old. What was their purpose? Were they so different from the colonies founded in Italy? Did they represent a new form of urbanism? To answer these questions, we need to examine two colonial foundations of the Augustan age: Aosta, within the newly conquered territory of the Salassi in the Italian Alps, and Mérida, the future centre of the Iberian province of Lusitania.

Aosta presents us with a contemporary image of the nature of a colony in the Augustan period (fig. 2.6). The campaigns of Augustus' general Varro against the Salassi resulted in their capture and large numbers were sold into slavery at Eporedia (Ivrea), a neighbouring colony previously

---

[63] Dio Cass. 54.25; see Keppie (1984).

established in 100 BC to suppress the region. Over 8,000 fighting men and a further 28,000 inhabitants were removed from the region. To repopulate the area 3,000 colonists were sent by Augustus and the city of *Augusta Praetoria* was founded on the site of Varro's military camp.[64] It is clear from Dio, however, that only the male Salassi of fighting age were enslaved with the provision that they would not be freed for twenty years.[65] The most productive land was allocated to veterans from the Praetorian Guard in 25 BC, with the establishment of the town itself slightly later in 23 or 22 BC. The Salassi appear in an inscription as *incolae*, or resident aliens within the town, and Keppie estimates that, if the valley was divided into fifty-*iugera* plots for the settlers, little land would have remained for the Salassi.[66] The former praetorians may have brought with them not just their immediate family but also their brothers and relatives within their extended *familia*. Laffi goes further and makes an argument for the *Salassi incolae* to have been composed of those members of this people who had deserted to Rome during Varro's campaign.[67] What is clear is that the local communities of the Salassi were destroyed and replaced by a colony which included a small number of the tribe as resident aliens with limited political rights. The fact that they appear in an inscription so soon after the foundation of the colony suggests that they were still a group incorporated into the town, as opposed to the defeated and dispossessed.

The city of Aosta (*Augusta Praetoria*) was situated at a central point within the valley of the Durias, in a region associated in antiquity with gold-mining, which was facilitated through the use of large quantities of water. Two Alpine routes converged at this point north of the colony of Eporedia.[68] The town was formed from the earlier military camp, with walls that enclose an area of 754×572 metres. Some would see the urban form as a prototype for other cities in the provinces.[69] The forum was located at the junction of the two routes through the Alps, with the other public buildings – a theatre built shortly after the foundation and an amphitheatre constructed in the first half of the first century AD – lying to the east, close to the Porta Praetoria and the route into Italy itself. These buildings and the forum complex took up about 17 per cent of the total area of the city within the walls (fig. 2.6). The presence of the town was an important factor in creating a Roman landscape and a sense of security in the former territory of a hostile people. The route from the town of Eporedia led up the valley with the crossing point of the river Buthier

[64] Strabo, 4.6.7.   [65] Dio Cass. 53.25.5.   [66] *ILS* 6753; Keppie (1983), pp. 206–7.
[67] Laffi (1966), pp. 178, 202.   [68] Plin. *HN* 3.123; Strabo, 4.6.7.   [69] Corni (1989), p. 52.

marked by the triumphal arch of Augustus. Six hundred metres further on were the town walls, and once within the town a decision over which route across the Alps would be taken had to be made at the forum in front of the temples. Taking either route led up to sanctuaries with *mansiones* (inns or stopping-points) at Summa Alpis Graia and Alpis Poenina at the top of the passes. Votive tablets have been found at these sites.[70] This combination of sacred places with a landscape that had been surveyed and divided amongst colonists, with a colonial town at its heart, marked a transformation of the place from wild mountains, associated with dangerous enemies, into a sacred landscape of victory and subjugation of those enemies.

Augusta Emerita (modern Mérida) is a town whose origins are inscribed in its very title, which is derived from the word *emeritus*, a veteran. It was built at the highest navigable point of the river Guadiana and was a bridging-point, as well as a point from which goods were exported and imported (fig. 2.7).[71] Veterans from V *Alaudae* and X *Gemina* were settled here at a date somewhere between 25 and 15 BC.[72] The laying-out of the town was celebrated on the local coinage, with issues showing a priest ploughing the *pomerium*, or sacred boundary of the city.[73] It is made clear by Cicero that the sanctity of the boundary produced in this way should not be underestimated.[74] The walls built along the ploughed line survive in places at Mérida but are better known from the local coinage that shows a double-arched gateway flanked by towers with the words *Augusta Emerita* emblazoned above the gates (fig. 2.8).[75] Some scholars have argued that these coins do not represent the city walls, but the camps of the legions. However, we need to remember that the first known army camp built from stone was that of the Praetorian Guard in Rome constructed later under the emperor Tiberius. These Augustan coins clearly represent the city's main gateway and defensive circuit of walls. The town itself was divided up with an orthogonal grid of streets, and not one but two fora were developed at central points in the city shortly after foundation (fig. 2.7). Both were dominated by temples to unidentified gods, but one of the fora also displayed a very distinctive iconography that is also found within the Forum of Augustus in Rome, such as *clipei* decorated with the heads of Jupiter Ammon and Medusa, as well as caryatids.[76] Some have suggested

---

[70] Barocelli (1932).   [71] Curchin (1991), p. 106.   [72] Dio Cass. 53.26.1.

[73] Burnett, Amandry and Ripollès (1992), pp. 69–73, nos 5, 6, 7, 11, 13.

[74] Cic. *Phil.* 2.102; see Gargola (1995) for a discussion of the formal rites of foundation.

[75] Burnett, Amandry and Ripollès (1992), nos 10,12, 20, 21–7, 30–3, 38, 41–4; see Perring 1991b on symbolism of city walls.

[76] See De La Barrera (2000) for a full catalogue.

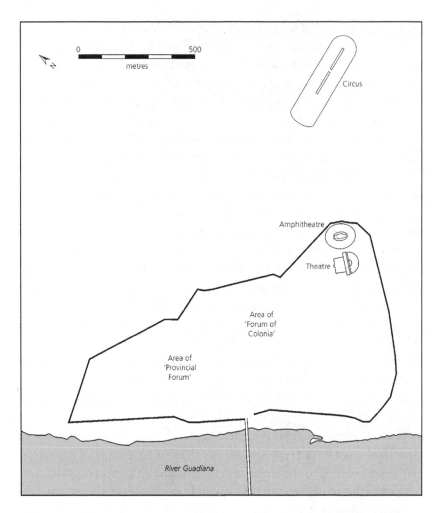

2.7 Mérida: plan of the Augustan colony: showing the distribution of monuments within the city, including the separation of amphitheatre and theatre from the fora (compare fig.2.4)

that the two fora had quite different purposes: one was for the colony and the other for the province. However, this explanation stems from a desire to distinguish two legal units as part of an explanatory framework which is only applied to the study of Roman urbanism in Spain (for example at Tarraco), and may not be applicable at Mérida. There is an alternative explanation that needs to be considered. The availability of space for the development of monuments was far greater at this green-field site than within the cities of Italy. The inclusion of two fora should instead be related to the development in Rome of two or more fora, and the fact that even the

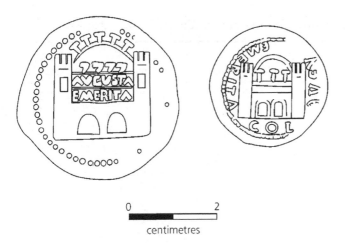

0   2

centimetres

2.8 Mérida: the image of the city as represented on coins minted by this Augustan colony. Both of these coins were minted after Augustus' deification in the reign of the emperor Tiberius.

Forum of Augustus was constructed with more than one function in mind: for the reception of embassies and for the accommodation of the significantly increased amount of legal business. The colonial setting at Mérida permitted the inclusion of two fora that need not be assigned specific jurisdictions at the date of their construction.

The importance of religion to the new settlers cannot be underestimated; the local coinage features a foundation rite and the city's walls.[77] However there are other religious symbols on the coinage: a river goddess issuing water appears on the reverse of several of the coins showing the ploughing of the *pomerium*.[78] There is a connection between the river deity and the sacred action of ploughing the boundary of the city. Like the appearance of river gods in other settings, the river goddess here is aiding the act of foundation, just as the Tiber aided Rome's foundation in the myth of Romulus and Remus. A religious link to the colony's past was made through issues that showed an eagle between the standards of the fifth and tenth legions. A theatre was built, or under construction, in 16 BC and the amphitheatre, which was funded by Agrippa and largely cut from the hillside, was complete or under construction in 8 BC;[79] the structures would have facilitated the retelling of the myths not just of the new city

---

[77] See Howego (2005) on the themes of local coinage.

[78] Burnett, Amandry and Ripollès (1992), nos 5–11; Howego (2005), p. 12 on river gods.

[79] See Durán Cabello (2004) for a full study of the theatre.

Table 2.1 Coinage referring to urban features from Spain (Augustus-Tiberius)

Town name	Status	Ploughing *Pomerium*	Walls	Altar	Local deity	Temple	Vexillum	Army standards
Mérida	*Colonia*	X	X	X	X	X		X
Italica	*Municipium*			X			X	X
Gades	*Municipium*					X		
Cordoba	*Colonia*							X
Acci	*Colonia*							X
Carthago Nova	*Colonia*				X	X	X	
Ilici	*Colonia*			X		X		X
Tarraco	*Colonia*			X		X		
Celsa	*Colonia*	X						
Caesaraugusta	*Colonia*	X				X	X	X
Abdera	?					X		

but also of Rome. Later, after Augustus' death in AD 14, an altar of *Providentia Augusta* appeared on the coinage at a time when we can assume the *colonia* to be established and we also find an image of a temple on a coin with the legend *Aeternitati Augustae*.[80] These could be seen as representations of buildings dedicated to the worship of the imperial cult within the *colonia* and therefore as expressions of loyalty to the new emperor. At this site, we are aided in our interpretation by the issue of coins. This phenomenon is not unique and, as Table 2.1 demonstrates, is also encountered at other towns founded in Spain during the Triumviral and Augustan periods.[81]

What we have at Mérida, and some of the other towns of Spain, is urbanism on a very sophisticated scale, and much of it constructed by or for the veterans within the first generation of the colony. The contrast with the erratic fortunes of Cosa's two hundred and fifty years of haphazard development is striking. Moreover, Mérida provides us with an understanding of what a town should be: a place defined by a ritual, a place of religion, a place that included an amphitheatre and a theatre, a place that had water led to it by an aqueduct, and a place that utilised marble in the decoration of its forum and other buildings. We have all that we might expect to find in a Roman town, and rather more than we could find in

[80] Burnett, Amandry and Ripollès (1992), nos 28, 34–6, 45–6 for the altar, nos 29, 47, 48 for the temple.
[81] Burnett, Amandry and Ripollès (1992); Ripollès (2005).

contemporary Cosa. It is as though urbanism had been thought through and made manifest in a single place. The form of urbanism has all the elements found in the more successful cities of Italy and employs the ideologies of architecture and myth found in the rebuilt Augustan capital. In the colony and in the capital, Rome, we can identify the same cultural style with a similar ideological basis. This would seem to have been fundamental to the Augustan period and cannot be found previously in the colonies of veterans, let alone in those colonies of earlier periods. The presence of the Augustan style of urban life within the colonies provides us with the first definition of a Roman cultural identity.[82] Colonisation no longer consisted of leaving a group of Roman citizens to get on with it at a specific location, but instead involved building a town with rites similar to those that were traditionally seen to be used in founding Rome.

Not every colony, let alone every city, developed an urban way of life in the manner of Mérida, with its close relationship to Rome and the actions of Agrippa and Augustus within it. What it indicates, however, is a notion or ideology of what a town should have and, in other towns across the Empire, we can find attempts being made to gain access to this form of urban life or to adapt it to local conditions or limited financial resources. For example, Conimbriga produced a forum, basilica, temple, small *curia*, baths and an aqueduct, yet had no Roman status.[83] Colonies such as Mérida, like the capital, would provide new meanings of the city that would be incorporated into those already existing within the Italian peninsula and Gallia Narbonensis.

THE COLONIES AND THE DEVELOPMENT OF ROMAN URBANISM

Much of the emphasis in this chapter has been on highlighting the fragility of the colonies, and the well-excavated and well-published example of Cosa tends to dominate the discussion. Hence, we now need to examine whether the colonies were producing a new meaning to Roman urbanism?

To begin to answer this question we need an example, and one exhibiting change through successive phases. The colony at Luni was founded in 177 BC and was developed with a forum and *capitolium* during the second century BC within a walled area of 560×438 metres (fig. 2.9).[84] A Tuscan three-*cella* temple was constructed at the highest point in this low-lying

---

[82] Keay (1995), p. 305.   [83] Richardson (1995), p. 348.   [84] Livy, 41.13.

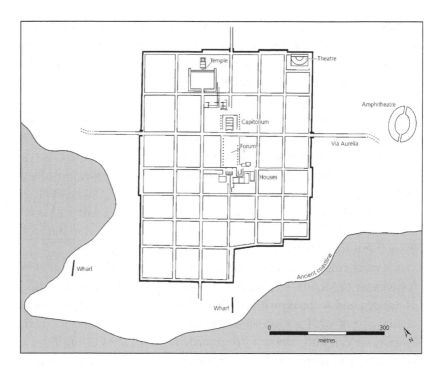

2.9 Luni: plan showing the relationship between the monuments of the city and the Via Aurelia, as well as the later monuments (amphitheatre and theatre).

coastal city in the second century BC.[85] The main road through the colony was aligned with the Via Aurelia, which was constructed in 109 BC along the line of an existing road.[86] A theatre was built over an existing *insula* block during the Republican period. The forum was completely remodelled in the first century AD with the *capitolium* as its focus, but continued to include shops.[87] The city continued to exist in a form similar to that established on its foundation, but with some elaboration and restoration of the existing structures, including the cladding of buildings in local marble. It was only in the second century AD that an amphitheatre was added outside the walls of the city. Luni reveals considerable continuity within its urban form and suggests that the continued definition of urbanism here was a place with a forum, at least one temple, walls and a grid of streets. What was different, though, was a fusion in the forum between the space of commerce and that of a sanctuary or religious site.[88] It had no parallels at Rome prior to the Fora of Julius Caesar and Augustus. Absent

---

[85] See Frova (1973) for the excavated material.   [86] Frova (1973), p. 34.
[87] Frova (1973), p. 192.   [88] Zanker (2000), pp. 33–7.

from the excavated remains of the forum at Luni is a *comitium*, unlike in the earlier colonies of Cosa, Paestum or Fregellae. It was this conception of the forum as a sacred place, as well as a place for business, that was reproduced later in Rome by Julius Caesar and Augustus, but it can be found earlier in the colonies and was reproduced in other cities at about the same time (for example at Pompeii; see Chapter 7 for further discussion). The construction of new towns was causing a rethink in how the shape of the city should be formed. Later, in an overview of the new Rome of the imperial period and the colonial foundations of that city, Aulus Gellius (*NA* 16.13) saw a direct relationship:

> But the relationship of the colonies is a different one; for they do not come into citizenship from without; nor grow from roots of their own, but they are as it were transplanted from the *civitas* (i.e. Rome) and have all the laws and institutions of the Roman people, not those of their own choice. This condition, although it is more exposed to control and less free, is nevertheless thought preferable and superior because of the greatness and majesty (*amplitudinem maiestatemque*) of the Roman people, of which these colonies seem to be miniatures and copies (*quasi effigies parvae simulacraque*).[89]

A distinction is being made by Gellius between the colonies and *municipia*, one of which many people seem to have had limited grasp (even those living in the colonies). Hence, he also provides an explanation of the different legal status of the inhabitants of a *municipium*:

> *Municipes*, then, are Roman citizens from free towns, using their own laws and enjoying their own rights, merely sharing with the Roman people an honorary *munus* or privilege...and bound by no law of the Roman people, except such as their own citizens have officially ratified...the rights of the *municipia* have become obscure and invalid, and from ignorance of their existence the *municipes* are no longer able to make use of them. (Aulus Gellius *NA* 16.3)

The colonies were seen as *simulacra* or copies of Rome because they employed the same legal mechanisms as Rome. At the same time, even in the first century AD, the foundation of a colony created a settlement of citizens who might act in the face of rebellion and inculcate respect for the law amongst Rome's allies.[90] Allied cities (*municipia*) were not necessarily very different from the *coloniae* and developed similar legal codes and

---

[89] Trans. Loeb.
[90] Tac. *Ann.* 12.32.5 makes clear that Colchester's veterans acted in an exceptional manner; in this case the veterans flouted the laws and oppressed the allies of Rome in the first 11 years from its foundation, see Tac. *Ann.* 14.31–2; *Agr.* 16.

systems of annual magistracies. Yet, by the Empire, the status of *colonia* was desirable and we find Italica petitioning Hadrian to be allowed to replace its current status of a *municipium*; Hadrian was to point out the advantages of local laws over the rights of the *coloniae*.[91] By the second century AD, to be a *colonia* was to be more Roman than a *municipium* and to buy into the 'greatness and majesty of the Roman people'.[92] What we see in the case of Italica in the second century AD, and in the writings of Gellius, is an invented tradition of the Roman *colonia*. Yet this tradition could be important in the shaping of the city on the ground. In the case of Italica, in order to be truly a *simulacrum* of Rome, expansion was necessary and new buildings were added that reflected developments in the architecture of Rome (fig. 4.5 and discussion in Chapter 4).[93] These may seem oversized for the city, but may reflect the conception of a *simulacrum* of Rome as it was in the second century AD; whereas earlier cities reflected a *simulacrum* of Rome from an earlier age, with rather smaller architectural structures. What changed was the image of the city of Rome that could be mirrored in the major developments in cities and colonies of the second and third centuries AD – particularly in the birthplaces of the emperors, notably Italica and Lepcis Magna (fig. 5.4). Different colonies reflected an urban image found in Rome in quite different periods, according to their date of foundation and their ability to concentrate resources for their development.

THE END OF COLONISATION

As we have seen, the distribution of veteran soldiers in colonial foundations, mostly on sites of existing settlement, resulted in a minor redistribution of land at a macro level, although at a local level the arrival of veteran colonists was far from welcome. The veterans still retained a military identity; at the end of the first century AD, Pliny would call Arles a colony of the sixth legion, Béziers a colony of the seventh legion, and Orange a colony of the second legion.[94] Julius Caesar's settlement of veterans in Italy resulted in the presence of a force of soldiers, who could be called on in the crisis following the dictator's death.[95] In some ways the veterans were a garrison in favour of their victorious general and attached to their former commander. The number of colonies of veterans founded in the period of

[91] Salmon (1969), pp. 70–1; Gell *NA* 16.13.   [92] Zanker (2000), p. 41.
[93] Boatwright (1997).   [94] Plin. *HN* 3.36.   [95] Rawson (1994), pp. 468–75.

civil wars can be seen as a function of the exceptional scale of military operations undertaken, and the need to demobilise a large number of soldiers.[96] Significantly, it is in this period that we find the development of the term *veteranus*,[97] which should be seen as a response to the process of demobilisation. The Triumviral and Augustan periods were the last when sustained veteran colonisation took place in Italy and the provinces.[98] There were some attempts to settle veterans in the cities of Italy,[99] but Tacitus saw such attempts as doomed to failure, due to the soldiers' desire to remain in the provinces in which they had served.[100] The twenty years of military service introduced by Augustus (and later increased to twenty-five years) as a standard feature of life within the army detached the army recruits from their original homelands. The civil wars of AD 69 did not involve the recruitment of veterans for the fighting, but instead relied on the existing armies of Rome's frontiers. As a result of their dispersal, as opposed to their concentration in a single site, the veterans continued to be a force that could be mobilised, but they were a less potent force for the development of urbanism.[101] Where soldiers were settled in colonies, this did not result in the growth of urban life in the first generation of settlement, as can be seen from an examination of their occupation of the former barrack-blocks at Colchester, amongst other sites (fig. 2.10),[102] and, if we are to trust our information from Tacitus, they maintained very militaristic attitudes towards the local inhabitants.[103] The Trajanic colony of Sarmizegetusa in Dacia was initially constructed in wood over a twenty-two-and-a-half-hectare site, and only later developed into a seventy-five-hectare walled area with two fora.[104] This implies that migration and population movements underpinned the development of new cities.[105] Indeed, a number of cases, not least Cosa, demonstrate that, without the reinforcement of the initial colonists through migration, the colony would fail.

THE SIGNIFICANCE OF ROME'S COLONIES

The colonies are a prominent feature of the texts written years after the foundation of cities in remote locations. Livy might write about the problems of peopling these distant places, but mostly the colonies are seen by

---

[96] Whittaker (1996), p. 603.   [97] Keppie (1983), pp. 46–7.   [98] Dio Cass. 54.25.5.
[99] Keppie (1984).   [100] Tac. *Ann.*13.31, 35, 14.17, 27.
[101] See the debate between Fentress (1979), (1983), (1984); Cherry (1998); and Shaw (1983).
[102] Creighton (2006); and the papers in Hurst (1999).   [103] Tac. *Ann.* 14.31.
[104] Diaconescu (2004).   [105] Eutr. *Brev.* 8.6; Dio Cass. 68.14 on migration to Dacia.

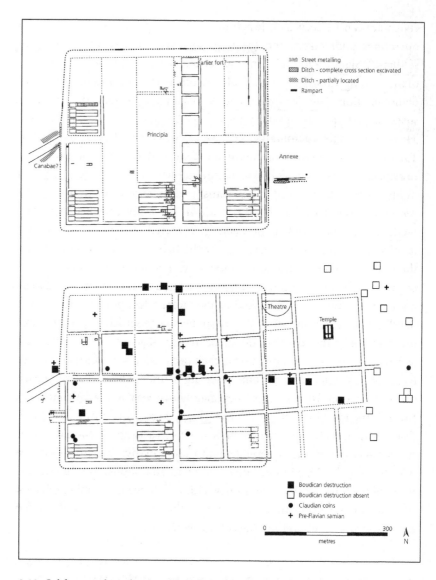

2.10 Colchester: plans showing (above) the legionary fortress and (below) the *colonia*. Some of the organisation of space in these two plans shows the continuity between living in the fortress as a soldier and living in a colony as a veteran.

writers of the first century AD as one of Rome's many achievements and a reflection of the majesty of the Roman people. These factors ensure the colonies a greater prominence in the literature on the urbanisation of both Italy and the provinces. After all, even for Pliny, the colonies may have been the most famous of places, but as a type of settlement they were in the minority: for example, in Spain 9 out of his 175 towns in Baetica, and 12 out of his 179 towns in the rest of Spain; or in Italy 4 out of his 49 towns in Umbria, or 6 out of his 26 towns in Aemilia.[106] What Pliny does is to follow Augustus' system of listing the colonies of a region first and then the other settlements.[107] Roman colonisation was not the factor producing the network of cities listed in Pliny. As we saw at the end of Chapter 1, a single individual, Aemilius Lepidus, could have a major impact on the development of cities. Not all cases are as explicit and there were probably other factors at work that are hidden to us but which might follow the examples discussed in Chapter 1. The settlements found in Pliny's list of the towns of Italy that include the word Forum (Forum Novum, Forum Clodii, Forum Livii, etc.) are a defined group of settlements in which markets, political meetings and legal cases were held.[108] The names suggest the founding of a new forum by a particular person, in the manner of the Elogium of Pola that states that a person whose name is now missing set up the *aedes* and the forum.[109] The places listed by Pliny were the successful foundations that survived, while many others may have failed (see Chapter 4 for discussion of the development of Forum Novum). In the processes of development in Italy and the Mediterranean provinces from the third century BC down to the second century AD, the Roman aristocracy was involved in numerous initiatives to develop its own properties; and it is not inconceivable that town foundation might have contributed to their enhancement, even at the level of the construction of a forum and a temple as a central place. We know of thirty-one Fora in Italy and a further seventeen from the western provinces.[110] The place-names Forum Traiani and Forum Hadriani provide firm indications that such places continued to be founded down to the second century AD. The forty-eight known examples should be seen as indicative of a more generic process of town foundation. This did not depend on the state taking the initiative to found colonies in all cases. Aristocrats, or the state, or the emperor, might found new towns.

Many of the colonies were constructed in already defined centres (for instance, Felsina in Italy was renamed as the colony of Bononia).[111] Nevertheless, the definition of a place as a colony or *municipium* mattered to the Roman elite and marked these places out in the provinces as having a higher status than the *oppida*, whose barbarian names Pliny could not easily express in Latin or which he designated as *oppida ignobilia*.[112] What the

---

[106] Plin. *HN* 3.7, 3.18, 3.113–14, 3.115–16.   [107] Plin. *HN* 3.46.
[108] Ruoff-Väänänen (1978); Laurence (1999), pp. 27–38; Festus 74L, see now Coarelli (2005) who sheds light on the subject using a fusion of archaeology and text.
[109] *ILLRP* 454.   [110] Ruoff-Väänänen (1978), pp. 76–9.
[111] Plin. *HN* 3.115.   [112] Plin. *HN* 3.1.8; 3.37.

geographical texts (Mela, Pliny, Ptolemy and Strabo) demonstrate is the sheer number of towns in the Roman Empire, which have been confirmed archaeologically in many cases. This has caused historians to suggest that the level of urbanisation, in terms of population, was higher in the Roman Empire than in any other pre-industrial society in history.[113] Colonisation distributed a population of Roman citizens in communities regarded as having a very strong Roman identity across the western Mediterranean and beyond; indeed, perhaps as many as 1,250,000 people may have been involved over the period of the last two centuries BC.[114] Colonisation established a series of cities that were expected to develop the traits of urban life in the future; at the point of colonisation, the site in many cases had more in common with a garrison than with a civilian settlement. Moreover, the sites of these towns were defined ritually with a boundary, as well as with a street grid that was sometimes larger than the needs or requirements of the initial settlers.

The colonies founded in Italy provide us with key information for the study of the Roman city. Those founding a colony were involved in a process of articulating what was needed in a city that was to be populated by citizens subject to Rome and her allies. At Cosa, we can see the definition of these needs to have been fairly basic – revolving around issues of defence, property and social hierarchy. The colony at Paestum involved some re-articulation of the existing urban form in which citizens and allies would live. At Cremona and Placentia, at the end of the third century BC, defence and protection from a hostile population were key factors, although they were not adequately dealt with and so many of the settlers took flight. The issues differ according to local conditions at a site. This causes difficulties for historians attempting to provide a long-term history of Roman colonisation, or to understand its form as a single unified phenomenon. Perhaps this urge for viewing colonisation as a unified phenomenon is derived from Velleius Paterculus and Livy, who produce histories of the Roman people that prominently feature the founding of colonies. Significantly, they do this in the early years of the Roman Empire, a time associated with a greater intensity in colonial foundation. This was the time when some of the colonies founded in Spain, including Mérida, produced images of city foundation that linked the founding of their city to that of Rome by Romulus. Indeed, they may have been the source of the idea that the colonies were *simulacra* of Rome. Yet we should perhaps recognise that

[113] Jongman (2003), pp. 101–2.
[114] Scheidel (2004), p. 19; but to be read with discussion by Erdkamp (2008).

the relationship between the city of Rome and the colonies ought also to involve a reflection of the colonies in the physical appearance of the city of Rome. Both Rome and the colonies were elements in considering the question of what was a city: something of considerable age in the case of Rome, or something that was new in the case of the Augustan colony; a place of considerable population in the case of Rome, or a place of a few thousand in the case of the colony. Whatever the dialogue might have been, both Rome and her colonies were cities and both were also highly valued as places more closely identified with Romanness.

3 | City foundation, government and urbanism

The town or city has been recognised as playing a vital role in the government of the Roman Empire. It was characteristic of the developed geography of the Roman West and was a feature that differentiated the Empire from the barbarian cultures beyond its frontiers. In this chapter we seek to outline the interplay between the city as a place of government and the city as a distinct geographical formation that was defined by means of its existence in time and space. We will begin by investigating the legal and geographical distinctions between the various types of towns, and then move on to examine the myths of town foundation that helped to define new cities and to create a sense of their past once they were established in the landscape. There follows a detailed examination of the rules of government found in the town charters: our focus will be on the charter from Urso in Spain. These charters give us a picture of the limits of government and the opportunities given to annually elected magistrates to develop their communities. The cities of the Empire were not, however, just places of politics and government. We will examine the holding of periodic markets and auctions which, quite apart from their economic functions, were a fundamental and jealously guarded legal privilege of the cities. The city also played a role as a place of justice, both locally for the community and for traders dealing with that community, and at a regional level where some cities gained status as the locations to which the provincial governor came to dispense justice. This takes the discussion of the city up to the level of the province and reveals two important roles for the city as a place from which tax was collected and from where recruits to the Roman army originated. These topics reveal the ways in which the local city was integrated into a wider vision of the Roman Empire as a territory held in common. Some cities, most notably Lyon, ancient Lugdunum, did develop as regional centres through their role as a meeting place for the worship of the deified emperors and the holding of sessions of the provincial council. We shall demonstrate that the cities of the Empire may have possessed local autonomy and a very local form of government, but could be integrated into a larger political geography at the level of the province or, more fundamentally, as part of a Roman territory that encompassed both the western and the eastern Empire.

CATEGORIES OF TOWNS

In the previous chapter, we looked at a particular type of town: the colony. However, the Roman Empire was not entirely composed of colonies. There was in fact an array of settlement types: at the top end were the *coloniae*, and the *municipia*, and then came three types of settlement that displayed less developed forms of urbanism: *praefecturae* (prefectures), *fora* (forums), and *conciliabula* (rural settlements). The colonies were distinguished from all other types of settlement by the legal language employed for their foundation. This is made clear in the *lex Iulia agraria* dated either to 59 BC or, later, to the period 47–44 BC: 'Whatever colony shall have been founded or whatever *municipium, praefectura, forum or conciliabulum* shall have been constituted' (*Quae colonia hac lege deducta quodue municipium praefectura forum conciliabulum constitutum erit*).[1] The legal language takes care to identify the various types of settlement and to use the relevant verb. Less care was taken in the description as an *oppidum* of the settlement of Cingulum founded by Labienus, but the care taken over the language used to refer to the act of Labienus that constituted the town and built it means that we should see the status of this town as that of either a *municipium* or a *forum*.[2] A similar dichotomy between colonies and other *oppida* or towns is found in the *lex agraria* of 111 BC and also in Livy (as demonstrated by Sherwin-White), and is found in a number of other writers such as Pliny in the *Natural History*, as we saw at the end of the previous chapter.[3]

The foundation of a colony was quite a different matter from that of the other towns. As we saw in Chapter 2, it was associated with the definition of a boundary or *pomerium* which divided what the Romans regarded as home, within the *pomerium*, from a zone of military action beyond the *pomerium*.[4] Intriguingly, the term *oppidum* is used to refer to this zone within the walls, or *pomerium*, of a colony and to the defined urban area within a *municipium*.[5] The military association of the colonies appears to have been absent from other cities. Significantly, Roman magistrates in the Republican period did not found *municipia*, but, after the Social War, they did provide towns with new law codes. The ability granted under the *lex*

---

[1] Crawford (1989); Crawford (1996a), pp. 763–72.

[2] Caes. *B Civ.* 1.15.2: *etiam Cingulo, quod oppidum Labienus constituerat suaque pecunia exaedificaverat.* See Gabba (1972).

[3] *Lex Agr.* 22; Crawford (1996a), pp. 113–80; Sherwin-White (1973), p. 72.

[4] Gargola (1995), pp. 111–12.

[5] For a colony see the *Lex Coloniae Genetivae* 84 and 85; Crawford (1996a), p. 404; for a *municipium* see *Lex Irnitana* 62; González (1986), p. 166.

Iulia agraria to constitute (*constituere*) implied anything from establishing and creating a new city, as in the case of the *oppidum* at Cingulum, to ordering an existing settlement.[6] It is clear, however, that Roman magistrates did not constitute *municipia ex nihilo*,[7] but would be much more likely to constitute a *praefectura*, a *forum*, or a *conciliabulum*. These settlements and others already in existence could become *municipia* at a later date.[8] The act of constituting involved the ordering of the town, including the provision of a new legal code or town charter, and was a procedure that continued in Italy throughout the first century BC and into the Imperial period (for instance, Crawford cites the example of Veii being constituted under Augustus), during the reigns of the Julio-Claudian emperors.[9] The results of the procedure can be found in the settlement types destroyed by the Boudiccan revolt in AD 60–61: Tacitus calls Colchester a *colonia*, Verulamium a *municipium*, and London a settlement that was full of traders and undergoing growth – but did not hold the status of the other towns.[10] Interestingly, however, Tacitus also refers to London with the anticipation that it would be raised not to the status of a *municipium*, but to that of a *colonia*.[11] Just as the people of Italica petitioned Hadrian to be raised in status from that of a *municipium* to that of a *colonia*,[12] other towns could do the same. Our record of this process is far from complete and there is more evidence for it from the reign of Hadrian than from any other. Mary Boatwright identifies eleven *municipia* that were raised to the status of *coloniae*: seven in Africa, two in Italy, one in Mauretania, and one in Baetica.[13] More impressive, perhaps, is the number of towns identified by her as raised to the status of *municipium*: ten in Africa, two in Noricum, two in Dacia, two in Pannonia, one in Moesia, one in Raetia, one in Hispania Tarraconensis and one in Mauretania. These examples are only the ones known to us and our very knowledge of them arises out of the pattern of the survival of evidence from antiquity, but they do point to the existence of an important phenomenon: the change of status of a city as a *beneficium* granted or confirmed by the emperor.[14] What developed was an official hierarchy of settlement types and a system of mobility within the hierarchy according to which settlements could move from one status to another,[15] subject to regulation by the emperor himself.

[6] Gargola (1995), p. 112.   [7] Gargola (1995), p. 109; Sherwin-White (1973), p. 170.
[8] Crawford (1995), p. 422.
[9] Cic. *Fam.* 13.11; Crawford (1995), pp. 422–3; Crawford (1996a) for the legal texts.
[10] Tac. *Ann.* 14.21–3.
[11] Tac. *Ann.* 14.22; Perring (1991a) for discussion of the development of London.
[12] Gell. *NA* 16.13.   [13] Boatwright (2000), pp. 36–41.
[14] *Dig.* 47.21.3.1; Plin. *Pan.* 37.3.   [15] For further examples see Syme (1981).

Looking at the different settlement types archaeologically, we would not be able to define which towns had been *coloniae* and which *municipia*. Legal status was something that the inhabitants of a place saw as defining themselves in relationship to Rome. For example, after the Social War, the towns of Rome's *socii* (allies) in Italy became *municipia* with their grant of citizenship. Scholars have suggested that this gave an impetus to the urbanisation of the settlements of Italy in a similar way to what occurred at Cingulum; constituting a town was associated with major building projects.[16] The connection in this case, however, seems to have arisen from a change in citizenship on the one hand, and the granting of a new legal code for the town on the other. The connection between this change of citizenship and the appearance of monuments in the towns of Italy need not be directly connected. Other literary texts, referring to the Imperial period, regard the change in legal status as a recognition of the development of urban amenities.[17] We need to appreciate some chronological distinctions: in the Republic and in the first century of the Empire, changes in status were generated from the top down, whereas in the second century AD the impetus came from the local communities.[18] Any relationship between the presence of particular monuments and a change in status appears to be a red herring, since monument-building in the cities (whether in the Republic or the Empire) was a far from uniform response to the various cultural changes occurring. The process by which a change in status came about was pretty haphazard; it depended in the Empire upon a desire or aspiration on the part of the inhabitants and the grant of this status as a gift or *beneficium* by the emperor.[19] The problem in both cases is that it is almost impossible to use the individual cases to make generalisations about responses to a new legal status or about the Roman recognition of a new status.[20] What a change in status does indicate, though, is an aspiration for recognition of a higher status. It is difficult to see what might have stimulated this desire for change, or the meaning of such a change of status at a local level. However, the change in status did matter – just as the designation of city status in the UK is campaigned for locally, with some success in the case of Sunderland and without success (to date) in the case of Reading. Both town charters from antiquity in their developed form and a town's status as a *colonia*, a *municipium* or a *forum* not only provided a means to understand a town but also created an ordered form of

[16] Gabba (1972).   [17] E.g. Tacitus on London; see Bowman (1996), pp. 355–6.
[18] Sherwin-White (1973), pp. 237–8.   [19] Dio Cass. 72.19.
[20] Sherwin-White (1973), pp. 234–6.

3.1 Curule Chair (*sella curulis*) and *fasces* on a funerary relief of a city magistrate Gaius Otacilius Oppianus (*quattuovir*) discovered in 1793 at Graveson, Bouches du Rhône (southern Gaul). Note that the *fasces* are a hybrid form, that have leaves surmounting them rather than an axe.

government – one that eschewed those forms of government seen as un-Roman, such as kingship and other barbarian modes of rule that were also reflected in the iconography of funerary reliefs (see fig. 3.1).[21] Mary Boatwright uses a comparison of two charters from the first century AD,

[21] App. *Hist. Pref.* 7.

the municipal charter of Irni and the colonial charter of Urso, to demonstrate that the legal constitution of *municipia* and *coloniae* was very similar in nature.[22] The charters of both types of towns were drawn up to facilitate their autonomy, providing a means whereby provincial governors, the Senate and the emperor were freed from dealing with the petty affairs of a local community.[23] A change of status, whether to that of a *municipium* or from that of a *municipium* to that of a *colonia*, may seem a fairly trivial issue, but it can be regarded as a means to give order to 'the formless enthusiasms of the provincial populations',[24] and was a phenomenon only found in Italy and the provinces of the western Roman Empire, perhaps most prominently in Africa, and was absent from the eastern Empire. *disagree!.*

THE CREATION OF CITIES AND CITY GOVERNMENT

The act of founding a colony or constituting a *municipium* defined a place or point in the landscape; it was recognised and categorised by its status and expected to continue to exist in the future, despite the problems of maintaining population that were mentioned in the preceding chapter. As we have seen, from its foundation the Roman city was a vehicle for the creation of order and stability. The day on which the city was founded was to be celebrated by a festival each year which referred either to a foundation myth or to a historical act from the Roman past. Foundation came with a set of laws or statutes that prescribed the government of the new city. These laws established annual elections of magistrates, who would be responsible for the government and collective finances of the city. The statutes need to be examined to understand the nature of government – and its limits – within these communities. During their year of office, magistrates could gain honour from financing games, new public buildings and other urban amenities, and indeed these activities were an obligation written into the statutes or town charter. As a result, not only did magistrates have an opportunity to enter the historical record, or at least the collective memory of the city, but also control over the architectural and spatial form of the city was handed to the elite. They might provide monuments, games and dinners for others, but these gifts should also be seen as signifiers of coercion, that reinforced and legitimated their control over the inhabitants

---

[22] Boatwright (2000), pp. 43–54.   [23] Boatwright (2000), pp. 53–4.
[24] Sherwin-White (1973), p. 234.

and the development of the physical fabric of the city. The town charters established an elite that would take on the burdens of development and ensure that the city might exist in the future. We do in fact tend to find that the person or persons who organised the constitution of a town were also often involved in building public monuments.[25] Equally important for the survival of the new town, and for towns in the longer term, was the holding of regular markets. As we shall see, the right to hold a market was something to be jealously guarded in the first century AD, and could be seen as a defining feature of the role of cities – hence it needs some attention. Alongside the market were other forms of business, most notably those involving the law. A fundamental feature of the city was that its forum or basilica was the place to which individuals might be summoned to appear. Hence our concern in this chapter is not so much with the legal niceties (thoroughly discussed by Crawford), but with the way in which the establishment of colonies and towns created an ordered form of urban living that might be described as distinctly Roman.[26]

The foundation of a city, whether a colony or a *municipium*, was an act that was to be recalled in the future. Many of the cities of the Mediterranean, such as Rome, are well-known for their complex myths of foundation and early development. It seems clear now that the myth of Romulus and Remus developed in Italy during the fourth and third centuries BC.[27] The date of the foundation of Rome appears in calendars of religious festivals and was celebrated publicly. This phenomenon was not unique to Rome itself. The inhabitants of other towns of considerable antiquity, such as Patavium, the birthplace of Livy, constructed their origins in parallel to those of Rome. Their myth of origin traced its ancestry back to the Trojan Antenor, which allowed them both to ally themselves with the myths of Rome, whilst at the same time establishing their own independent Trojan ancestor.[28] The retelling of foundation myths resulted in the development of new versions and points to a dynamic of re-invention of stories about city foundation that caused these myths to retain a relevance with the passage of time.[29]

Those towns founded by Rome, the Latin and Roman colonies, did not have myths like these to recall. Yet their date of foundation was important not just in the local history of the place but also in the history of the Roman people as a whole. Velleius Paterculus lists the foundation dates of Roman

---

[25] E.g. Caes. *B Civ.* 1.15.1 and see Crawford (1995), pp. 421–2 for other examples.
[26] Crawford (1996b).   [27] Wiseman (1995).
[28] Harris (1977); Laurence (1998).   [29] Wiseman (1995).

colonies in a section of his *History of Rome* in order to explain the majesty of the Roman people.[30]

As we saw in Chapter 2, the definition of the space of the town in the act of foundation was recalled or retold visually by a cow and a bull ploughing a furrow; because the bull would be stronger the plough would be directed in a circular motion.[31] The plough was thought to have been lifted up at the places earmarked for the future gates of the city.[32] What this action created was a sacred boundary, or *pomerium*, for the city that determined which things and people were within the city and which outside, and this was to be maintained for the future; violators faced capital punishment for transgressing the sacred boundary – including, for example, encroachment on the space of the *pomerium* through building.[33] The moment of foundation was recalled each year and was treated as a cause for celebration. In 57 BC the colony of Brundisium in southern Italy was celebrating its foundation when Cicero returned from exile in Greece. He recorded that the city was full of people that day – a day that coincidentally was the birthday of his daughter Tullia.[34] A cycle of commemoration underlay that event, however, so that it was possible to know exactly when the commemoration of the town's foundation would take place, thereby enabling Cicero to return to a city full of people in celebration.

A city was not simply founded through a division of space. It also needed a set of statutes to create the conditions and rules for the government of the new town. Fundamental to the government of all the cities founded by Rome was the principle of the annual election of magistrates, who would oversee the running of the city for the period of a single year. This principle of annual election was not unique to Roman cities and can also be found in the cities of the Italian peninsula that have the names of magistrates and their offices recorded in Oscan or Greek. Several statutes referring to the government of cities survive from antiquity. They were inscribed on bronze tablets, but in no case does an entire document survive. The most complete was found at the colony of Urso in Spain and dates to the late first century BC. Similar statutes were applied to all colonies and *municipia*.[35] They were issued either by the Roman people in Rome, or by magistrates in Italy or the

---

[30] Vell. Pat. 1.14–15.

[31] Rykwert (1974), pp. 65–6 reconstructs the procedure from the following texts: Plut. *Rom.* 11; Cato in Serv. *ad Virg. Aen.* 5.755; Macrob. *Sat.* 5.19; Varro, *Ling.* 5.143; Ov. *Fast.* 4.819; Columella, *Rust.* 3.1; Tac. *Ann.* 12.24; Dion. Hal. *Ant. Rom.* 1.79.

[32] Serv. *ad Virg. Aen.* 2.730; Cato *apud Isid. Etym.* 1.15; Plut. *Quaest. Rom.* 27.

[33] See *Dig.* 1.8.11, 1.81, discussed by Esmonde Cleary (2003), p. 79.

[34] Cic. *Att.* 4.1, *Sest.* 131.   [35] See Crawford (1996a); González (1986).

provinces.[36] To modern legal experts the statutes can appear to be poorly drafted, or simply lifted from sections of other legal codes,[37] yet they produced a fairly standard pattern of urbanism. There was room for the survival of earlier practices, particularly in cities previously governed by Greek practices.[38] However, the statutes that do survive provide us with guidelines as to what we might expect from, or how we might begin to define the nature of, the Roman city.

THE URSO CHARTER

The *lex Coloniae Genetivae Iuliae* from Urso in Spain, a colony founded by Julius Caesar, will be the focus of the discussion here,[39] but there will be reference to other statutes where they inform us about other practices associated with the city and its government by the elite. The population was deemed to include not just the colonists, but also resident aliens (*incolae*), guests (*hospites*) and visitors (*atuentores*) (126). All of these persons were involved in the life of the city and attended the games and also defended the city if it came under attack (103). All adult males aged between fourteen and sixty living within the city and its territory were required to spend up to five days each year working on public construction projects (98). The statute explicitly expects the wives of colonists/citizens to obey the rules as set out (133). This reveals the legal composition of the colony, comprising those who were citizens and others who were resident or were married to citizens. There was ample room, even in the minds of those who drafted the statute, for the future migration and integration of others into the nascent colonial town. We find in the statute from Heraclea (42–56) that records of those who lived in the town were kept and included all citizens' names, their property and their age, and that copies of this information were sent to Rome. To avoid the census was a crime, and was punished in Bantia by flogging in front of fellow citizens and the confiscation of estates.[40]

The statute from Urso also sets out divisions and regulations to sustain the city and manage its territory, and to prevent damage from being done to either of these. The dead were not to be buried or cremated within the

census results sent to Rome

---

36 Livy, 34.51.6.   37 For a full discussion see Crawford (1996a).
38 See Lomas (1993); Crawford (1996b).   39 See Crawford (1996a), no.25 for the full text.
40 Crawford (1996a), no.13.

sacred boundary that had been ploughed on foundation (73). Places for cremation were to be kept at a distance of five hundred paces from the city itself (74). Thus the dead and their disposal were established beyond the defined area of the city, yet in close proximity to that newly defined space. Within the city itself, nobody was to be permitted to dismantle a building without giving a guarantee to the magistrates of the town that it would in due course be rebuilt (75). Tile-works 'having the capacity to produce three hundred tiles' were to be restricted to areas outside the city (76). Access across the territory of the city was to be established by means of public roads and access to water within the territory was to be granted as a general right (78–9). There is also a clause to establish that lands, woods or buildings that were held by the colony for public use could not be sold or leased to private individuals for more than a period of five years (82). Property boundaries within the territory of the colony were to be established (104). We may note here that the statute from Tarentum highlights the fact that the city owned public and sacred monies as well as public property.[41]

The principal features of the government of Roman cities by the end of the first century BC were a city council or *ordo* of decurions and annually elected magistrates – usually *duumviri* (the two men) and *aediles*. These persons are defined within the clauses of statutes that survive from Tarentum (26–31) and Heraclea (89–97, 110–12) in southern Italy and were required to own a large house (roofed with more than fifteen hundred tiles) and to reside within the city, or a mile from the city in the case of Urso (91). How many decurions were there in a town? The statute of Urso specifies the numbers to be present on certain specific matters: three-quarters, twenty, fifty, half, two-thirds are some of the figures, but there is no mention of the actual number of the *ordo*. We might assume in the region of a hundred persons.[42] Magistrates needed to be over the age of thirty at Heraclea and to have completed six military campaigns as a foot soldier or three campaigns fighting on horseback. No one could become a magistrate if he had been condemned for theft, was insolvent, was a debtor, had ever been or had trained as a gladiator, had ever been an executioner, a prostitute or an actor, or had run a brothel. Nor could he be drawn from the ranks of freed slaves (105), although Crawford has noted that some freedmen were magistrates in Caesarian and Augustan colonies.[43] The intention was to include only those who had proven themselves valuable to the community and had a level of wealth or a wealthy lifestyle sufficient to support their

---

[41] Crawford (1996a), no. 15: 1–6.
[42] Duncan-Jones (1982), pp. 283–7 for variations in number.   [43] Crawford (1996a).

new status as a magistrate within the community. Those who were not worthy should never become decurions or hold a magistracy.

The annually elected magistrates performed their roles in conjunction with the *ordo* of decurions. The *duumviri* (who tended to be older and more senior) took a leading role in all matters that needed to be carried out during their year of office. At Urso they settled the dates for the festivals and sacrifices and let out any contracts for sacrifices in consultation with the *ordo* of decurions – the statute specifies how many needed to be present on each occasion that the *ordo* met (64 and 69). The magistrates were sworn in during an assembly on market-day to undertake to keep accounts and to guard public money, and their scribes swore similar oaths (81). The decurions, however, could raise matters of finance with the *duumviri* for discussion (96). The magistrates were also the figures who administered justice in the town (93–4) and enhanced public property such as the roads (77).

It is clear that the *duumviri* could not simply act on their own and that all public matters needed to be brought to the decurions (e.g. Urso 99). In particular, public matters involving outsiders needed the careful consideration of the decurions and hence were brought to them by the *duumviri*; examples include the appointment of a patron or the sending of embassies (97 and 92). The *duumviri* can also be seen as instruments for carrying out the will of the decurions (e.g. 128). Their status in this role is symbolised by their wearing the *toga praetexta* (toga with purple stripe or trim) and being accompanied by two lictors. In addition, in order to carry out their role, they were assigned a staff of citizens: a servant, two scribes, two messengers, a clerk, a crier, a *haruspex* (expert who interpreted entrails of sacrificial animals) and a flute-player, at a cost of at least 11,100, and at the very most 44,400, sesterces per annum (62). The *aediles* as more junior magistrates were not preceded by lictors but wore the *toga praetexta*. Their staff included: a scribe, a crier, a *haruspex* and a flute-player, plus four public slaves for heavy work. The annual overall cost of this staff was at least 4,600 sesterces and at most 18,400 sesterces, in addition to which there was the upkeep of eight slaves (62). The role of all magistrates in public sacrifices was emphasised by their dress, the presence of a *haruspex* and a flute-player on their staffs and the provision of torches and tapers for their use (fig. 3.2). They were there to carry out the sacrifices as agreed by the *ordo* of decurions, even though there were pontiffs and augurs within the colony (66).

Both *duumviri* and *aediles* were required by statute to organise shows and dramatic festivals in honour of the gods: Jupiter, Juno and Minerva, alongside other ancestral gods. The *aediles* in addition organised a day in the circus or the forum in honour of Venus – the key ancestral figure of Julius Caesar, the

3.2 Magistrate sacrificing with toga drawn over his head with assistants, including a boy (*camillus*) and *victimarius* (with hammer) from the temple of the Genius of Augustus at Pompeii.

founder of the colony. In every case the magistrates were required to spend a minimum of two thousand sesterces of their own money and to have access to specified sums of public money less than this amount (70–1). The games had to be held for the greater part of the day. The seating arrangements were set out so that the decurions and magistrates could enjoy prominence and a preferential view of the performance (125–7), in terms both of proximity to the performers and of the angle at which the audience viewed the performers (see fig. 3.3 for a comparison of views of the stage). The decisions of the decurions were to be obeyed by all, including the magistrates and the decurions, with a heavy fine every time a person did not conform (129).

THE TOWN AS A MARKET

One of the *aediles'* roles was the inspection and control of the city's markets (*nundinae*).[44] These were held periodically in the city at times

---

[44] For *municipia* see the *Lex Irnitana* 19.

(a)

(b)

3.3 View of the stage, upper image from the seats of the *ordo* of decurions and lower image from the middle of the *cavea* (seating area) – small theatre at Pompeii.

determined by the *aediles* (according to the *lex Coloniae Genetivae Iuliae*) and our concern with them here is that they were a legal privilege accorded to certain places and thus marking them out; we are not as much concerned here with their more strictly mercantile aspects. The presence of a market drew people in from the surrounding countryside and integrated them socially and economically at the site of the city.[45] Significantly, the charter from Urso specifies that the *duumviri* should swear oaths of entry into office on a market-day, presumably to ensure a large number of witnesses to the oath. De Ligt has established through an analysis of the use of the words for market in antiquity that there is a connection to the development of towns; it is noted, for example that the words *fora* and *nundinae* are similar in their usage and that both might signify an urban settlement in the mid-Republic.[46]

Our knowledge about the holding of markets comes from the period just after the introduction of the Julian calendar, and a switch from the calculation of dates based on a lunar calendar. The change to a solar year of 365 days, with an extra day every four years, raised concern over the calculation of when market days would take place, and items to aid the calculation can be found in central Italy. These inscribed stones, known as *parapegmata*, list the days on which markets or *nundinae* were held.[47] The most elaborate example provides detailed evidence of how the solar year was integrated into an existing cycle of markets (fig. 3.4). The days of the week – Saturn, Sun, Moon, Mars, Mercury, Jupiter and Venus – are marked across the top of the stone. In the centre is a decorative listing of the days of the month, with a drill hole perhaps for marking the current day or the next market-day. On the left and right the word *nundinae* (markets) appears. On the right-hand side the names of eight places are inscribed: Aquinum, in the *vicus* (village), Interamna, Minturnae, Rome, Capua, Casinum, and Fabrateria. This leaves the use of the document open to interpretation. If, however, we read it as a tool for converting the cyclical sequence of markets into solar time, we may begin to understand the logic of the text. Spring is marked from thirteen days before the Kalends (first day) of February until twelve days before the Kalends of May – a total of ninety-one days; summer from eleven days before the Kalends of May until ten days before the Kalends of August – ninety-four days; autumn from nine days before the Kalends of August until eleven days before the Kalends of November – ninety-one days; and winter from ten days before the Kalends of November and fourteen days before the Kalends of February – eighty-nine days.

---

[45] Shaw (1981); Frayn (1993); De Ligt (1993); Morley (2000). [46] De Ligt (1993), pp. 113–15.
[47] Frayn (1993); De Ligt (1993); Degrassi (1963), nos 49–54.

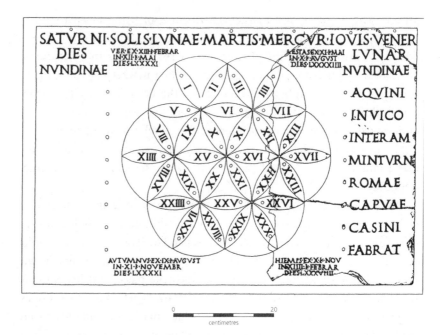

3.4 An inscribed listing of markets in Campania and Latium. Across the top are the days of the week, in the centre the days of the month and on the right-hand side a list of towns. Holes were incised to permit the positioning of markers to show the date and place of a market.

This seasonal division of a 365-day year into four parts was included for a reason. This might be that the holding of *nundinae* varied according to the season and the availability of agricultural produce.[48]

Under the Empire the holding of markets was tightly regulated by the government in Rome, and even the emperor needed to apply to the Senate to hold a market on his own estates.[49] We know from the *Letters* of Pliny that the establishment of new markets ran against the interests of towns with existing markets.[50] The town of Vicetia paid considerable legal fees to oppose a local senator setting up a market close by on his own estates. This would suggest that towns with the rights to hold markets had some sort of advantage that the town council would protect even when that protection involved considerable expense. De Ligt persuasively suggests that it was the right of any city to impose taxes or customs on goods coming into the town

---

[48] Storchi Marino (2000), p. 101; also Ziccardi (2000).
[49] Suet. *Claud.* 12.2.   [50] Plin. *Ep.* 5.4, 5.13.

or for sale at market.[51] Additional revenue could have been gained if auctions also took place on the same day. Hence, the people of Vicetia were probably trying to protect this revenue in seeking to prevent the establishment of a competing commercial centre. The fact that a *ius nundinarum* had to be granted by the Senate or emperor indicates that tight control was maintained over where and when a market could be established. There may have existed a fear of the congregation of people that could lead to rebellion.[52] However, the right to hold a market was also seen as a *beneficium* that could be granted by the emperor and, as De Ligt argues, by a provincial governor as well.[53] The granting of the ability to hold a market also implies the use of a temporal framework which permitted the holding of markets at different places on different days rather than in competition with one another. That temporal framework was derived from the adoption of the Julian calendar. There were clear advantages for any settlement with a market, and this should be regarded as one of the central features of the city that needed to be both organised and controlled by the annually elected *aediles*.

Markets were held not only in towns but also in *vici* (villages) or *praefecturae*.[54] The cases that are known tend to have been in regions that lacked the infrastructure of cities or places defined as *municipia* or *coloniae*.[55] Shaw has suggested that in North Africa the *nundinae* performed the function of a *civitas* or city, with markets held at regular intervals of between a year and every eight days.[56] The combination of a regular market and a temple or religious centre on an estate, alongside a population of estate workers, could represent a demographic and economic formation which might develop into a town. The classic example attested in the literary sources is that of Lucus Feroniae in the Tiber Valley, where people from other cities went to the temple, merchants, craftsmen and farmers made money from the festival and eventually its markets became the most famous in Italy.[57] Such a scenario is archaeologically attested at the Forum Novum, while we might postulate a similar process of development for the small towns of, for example, Roman Britain.[58] The difficulty is to determine at what point these settlements became recognisably urban, rather than existing as *vici* (villages) with magistrates. The addition of a town charter

---

[51] De Ligt (1993), p. 208.

[52] Shaw (1981). A similar regulation of communal gathering can be found in the legislation on *collegia* discussed by Diosono (2007), pp. 33–8.

[53] *Dig.* 50.11.1; De Ligt (2000); *CIL* 8.19337; *SEG* 32.1149.

[54] *vicus* – Festus 502L; *praefectura* – Festus 262L.   [55] Festus 127L.   [56] Shaw (1981), p. 60.

[57] Dion. Hal. *Ant. Rom.* 32.1.   [58] Burnham and Wacher (1990), pp. 43–50; Whittaker (1995).

created magistrates, an *ordo*, scribes, a *haruspex* or equivalent and the other trappings of Roman urbanism, including a city territory. It would seem to have been contrary to the interests of existing centres to have other competing centres develop in this manner. A benefit for the elite who held office was the grant of Roman citizenship, a tangible return for expenditure on office-holding that along with the giving of games is categorised as euergetism by scholars today – a process by which the elite reinforced their status through office holding and expenditure. For others, it is hard to understand what advantages the inhabitants of such organic settlements might gain from the new status of an autonomous city.

ADMINISTRATION OF JUSTICE

The forum of a city was not just a place to hold markets. The central space of the city was also the location for legal business. The unique evidence from the archive of the Sulpicii found at Murecine, outside Pompeii, sheds light on how the forum functioned as a place to which persons were summoned on a particular day.[59] The summons tended to be quite detailed, mentioning a particular time and a very specific location within the forum: an altar, a statue or a particular building. The time of summons varied from the first hour through to the ninth, with the most common time being the third hour. For the forum to function for the purpose of legal business, there needed to be an understanding of the solar calendar. Its use in the case of the Sulpicii archive can be demonstrated only for the cities of Capua, Puteoli and Rome, the evidence for which is presented in Table 3.1.

In the provinces, the Roman state appears to have imposed a system of cities, at the heart of which was a Roman sense of place and time. For example, Augustus ordered the Asturians and Cantabrians to occupy and cultivate the area around his military camp on the plain rather than their mountain refuges.[60] This created a centre of government in which a Roman governor might hold assizes and review legal cases. The holding of markets and public assemblies on a regular basis in the new towns of Germany under Augustus was seen as one of the features that transformed the barbarians into Romans.[61]

The forum was no doubt the place where the magistrates of Rome made their appearance in the cities of the Empire, whether as governor, *procurator* or *iuridicus* (regional judge). Those cities designated as places to which

---

[59] See Camodeca (1999) for the relevant texts.   [60] Flor. 2.33.   [61] Dio Cass. 56.18.2–3.

Table 3.1 The use of time and place in the Sulpicii Archive

City	Place	Location	Time	Reference
Puteoli	Forum	Hordionian Altar	3rd Hour	TPSulp.1
Puteoli	Forum	Hordionian Altar	3rd Hour	TPSulp.2
Puteoli	Forum	Hordionian Altar	3rd Hour	TPSulp.3
Puteoli	Forum	Hordionian Altar	3rd Hour	TPSulp.4
Puteoli	Forum	Hordionian Altar	3rd Hour	TPSulp.5
Puteoli	Forum	Hordionian Altar	3rd Hour	TPSulp.8
Puteoli	Forum	Suettian Altar of Augustus	3rd Hour	TPSulp.9
Puteoli	Forum	Hordionian Altar	9th Hour	TPSulp.10
Capua	Forum(?)	Basilica	1st Hour	TPSulp.12
Rome	Forum of Augustus	Statue of Gaius Sentius Saturninus	5th Hour	TPSulp.13
Rome	Forum of Augustus	Statue of Gaius Sentius Saturninus	3rd Hour	TPSulp.14
Rome	Forum of Augustus	Altar of Mars Ultor	4th Hour	TPSulp.15
Puteoli	Forum	Hordionian Altar	3rd Hour	TPSulp.16
Puteoli	Forum	Hordionian Altar	3rd Hour	TPSulp.17
Puteoli	Forum	Suettian Altar of Augustus	3rd Hour	TPSulp.18
Rome	Forum of Augustus	Statue of Gracchus, on 1st step by 4th column	9th Hour	TPSulp.19
?	?	?	3rd Hour	TPSulp.20
Rome	Forum of Augustus	Statue of Gaius Sentius Saturninus	3rd Hour	TPSulp.27
Puteoli		Octavian *Chalcidicum*	3rd to 5th Hours	TPSulp.35
Puteoli		Hordionian *Chalcidicum*	3rd to 5th Hours	TPSulp.36
Puteoli		Hordionian *Chalcidicum*	3rd to ? Hours	TPSulp.37
Puteoli		Hordionian *Chalcidicum*	3rd to ? Hours	TPSulp.38
Puteoli		Hordionian *Chalcidicum*	3rd to ? Hours	TPSulp.39
Puteoli	Forum	Hordionian Altar	3rd Hour	TPSulp.40
Puteoli	Forum	Caesonian *Chalcidicum*	3rd Hour	TPSulp.85

these magistrates made visits were defined as *conventus* (place at which courts could be convened) or a centre for a *conventus*.[62] These were the places to which provincial governors travelled to hear legal cases and to

[62] Bowman (1996), p. 353.

make judgements.[63] Famously, when governor of Africa, Vespasian was pelted with turnips during his attempt to hold assizes at Hadrumetum.[64] Clearly a city that was a centre for the governor's assizes experienced regular visits of the governor and of people wishing to encounter the governor.[65] In another example, Apuleius travelled from Oea to Sabratha to have his case heard before the proconsul Claudius Maximus in AD 159–60.[66] In his account of the towns of Baetica, Pliny lists four cities as *conventus* with some form of regional jurisdiction: Gades, Cordoba, Hispalis and Astigitana.[67]

A governor could also intervene in any city's financial or administrative affairs.[68] It is significant that, rather than practising a blanket form of government across a whole province, the governor directed his interventions at the level of the city. His powers, as Graham Burton concludes, were limited by the need to appear in person at places where assizes were held and to intervene in cases that might involve people from beyond the jurisdiction of that city.[69] This gave a special importance to *conventus* centres compared with other cities; they experienced a temporal geography that included a formal visitation from the governor, which also entailed a temporary increase in their population. Such occasions could be also the occasion for conflict and rioting, as Vespasian discovered at Hadrumetum.

TAXATION AND ARMY RECRUITMENT

Even the lowest grade of urban settlement, a *conciliabulum* (a public meeting place), played a part in the apparatus of the state. According to Livy, it was from the *fora* and *conciliabula* that taxation was collected and army recruits were drawn in the early second century BC.[70] These taxes were later suspended in Italy, and instead the revenue was collected from the provinces. There the *conventus* centre played a part in the collection of taxation, a model that can be traced back to the second century BC.[71] Taxation and

---

[63] Cic. *Att.* 6.3.3; Burton (1975); Bowman (1996), pp. 365–6.

[64] Suet. *Vesp.* 4, also compare Suet. *Galba* 9 and the movement of Pliny as governor of Bithynia in *Ep.*10.

[65] Burton (1975), p. 97 suggests a single annual visit per *conventus* on the basis of *Dig.* 1.16.7 *pr.*

[66] Apul. *Apol.* 41, and see other examples in Burton (1975), p. 96.

[67] Plin. *HN* 3.6–15; compare the seven *conventus* in Tarraconensis listed in Plin. *HN* 3.18.

[68] See Plin. *Ep.* 10 for examples.   [69] Burton (1975), p. 106.

[70] Livy, 25.5.6, 29.37, 39.14.7, 40.19, 43.14.6–10; Laurence (1999), p. 35.

[71] Livy, 45.16; 45.28–40.

Table 3.2 Recruitment into the imperial legions (data
from Mann 1983)

	Recruitment to AD 69	Recruitment AD 69–117	Recruitment AD 117–238
Bononia	12	4	–
Brixia	11	7	2
Mérida	2	8	3
Lyon	7	9	2
Forum Iulii	12	4	–
Cirta	3	1	47
Utica	1	3	12
Carthage	1	7	95

army recruitment were features of urban living and were a means by which
a city was integrated into the Roman Empire. Taxation would have created
a series of flows of persons and goods to these regional centres. From this,
there developed the idea of certain cities heading regions and becoming
places in which meetings might be held of a body referred to as the
consilium (advisory council) of the *conventus* (which in the case of Clunia
elected a senatorial patron in AD 222).[72]

The recruitment of soldiers into the legions was focussed on Roman
citizens, and during the Republic affected all cities in which there were sons
of citizens.[73] Recruitment in the Empire involved the governor enrolling
the recruit and doing the paperwork, but there were also recruiting officers
in the provinces who selected recruits from individual cities.[74] Individual
cases are known from inscriptions and these reveal a shift in legionary
recruitment from Italy to the provinces.[75] Table 3.2 provides eight examples of cities in Italy, Gallia Narbonensis, Spain and Africa. The evidence is
fragmentary but demonstrates that every second year the cities continued
to be the focus of army recruitment.[76] The contact between a city and the
army did not create a relationship between that city and a particular legion
or province.[77] Recruits from Brixia served in Spain, Britain, Dalmatia,

[72] On the role of taxation in the provinces Hopkins (1980) continues to be a prominent model; but
see also Bowman (1996), pp. 362–5; *CIL* 6.1454.
[73] Brunt (1974).   [74] Gilliam (1956); Davies (1969), esp. p. 218; on selection, Davies (1989).
[75] Mann (1983) for discussion and epigraphic data. Unfortunately we do not have adequate data to
establish the role of cities in the supply of manpower to the auxiliary units, but no doubt these
cities played a role in this process.
[76] Forni (1953), p. 24.   [77] Davies (1969), p. 225 for evidence of letters from son to mother.

Table 3.3 Settlement of veterans in cities (data
from Mann 1983)

	Settlement to AD 69	Settlement AD 69–117	Settlement AD 117–238
Bononia	–	–	–
Brixia	3	2	2
Mérida	1	1	6
Lyon	–	–	16
Forum Iulii	–	–	–
Cirta	3	–	4
Utica	–	–	–
Carthage	–	2	4

Pannonia, the two Germanies, Moesia and the East.[78] At least during the
early Empire, soldiers tended on discharge to return to their home cities or
to settle in the provinces where they had served.[79] The data are much more
fragmentary for this process than for that of recruitment into the army.
However, Table 3.3 demonstrates that veterans might have been attracted
to certain cities. This would appear to have been the case with Lyon, a
regional centre for the Three Gauls. The alternative destination for veterans
appears to have been to towns or places developing into urban centres in
the frontier zone.[80] The discharge of an average of three thousand veterans
a year would not have created a regular flow of veterans arriving in any one
city, and veterans can be expected to have been present within any city.[81]
They were part of the urban scene and valued their military past and
connection to a named legion.[82] At Mérida tombstones have been found
belonging to veterans of *VI Victrix* and *VII Gemina* who lived to the ages of
55, 61, 70 and 86.[83] Their role in the city is unclear, but their connection to
their legion was recorded long after their retirement from the military and
must be understood as an important aspect of their identity. No doubt they
formed a significant proportion of the population in numerous cities:
Fentress calculates that 10 per cent of the population of the *vicus* around
the fort of Lambaesis were veterans.[84] Recent studies of inscriptions mentioning veterans have shown that a significant number became magistrates

[78] See Mann (1983), for data.   [79] Mann (1983), p. 58.
[80] Dondin-Payre and Raepsaet-Charlier (1999).
[81] See Mann (1983), p. 59 for the calculation. Shaw (1983); Cherry (1998).
[82] For example *CIL* 5.4365.   [83] *CIL* 2.489, 490, 491, 5212, *AE* 1946: 195, 200.
[84] Fentress (1979), pp. 132–3 argued on the basis of *CIL* 8.18234.

(10 per cent of veterans known from inscriptions).[85] Those of a more senior rank, the centurions and *primipilares* (senior centurions), had a more prominent role and certainly constructed more elaborate tombs.[86] Indeed a legionary centurion who saved his pay could accumulate, along with his discharge bonus, more than 400,000 sesterces, the equivalent of the capital required to be an *eques*. In contrast, ordinary legionaries could have accumulated between 4,000 and 18,000 sesterces.[87] The veteran was also exempted from certain *munera* or services to his city, and Roman law developed a distinction between the honourably discharged soldier and other civilians.[88] Hence veteran centurions were well placed to become municipal magistrates and veteran legionaries would have had the capital to become perpetual priests.[89]

The connection with the military was particularly strong in the Augustan colonies of Spain. These towns in the early first century issued coins whose imagery commemorated not just the act of foundation but also the legions from which the colonists came (see Table 2.1). The identity of these cities depended on their foundation and the origins of their first inhabitants in the V and X Legions. The inscriptions referring to recruits from Mérida, however, do not reveal the maintenance of a connection with these two legions; instead we can identify the *VI Victrix*, *VII Gemina* and *XX Valeria Victrix* as the legions to which they were assigned.[90] It seems likely that their city of origin was also the point from which they were recruited. Once recruited into a particular legion, their civic identity was maintained even when outside the province and across the Ocean in Britannia.[91] The same was also true of the auxiliary units; if serving within their own province they were described as from a particular place, if serving outside their own province they were described as from their home province.[92] The experience of service in the army included encountering soldiers from other parts of the Empire and living on the frontiers of the Roman world for the central part of their lives from their early twenties into their mid- to late forties.[93] They possessed a different identity if they returned to their home city, such as Mérida.[94] They had been soldiers and absent from the town in which they had grown up. The period of military service

---

[85] See Mrozewicz (1989), pp. 81–90; Ardevan (1989), pp. 65–80; Dupuis (1991), pp. 343–54; Bérard (1992), p. 169; Todisco (1999), pp. 214–16; Keppie (1983), pp. 104–12; Fentress (1979), pp. 124–49.

[86] Coarelli (1967).   [87] Fentress (1979), p. 152 for the calculation.   [88] *Dig.* 49.18.1–5.

[89] Fentress (1979), p. 153.   [90] *CIL* 2.489, 490, 491, 5212; *AE* 1946: 195, 200; *RIB* 501, 502.

[91] *RIB* 501, 502.   [92] Speidel (1986).

[93] See Forni (1992), pp. 116–41 for his refined list of the origins of legionaries.

[94] For comparison see Keppie (2000), p. 236.

dislocated their connection with the civilian community, which might explain why the aged veterans in Mérida were commemorated in three cases by their freed slaves,[95] heirs from outside their own *familia* in a single case,[96] in one case by a home-born slave,[97] and by their descendants in only two cases.[98]

REGIONAL CENTRES

Some cities in the provinces appear to have assumed the role of a regional capital, expanding their role as a *conventus* centre to include meetings of the provincial council and religious cult of Rome and Augustus. Lyon was a regional centre for a number of reasons, but illustrates the difficulty of identifying regional centres on this basis. Strabo picks it out as the most populous city other than the colony of Narbo and explains that it is an *emporium* (port of trade), as well as the place where the Roman governors mint gold and silver coins.[99] The city had been founded as a colony in 43 BC. It was later in Lyon that the sixty peoples of Gaul dedicated not just an altar to Augustus, but a temple as well (fig. 3.5).[100] There was also a major festival celebrated from 12 BC to the third century AD, which was a moment at which the city was full of visitors from elsewhere.[101] The festival would have involved a meeting of the sixty peoples from the Three Gauls who held the altar and temple to Augustus in common.[102] It was at this festival that Caligula held oratory competitions in both Latin and Greek.[103] The presence of the mint and an urban cohort drew Lyon closer to Rome than the other cities of Gallia Comata or the Three Gauls, and its population included a number of senators prior to Claudius' admission of prominent citizens from the rest of the Gallic provinces into the Senate during his censorship in AD 48.[104] The combination of these additional features marked Lyon out as a particularly prominent city (it is significant that the only other provincial city that was garrisoned by an urban cohort was Carthage, which was the dominant city in the province of Africa). That prominence depended on its identification by the Roman government as a colony in which additional functions of government and cult could be permitted.

---

[95] *CIL* 2.490, 491, 5212.   [96] *AE* 1946: 195.   [97] *CIL* 2.489.

[98] *AE* 1946: 200; *AE* 1911: 91.

[99] Strabo, 4.3.2; Burnett, Amandry and Ripollès (1992), p. 150, have also demonstrated that Narbo also minted bronze coins.

[100] Strabo, 4.3.2; Livy, *Epit. Per.* 139; Dio Cass. 54.32; Suet. *Claud.* 2.

[101] Euseb. *Hist. Eccl.* 5.1.47.   [102] Strabo, 4.3.2.   [103] Suet. *Calig.* 20.

[104] *CIL* 13.1668; Tac. *Ann.* 11.23.

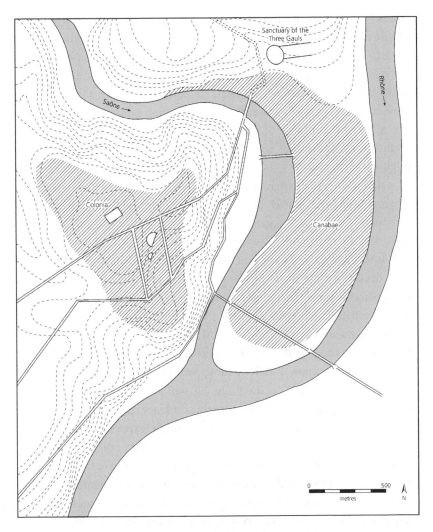

3.5 Lyon: plan showing the location of the major monuments of the colony in relation to the Sanctuary of the Three Gauls and the *canabae*.

It is possible to identify other regional centres. In AD 15 the province of Tarraconensis made a request to found a temple of Augustus within the colony of Tarraco or modern Tarragona (see fig. 4.4). The request was granted and Tacitus sees this foundation as setting a precedent for other provinces.[105] Duncan Fishwick argues for the possibility of similar cult sites at regional centres located across the western provinces: Mérida, Córdoba, Narbonne, Colchester, Gorsium, Sarmizegetusa, Carthage and a number of

[105] Tac. *Ann.*1.78.

others.[106] The evidence points to these places as cult sites, but it might be unwise to regard them as provincial capitals with all the implications of that modern term;[107] after all, as we saw earlier, the governor of a province was not located in one place but moved on a circuit between the assize centres of his province. What we do find, though, is evidence that individual provinces took action as a collective body. For example, between 2 BC and AD 14 the province of Baetica set up an inscription in the Forum of Augustus in Rome that referred to its gift of gold made in return for Augustus' *beneficia* or gifts and the peacefulness of their province under his guidance.[108] The province petitioned for the right to set up a temple to Tiberius and Livia in AD 25.[109] Provincial meetings were a time for an exchange of views and to gather information from further afield; interestingly, in AD 25 the people of the province of Baetica were aware that a temple to Tiberius and Livia had been permitted in the province of Asia.[110] How decisions were made by the province is unclear, but what it needed was a place in which they might be taken. Later, from the second century, the council of the province set up statues in both fora of the colony of Córdoba and in the *municipium* of Mellaria and the colony of Astigi.[111] This decision suggests the rather decentralised nature of the council; it may have met at Córdoba, but its actions included the commemoration of individuals outside that central point. So, while the council of the province could be an important body, the available evidence suggests that the notion of a provincial capital was weaker than we might expect.

If the regional meeting places found at Tarragona and Lyon were also present in other provinces, we should expect them to have been located in or outside a *colonia* and to have been associated with a meeting of the peoples of the province at a festival focussed on the worship of Rome and Augustus. It is, however, difficult to establish the regional centre in every province on this basis because of the paucity of the evidence in some cases, and it is also apparent that some cult centres, such as the colony at Colchester, did not develop as the regional centre for the province. Perhaps this was because, unlike Tarragona and Lyon, they lacked the trading function of an *emporium*; this was certainly absent from the colony of Colchester but present at nearby London. Both features drew people to these cities, but it was only when these and other functions combined that regional centres began to develop. Clearly, from the example

---

[106] Fishwick (2004), pp. 1–220.   [107] See Haensch (1997).
[108] *CIL* 6.31267.   [109] Tac. *Ann.* 4.37.   [110] Tac. *Ann.* 4.37–8; 1.15.
[111] Cordoba: *CIL* 2²/7. 254, 255, 258, 282, 291, 292, 293 and 295; Mellaria: *CIL* 2²/7. 799; Astigi: *CIL* 2²/7.1171.

of Colchester, we cannot assume that being a centre for the imperial cult automatically led to a place becoming a regional capital. Colchester has been viewed by Fishwick as following in some ways the model of Lyon, with a cult centre being set up for the province.[112] The rejection of the cult centre at Colchester, however, which was seen as a catalyst for the Boudiccan revolt of AD 60, points to a different situation in Britain from that found in the Three Gauls.[113] After the revolt, Colchester was maintained as a cult centre and developed a rare monument, a circus, in the second century AD (see fig. 2.10). Yet, as a regional centre, it was eclipsed by the new foundation of London, which was an *emporium*.[114] Other examples of the problematic development of regional centres can be found. For example, Mérida's population needed to be reinforced by the settlement of new families in AD 69.[115] The development of a cult centre within a city and a site at which the provincials might display their loyalty to Rome was not enough for that city to develop as a regional centre; it also needed to be located in a place that was central to trade. Cities that included all three of these elements were rare: Tarragona is one example and Carthage might be seen as another, but in Britain it was London rather than Colchester that developed as a regional capital for the province.

THE ELITE AND URBANISM

We have seen that the city was controlled by the *ordo* of decurions, who decided, among other things, what buildings should be built, whether a statue should be set up and whether a tomb plot should be given to an individual on behalf of the city. The statute or town charter created the *ordo* as the decision-making body, to which the annually elected magistrates were answerable. It was a structure that was akin to the formation of a provincial council with a priest at its head. The town charter established what should not be included within the built-up area of the city, or *oppidum*, and what should be relegated to the city's territory. The roles of magistrates were defined in the town charter, including the sums of money that should be spent on the festivals. The charters reveal an emphasis on religious celebration, a necessity for the survival of the city, specific ways of organising government within the city and annually elected magistrates.

---

[112] Fishwick (1987), pp. 195–218 for a full discussion of the evidence, also note Tac. *Ann.* 12.32 and Sen. *Apocol.* 8.3 on the role of the temple in promoting loyalty in the new province.
[113] Tac. *Ann.* 14.31.   [114] Tac. *Ann.* 14.33.   [115] Tac. *Hist.* 1.78.

These might be seen as the crucial ingredients of Roman urbanism. The Roman city was more than this, however. The periodic market and the conduct of legal business in the forum were fundamental to the definition of urbanism. These last two features seldom leave a strong presence in the archaeological or epigraphic record, but had greater importance in the day-to-day business of the city and the lives of most of the population than the inscribed stones recording the prestige of members of the *ordo* found on statue-bases and building inscriptions. The latter visibly commemorate individuals from the past whose actions may have transformed the city's shape. The town charter provided a means by which the elite could transform their city and be recognised for their contribution by other members of the elite, who might have statues erected or money provided for tombs and funerals at a later date. These actions left a physical imprint on the city at a local level that will be discussed in Chapters 5 to 10, and developed the city as an arena or backdrop for government and religious celebration.

There is a danger that the detailed evidence found in the town charters could lead us to characterise each city as a hermetically sealed entity. This flies in the face of the less tangible evidence pointing to the integration of individual cities within wider regional and provincial structures. The enrolment of a city's youth into the Roman army was one way in which a city could have had contact with the world of the frontier. Numerous veterans appear to have settled not just in the frontier regions but also in other cities of the Empire or to have returned to their home cities. The veterans were a reminder of Rome's military power and the existence of a wider conception of Romanness that included the world outside both the city and the province. The role of the governor's assize circuit created points in time and space where justice could be administered. A city on the assize circuit may have experienced a rather different form of urbanism from one that was not. Taxation may have been one of the more exploitative features of the government of the provinces, yet, like the recruitment and discharge of soldiers from the military, it created a tangible contact between the individual subject and the army on the frontiers. Romanness may have been formulated on the basis of the maintenance of peace and the absence of a requirement for a local militia, and it was taxation that paid for this distant army.[116]

---

[116] See Aristides, *Orationes.* 26.74–8.

4 | The reception of Roman urbanism in the West

> Greatest of censors, prince of princes, though Rome owes you so many
> triumphs, so many temples coming to birth, so many reborn, so many
> spectacles, so many gods, so many cities.
>
> (Mart. *Ep.* 6.4)

Rome held an empire in which there were cities, and the Roman governors
of the West expected to view a provincial landscape in which there were
cities that could be recognised as having distinctly Roman urban forms.
This chapter seeks to examine how the Roman concept of the city was
received and reproduced across the provinces of the former barbarian
West. In the past, the excavated remains of the cities of the Roman
Empire have been used to establish the spread of civilisation across the
West.[1] The straight lines of the grid-plan of the towns were equated at the
turn of the twentieth century with the notion of a rational city, whether in
the past, present or future. The Roman city in the West was perceived as a
bringer of civilisation to the barbarians (see Chapter 5 for further discussion). This perception of the past has been adjusted, but the narrative of the
Roman provinces continues to focus on the role of cities and urbanisation.[2]
The question for us in this chapter is what features of the Roman conception of urbanism were attractive to these former barbarians in the first
or second century AD? Equally important is the question of whether their
conception and development of urban forms in the former barbarian West
(that is, the Gauls, the Germanies and in Britain) was so different from
what was occurring at the same time in other more developed parts of the
Mediterranean such as Italy, Spain or North Africa. This chapter will
therefore explore the conception of Roman urbanism viewed from the
former barbarian provinces of the West rather than from Rome or Italy
(a view expressed in the opening quotation, from the late first century AD).
These questions have perplexed those studying the origins of towns, particularly in Britain, and have been subject to a reworking of hypotheses and

---

[1] Haverfield (1913); Laurence (1994).   [2] Millett (1990).

the development of new theories of urbanism.[3] This is an exciting field full of new possibilities; a recent hypothesis is that of John Creighton, who tries to make a link between the type of town and the identity and aspirations of its inhabitants.[4] Governors would have had different expectations or life experiences of the town from those of soldiers or provincials. Ex-soldiers may have been content to continue to occupy former barrack blocks (as in Colchester or Gloucester, see Chapter 3), but the governor was more likely to produce a city in the image of a Pompeii or other Italian cities (for instance, London). It needs to be remembered, however, that all these groups understood that there would be other viewers of, or visitors to, their town. It also needs to be pointed out that the city in Italy may have been a little more fragile or even underdeveloped as a universal experience than Creighton allows.[5] As we have seen and shall see again, attempts to found cities in Italy did not always result in settlements of the magnitude of a Silchester or a Pompeii (see Chapter 2). We wish to shift this debate away from the life experience of the inhabitants towards an understanding of the Roman city in the provinces as a manifestation of the urban way of life of the inhabitants, and to the forms of building or settlement type that signified a town or city to others, or were thought to be emblematic of the status of an *oppidum* or Roman town. As part of this analysis we will also examine whether legionary forts, which in their physical form shared many aspects of what we think of as Roman cities, should in fact be regarded as being cities.

TEXTS AND TOWNS

At the edge of the Empire in Germany, under Augustus territory had been subdued and soldiers were encamped in winter-quarters. Alongside the military presence towns were being founded and the barbarians were holding markets and assemblies as signs of the change that Rome had brought, while the barbarians did not forget their own customs.[6] Cassius Dio suggests that the recently conquered barbarians underwent a phase of unlearning their customs and adjusting their lifestyles to those of the city, markets and assemblies. The find of a settlement with a forum at Waldgirmes, some 100 km to the east of the Rhine, provides contemporary archaeological evidence for such a process.[7] Dio is clear on the speed of change; it was gradual and needed to be overseen by the governor, but

---

[3] Esmonde Cleary (1998); Creighton (2006), pp. 71–8.   [4] Creighton (2006).
[5] Creighton (2006), pp. 13, 79–80.   [6] Dio Cass. 56.18.   [7] Rasbach and Becker (2003).

intervention on his part would have caused problems.[8] In AD 9 P. Quinctilius Varus wanted to speed up the process of change in Germany. This would seem to have been justified since he commanded a huge military force on the Rhine. However, rather than encouraging the provincials in their own endeavours to change to Roman ways, he issued orders and levied money to promote change. This was fatal and led to open revolt that resulted in the loss of three legions. There was an almost immediate return to the policy of quiet or passive observation of the barbarians as they transformed themselves and adapted to the Roman forms of city, markets and assemblies.[9] The direct parallels for Varus' actions lie in the events leading up to the revolt by Boudicca and in the actions of Agricola in the encouragement of urbanism.[10] There is another parallel for the actions of Varus at Cherchel (Iol Caesarea) in Mauretania, where we find an example from the late second or early third century that confirms Dio's view: an imperial official had encouraged the town to pave the street leading to the town and the grateful citizens duly acknowledged this sound advice in an inscription.[11] Governors and procurators should not thus be seen as inactive in the development of towns; rather they observed and offered advice. The examples of Varus and Agricola demonstrate that the transformation of barbarians into provincial town-dwellers adopting or adapting Roman forms of urbanism was not a straightforward process, but it was expected to occur.

It is Tacitus' biography of his father-in-law Agricola, governor of Britain under Domitian in the late first century AD, that furnishes what is perhaps the most famous analysis of the process of change. Britain, like Germany, had been the site of a major revolt: that of Boudicca in AD 60/61, which was precipitated in part by the foundation of the Roman veteran colony at Colchester, along with subsequent abuses by the colonists and in part by the recall of very large loans made to the provincial elite by high-ranking Romans such as Seneca, presumably amongst other things to finance the adoption of Roman customs.[12] So subsequent governors may well have appreciated the need to work with rather than against the grain of the British elite. Tacitus' structuring of Agricola's governorship is a classic portrayal of a Roman instilling fear through military conquest and respect through *clementia*, or clemency.[13] The bulk of the narrative is concerned with the summer campaigns, but the winters are filled with the actions of a

---

[8] Dio Cass. 56.18; Vell. Pat. 2.118; Wilson and Creighton (1999), pp. 16–20.
[9] Dio Cass. 56.24.6.   [10] Dio Cass. 62.1–6; Tac. *Agr.* 20–21.
[11] *CIL* 8.10979 = 20982.   [12] Dio Cass. 62.2.   [13] Tac. *Agr.* 20.

good governor. Agricola was credited by Tacitus as the first governor to check the abuses of an undisciplined army and corruption in the levying of taxes.[14] In the winter, as in Augustan Germany, Agricola promoted the building of temples, *fora* and good houses. He did not, however, compel or order the provincials to undertake such projects. Instead he encouraged them and promoted the ideal of town-building, almost as a competition from which individual Britons gained in status – a process seen by Tacitus as being nearly as effective as compulsion.[15] This rosy picture of a governor interacting with the provincial elite is practically a manifesto for good practice in governing one's province, but there was more to this than just the building of an urban fabric of temples, a forum and some houses at various locations across the province. With these manifestations of Roman urbanism came others: the Latin language and the toga. There were also other aspects of Roman urbanism that came with the foundation of these new settlements: the *porticus*, baths and sumptuous banquets.[16] These last three aspects are of interest and contrast with the earlier list of three urban aspects: temples, *fora* and houses. This shows us the classic two-sidedness of Roman urbanism – the traditional elements: forum, temples and homes, and the corrupting luxuries: the *porticus*, baths and dining. For Tacitus, the latter had enslaved the Britons and were a consequence of the introduction of the virtuous elements of the city promoted by the governor.[17] What is clear from this passage of the *Agricola* is that the attractions of Roman urbanism were as much the discussions conducted in a *porticus* or *palaestra*, the ability to clean oneself and to groom the body in a Roman manner, and to eat or dine in a manner that was Roman rather than barbarian, as much as the benefits conferred by more sophisticated housing, monumental piazzas and religious practice enhanced by a stone structure. On top of this there was a change of dress and language. The result was, as far as Tacitus and his readers were concerned, a network of developing cities with public buildings and toga-clad, Latin-speaking, bathed and groomed Britons. The process initiated by Agricola in those parts of the province that lacked towns took place some thirty-five years after Claudius' triumphal entrance into Camulodunum. This process of change can also be seen in the case of Orcistus, a *vicus* in Phrygia, which, under Constantine, successfully attained the status of an *oppidum* on the following grounds:[18]

- the *vicus* had flourished;
- there were annually elected magistrates with *fasces*;

---

[14] Tac. *Agr.* 19.   [15] Tac. *Agr.* 21.   [16] Tac. *Agr.* 21.   [17] Tac. *Agr.* 21.   [18] *CIL* 3.352.

- there were a suitable number of decurions;
- there was a full population of citizens;
- the location was at the junction of four roads and the town contained a *mansio* (inn) that was functional and comfortable;
- there was an abundance of water for the public and private baths;
- there was a forum adorned with statues of the emperors of old;
- there was a sedentary population, 'so numerous that all the seats [in the theatre] as are there are easily filled up'.

The people of Orcistus petitioned the governor for the change of status; it is the governor whom Tacitus and Cassius Dio see as the promoter who encourages the development of urbanism during the winter months when campaigning is over. This did not mean that Roman governors built the cities of the provinces with their soldiers' labour. In fact there is evidence suggesting that not everyone may have approved of the idea of giving people a city. In the middle of the first century AD a story circulated in Rome about Alexander the Great, in which he was said to have given a man a city. The man turned him down, however, because the gift was too great for him to receive without incurring the jealousy of others. Alexander regarded the gift not from the recipient's point of view but as something that reflected his own greatness.[19] The story has relevance for understanding the relationship between the governors and provincials, where the former was involved in the promotion of an urban culture; you can only give a gift that a recipient might receive and regard as something of utility and not beyond their own requirements. Hence, when we view the urban forms of the Roman West, what we should be looking for is not the replication of the urban forms of, say, Pompeii or Cosa, but a form of urbanism that reflects the utility of the individual elements of the city in the local situation.

CITY FORMATION AND DEVELOPMENT

The discussion so far has primarily used textual evidence; we need now to try to understand the process of city formation and development on the ground using the archaeological evidence. It needs to be noted at the outset that there is an intrinsic problem with the available data for city formation: very few sites have been excavated with a view to establishing the origins of

---

[19] Sen. *Ben.* 2.16.

the city. Indeed, at many sites the fully developed city has been of such magnitude that excavation through these remains would have resulted in the destruction of heritage or, alternatively, the larger data sets from later periods, when the city had developed, have preoccupied the excavators and their teams. Our discussion will focus on three sites: Saint-Bertrand-de-Comminges in south-west France, Forum Novum in central Italy and Silchester in southern Britain. We wish to highlight the elements of town formation that were selected or emphasised at these sites that have been the subject of considerable archaeological exploration in recent years. Finally, we will place developments at these 'new towns' in a wider context, by examining the development of two more established cities in the provinces: Tarragona and Italica. We shall show that there was a difference in the scale of development across these five cities, but we shall also reveal that there was a consistent understanding of what made a Roman city in the provincial context.

Saint-Bertrand-de-Comminges, or Lugdunum of the Convenae, is situated in Aquitania in the foothills of the Pyrenees.[20] There was a strong tradition that Pompey the Great founded the town in 72/71 BC[21] during action to strengthen the defences of southern Gaul.[22] He appears, like the good governor Agricola, to have founded cities whilst taking war to an enemy. A first look at the plan of the excavations (fig. 4.1) reveals the disjuncture between Saint Bertrand and the orthogonal grid-plan of streets that characterised so many of the Roman towns of Italy. It would seem to have been built on a green-field site, but the street pattern established in the late first century BC was far from regular and was realigned in the Augustan period.[23] The town appears to have been laid out with respect to the junction of some major routes across the province of Aquitania: a north-west to south-east route along the front edge of the Pyrenees; a route to the west; a route to the east along the valley of the River Garonne; a route to the north-east towards Toulouse; and a route to the north that led to a crossing-point of the River Garonne. This prevented the formation of the expected grid pattern of streets with the existing roads joining together at the entrance or gateway of the city. It should be noted that excavations at the site have tended to concentrate on the monumental buildings of the town centre, but this is a bias which suits our purposes here. The earliest

---

[20] For a general treatment see Esmonde Cleary (2007).

[21] Strabo, 4.2; Jer. *Contra Vigilantium* 4.

[22] Cic. *Font.*13. This may be linked to the foundation myths of cities such as Italica discussed above in Chapter 1.

[23] Paillet and Petit (1992).

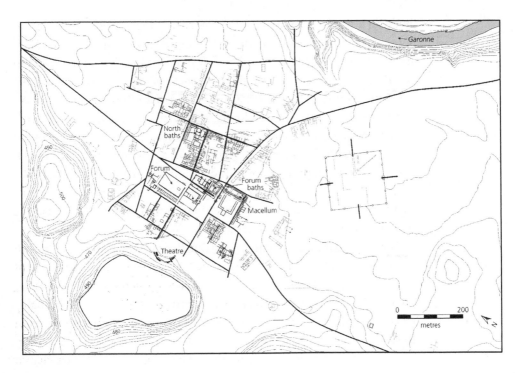

4.1 Saint Bertrand: the plan shows that the grid of streets is fitted around a combination of routes through the site and the development of monuments aligned with reference to these routes, with the exception of the theatre constructed to the west against a steep hillside.

major surviving building at the site was a set of baths (Forum Baths État I), with hot and cold rooms and a *palaestra* for exercise.[24] This structure was important not only for the passing travellers using the roads, but also for the creation of clean and groomed male and female inhabitants, who may have spoken Latin and appeared little different from the Roman governors' entourages which passed through the city and used the baths. The success of this structure in fulfilling its function is attested by the upgrade to the facilities undertaken in the middle of the first century AD, when we find some evidence of marble veneer and brick columns – features of contemporary bath buildings in Pompeii (see Chapter 8). What enabled the bath-building to function, of course, was an aqueduct capable of supplying 3000 m^3 a day. Clean water was an essential feature of the baths that were a key feature of Roman urban life, and this was to be displayed to travellers passing through the city who needed access to bathing facilities.[25]

[24] Aupert and Monturet (2001).   [25] Vitr. *De arch.* 8; Frontin. *Aq.* 2.92.

Built on a similar alignment to the baths, across the major north-west to south-east route, was a slightly later temple facing out over the major metalled area at the road-junction.[26] Just across the Toulouse road from the Forum Baths, a market building (*macellum*) was constructed in the early first century AD with permanent shops as a feature of its structure. We can therefore observe the development of a city at a major road-junction with its public buildings built around the transport node, a fact symbolised by the construction of a circular monument at the intersection of two of these routes; perhaps some form of dedication to the deities of the cross-roads (*Lares Augusti* or *Lares compitales*).[27] Whatever the monument's significance, it designated the heart of the city and the city's origins at the junction of two major urban streets.

The combination of buildings at Saint-Bertrand coincides closely with those identified by Tacitus in the second century AD as the buildings that created the conditions for Roman urbanism. Interestingly there is no mention in this list of a theatre. At Saint-Bertrand, the theatre was probably originally constructed in the early first century AD and made use in part of the convenient outcrop of a hill to support a substantial part of the seating. This is an important reminder for us when looking at plans of cities: that so often the theatre and, indeed, some amphitheatres were located according to the pragmatic convenience of a rocky outcrop or hill that could be quarried for new material and shaped into the iconic architectural forms for the holding of spectacles, rather than according to the dictates of some preconceived ideology of where such structures should be situated. Not surprisingly, at Saint-Bertrand the theatre was constructed nearby using the most convenient outcrop for its construction, which would have reduced the structure's cost. The theatre's position may have been determined also by the presence of a settlement on the hill which overlooked the excavated area of Roman remains and was the focus of the late antique town. We should also note here the presence of what was probably a *palaestra* with *natatio* (swimming pool), aligned with the north-west to south-east road and presumably largely geared to moulding the bodies and minds of, at least, the elite young men of the city in a Roman way. The *palaestra* is a facility alluded to by Tacitus in his discussion of urban development in Britain under the Flavians, but it is in fact a building-type rarely identified outside Italy and so may reflect Tacitus' Italian urban view rather than the realities of western provincial cities. What we see at

---

[26] Badie, Sablayrolles, Schenck (1994).
[27] For discussion of the evidence from Rome see Lott (2004).

Saint-Bertrand in its early phase is the construction of baths, a temple, a forum and a market-building. The four public buildings of Saint-Bertrand – five, counting the theatre – provided all the facilities required by passing travellers and the production of a Roman culture, in which the population groomed and cleaned itself in the baths, sold goods to others in the market-building, held meetings in the forum, worshipped at a temple and even retold their myths in a theatre with a sun-shade or *velum*. The addition of the *palaestra*, the provision of a second set of baths (the North Baths) perhaps associated with a major shrine, the enlargement of the theatre, the rebuilding of the forum and the Forum Baths after a fire and the increasing use of the local marbles to adorn the city speak also of the cumulative nature of provincial urbanism. Town-foundation was not a once-for-all act, and each city continued to redefine itself and the citizens it produced as fashions changed and resources allowed.

Town-foundation was not a phenomenon unique to the provinces in the first century AD but was still under way in Italy. Another road-junction, this time at Forum Novum in the Middle Tiber Valley, had developed as a town by the Augustan period and was listed as such in official records.[28] Excavations and inscriptions at the site have revealed an aqueduct, a basilica and forum complex, a number of temples, baths, a *campus*, a wooden amphitheatre, and a number of large monumental tower tombs (fig. 4.2). A single benefactor, P. Faianus Plebeius, provided the water-supply to the city from his own land, constructed the fountains in the town, and connected the water to both the baths and a *piscina* or swimming-pool.[29] Filippo Coarelli has argued that the town was in fact an extension of Plebeius' property, located on a key transhumance route, with a market for the sale of sheep.[30] The geophysical survey conducted by the University of Birmingham revealed a town that lacked not only houses but also any definition of the limits of settlement.[31] The large villa that seems not to have been completed fell quickly into disuse, as did the amphitheatre and the baths by the third century AD. Here was a town being developed through the energies of one person, within reach of Rome, on productive land and with good transport facilities by both road and river, that failed to develop beyond its nucleus of a crossroad with some public buildings, a market, and a place for the worship of the gods. In effect it remained an appendage of an estate on a transhumance route, rather than seeing development into a city.

---

[28] Plin. *HN* 3.107; *Liber Coloniarum*, 2.255.21.
[29] *CIL* 9.4786. The man himself may have come to prominence as an *eques*, who was accused of treason in AD 15. Tac. *Ann*.1.73; Coarelli (2005).
[30] Coarelli (2005).   [31] Gaffney *et al.* (2001).

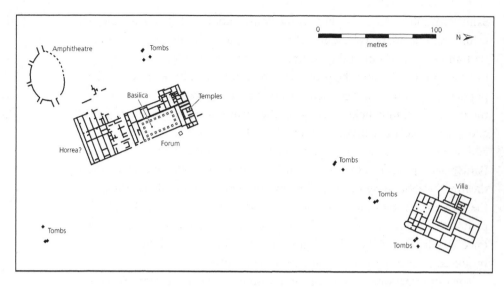

4.2 Forum Novum: plan showing the development of urbanism (first century AD) in the form of a basilica, small temples, monumental tower-tombs and a villa, but with little other evidence for habitation.

It is difficult to assess fully the development of urban centres in north-west Europe because few sites have been investigated to reveal the extensive remains of timber as opposed to stone buildings. The excavations at Silchester (or Calleva) allow us to begin to understand the process of transformation at one site and the degree to which a street plan and the urban form could be subject to change. The town in its final form featured an orthogonal grid aligned to the points of the compass and a set of walls (dating to the third century AD but fronting a set of earthwork defences of nearly a century earlier), but excavation has revealed that an earlier, mid-first-century AD, phase of the site displays a quite different form (fig. 4.3). For a start, excavations under the later forum-basilica[32] have shown elements plausibly belonging to a grid of metalled streets laid out in the first half of the first century AD, comfortably before the Claudian invasion, and at an angle of about 51 degrees to the later street-grid. Even in the plan of the fully developed Roman city as revealed by the Victorian excavators it is possible to discern a number of structures that share this alignment, and continuing excavations on Insula IX of the city show that some at least date back to the mid-first century, if not earlier.[33] But at about the time of the Roman conquest (the dating evidence is not precise enough to establish

[32] Fulford and Timby (2000).   [33] Clarke and Fulford (2002).

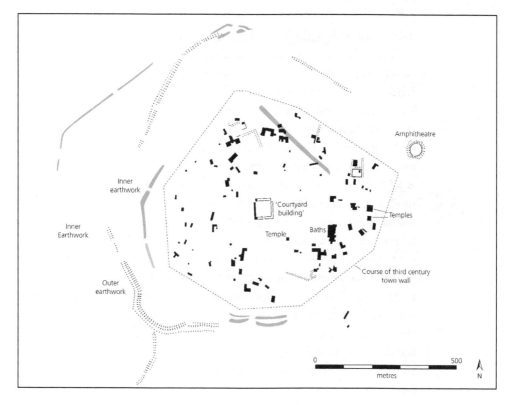

4.3 Silchester: plan showing the distribution of monuments in the pre-Flavian phase. The street grid in this phase, demonstrated by the building alignments, is orientated quite differently to that of the N-S, E-W orientation found in the later phases of this site.

whether before or after), a major timber structure was built under the later forum-basilica and aligned north-south.[34] The purpose of this structure is unclear and has been much debated. Was it connected with the Roman military or constructed by a local magnate?[35] From the *insula* to the west of the forum the Victorian excavators recovered a collection of mid-first-century architectural and decorative stonework, out of any original context but perhaps indicative of a major high-status complex at this date, part of which was a set of baths.[36] How these developments relate to the presence of bricks stamped with the name of Nero is still an open question, but it is not hard to see the evidence for a major restructuring of Calleva in the generation after the Claudian invasion as a response by a local leader, or leaders, to the new realities, possibly with high-level (gubernatorial or imperial) encouragement. By the end of the first century Silchester also

[34] Fulford and Timby (2000), pp. 37–44.
[35] Fulford (2003), Creighton (2006), pp. 64–8.   [36] Fulford (2008).

displayed a set of baths, a wooden amphitheatre (quite similar to that found at Forum Novum), a number of temples and a courtyard building that could be interpreted either as the basilica of a timber forum or as part of a residence similar to the legates' *praetorium* in the double-legionary fort at Vetera in Germany.[37] Its orientation, however, following that of the timber structure mentioned above, is close to the final north-south, east-west axis of the grid of streets established under the Flavians towards the end of the first century AD. The baths were built on a different alignment (though not at a 51 degree angle to the Flavian grid) and the entrance *porticus* had to be modified to make way for the new street within the orthogonal grid. There was no destruction or fire to explain why the new grid was constructed. Instead there is evidence of the existing structures on earlier alignments continuing or adjusting to the new condition of a street grid on a totally different alignment.[38] The source of that alignment can be identified as that of the central courtyard building/forum-basilica complex and the road running from its midpoint out of Silchester towards London.[39] However, the desire to reorientate the grid is harder to understand. Perhaps it is significant that the new grid was orientated on the cardinal points – north-south and east-west – and perhaps it should be read as having a cosmo-logical significance. What is clear, though, is that those travelling through the city entered a distinctly urban network of streets, with facilities for the traveller and for the production of a clean and groomed population.[40]

The examples of town-formation at Saint-Bertrand, Forum Novum and Silchester demonstrate that there was no single vision for the format of the city; whether or not it was to have a grid-plan was the most pertinent question posed to the architects (we return to the subject of planning in the next chapter). Choices had to be made over what was seen as essential: baths, temples, and a central space or forum. All three examples were located at the junctions of major roads and should be seen as meeting not just the needs of the local inhabitants but also those of travellers, including the governor, the procurator (the province's chief financial officer) and their entourages. The governor or procurator may have overseen the transforma-tion of Saint-Bertrand or Silchester, and may have arranged for the sale or supply of stamped tiles to the people of Silchester under Nero. They were not, however, always interested in intervening directly in the development of the cities of the provinces. We can imagine a scenario in which the governor or procurator might express a view on the development of a place to a

[37] Fulford (1989), p. 186; (2003), pp. 100–2; Esmonde Cleary (2001).
[38] Clarke and Fulford (2002).   [39] Bewley and Fulford (1996).   [40] Frere and Fulford (2002).

member of the local elite, but this is interaction as opposed to intervention. There were individuals in Britain and Aquitania who felt, like Faianus Plebeius at Forum Novum, that they needed the forms of urbanism that they had seen or heard about: a forum, baths, good houses, theatres, amphi-theatres, a *porticus* or a *palaestra*, as well as an orthogonal grid of streets.

We have concentrated up to this point on town-formation, but need to bear in mind that the existing cities of the West did not just simply stagnate once they had been defined architecturally and constitutionally. At Tarragona (fig. 4.4), by the period of the Flavian emperors in the late first century AD, the upper town had been redeveloped as a series of three terraces: the lowest held a circus (340 by 116m), the second contained a rectangular space (300 by 120m) bounded on three sides by porticoes, identified by some as the Provincial Forum, and finally there was the precinct of the temple of Rome and Augustus (140 by 120m).[41] The skyline of the old Republican city had been transformed into a sanctuary site declaring the dedication of the people of Tarragona and the province of Tarraconensis to Rome and its emperors.[42] The format and connection between the spaces of the circus, the 'Provincial Forum' and the temple complex are reminiscent of the sanctuaries of Hercules at Tivoli or Fortuna at Palestrina, but with the important difference that the theatre was replaced with a circus (see Chapter 8 below). This was a religious space for large numbers to attend chariot racing in the format known from the Circus Maximus at Rome. And it was also the location of statues com-memorating the famous men or *summi viri* of the province: priests, ambassadors to Rome and other prominent individuals as in the Forum of Augustus at Rome.[43] The development of this temple site on such a scale may have reflected the fact that Tarragona was the very first city to gain permission to construct a temple of Augustus in AD 15, an example followed in all the other provinces.[44] The scale of architecture at Tarragona in the Flavian period had more in common with Rome than with either Saint-Bertrand or Silchester, yet there were other elements that were of a similar scale to them: the forum and theatre in the lower town and the grid plan of the city's streets. What had occurred was a demand by the population of the city and of the province to construct an architecture for the cult of Augustus on a new scale so that Tarragona could continue to win fame as the earliest and preeminent cult centre for the worship of Augustus as a deity.[45] As we have already seen in the case of some other towns,

---

[41] Dupré i Raventós (2004). See Chapter 3 on the role of Tarragona as a provincial capital.
[42] Mart. *Ep.*10.104.   [43] Fishwick (2004), p. 33.   [44] Tac. *Ann.*1.78.
[45] According to S.H.A. *Sev.* 3 the temple was in need of restoration in AD 178.

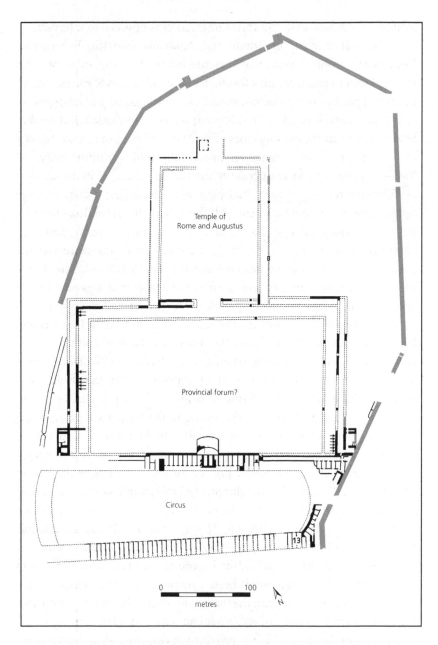

4.4 Tarragona: plan of the Temple of Rome and Augustus (first century AD), in front of which stood the city's second forum, and in front of that, a circus.

Tarragona may also have constructed its identity around the figure of Scipio Africanus, whose winter base was situated here in 218 BC, meaning that Tarragona could make a claim to be the earliest town in the Spanish provinces. In the political context of the new Flavian regime at Rome,

Tarragona as the 'provincial capital' seems to have been attempting to maintain its prominence following the civil wars of AD 68–9 (during which Tarragona was a base for Galba's claim to the imperial throne): the rebuilding created a visual and physical reminder of the strategic importance of the city.[46]

The difference between Silchester and Tarragona is a difference of location and history; one had a long history of urbanism stretching back to the first century BC or earlier and was located on the Mediterranean, while the other was located in the north, at the edge of the Empire, with a far shorter history or experience of Mediterranean urbanism. Both cities pursued a course of urban development that would lead them to a position of local prominence, but the scale or sophistication of that development varied, as did the expectations of the visitor or even the Roman governor setting eyes on either city for the first time. Silchester did have temples, a grid of streets, and an amphitheatre; unlike some towns such as Panopeus in Asia minor, which Pausanias famously found to be lacking government offices, a gymnasium, a theatre, an *agora*, and an aqueduct to feed the water-fountains.[47] At about the same time, Pompeii remained under reconstruction or in restoration through to its final destruction in AD 79, yet the fact that much of this work was incomplete did not cause the city to cease to exist. Instead it was rebuilding for a new future with a new architectural form that would continue to highlight the city's ambitions, and new facilities that resembled some available in Rome, such as the well-lit Central Baths (fig. 8.3).[48]

A vexing question in the literature on the formation of towns in the Roman West is whether the town was a feature of what has been termed 'Romanisation', which is considered by most scholars to denote a process by which the former barbarians engaged with Roman culture.[49] Tacitus and Cassius Dio certainly saw the presence of a town, markets, fora, temples and baths as signs of a change towards the ways of the Romans. However, the use of a certain kind of material culture or urban architecture does not necessarily imply a convergence between cities across the Empire and the possibility of defining a city type.[50] The use of the fabric of the city does not coincide with the spread of Roman citizenship, and indeed the city in the Roman Empire appears at once as a global phenomenon and at the same

---

[46] Dupré í Raventós (1995).   [47] Paus. 10.4.4.   [48] Dobbins (1994).

[49] For a bibliography on Romanisation see Mattingly (2004).

[50] As Williamson (2005), p. 23 reminds us in connection with debates on the production of local coinage.

time as a local adaptation of that phenomenon.[51] There is no hint of a close relationship between juridical status on the one hand and physical form and the provision of particular monuments on the other. There was no 'package' of public structures proper to a *colonia* as opposed to a *municipium*; all were usable if they fitted the ambitions and pockets of the local elite. Forms as varied as Tarragona, Silchester, Forum Novum and Saint-Bertrand are local responses to an idea of the city and an ideal of urban life. The city was a means of demonstrating to others, and to its own inhabitants, the local acceptance and manifestation of urban life, and was a feature to be observed and responded to by provincial governors, whether a Varus or an Agricola.

An insight into the expectations of the Roman viewer of the provincial city can be gained from an examination of the redevelopment or even refoundation of Italica, the birthplace of the emperors Trajan and Hadrian (fig. 4.5).[52] The original city of thirteen hectares, which contained a forum, baths and a Tiberian theatre restored and expanded under Trajan,[53] was extended over an additional area of thirty-eight hectares. The extension of the original city was laid out across an orthogonal grid that was orientated around three major public building projects: a large temple dedicated to the deified emperor Trajan, a colossal set of baths covering 32,400 m², which was supplied by a new aqueduct, and a large amphitheatre to house some 25,000 spectators.[54] Much of the new Hadrianic city was to be abandoned about a century later,[55] but it is clear from the geophysical survey conducted in the 1990s that the new city contained housing as well as the major monuments.[56] Whether Hadrian was the inspiration behind these developments is debated: Cassius Dio remarks that Hadrian granted both honour and gifts to his place of birth; yet the same author notes that Hadrian, as emperor, never visited Italica, in contrast to Tarragona, where he spent a winter and restored the temple of Augustus.[57] However, the expansion of Italica appears to have been an imperial benefaction, which sat alongside its new status as a colony, *Colonia Aelia Augusta Italica*, and Hadrian's occupation *in absentia* of the office of *duovir quinquennalis* (pair of senior magistrates elected every five years).[58] It needs to be remembered that colonial status was awarded at the inhabitants' insistence rather than being initiated by the emperor.[59] This would

---

[51] Williamson (2005), p. 23.   [52] See Chapter 2.
[53] See Keay (1998) for the debate over dating; Blázquez (2003), pp. 134–7.
[54] Rodríguez Hidalgo (1997); Boatwright (1997).   [55] Rodríguez Hidalgo (1997), p. 108.
[56] Rodríguez Hidalgo (1997).   [57] Dio Cass. 69.10; S.H.A. *Hadr*.12.
[58] S.H.A. *Hadr*.19; Boatwright (1997), p. 119.   [59] Gell. *NA*16.13; Boatwright (2000), pp. 42–3.

Baths of
Hadrian

Amphitheatre

HADRIANIC CITY

Trajaneum

Republican
temple

Baths of
Trajan

REPUBLICAN
CITY

Theatre

0   300

metres   N

4.5 Italica: plan showing the extension of the city in the second century AD, including the cult centre of the deified emperor Trajan.

have brought the city Roman law, citizenship and access to recruitment into the legions, rather than into the auxiliary units. The status of *colonia* in effect gives the place a greater Romanness than when it was a *municipium*. The scale of the new Hadrianic architecture at Italica was far larger than in other cities in the West, having much in common with Hadrian's projects in Athens, but still reveals similar concerns to those found earlier under the

Flavian emperors at Silchester: an amphitheatre, baths, a temple and an orthogonal grid of streets mapped around these three mega-structures. This was of course in addition to the existing facilities of a theatre, a forum and another set of baths. What is somewhat different is the emphasis on Italica as a place of veneration: the temple or *Traianeum* has inscriptions indicating not just the worship of the emperors but also of the *genius* (patron spirit) of the *colonia* that had produced them.[60] Just as Tarragona was the first place to have its temple of Augustus, so Italica would appear to be the first city with a priesthood and cult of the deified Trajan.[61]

ARE LEGIONARY FORTS CITIES?

At this point we wish to shift the focus slightly. We have found, whether in central Italy, south-west France, southern Spain or southern Britain, that the Roman city might be defined by the presence of temples, a forum, baths and the option of a grid of streets with houses. These elements of urbanism can also be identified in the army camps of the legions and auxiliaries that have been excavated in the provinces. John Creighton has drawn our attention to the fact that the colonists in Colchester and Gloucester inhabited a series of former barrack-blocks (fig. 2.10).[62] This raises a problem of definition: was the army camp of the legions a form of urbanism? In his *Geography* of the second century AD, Ptolemy includes the camps of the legions within the lists of towns, and we find for Britain the following entries: *Deva Legio XX Victrix, Eburacum Legio VI Victrix,* and *Isca Legio II Augusta.* Similar entries can be found for the location of other legions in other provinces. Hence for this Mediterranean writer the legionary fort was a form of urbanism.[63] In terms of the life experience of the recruits, many came from towns that had been colonies, places like Mérida, discussed in Chapter 3. The longevity of some of the sites of legionary forts is significant, such as Caerleon from AD 74 through to the end of the third century. This was a stable settlement that was the base for five to six thousand soldiers, and their associated suppliers, workers, and hangers on. There were, of course, periods when the legion was absent and involved in the construction of Hadrian's Wall and, in the second century,

---

[60] Boatwright (2000), pp. 165–6.   [61] *AE* 1982: 520, 521.

[62] Creighton (2006); Crummy (1988); Hurst (1988).

[63] Laurence (2001b); but note the difference in terms of form of local government. Compare Chapter 3.

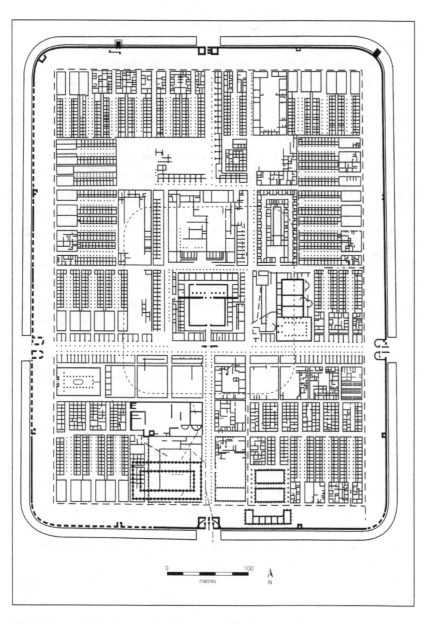

0   100

metres   N

4.6 Neuss: plan of the legionary fortress: showing the organisation of space and the buildings contained within such permanent military settlements.

campaigns in Scotland that culminated in the construction of the Antonine Wall. In any case, it would have been rare that all the legionaries were in residence at the same time. The fort was a base rather than the place of permanent residence of the entire legion (fig. 4.6 for a plan of an excavated legionary fort). What is interesting in terms of urbanism is how the site developed over a period of time. The phases of development demonstrate that the establishment of a permanent place of settlement, even with the labour force of the soldiers, was undertaken in a piecemeal fashion and that it took more than one generation for those features to appear that we expect to see in a Roman fort or a Roman town.[64] The early fort featured an area of land surrounded by a ditch and palisade[65] and with streets that were engineered to last. This should be seen as a sign of the intended permanent nature of the settlement, and involved a significant input of human labour.[66] The construction of the barracks, baths, *principia* and other buildings was a gradual process. Interestingly, one of the earliest buildings in stone within the fort was the baths, a necessity if they were to be heated by fire,[67] and another was the amphitheatre. What was being established in the fort was a defined area similar to that of a town, with the facilities that would replicate a mode of living that included bathing and worship of the gods (including the staging of games in the amphitheatre), all of which reproduced a Roman identity for the citizen soldiers in the Second Legion.[68]

The importance of bathing for the reproduction of this identity cannot be underestimated (a full discussion of bathing and urbanism can be found in Chapter 8). *II Augusta* had previously been based in Exeter, where the remains of the bathhouse have been excavated, and bathhouses are known at the forts of Chester and York, while provision was being made for the necessary water-supply when construction of the fort at Inchtuthil was abandoned.[69] Baths may have developed within legionary forts rather earlier than the Flavian period, as suggested by their presence within the Claudian fort of Vindonissa. The baths at Caerleon covered an area of one hectare and included a basilica, as did the baths of *II Augusta* at its earlier base in Exeter, and there was at least one other major set of baths outside the defences at Caerleon (the Castle baths).

Some questions remain, however. How did those who were not legionaries or Roman citizens view the fort? Did they, like Ptolemy, regard the fort as a town? These questions are impossible to answer, but what we can say is that the fort at Caerleon attracted settlement around it.[70] It must be remembered that the fort would have housed, or been used by, a variety of other people attached to the legion. The legionary legate would, of course,

[64] On the labour requirements of construction see Shirley (2000), (2001).
[65] Evans and Metcalf (1992).   [66] Boon (1972), p. 25; Shirley (2001), pp. 82–4.
[67] Zienkiewicz (1986).   [68] *RIB* 319–24.   [69] Bidwell (1979), (1980).
[70] Evans (2000); also Sommer (1984).

have had his *familia* with him, comprising not only his wife and children but also the household slaves and other dependents of such a notable man. Slaves and other attendants such as farriers and ostlers are amply attested at Roman military sites. Now that the 'ban' on the marriage of serving soldiers can be seen to be a modern fiction,[71] we must envisage large numbers of women and children attached to a garrison fort, and the question of whether they necessarily lived outside the walls in the *canabae* (a settlement dependent on a fort) is one that has yet to be resolved. Moreover, evidence from Vindonissa attests to the presence of women inside the fort, one apparently operating a bar.[72] Traders and other professions servicing soldiers and their needs have long been recognised as indispensable components of the wider population of a fort. So in terms of the heterogeneity of its population, a long-term army garrison may have been more similar to a city than has previously been allowed. The fort acted as a focal point in the landscape, as well as reproducing a culture of Romanness for the citizen-legionaries.

Interestingly, the abandonment of the fort at Exeter reveals a dramatic disjuncture between the military use of the site and its civilian reoccupation. The street grid remained the same, but the bath-building and its *palaestra* were replaced with a forum-basilica complex and a new set of baths was constructed in an adjacent block.[73] Bidwell suggests that during the period of disuse the *palaestra* of the baths and the *frigidarium* could have been utilised in the manner of a forum and a basilica respectively.[74] The baths were probably damaged in the general destruction associated with the abandonment of the site by the Second Legion.[75] The gap between the abandonment of the fort and the reoccupation of the site as a civilian settlement may explain the decision by the new civilian authorities to construct a forum-basilica complex and a new set of baths in an adjacent *insula* (i.e. because the military baths had ceased to function). Alternatively, these new authorities were seeking to create a different sort of settlement, one in which the forum occupied a central point in the grid, and the baths were in the way of this development. Interestingly, a very similar sequence can be seen at the other legionary fort in Britain which was turned into a *civitas*-capital rather than a *colonia*, Wroxeter. There again, the forum was constructed over the legionary baths and an entirely new set of baths created across the new *decumanus maximus*, although again the main

---

[71] Phang (2001).   [72] Allison et al. (2005).
[73] Bidwell (1979), pp. 69–70.   [74] Bidwell (1980), p. 56.
[75] See Holbrook and Bidwell (1991), pp. 7–8 on the process of abandonment and evidence for it.

armature of the fort's street system was substantially preserved into the civilian phase.[76]

Although disjuncture can be found at Exeter and Wroxeter, where the legionary bathhouses were redeveloped into the forum-basilica complex perhaps in order to create a new form of urbanism that did not coincide with the previous conception of the place as a legionary fort, it needs to be stressed that Wroxeter utilises the existing grid of streets to create the new forum and its basilica as a central space, while the fort of *II Augusta* at Exeter (and that at Caerleon) displayed most of the features of Roman urbanism: baths, a central place, an amphitheatre, worship of the gods, a grid of streets and the use of Latin. As the children of citizens, the legionaries had a life experience of the city (often of cities in Narbonensis and Italy) prior to recruitment into the army camp in their late-teens or early twenties. Bathing, worship of the gods, use of Latin, and an organised settlement pattern based around a grid of streets were the normative life experiences of these soldiers. Going beyond the city, or losing the opportunity to bathe or to worship the gods, was to step into a different world, that of the barbarian. Both the military fort and the Roman city consciously recreated an interpretation of what it was to be Roman. The fact that the versions produced at Silchester and at Caerleon coincide should not really surprise us, because each reproduced a structural hierarchy of power; in descending order this consisted of legate, military tribune, centurion, legionary, or *duovir quinquennalis, duovir, aedile, ordo* of decurions, citizen, resident alien. Interestingly, veterans crossed from one hierarchy into the other with centurions becoming important members of the elite.[77] The relationship between a veteran colony and a Roman fort appears to have been closer than that between a fort and other towns, since the grid formation is a feature of these settlements – particularly in the German provinces close to the Rhine frontier.[78] Perhaps the distinction between a fort or military base for a legion of citizens and a veteran colony of citizens should not be so sharply drawn, since both types of settlement were involved in the production of a stable Roman identity through time. These were both places expected to last into the future.

There is still a difference, however. If the legion were to relocate to a new site, the fort would be abandoned with a degree of destruction but might be converted into a town.

---

[76] White and Barker (1998), pp. 70–101.

[77] Patterson (2006), pp. 233–5 notes their increased significance following periods of civil war and land redistribution.

[78] Carroll (2001), p. 45.

ROMAN URBANISM IN THE PROVINCIAL CONTEXT

This chapter has demonstrated that a number of assumptions about the nature of Roman urbanism need to be questioned. A Roman town did not need to have an orthogonal street-grid, as we saw in the case of Saint-Bertrand and Forum Novum. The presence of a new street-grid on a new orientation at Silchester highlights the level of central control and desire and the labour resources involved in the reorientation of the public spaces of that city; interestingly, the new grid was developed after the town had become established. Saint-Bertrand developed a pseudo-grid of streets through the expansion and adjustment of the network of existing roads, but the urban managers (whoever they were) did not embark on a full reorientation of the public streets. There may have been a crucial difference in the powers of the local authorities at each place, so that those at Silchester were able to impose a more radical solution than at Saint-Bertrand, where change evidently had to be negotiated in a more piecemeal fashion.

What is laid out in these early urban formations is a condensed code of the city that was later elaborated upon with the addition of new buildings, as we saw in the cases of Tarragona and Italica. The influence of finance from the centre of the Empire at these sites might have produced a difference in the scale of the public buildings and their architectural sophistication, but it did not produce new forms of urbanism. This points to there being a definition of what it was that made a city, which coincided with the concepts found in Cassius Dio and Tacitus: temples, fora, baths and optional extras: a theatre, an amphitheatre, walls, a street-grid. The quality of the housing-stock was also an important consideration for Tacitus, but it seems to have been less important for those using the city for markets, public meetings and religious worship than modern authors might anticipate.[79] One of the main attractions of Roman urbanism was the ability to bathe. It marked the difference between Romans, whether soldiers (auxiliaries and legionaries) or civilians (citizens and provincials), and the barbarians, whether they lived beyond Rome's frontiers or in rustic squalor within the Empire. This essential feature of Roman identity was associated by elite moralists with the other luxuries of the *porticus* (corresponding to the Greek gymnasium) and sumptuous dining. This view of the city from

---

[79] Creighton (2006).

the early second century AD is confirmed by another writer at the end of the second century – Tertullian. In a justification of the Christian life, he pointed out that a Christian lived no differently from a pagan apart from in the thorny matter of religious observance. Like other city dwellers, a Christian used the forum, the food market or *macellum,* the baths, the *tabernae,* workshops and stables and attended market days in the city.[80] This was a reaction to a form of persecution that excluded Christians from the use of the forum, the baths and the houses of a city, such as that at Vienne in AD 177, which in effect excluded them from civilisation.[81]

---

[80] Tert. *Apol.* 42.2.   [81] Euseb. *Hist. Eccl.* 5.1.5, 5.4.2.

Town planning, competition and the aesthetics
of urbanism

Everywhere is full of gymnasiums, fountains, gateways, temples,
handicrafts and schools. And it can be said in medical terms that the
inhabited world was, as it were, ill at the start and has now recovered.
Never does the flow of gifts from you [Rome] to these cities stop, nor can
it be discovered who has received the greater share, because your
generosity is equal toward all. Indeed, the cities shine with radiance and
grace, and the whole earth has been adorned like a pleasure garden.

(Aelius Aristides *Orations* 26.97–9)

FROM 'TOWN PLANNING' TO A NEW URBAN AESTHETIC: ARMATURE

One of the most distinctive and widely remarked elements of the Roman
city is the presence at very many sites, from the middle Republic in Italy
onwards, of a regular, orthogonal grid of streets; particularly noticeable of
course to modern scholars working from two-dimensional plans of these
sites. Because of the ubiquity of such sites with street-grids and the way in
which those grids control the placing of buildings and other features of the
urban landscape, they have been accorded great importance in the modern
literature on Roman urbanism. Several books have presented the plans of
Roman cities and created a value to the orthogonal grid of streets found
frequently, across the Mediterranean and beyond, as a form of town
planning.[1] At the level of the plan as derived by archaeological investigation, the analysis works to determine the city walls, the alignment of the
streets, the position of the forum and the location of other public buildings.
The grid is accepted as an organising feature and major characteristic of the
Roman city which was deterministic in the development of Roman urbanism. We wish to question this viewpoint. Our grounds for doing so draw on
the work of William MacDonald.[2] He did not contest that the layout of

---

[1] See Haverfield (1913); Ward Perkins (1974); Owens (1991); Anderson (1997), pp. 183–240;
Sommella (1988). For a critique of these views see Laurence (1994).
[2] MacDonald (1968) and (1986).

towns with a grid-plan and a forum was a feature of the early towns and colonies of Italy and the provinces, but what he suggested was that the grid developed what he calls an armature of major street(s) on which the principal buildings of the cities were sited.[3] This feature created for a visitor to a city a sequential view of public monuments as they passed through the city. What this represents in terms of planning is a shift from geometric space based on a grid to an emphasis on experiential space, in which the seemingly unplanned or disorderly arrangement of monuments in terms of geometry had a spatial logic that was based on the movement along an armature or major street and the connectivity between monuments.[4]

What we wish to suggest is that the grid of streets was an easy way in which to provide a shape to the space within the walls of a city (see Chapter 6 for discussion), but it was not intended as a planning tool in the manner of the layout of Manhattan in 1807 with a view to the future expansion of the city over the 2,028 blocks of Manhattan Island.[5] Underlying the surviving ancient texts that refer to the layout of new cities, such as Aristotle or Vitruvius, there would seem to have been a wider debate involving other writers (whose work does not survive) over the layout of a town and the utility of a grid of streets.[6] The need to compromise over the shape of the city with reference to defence, the position of temples, health and the image of the city concerns these writers far more than the determination of a grid and, where it is mentioned, it does not appear to have been seen as the tool for the planning of the city.[7] From the perspective of archaeology, we can see that the determination of the size of the grid for a new city's population was a pretty hit-and-miss affair. There are numerous cities whose grid did not fill up with housing, such as Cosa,[8] and there are others where the city's grid and walls swiftly became irrelevant as the area of habitation expanded, such as Timgad or Djemila.[9] It is difficult to describe this process as planning and we wish to set the debate over the town plan in a wider context of the experience of urbanism at ground level and to develop a thesis of the aesthetics of Roman urbanism.

The question remains: how early did this aesthetic of connective space develop? Claude Nicolet and Pietro Janni have suggested that the Roman approach to space, even as early as the first century BC, was one in which movement through space took precedence over the representation of space

---

[3] MacDonald (1986), pp. 17–19.

[4] Both public buildings and water features; MacDonald (1986), pp. 22–3.

[5] Koolhaas (1994), pp. 13–27.

[6] Arist. *Pol.* 1276b.24, 1330a.34–1331b.10 or Vitr. *De arch.* 4.1.9, 1.3.1, 1.6.7, 4.5.

[7] Laurence (2000).   [8] Fentress (2000).   [9] MacDonald (1986), pp. 25–9.

as an area of territory.[10] The dominance of this mode of representation can be found in Pliny the Elder's description of Rome from the second half of the first century AD.[11] He can describe the circumference of the city – 13 miles and 200 paces – and say that the area enclosed by this was divided into fourteen regions, but after that he concentrates on describing the length of routes leading from the milestone in the Forum Romanum to the gates. What he does not do is account for the city's regions in terms of their size or as divisions of space. It is a spatial logic that can be found in other geographical descriptions from the ancient world, including the Antonine Itineraries, the Vicarello Goblets and the Peutinger Table.[12] This linear logic of space existed alongside another spatial concept of area associated with being within or outside the urban boundary (pomerium) or within a particular neighbourhood (a vicus).[13] The intersection of the linear and area-based conceptions of space could cause the term vicus to be associated with both the linear space of the street and an urban area or neighbourhood. Ultimately the linear conception had greater hold on space, partly due to its utility for navigation through the city. It is at the level of the street that we can see how this linear conception of space linked monuments to build up into an urban schema that might be described as a 'connective architecture' associated with the Roman city.[14]

Writers in antiquity were very conscious of the absence of beauty in the streets of Rome, prior to the great fire of AD 64. Rome was characterised by ugly buildings and narrow winding streets or vici. It was a city filled up rather than laid out and thus unlike both the colonies founded by Rome and Italian cities, such as Pompeii, and the cities founded by provincials.[15] The great fire of Rome in AD 64 led to a new form of urbanism at Rome: rows of measured streets with broad thoroughfares, a restriction on the height of buildings, open spaces, and the addition of colonnades in front of the apartment blocks.[16] It is dubious whether these measures were fully implemented, but Tacitus is quite clear that the measures created a different form of urban experience in Rome – gone were the shady, winding streets, and towering buildings, and instead they were replaced with broad

---

[10] Nicolet (1991) and Janni (1984).   [11] Plin. *HN* 3.66
[12] See Brodersen (1995) for a full discussion and Brodersen (2001) for a summary in English; also see Salway (2001).
[13] See Haselberger (2007) on the application of boundaries and the creation of new boundaries in Augustan Rome.
[14] See Laurence (2008).
[15] Tac. *Ann.*15.38; Suet. *Ner.* 38; Dio Cass. 62.16; Livy, 5.55, Diod. Sic. 14.116; Plut. *Cam.* 32.3; see Cic. *Leg.* 2.35.95–6 for a comparison of Rome to Capua.
[16] Tac. *Ann.*15.43.

streets with colonnades and lower buildings.[17] This was a new aesthetic for Rome, described by Tacitus in the second century AD, but one that can be found in other cities in the Empire. The so-called *decumanus maximus* at Ostia is one such broad avenue, with shaded colonnades for pedestrians in front of apartment blocks. It is utterly different from even the broadest street in Pompeii of the first century AD, which was characterised by a roadway in which it would have been difficult for wheeled traffic to pass. Even a community in Narbonensis, the Vocontii at Vaison-la-Romaine, constructed a colonnade along one side of the main street. What Nero introduced into Rome was not so much orthogonal planning, but a system that created a new vision of urban utility: wider streets, colonnades and careful layout. This was the basis of the new Rome that Tacitus could describe as a city of beauty.[18]

ARCHAEOLOGICAL EXAMPLES OF THE EARLY APPEARANCE OF ARMATURE

Naples (Neapolis) provides an example of how we can use this form of analysis on actual sites. The city's walls and grid date back to the fifth century BC (fig. 5.1) and it has been occupied continuously until the present day.[19] The major armature of the city splits it in half and connects the east and west gates to the forum located at the Church of San Lorenzo Maggiore, built over the Roman *macellum*, and the Church of San Paolo Maggiore, the former temple of the Dioscuri. The odeon and the theatre were located within this area. The presence of walls caused traffic to be funnelled through gates. Once within the walls, that traffic did not disperse throughout the grid but was concentrated towards its destination, whether out of the other side of the city, to the forum or to some other point within the grid, such as temples, houses of prominent individuals and so on. Thus in Naples traffic was concentrated towards a number of specific locations along relatively few major routes with the other streets taking on a secondary role or being relegated to the status of alley-ways.[20]

The simple grid of streets and public buildings found in Naples gets us only part of the way. To take this further, we need to have a fuller understanding of the urban elements that were distributed across cities to create a

---

[17] Tac. *Ann.*15.38.
[18] Tac. *Ann.*15.41; see Wallace-Hadrill (2003) on the intersection between the newly planned Rome and the city of winding streets.
[19] Arthur (2002).   [20] Compare Wallace-Hadrill (2003), p. 196 on Rome.

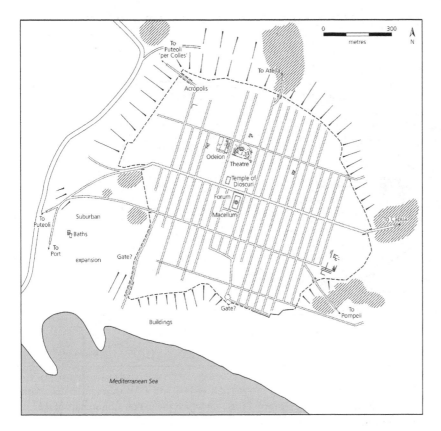

5.1 Naples: plan showing the organisation of the street grid in relation to the monuments, city walls and harbour (shaded areas are cemeteries). The major east-west route through the town connecting Capua with Puteoli creates an urban armature on which the major monuments were built.

visual display or sequence of features which confirmed the inhabitants' sense of urban life. Not every site can provide us with enough information for an understanding of these features. Simon Keay and Martin Millett's survey of Falerii Novi produced the most complete plan of a city from Italy (fig. 5.2).[21] The lack of excavation associated with the project creates problems of interpretation as there is an absence of data on chronological development but, as currently revealed, the site displays the features of a number of phases and includes a general distortion of the orthogonal grid to allow the Via Amerina, running south-north through the city, to exit via the north gate. The layout of the site, however, highlights a concern to create visual impact using the sequence of spaces and views of the

[21] Keay *et al.* (2000).

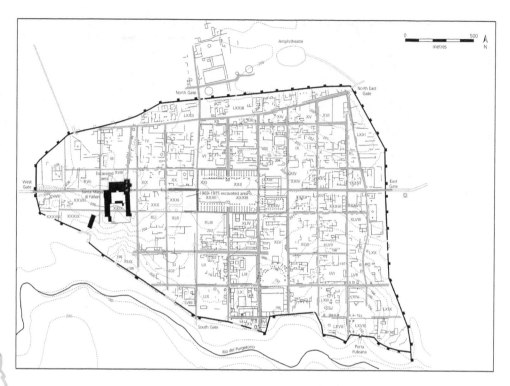

5.2 Falerii Novi: plan showing intersection of N-S and E-W through-routes on the forum, which create two axes (armatures) on which the major monuments of the city are arranged.

architecture of the town. The forum is located on the original east-west linear route, and is placed at the highest point of the ridge that coincides with the centre of the grid of *insulae* within the walls of the city. The only higher point in the city is to the north of where this road exits the city via the west gate; there is a strong indication that a temple or *arx* similar to that found at Cosa or Norba was located here.[22] The southern approach to the city (i.e. from Rome) had been amplified as a result of the quarrying and sculpting of the landscape to create a series of cliffs onto which the walls of the city were constructed. These walls provided a vision of urbanism that was further enhanced by the visibility of the *capitolium* on the *arx* in the west of the city. For those travelling on the Via Amerina, passage across the city featured a rise of thirteen metres to the western edge of the forum up a slope with a gradient in the region of 1 in 15 to 1 in 20. The forum at the brow of the hill presented a natural pause for the traveller, just as it would

---

[22] Quilici Gigli (2003).

have done for those travelling down the hill. This street would have been paved, so any driver of a wagon or cart would have undertaken the slope with care.[23] From this stopping-point on the road, the passer-by could have looked either along the colonnaded forum to the temple(s) and basilica at the other end of the piazza or towards the west gate located down the long street which articulated the grid system of the town. Moving northwards, at the next intersection the *capitolium* would have come into view. Leaving the city on the Via Amerina, the amphitheatre would have become visible across the cemetery to the north that contained some massive monumental tombs. Elsewhere in the city, the natural topography was exploited with a theatre being built into the hill's southern slope. It is also notable that the layout of the forum created a point of intersection between the street leading to the theatre and that leading to the *capitolium*. The two principal entrances, symmetrically placed on the north and south sides of the forum, would have constructed a monumental route through the complex, whilst removing through traffic to the Via Amerina beyond the southern limit of the piazza. Simon Keay and Martin Millett suggested a tentative chronology for these developments:

(1) the layout of the central area of the orthogonal grid and Via Amerina;
(2) the development of the irregular route around the northern, eastern and western sides of the grid;
(3) the construction of the *capitolium*;
(4) the construction of the town walls that cut through earlier tombs;
(5) the expansion of the central grid over the area of the walled enclosure.

The sequence of construction, and the placement of the forum at a site that was a natural stopping-point, highlight the need for a city to display itself to passers-by and ideally to cause them to break a journey. After all, any journey within the Empire was articulated or broken up via the encounter with cities, which form the basis of the measurement of journeys in the Antonine Itineraries. If the city did not look like a city, it might have been overlooked as a suitable place for travellers to stop, to rest and to bathe. These are all features that helped Orcistus in Phrygia to gain recognition as a city (cf. Pausanias 10.4 on Panopeus in the second century AD), but we might extend the menu of urban elements from that city to interpret the nature of urbanism at other sites recovered by archaeological methods. What we see in the cities across the Empire is an assemblage of urban elements, the nature of which varied from region to region and period to

---

[23] Davies (2002), p. 79.

period. Even though we can identify variation and difference, there is also a sense of likeness that caused the construction of some elements, especially public buildings, in a very similar form – whether in Britain, Italy or North Africa.

URBAN COMPETITION AND THE AESTHETICS OF URBANISM

The process of development of cities and, in particular, the elements of beauty or urban aesthetics that underlie William MacDonald's thesis, can be identified in texts of the second century AD, most notably that of Aelius Aristides in his oration *On Rome*, which envisages a world of beautiful cities that competed for recognition by means of the construction of gymnasia, fountains, monumental approaches, temples and other buildings. These texts also reveal the tensions involved in city development: financial for the most part, but also a certain scepticism that the projects would actually come to fruition and not leave the city in a worse state with numerous citizens deprived of their homes.[24] However, we suggest that the inter-city rivalries that can be found in the mid- to late first century AD indicate the process already at work. The collapse of central authority during the civil wars of AD 68–9 allowed cities to look enviously at each other. A dispute over the theft of crops and cattle between Oea and Lepcis Magna led to open warfare, with Oea enlisting the aid of the barbarian Garamantes, whereas at Placentia the soldiers of Vitellius burnt down the amphitheatre located outside its walls.[25] The explanation of the burning of the amphitheatre, as reported by Tacitus, includes a role for the inhabitants of neighbouring colonies or cities, who were jealous of Placentia for having the amphitheatre that qualified as the largest building of its kind in Italy.[26] Such rivalries existed in peace as well. Pompeii and its neighbour Nuceria had a close relationship in many ways, including attending games at each other's city. However, their rivalry spilt over into a riot at a gladiatorial show in AD 59 that left numerous Nucerians maimed or dead.[27] This event was commemorated by a famous fresco in the peristyle of the House of Actius Anicetus and referred to by numerous pictorial graffiti.[28]

---

[24] Aelius Aristides, *On Rome*, 26.97. Other references to such amenities include: Paus. 10.4; and Dio Chrys. (*Or.* 40.5–11, 45.12–16, 47.10–25) who makes clear that this view was held not just by himself as a citizen of Prusa but also by the provincial governor – a view confirmed by Plin. *Ep.*10.17b, 23, 24, 31, 32, 37, 38, 39, 40, 41, 42, 49, 50, 54, 55, 61, 62, 70, 71, 75, 76, 90, 91, 98, 99.
[25] Tac. *Hist.* 4.50.   [26] Tac. *Hist.* 2.21.   [27] Tac. *Ann.*14.17.   [28] E.g. *CIL* 4.1293.

Aelius
Aristides

The physical defeat of those belonging to a neighbouring city was a source of pride.

Moving beyond the Mediterranean, the introduction of the technologies of the city to areas that had little experience of monumental architecture or the use of marble could have created new images of the powerful, or a new means to express power. The city was an agent of domination, as much as veteran settlers or Rome's armies.[29] The assimilation by the local elites of the language of Roman urbanism is striking and created a means for elites in different locales to compete to create a city that might be described as an object of beauty or of monumental splendour. The four examples above can be described as inter-city rivalry, or what anthropologists have termed peer-polity interaction, also known as competitive emulation.[30] Urbanism  was a competitive business, in which the magistrates and decurions set out to demonstrate not only their individual worth within the city to their electorate of citizens through the construction of public monuments, but also to represent their place of residence as a place of urban living to surpass that of their neighbours. A motivation that produced a large amphitheatre in Placentia would have been the need to assert the city's supremacy over its neighbours, which could be expressed in built form and regarded with jealousy by those living in other cities within close proximity to the city. In areas where there was a higher density of cities, there would have been a greater sense of competition between neighbours. Equally, in founding new colonies or settling veterans, there was an impetus for the state or the city founder(s) to create places of higher status than the surrounding settle-ments. It may come as no surprise that a distinctive feature that is far less common in *municipia* in first-century BC Italy was an amphitheatre, a structure that at the time was almost exclusively a feature of the cities that contained veterans, such as Pompeii. Documented examples of such rivalry from antiquity are a rarity, but remind us of the competitive nature of urbanism and that a city's status or image was always negotiated in relation to the developments occurring in other neighbouring cities. The similarity of the Flavian amphitheatres of Arles and Nîmes may betray just such rivalry, as may the proximity of the circuses of Lyon and Vienne. Competition can therefore be understood as a motivation for the building of new monuments. Competition was the impetus behind the development of the city and the very idea of beauty within urbanism.

---

[29] E.g. Tac. *Agr.* 20–2. On the view of the local elite and the provincial governors see Dio Chrys. *Or.* 40.5–11, 45.12–16, 47.10–25 and the exchange of letters between the governor of Bithynia and the emperor Trajan in Plin. *Ep.*10.

[30] Renfrew and Cherry (1986).

THE SEVERAN CITY

When looking at the outcome of Roman urbanism in the West under the Severan emperors, we can begin to see the results of a shift in the nature of urban design from a grid with a number of streets that connected the main monuments of the city together, to a spatial design that was focussed on the integration of new monuments into routes that connected architecture. Indeed, it was under the Severans that we see a complete break away from the grid and the reshaping of that grid by means of the inclusion of additional monuments. What was set up in its place was a sense of urban design based on the development of new buildings and the redesign of the streets connecting to them, placing more emphasis on the vista and the sense of progress through the city towards a visual stopping-point. These features can most easily be seen in the projects in Rome and Lepcis Magna put in place under Septimius Severus and Caracalla.

The public buildings for which Septimius Severus was remembered in Rome that survived into late antiquity were the Baths of Severus and the Septizodium at the foot of the Palatine (fig. 5.3).[31] The latter was constructed in AD 203 (*CIL* 6.1032) and was composed of a colossal *nymphaeum* in the form of an elongated *scaenae frons*, perhaps even 180 metres in length, but it was also built as an entrance into the emperor's palace; until the city Prefect placed a statue of Septimius in what was to be the entrance, which was later seen to have been designed to make an impact on those arriving from Africa.[32] The monument was to be experienced by those arriving in the city: it was not a static entity but integrated into an ideal of display and visual impact on the viewer. It is a monument which finds parallels in examples from Africa and in the tomb of the Severi on the Via Appia.[33] Septimius Severus was also involved in the erection of buildings in the cities across the Empire.[34] His son would build a portico or colonnade in which Septimius' achievements and wars were celebrated, as well as the famous marble-clad Baths of Caracalla that still stand today, and a new street leading to it that would be described later as the most beautiful in Rome, and which was further embellished by works that included a *porticus*.[35] As with the Septizodium and its associated road, the route

---

[31] S.H.A. *Sev*.19; Cassiod. *Chronicon*. 144.879.

[32] Septizodium – *CIL* 6.1032; *nymphaeum* – Amm. Marc. *Res Gestae* 15.7.3, see Pisani Sartorio (1999), pp. 269–72 for a discussion; entrance/statue – S.H.A. *Sev*. 24; discussed by Thomas (2007).

[33] Africa – *CIL* 8. 2657, 14372; tomb of the Severi – S.H.A. *Geta* 7.   [34] S.H.A. *Sev*. 23.

[35] DeLaine (1997); S.H.A. *Carinus* 9, *Heliogab*. 17, *Alex. Sev*. 25.

5.3 Engraving of the Septizodium, showing its relationship with the Palatine Hill to its rear and the Arch of Constantine (built over an earlier Flavian Triumphal Arch). The Septizodium was the focus for the new connective Severan architecture that linked the baths of Caracalla – the Circus Maximus – the Palatine – the Colosseum, as a route through the city.

leading to the Baths of Caracalla was part of the architectural scheme to provide a means for people to view the beauty of the monument and also the beauty of the route leading to the monument.

The contemporary senator and historian, Cassius Dio, observed the actions of Septimius Severus at first hand. Dio was a far from unbiased commentator and sought to find fault with much that Septimius did; he disliked the fact that the world had changed and that the supremacy of the Senate and Italy had been replaced by that of a general and his soldiers recruited in the provinces.[36] Septimius' attitude to the cities of the Empire was a partial one. Those who had supported him were rewarded, those who had not were punished.[37] For example the walls of Byzantium were torn down and the city was incorporated into the territory of the Perinthians – all observed by Dio in person.[38] The senator's attitude to the building programme of Severus is intriguing – he strongly disapproves of the Emperor's actions:

[36] E.g. Dio Cass. 76.7–8; Dio Cass. 75.2 on soldiers.   [37] Dio Cass. 75.8.   [38] Dio Cass. 75.14.

He [Severus] restored a very large number of the ancient buildings and inscribed on them his own name, just as if he had erected them in the first place from his own private funds. He also spent a great deal uselessly in repairing other buildings and in constructing new ones; for instance, he built a temple of a huge size to Bacchus and Hercules.[39]

The problem for Dio was one of expenditure and a view that money was wasted, even though he admits in the next sentence that Septimius left the Roman state with a vast fortune. Dio expresses his view on the construction of monuments in a speech that he gives to Maecenas, the cultural supremo under Augustus:

So far as funds are concerned, therefore, a great abundance would be supplied from these sources. And I advise you to conduct the administration as follows. Adorn the capital with utter disregard for expense and make it magnificent with festivals of every kind ... The other ... cities should not indulge in public buildings unnecessarily numerous or large, nor waste their resources on expenditures for a large number or a variety of public games, lest they exhaust themselves in futile erections and be led by unreasonable rivalries to quarrel amongst themselves. They ought, indeed, to have their festivals and spectacles ... but not to such an extent that the public treasury or the estates of private citizens shall be ruined thereby, or that any resident stranger there shall be compelled to contribute to their expense ... For it is unreasonable that the well-to-do should be put under compulsion to spend their money outside their own countries.[40]

What concerned Dio, as expressed in the fictional speech of 29 BC and in his critique of Septimius, was the cost of the projects. It was an attitude that was beginning to engulf the Empire and can be seen in the significant decrease in the building of new monuments and, in particular, monuments that were of some considerable size. He sees the phenomenon of urban development as ruinous financially and as creating an unhealthy level of competition locally. This speech reflects Dio's own world, in which competition over the building of new monuments could bring about the financial ruin of the elite of the cities of the Empire, and it also reflects a rejection of the need to develop the city with new projects. The attitude could even shape Dio's interpretation of Augustus' famous dictum 'I found Rome a city of brick, I leave it to you a city of marble'; the third-century senator was adamant that this statement did not refer to the city of Rome but was instead a metaphor referring to the strength of the Empire.[41] A century before, Suetonius had placed this boast in that

---

[39] Dio Cass. 75.16.   [40] Dio Cass. 52.30.   [41] Dio Cass. 56.30.3–4.

section of his biography of Augustus that dealt with the Emperor's endeavours to embellish the city with new public buildings.[42] The contrast between Dio and Suetonius reflects a change in the attitude to such matters and a new culture in which the provision of such monuments was frowned upon.

Nevertheless, the Severan projects in Rome and elsewhere were spectacular: none more so than those in Lepcis Magna (fig. 5.4). Procopius looked back approvingly at the formerly large area of the city and its abundant population, as well as the Severan palace.[43] By the sixth century, when Procopius composed his text, Lepcis as refounded by Justinian was on a much smaller scale with strong walls, a bath-building and five churches – a smaller, yet stronger, city for a sixth-century world.[44] The Severan city has in part been rediscovered archaeologically, with numerous relevant inscriptions recovered, and can be seen to be an – albeit atypical – imperially sponsored example of early third-century urbanism from which we may elaborate at least a notion of what was considered to be aesthetically pleasing (fig. 5.4). However, the effort involved in building the architecture that so impresses us was a short-lived one and may have fulfilled the criteria according to which Dio saw folly in such an endeavour; for some scholars the third century saw a significant decline in the fortunes of the town.[45]

There were already numerous monuments in the city of Lepcis prior to the birth of Septimius Severus: an early forum[46] and a grid of streets that demonstrates several phases of expansion. The first century AD had seen the development of a market, a theatre,[47] an amphitheatre, a *chalcidicum* and an arch dedicated to Augusta Salutaris;[48] while the second century saw the grant of colonial status,[49] the building of the extensive baths under Hadrian[50] and a circus.[51] Onto the existing monuments was grafted a Severan building scheme that parallels those found in Rome: a new forum and basilica with a colonnaded street including a monumental exedra and *nymphaeum* linking the new structure to the Hadrianic Baths and the newly redeveloped 'Severan' port (fig. 5.4). This should be seen as a single project,[52] a feature of Severan urban design that can also be found in Rome in the design for the Baths of Caracalla and its beautiful

---

[42] Suet. *Aug.* 28.   [43] Procop. *Aed.* 6.4.

[44] Goodchild and Ward-Perkins (1953); Pringle (1981).   [45] Ward-Perkins (1948), p. 60.

[46] Masturzo (2003).   [47] Caputo (1987), pp. 24–5.   [48] *IRT* 319, 321–4, 308.

[49] Reynolds and Ward-Perkins (1952), p. 77.   [50] *IRT* 357, 361.

[51] Humphrey *et al.* (1973–4), Humphrey (1986), pp. 25–55, 295.

[52] Ward-Perkins (1948), p. 61.

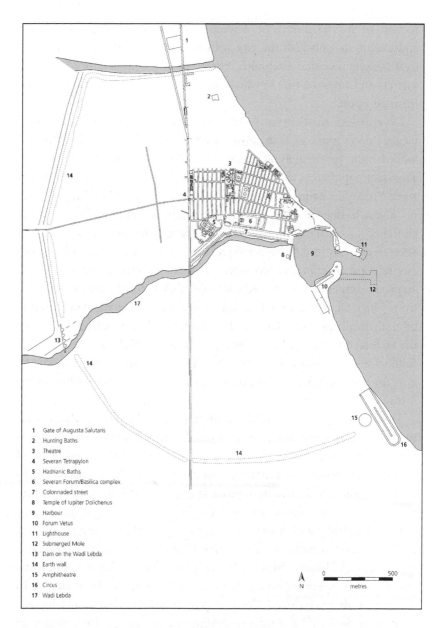

5.4 Lepcis Magna: plan showing the development of Severan monuments and in particular the concentration of these between the harbour (9) and the baths of Hadrian (5), which included the colonnaded street (7) and a new forum (6).

street that integrated the new baths into the existing topography of the city. The Severan forum at Lepcis included a basilica at its eastern end and a temple at its western end. The central space was surrounded with colonnades. It is likely that the project was originally planned to have a double

Table 5.1 Statues of Septimius Severus in Lepcis

Date	Number
197–200	10
198 or later (undated)	13
201–203	24
204	3
209–11	3
Total	53

forum with the basilica as the central monument.[53] The expanded 'Severan' port was now a monumental entry-point into the city with a *pharos* or lighthouse, two temples and twelve hundred metres of colon-naded wharves; in other words a harbour about one-third the size of that of Portus, imperial Rome's principal port (fig. 5.4).[54] The work on the port was part of the project that included the colonnaded street and the new forum and was integrated with the overall redevelopment of the city.[55] There were two destinations within the design: the forum, with its sculp-tural friezes of violent deities overcoming the giants and the labours of Hercules (allegorically identifying Septimius Severus with the mythical hero, for bringing order from the chaos of the civil wars and for the defeat of the Parthians),[56] and the Hadrianic Baths. The operation to supply Lepcis with marble for the embellishment of the new Severan buildings is attested epigraphically on a block of black marble and by numerous other quarry marks.[57] Marble had first been utilised in building projects in the city in the second century, featuring in the restoration of the theatre,[58] yet never had it been used on the scale of the new project, with its alien eastern craftsmen who left their marks on the imported columns of Carystian marble and red and black granites.[59] The scheme would have taken between twenty and thirty years to complete.[60]

At the same time, many statues to the emperor and his extended family were constructed across the city and demonstrate an enthusiasm for the new imperial household under Septimius (Table 5.1).[61] The majority of these were set up in the existing public spaces of the city: the theatre and the

[53] Di Vita (1982a).   [54] Bartoccini (1958), p. 11.   [55] Bartoccini (1958), p. 15.
[56] Squarciapino (1974) for the relevant catalogue; also see Vittozzi (1994); Brouquier-Reddé (1992), pp. 88–91; Levi della Vida (1942); *IRT* 288, 289, 297, 298, *IPT* 25.
[57] *IRT* 530a; Ward-Perkins (1951).   [58] Walda (1985), p. 48; Walda and Walker (1988).
[59] Ward-Perkins (1951), pp. 95, 101, 103; Walda and Walker (1984); Ward-Perkins (1993).
[60] Ward-Perkins (1993), p. 88; *IRT* 427 and 428.   [61] Barton (1977).

old forum.[62] However, we should resist the view that there was a general renewal of all the public buildings under the Severans, since there is little or no evidence for such an intervention in the circus.[63] After its establishment, the new Severan forum became the primary location in the city for the placement of statues of the emperors, and in the longer term, into the third and fourth centuries, it took over as the central space for the display of statuary.[64]

The entire project from harbour through to colonnaded street was designed as a single entity, with a view to enhancing the experience of arrival and first contact with the city of the Emperor's birth. It should also be noted that the experience of travelling through the city by road was enhanced by the erection of a monumental *tetrapylon* arch (arch or gateway over a crossroad with an arch on each side to enable access through the structure) dedicated to Septimius on the junction of the main coastal road from Africa to Cyrenaica and the *via triumphalis* that led from the interior of the city's territory and the old forum.[65] The existing city became an appendage to the new project, which, like the Septizodium in Rome, created a point of arrival and connection between the port and the rural hinterland, the new forum and the extant baths. This feature highlighted a new architecture of urban form that emphasised the ability to redefine the spatial structure of a city by means of urban extension or redevelopment, whether in the example of the Baths of Caracalla or here in Lepcis. Within this new architecture was an aesthetic of movement through space and street development, to create new armatures and the ability to link together the architectural elements of the city: a forum, a bath-building, a temple etc. Previously these elements of the city had been constructed at various locations across cities in the West, but few had been linked into the street grid through a redevelopment of the street(s) leading to them. For example, we do not find such a conception in Vitruvius, but only the elements of public architecture rather than the totality found at Lepcis.[66] Septimius' intentions could be characterised as the building of an imperial forum, based around that of the Forum of Trajan, in his home city.[67] There was more than this, however. The significance of the Severan redevelopment of Lepcis was that it created a unified linear architectural form of armature linking the harbour to the new forum and on to the Hadrianic Baths via a

---

[62] Condron (1998), p. 47.   [63] Humphrey *et al.* (1973–4), p. 12.   [64] Condron (1998), pp. 46–8.
[65] Bacchielli (1992).   [66] MacDonald (1986), p. 248.   [67] Ward-Perkins (1982), p. 36.

colonnaded street. It is the road's very size – with its carriageway of 20.5 metres and colonnaded walkways, each 10–11 metres in width with some 220 marble columns (all imported) flanking the carriageway – that demonstrates the importance of the route and its architectural significance within the Severan schema for the new city.[68] We should note, however, the abandonment of the original project of a double forum or additional public buildings adjacent to the colonnaded street.[69] Perhaps Cassius Dio understood the limits of urbanism, and in particular the limits of the imperial revenues, for the embellishment of the cities of the early third century AD.

THE NORTH AFRICAN CITY

Turning to sites in North Africa that did not feature the scale of imperial patronage found at Lepcis, we can still assess the impact of the new aesthetic of connectivity across the city, or the ability of new architecture to be incorporated into the existing plans of the cities of North Africa. Unlike many regions of the Empire, North Africa and its cities followed a rather different trajectory of monumental urban development. Away from the old Punic foundations, it was for the most part a second-century AD phenomenon, which can be seen to peak with the presence of the Severan emperors and to continue to make an impact on the epigraphic record in the third century (see fig. 5.5).[70] By contrast, urban development in Spain, Gaul and Italy tended to end or substantially decrease in the third century, both in the archaeological and the epigraphic record. We need, however, to recognise that the Roman development of the cities in North Africa occurred at sites that, in some cases, had an urban history that stretched back to the eighth century BC. Our interest here lies in the developed form of urbanism, which is the basis for William MacDonald's understanding of the development of a view of the Roman city based on an armature of interconnected monuments.

　　Africa under the Severans was the impetus for William MacDonald's development of the concept of armature that contrasted so sharply with the rectilinear plans of earlier urban layouts based on the grid (see Chapter 6). At another city in North Africa, Djemila (Cuicul), we can see the gradual

---

[68] Parisi Presicce (1994).　　[69] Di Vita (1995), p. 73.
[70] Table based on Jouffroy (1986), pp. 174–283; see also Duncan-Jones (2004), pp. 35–6.

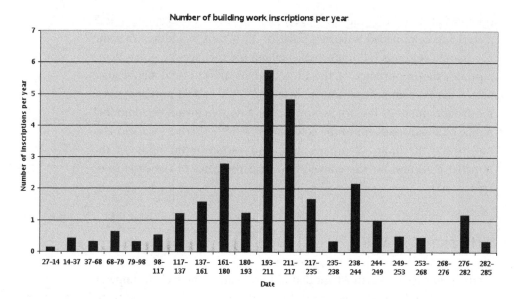

5.5 Graph showing the number of building inscriptions *per annum* in North African Provinces. Note the Severan peak in numbers of building inscriptions.

development of an armature without recourse to imperial intervention (fig. 5.6).[71] Unlike Lepcis with its long history of urbanism, Djemila was a foundation of the Emperor Nerva at the end of the first century AD, with the development of a forum with temple and *curia* alongside a linear route and a grid of streets. What interests us here are the Severan developments: a new forum placed just outside the city walls, in which a temple of the Severans was constructed, a *nymphaeum* or water fountain and an arch dedicated to Caracalla. This new forum became the centre of the city from which major roads extended to the theatre, to the large, late-second-century baths and back to the old forum with its adjoining *macellum*. What was created here was a form of urbanism or urban planning based on the extension of urban space and the integration of the parts of the city through the development of major routes.[72] It is unclear to what extent the developments were underwritten by the Severan emperors, but they were certainly present in Africa, and elsewhere their foundation of a new town is attested by an inscription found at Djédar de Ternaten in the province of Mauretania.[73]

[71] See MacDonald (1968) for a summary of his thinking.
[72] See MacDonald (1986), pp. 5–14 for a full articulation and study of Djemila.
[73] Salama (2005), pp. 97–9; *CIL* 8. 21545.

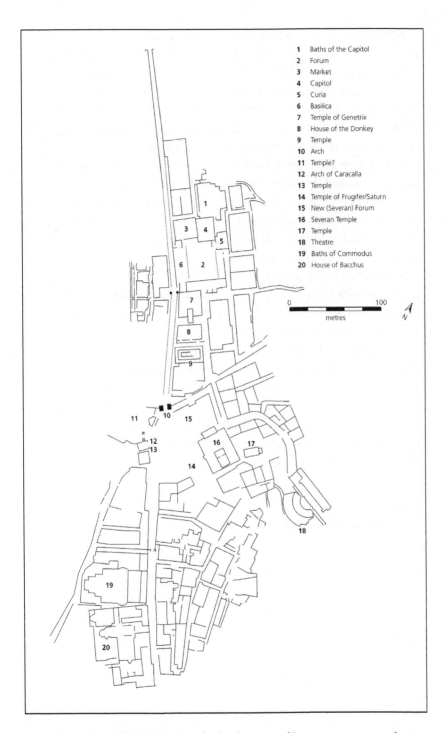

1 Baths of the Capitol
2 Forum
3 Market
4 Capitol
5 Curia
6 Basilica
7 Temple of Genetrix
8 House of the Donkey
9 Temple
10 Arch
11 Temple?
12 Arch of Caracalla
13 Temple
14 Temple of Frugifer/Saturn
15 New (Severan) Forum
16 Severan Temple
17 Temple
18 Theatre
19 Baths of Commodus
20 House of Bacchus

5.6 Djemila: plan of the city showing the development of Severan monuments: the new forum (15), with its new temple (16).

Not only do we find a new form of urban development in North Africa under the Severans, but we also discover that the Severans' actions gave a new impetus to urban development across North Africa. This factor needs to be remembered when viewing the epigraphic profiles that see a severe decline in the number of building inscriptions elsewhere, but some continuity in the African provinces. Urban development in Africa had a different trajectory due to the impact of the Severan dynasty, that created new spaces that needed to be filled with statues and other adornments of the kind that marked the other parts of the city. The result for Africa was that the level of construction of public monuments from the Severans to the end of the third century replicated the pattern found earlier in the second century, which points to a difference between the African cities and those of Italy and the other western provinces.[74]

Across the western provinces it is easy to view the shift over time from a town-plan with its grid of streets to a system of armature. As we have seen, however, in the discussion in this chapter, a city and its grid did not exist in isolation. There were inevitably streets that were of greater significance than others, and these might be described as the through-routes of the city.[75] What deceives us when viewing town plans with streets drawn to a similar width is that the streets are undifferentiated. There were always routes through and within the city that connected important monuments together. What is intriguing, though, is the whole question of why a grid of streets was viewed as a desirable form for a city – a subject that will be discussed in the next chapter.

[74] Jouffroy (1986), p. 406.
[75] For further discussion see Laurence (2007).

> In some colonies they laid out the *decumanus maximus* so that it contained the highway (*via consularis*) running through the colony, for example, in Campania in the colony of Anxur (Terracina). The *decumanus maximus* is seen along the Via Appia. Land capable of cultivation has received limits; the remainder is surrounded by rocky crags, and its outer boundary is demarcated...by landmarks and place names.
>
>   (Hyginus 2 *Constitutio Limitum* = Campbell 2000: 143 lines 34–9)

> In some colonies that were established later, for example, Haïdra in Africa, the *decumanus maximus* [main street] and the *kardo maximus* [cross street] start from the town and are drawn on *limites* through the four gates as in the case of a military camp, like wide roads. This is the most attractive system of establishing *limites* [boundaries]. The colony embraces all four areas of the allocated land and is close to farmers on every side, and all the inhabitants have equal access to the forum from all directions. Similarly in military camps the *groma* [surveying instrument] is set up at the crossroads where men can assemble, as to a forum.
>
>   (Hyginus 2 *Constitutio Limitum* = Campbell 2000: 143 lines 40–6)

The previous chapter questioned the basic premise of Roman planning, the grid of streets, as the major feature of Roman urbanism in its most developed form. However, we need to explain why, in the earliest phases of the development of Roman urbanism, the Romans chose to use a grid at those places that were new towns or colonies in Italy. There is another feature of some of these new towns: the city walls which bounded the grid and created a distortion of the evenness of the grid with an emphasis on routes that led from the gates of the city to its centre, to temples or through the city via another gateway (see fig. 6.1). Fundamental to the Roman conception of these new towns was the relationship between the city and the gods, most obvious in the temples that were sited at prominent points, often raised high above the city's walls or sacred boundary (*pomerium*), and overlooking the landscape beyond the city (see fig. 2.5). These three features in combination provide the earliest formats for urbanism in

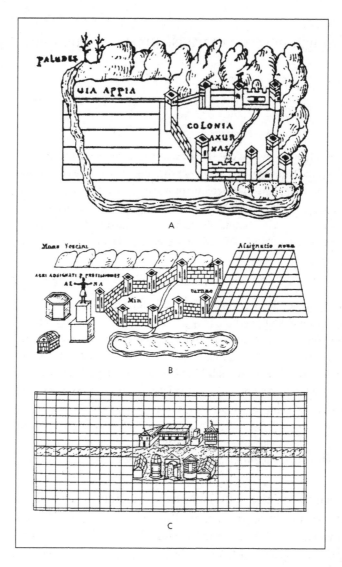

Agrimensores

6.1 Illustrations from texts of land surveyors (*Agrimensores*): (A) Terracina, (B) Minturnae, (C) a text-book example of a city.

colonies on the Italian peninsula and can be identified in the veteran colonies of the first centuries BC and AD. However, the apparent homogeneity of these three phenomena may not date back to the period of the mid-Republic and may have been retrojected by some of our sources to make sense of the earlier phase of town foundation.[1] As is becoming clear from the previous chapters, we would do well to remember that there need

---

[1] Bispham (2006); Bradley (2006); Patterson (2006).

not have been a single formula for laying out the city and that variation, both chronological and geographical, was a feature of Roman urbanism. Despite this, by the end of the first century AD and certainly by the second century, there was a definitive understanding of the city and an attempt to define colonies as homogenous, as little Romes – a factor that needs to be remembered when viewing the physical manifestation of the city.

When we turn to the provinces, we find a rather different patterning of these three features, which we will discuss with reference to examples from Gaul and North Africa. In Gaul, we discover that the grid of streets was a common format on green-field sites, but that walls were singularly absent from the design of these cities. Many of these cities had a characteristic suite of monuments: forum, major temple, baths, theatre/amphitheatre (figs. 6.6 – 6.10). But in addition they also had a major religious focus, generally an existing rural sanctuary situated at a distance from the city and also a focus of monumental construction, with temples, baths and theatres or theatre-amphitheatres. At other sites, for example Saint-Bertrand (see Chapter 4), the grid did not occur initially and can only be identified as an evolution or harmonisation of existing street systems; it may have stemmed from a later desire to produce a town with what might appear to a visitor or inhabitant as a grid of streets. What we find at these sites is a variation on the patterns of urbanism found in Italy and a degree of adaptation to the local situation, which has been defined through recent archaeological excavation. A rather different variation is found in North Africa. Sites can be identified with street-grids and walled circuits, but often the latter arose as a result of quite localised circumstances (figs. 6.11–6.15). In Africa the street-grid was not the fundamental feature of cities and could even be ignored as the city expanded, for example at Timgad (see below and fig. 6.12). Instead the epigraphic evidence reveals a rather different pattern from that of Italy: there was a continual focus within the city plans on building monuments dedicated to the gods and to the emperors, with the construction of rather fewer amphitheatres than on the Italian peninsula.

UNDERSTANDING THE UTILITY OF STREET GRIDS

The foundation of new towns, in the form of colonies in Italy, was by the first century AD seen as a fundamental feature of the history of the Roman state.[2] Beyond Italy, in the provinces, town-foundation often occurred in

---

[2] Vell. Pat. 1.14.

places that had not experienced Mediterranean-style urbanism (for a discussion see Chapter 4).[3] As a phenomenon, town-foundation is a defining feature of the history of urbanism in the western Empire, and needs to be analysed with a view to understanding the spatial form, as much as describing the spread of urbanism in relation to Roman imperialism (see Chapter 2). The nature of town-foundation and the definition of an area of land that was to become urban, as opposed to forming part of the territory, provide us with examples of what the Roman state and its subjects saw as the ideal, or desirable, spatial forms for towns. In studying the historical culture of cities, the spatial form of urbanism should not be reduced to a mere detail, or map, or town-plan, onto which monuments were laid out. Space, particularly urban space, is a 'fundamental material dimension' of any society.[4] Moreover, the town-plan, or grid of streets, would have been 'the most powerful determinant of urban movement',[5] but was subject to alteration by the inclusion of 'attractors' or 'magnets' such as temples, bath-buildings or theatres.[6] The grid of streets, whether enclosed or unenclosed by a city's walls, must therefore be analysed as a key aspect of Roman urbanism. It was in effect a form of 'spatial engineering' which permitted or allowed people to live at a certain density and which, at the city's foundation, predicted a continued existence for the city within the spatial form or setting originally designed or defined.[7] The grid of streets has been analysed today as a spatial form that facilitates movement in order to optimise the contact between persons travelling across the city in question, just as was foreseen in the opening quotation taken from the work of Hyginus, one of the writers on Roman land-surveying.[8] Some modern architects will even suggest that the street institutionalises human movement and that the community accepts that the street and its neighbouring network of other streets are something held in common and which rely upon a connection between people on journeys across or through the city.[9] The grid for the land-surveyor from Rome facilitated human interaction and could, in an ideal situation, facilitate equal access to the city and the forum.

Most cities in the Roman world did not conform to this ideal (as we saw in Chapter 5). The grid was not an undifferentiated landscape of streets of a similar nature. The plans of urban sites produced in modern books seldom manage to reflect the differences in street-width that are only too apparent

[3] Tac. *Agr.* 20–2.   [4] Castells (2003), p. 59.   [5] Hillier (1996), p. 152.
[6] Hillier (1996), p. 161.   [7] Hillier (1996), p. 179.   [8] Hillier (1996), p. 180.
[9] Rykwert (1978), p. 15; compare Wallace-Hadrill (2003) on streets in Rome.

when visits are made to these archaeological sites. More importantly, it has
been observed for almost half a century that urban space, even an urban
grid of streets, is not neutral but is characterised by a series of paths, edges,
districts, nodes and landmarks, partly created through a reordering of the
grid for human interaction (see fig. 6.1 for representations of this phenomenon).[10] The problem today is to find a way to characterise these features of
the urban grid. No ancient author discusses the use of city space in any
depth. However, there is a series of writings on the way in which surveyed
rural grids were utilised and appropriated through the actions of individuals. These are known collectively as the writings of the *agrimensores* or
land-surveyors.[11] They did not just survey land for enclosure, but were
involved in the unravelling of disputes, illegal occupation, or the location of
former boundaries themselves in lands that had often been divided into a
grid of rural plots allocated to colonists. Their observations of the practice
of individuals allow us to determine a level of human agency within a
spatial grid of Roman colonisation, which can be combined with archaeological examples to reveal further the nature of the changes initiated by
human agency to the regular grid forms found in cities in the Roman West.

The *agrimensores* or land-surveyors define different types of land, forms
of measurement and the nature of land disputes, to produce a very rich
array of examples known from parts of the Empire as diverse as Italy,
Africa, Dalmatia, Gaul and Germany. We are not concerned here with
summarising the texts, but instead wish to pick out the process of adaptation of the grid of land-holding and the nature of human interaction within
a grid of roads. The apparent uniformity of land-division as a result of
centuriation (*limitatio*) disappears on examination of these texts, because
the writers are at pains to state that even the practice of marking boundaries
varies from region to region.[12] Moreover, the writers frequently allude to
the changing shape of the boundaries, from the point of survey or centuriation to the present in the second century AD, as a result of land sales.[13] A
primary factor in shaping the grid of roads was a hierarchy in which the
public road was at the top, the local road was second, and the privately
owned road came at the bottom.[14] The nature of ownership of public space
could also be a factor present in the urban context – a public road could
form the major route through the city, while the other streets would fall

[10] Lynch (1960), pp. 46–90
[11] See Campbell (2000) for an introduction, text and translation of the *agrimensores*: references are
    to page numbers in this work and line numbers on the relevant pages.
[12] Campbell (2000), p. 93 line 28.   [13] E.g. Campbell (2000), pp. 119–21.
[14] Campbell (2000), p. 95 lines 6–7, p. 113 lines 11–42.

under the city's jurisdiction, apart from those streets that were private.[15] The hierarchy of roads in the countryside and streets in the city was also differentiated by the width of the space for traffic.[16] The *decumanus maximus* and *kardo maximus* of the land-survey were the widest roads of the centuriated grid – Augustus had stipulated that the *decumanus maximus* should be forty feet wide, the *kardo maximus* twenty feet wide, and the other *limites* either twelve or eight feet wide according to their position in the grid.[17] Hence, the grid of roads in centuriation was differentiated and a hierarchy of routes was established across it.

The grid was also subject to further differentiation via the establishment of shrines or sacred spaces (compare fig. 6.1). Dolabella suggested that a shrine could be placed at the junction of four properties and would have been expected to have four altars for each neighbour's sacrifice.[18] The layout of the grid also respected existing religious sites, such as public groves on mountains, temples and tombs surrounded by gardens.[19] Roads, we are told, often mark a boundary, and the space adjacent to them was frequently defined as a place of sacrifice and embellished with trees with luxuriant foliage, presumably to provide shade or enhance the place of sacrifice.[20] In addition, at Gabii (twelve miles from Rome) tombs of veteran soldiers lined the roads and coincidently marked the property boundary.[21] We may assume that not all roads were marked in this way and instead only those that were seen to have greater phenomenological significance to landowners, or were subject to the greatest number of viewers or passers-by. The effect was to mark certain roads in the grid system as having greater importance than others. These examples of spatial practice from the writings of the Roman land-surveyors would have caused or reflected a difference in the amount of movement through the various sections of the grid of streets in the city, or roads in the city's hinterland.[22] The apparent uniformity of the grid of streets featured in the town-plans of Roman cities (sometimes simply an artefact of modern cartography) was subject to similar social forces that created a differentiation of space within the grid. The presence of sacred sites and the sacred boundary of the city were two of the fundamental determinants of ways in which grids were subjected to social differentiation, and will be subject to further analysis in this chapter with reference to archaeological examples. In addition, the very organisation

---

[15] Note examples from Pompeii; Laurence (2007), p. 54.   [16] Campbell (2000), p. 137 lines 1–15.
[17] Campbell (2000), p. 153 lines 25–30.   [18] Campbell (2000), p. 223 lines 18–24.
[19] Campbell (2000), p. 9 lines 3–9, p. 87 lines 42–6, p. 125 lines 7–13.
[20] Campbell (2000), p. 31, lines 5–14.   [21] Campbell (2000), p. 257 lines 21–5.
[22] Compare Penn and Dalton (1994).

of the grid with reference to physical features such as rivers, hills and the centuriation of the hinterland needs further discussion and will also be dealt with below.

The differentiation between what was within a city and what was in its hinterland came in many cases from a set of walls enclosing the urban area (see fig. 6.1). Walls were a characteristic feature of many cities of the Roman Empire, a view confirmed by Vitruvius, who wrote with the civil wars of the late first century BC in mind.[23] However, a city's walls were concerned with much more than just defence, because they divided the living within the city from the dead buried outside in the cemeteries. Many towns, however, did not have a circuit of stone walls. This is true not just of the provinces but also of Italy, as can be seen from the section of the *Liber Coloniarum* dealing with 'The Communities of Campania from the Book of Regions'.[24] The cities and towns listed in this work are accompanied by a note of their status – *colonia, municipium, oppidum* – and many of these entries specifically include a mention of their walls. Of the sixty-four settlements mentioned, twenty-six were *coloniae* with walls; seventeen were *oppida* that had been fortified; thirteen were unfortified *oppida*; four were unfortified *municipia*; three *coloniae* were included with no mention of walls; one *municipium* was singled out as having had walls added to it; and a further five settlements had walls but their status was uncertain. Forty-four out of the sixty-four towns and cities from this list were certainly fortified, and their walls were a feature of urbanism worth mentioning, unlike any other form of public architecture. Walls distinguished a place as much as its status as a *colonia*, a *municipium* or an *oppidum*.

CITY WALLS AND URBAN LAYOUT 1: ITALY

The layout of colonies or new towns took into consideration the existing terrain and physical features of the location in which they were to be founded. This is in marked contrast to the Roman army camps described by Polybius, which eschewed the topographically determined setting of fortifications that underpinned the location of Greek army camps in favour of creating a familiar rectilinear grid within an artificial rampart, in which each person in the army would have been familiar with his location (said by Frontinus to have been adopted from a Epirote camp of Pyrrhus captured

---

[23] Vitr. *De arch.* 1.5.   [24] Campbell (2000), pp. 179–89.

in 275 BC).[25] The camp was a temporary formation that artificially recreated the familiarity of previous temporary camps to foster a spatial community over time.[26] The colony, unlike the military camp of the second century BC, was a place that would be permanent and was integrated into the landscape. In consequence, its shape and formation were adapted to the physical geography and phenomenological meaning of that landscape. The need for a water-supply in some cases led to colonies being sited close to or bounded by mountains, or close to the sea.[27] This led to a layout that was very different from the symmetrical plan of Haïdra in the opening quotation, with the shape of the city, and its associated grid of *limites,* being squashed or laid out in a single direction with the grid aligned to the cardinal points of the compass.

The Latin colony founded in 492 BC at Norba provides an indication of how a settlement utilised its physical setting for defence and visibility.[28] The colony was placed on a hill 450 metres above sea level and established as a citadel to dominate the Pontine plain; indeed, it has been associated by a recent study with the building of a walled acropolis (fig. 6.2).[29] The most prominent surviving feature is a set of walls 2.5 km in length enclosing an area of about forty hectares. The masonry is made from limestone, a material with a natural jointing that makes it particularly suitable for the construction of walls made from large polygonal (as opposed to quadrilateral) blocks (fig. 6.3). The jointing also facilitated the placing and stability of the facing blocks on sloping ground. These walls, constructed by the end of the fourth century and certainly by the mid-third century BC, reveal much more than a mere point about the nature of Roman construction; a statement can be read within the structure about the nature of urbanism in this early period.[30] The site had been chosen for its prominence in the landscape.[31] The addition of an extensive circuit of walls enhanced the importance of the location of Norba,[32] which offered little by way of the comforts of urban life.[33] The walls and, more importantly, the human effort put into their construction made another statement: the city of Norba was to endure through time. The walls defended the city notably in the civil wars between Marius and Sulla some four hundred years after the colony's foundation, which was only terminated by a Masada-like mass suicide and the total destruction of the city.[34]

---

[25] Polyb. 6.41–2; Frontin. *Str.* 14.1.14; but see Plut. *Pyrrh.* 16 for the opposite opinion.
[26] See Creighton (2006), pp. 86–92.   [27] Campbell (2000), p. 145 lines 1–11.
[28] Livy, 2.34.6.   [29] Quilici and Quilici Gigli (2001).
[30] Quilici and Quilici Gigli (2001).   [31] Livy, 2.34.6.   [32] Livy, 27.10.7.
[33] Livy, 32.2.4.   [34] App. *B Civ.* 1.439; Plin. *HN* 3.68.

6.2 Norba: layout of the city showing positions of temples and division of space within this fortified hilltop settlement.

The ability to create an urban area on Norba's inaccessible site was determined by the ability to construct routes up to it, which resulted in three rather asymmetrical entrances to the site. The inside of the city was dominated by two *acropoleis* overlooking terraces cut from the rock for the construction of temples (fig. 6.2). These temples were sited with reference to the grid of streets. The temple of Diana on the northern *acropolis* faced south-east, whereas the larger temple on the eastern *acropolis* faced north-west – in other words literally overlooking the major routes within the grid of streets. In addition, the location of the temples at the high points of the city facilitated an overview of the walls of the town as well as the taking of the *auspices* (divination using the flight of birds) from these sacred points with reference to a *templum* defined by the physical features of the surrounding landscape. The linear grid helped to define the urban space to the right and left of the line of the major street leading from the temples, while

6.3 Norba: the city walls were constructed from polygonal limestone.

the walls provided an additional division between being inside and outside the *pomerium*.[35] The effect was to create four quadrants within which birds could be placed and their movement interpreted.[36] The site, as Livy states, was a citadel dominating the landscape and is easily picked out today from a considerable distance, even without the aid of the architecture of temples on its high-points.[37] The coincidence between the division of space into quadrants for augury and the actions of the surveyor setting out a grid was noted by the land-surveyors.[38] Like the augur, the surveyor observed the terrain and divided it up into quadrants, a format which seems to have been ubiquitous in the Roman interpretation of space.

The location and shape of Norba differ completely from those of the town founded at Minturnae in 296 BC, which by contrast follows the principles of urban layout found in the discussion of Ammaedera. This small Roman colony of three hundred citizens was established after the construction of the major route of the Via Appia across the Pontine plain and at the crossing of the River Liris, which enabled it to develop

---

[35] See Livy 1.18.6–7; Varro, *Ling.* 7.8–9; Gargola (1995), pp. 44–7 for discussion.
[36] Cic. *Div.* 1.17.31.   [37] Livy, 2.34.6.   [38] Campbell (2000), pp. 9, 135, 137.

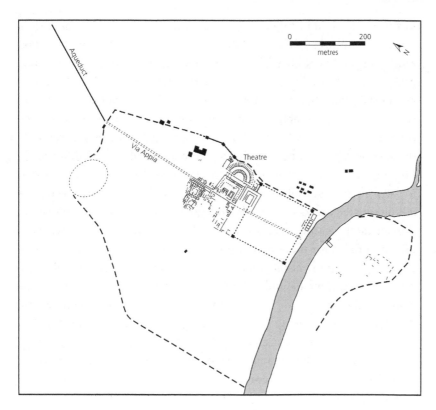

6.4 Minturnae: shows the expansion of this city from the nucleus of a small colonial fortress adjacent to the river Liris and the building of monuments along the line of the Via Appia.

river port facilities (fig. 6.4).[39] The rectilinear circuit of walls of polygonal masonry surrounding the original settlement, 182 metres by 155 metres, was tiny when compared to Norba, and the interior was wholly lacking in civic amenities, including a forum. Like other maritime colonies, such as Ostia, it was a fort laid out to house a small garrison of Roman citizens, and Dionysius of Halicarnassus views Minturnae and Ostia as having marked out an area of Roman domination between the rivers Liris and Tiber.[40] The colonists were, in effect, a permanent garrison that guarded the coast from piracy and, unlike the colonists sent to Norba, they were exempted from other forms of military duty (during the Hannibalic invasion of Italy, the *iuniores* aged seventeen to

---

[39] Livy, 9.25.9, 10.21; Vell. Pat. 21.14; Dion. Hal. *Ant. Rom.* 1.9.
[40] Dion. Hal. *Ant. Rom.* 1.9. See Zanker (2000) and compare with Bispham (2006).

forty-six were bound by oath to reside within the colony).[41] Due to its function, Minturnae followed Polybius' observations on the nature of the army camps of the Romans; like a Roman camp, it was organised around a central space. It would be easy to see maritime colonies such as Minturnae as an urban form that prefigured that of later Roman cities, or even army camps and forts, notably the Augustan foundations for veteran soldiers such as Aosta (see Chapter 2 above) but Bispham demonstrates the disjunction between the colonies of the mid-Republic and those of the Empire.[42] Like Minturnae, these later colonial settlements of veterans were to garrison the peninsula of Italy.[43] The veterans settled in new towns that, if built on green-field sites, displayed a spatial structure similar to that of a Roman camp. A town founded on a military site continued to reflect its military origins for more than a single generation from foundation; subsequent generations of inhabitants might reshape the city through monumental developments and the rebuilding of houses, but these did not obliterate the military form of the city's spatial arrangement (compare the discussion of later veteran colonies and legionary forts in Chapter 4).[44]

Minturnae began as a strategically located central place, but it grew and expanded beyond the original walls of the settlement.[45] Not only was it located at the crossing-point of the Via Appia over the River Liris, but it was also an important river port and was located close to a sanctuary of the Aurunci dedicated to the goddess Marica.[46] In terms of its organisation, the settlement, unlike many Latin colonies, did not initially require a forum because the city was defined as a garrison of Roman citizens rather than as a semi-autonomous city and the Roman citizens' forum was located in Rome.[47] By 207 BC the temple of Jupiter had been constructed over the walls of the city and aligned with reference to the Via Appia (fig. 6.4).[48] Later, in the first century BC, another temple was located outside the line of the original wall of the city. These temples faced towards the sea, and it remains uncertain how the *templum* for the observation of the flight of birds by an augur would have been constructed with a view across the marshes towards the sea. At some point a forum was laid out to the south of the Via Appia beyond the wall of the original *castrum*, and by the end of the first century BC a theatre and an aqueduct had been established. The city also spread

---

[41] Livy, 27.38, 36.3.   [42] Zanker (2000), pp. 26–9; Bispham (2006).

[43] Suet. *Aug.* 46; Augustus, *Res Gestae Divi Augusti*, 28.   [44] Keppie (1983), p. 130.

[45] Coarelli (1984), pp. 368–80; Johnson (1933), (1935).

[46] Livy, 27.37; Plut. *Mar.* 57–40; Plin. *HN* 3.36; Verg. *Aen.* 7.47–8, Serv. *ad Virg. Aen.* 7.47; Hor. *Carm.* 3.17.5–9; Mart. *Ep.* 10.30, 13.83; *Dig.* 19.2.13.1; Val. Max. 1.5.5; Strabo, 5.3.6.

[47] Zanker (2000), p. 27.   [48] Livy, 27.37, 36.37.

across the River Liris along the line of the Via Appia;[49] later, additional lands were surveyed and divided into centuries on this side of the Liris.[50] There was a further extension of the city to the south along the banks of the river towards the coast. To the north, a gate that carried the aqueduct marked the transition into the city and this spatial ideology was amplified by the sheathing of the gateway with a monumental façade in the form of an arch, that included at least one monumental inscription (illegible on recovery) and decoration that may have included statuary as found at other sites.[51] For those travelling south through the marshes, arrival in the city was anticipated by the vista of the aqueduct running at forty-five degrees to the Via Appia and entering the city at the same point as that of the thirsty traveller. Minturnae was a city that, just like Ostia and Pyrgi, developed from a tiny defensive settlement into a major city with all the trappings of Roman urban life. What is also interesting is that, in the expansion of the urban area, the walls and original boundary between the city and what had been a potentially hostile hinterland could be redefined.

As was discussed in the context of Mérida in Chapter 2, the boundary between the city and what was seen as not the city, i.e. the 'countryside', was marked not just by walls but also by a *pomerium* (sacred boundary).[52] This need not have taken the physical form of a linear boundary, but, at least in Rome, was marked by stones which indicated to the viewer that they were about to cross this boundary and enter a different type of space. Moreover, the area in front of the *pomerium* was a space that was measured out and had definite dimensions. Often the *pomerium* lay in front of the city walls;[53] whatever its nature, it was to be left free of private dwellings and could not be interfered with even on the authority of the *ordo* of the decurions, but was always being discussed by land-surveyors in relation to possible encroachments upon it.[54] Not only was the *pomerium* subject to encroachment, so too were the spaces beyond it in the *suburbana* that were dedicated to the burial of the poor and punishment of criminals.[55] Hence, although the boundary of a city was defined, it was subject to encroachment as a result of urban expansion beyond the original limits of the city. The definition of what was inside and outside the city could become blurred around the edges through expansion over the very walls that originally

---

[49] Plin. *HN* 3.36.   [50] Campbell (2000), p. 143 lines 10–15, p. 185 lines 11–13.

[51] Richmond (1933), pp. 154–6, 172–4.

[52] See Andreussi (1999), pp. 96–105 for sources and a discussion of debates over the *pomerium* in Rome.

[53] Campbell (2000), p. 67 lines 24–31.   [54] Campbell (2000), p. 7 lines 7–25.

[55] Campbell (2000), pp. 44–5; 69–70.

defined the city. This can be seen today at Pompeii or Timgad, where houses were built over the walls and tombs already built in the pomerial space. Urban expansion also seems to have been quite common in the maritime colonies, such as Minturnae. The defined city limits could be expanded, and it is possible that the *pomerium* would have been expanded at the same time. This reshaped the area of the city, and it makes sense that this should occur when a colony of veterans was founded on the site, thereby marking a new beginning for the city in question (as happened, for example, at Minturnae).[56]

Colonies continued to be founded in Italy well into the first century AD. Fanum Fortunae, modern Fano, was located on the Adriatic coast at the point where the Via Flaminia met the sea and turned north towards its terminus at Rimini. Fanum Fortunae appears to have possessed a Republican nucleus, and what had been a forum or *conciliabulum* was reconstructed or redefined as a colony in the Triumviral or Augustan period; this indeed was a city whose basilica was designed and built by Vitruvius.[57] The presence of mountains and the sea at right angles to each other facilitated the laying-out of the centuriation grid with reference to these physical features rather than the points of the compass.[58] The grid of the town was also laid out with respect to the right-angled turn in direction of the Via Flaminia. The effect was that the spatial logic of this colony was worked out with respect to its physical geography and to this vital transport link to Rome. As at Minturnae, the entrance to the town was marked by a monumental entrance, which incorporated an inscription recording the gift of the walls of the city by Augustus.[59] The gate was one of the earliest three-portalled structures that can be dated to the Augustan period.[60] The walls are 1.76 km in length with twenty-four rounded towers, which surround an urban area divided up into a grid of streets. The internal topography of the town remains less than certain due to continuous habitation on the site.

The need for such extensive walls for defence could be questioned by this period; the town had originally been established without walls and the contemporary new town founded at Carsulae in Umbria had no walls. Instead, the latter's urban area was marked at its northern edge by an arch.[61] Beyond this arch were the tombs of the dead, whereas on the other side was the area of habitation. This highlights the fact that there

---

[56] Campbell (2000), p. 185.　　[57] Luni (2000), pp. 57–73.

[58] Campbell (2000), p. 11 lines 18–21, and see also p. 197 lines 11–13 for a combination of Gallic *limites* and ordering to face the sea.

[59] *CIL* 5.6232 dated to AD 9–10.　　[60] Richmond (1933), pp. 156–7.　　[61] Morigi (1997).

[handwritten margin note: via consularis = highway]

was a need to mark the limits of the city. Walls were not solely defensive, but were physical markers of a boundary between the city of the living and the cemeteries of the dead. The need for walls at Fanum may have derived from a conception of the city as a place similar to a military camp (as discussed above in Chapter 4). After all, until the first century BC all citizens were in effect also soldiers – a point felt all the more in colonies. This tradition of the city continued when new colonies were created as at Fanum. In order for this place to feel like a city, it needed to have walls, using a traditional means for expressing permanence, whether or not those walls were intended to have a serious defensive function.

Cities with walls had a different form of urbanism from those that did not. The stone circuit gave a shape to the plan of the city. Walls constrained movement or channelled it into and out of the city. This caused the streets within the city that led to gateways to become more intensively used as channels of movement and access.[62] In contrast, parts of the city isolated from such routes also became isolated from the main areas of movement. This is a different spatial form of urbanism from that found in towns and cities that did not have a walled circuit. Moreover, the presence of a major road or *via consularis* (highway) running through a city altered the structure of space to produce a linear route along which monuments were displayed to the traveller. This could begin at the city gate, which could be embellished with statuary as an entry point, as we can see from the example of Rimini (fig. 6.5). The long-distance roads of Italy tended to run through towns, either bisecting them or running close to the forum, as documented for Terracina by Hyginus in the opening quotation of this chapter or as found at a number of other towns, such as Alba Fucens or Brescia (see Chapter 7). For travellers, the sequence of urban vistas would have commenced with the sight of an increasing number of tombs along the road and, perhaps, glimpses of the town's aqueduct (as at Minturnae above). This was followed by entry into the city via a gate, from where the major route would have led towards or close to the forum. From the forum the route led through the city and out through another gate and gradually the number of tombs diminished as the traveller proceeded away from the place. These nodal points of transition punctuated the journey through the city. It is possible that the orientation of field systems may also have changed as the traveller left one city's territory and entered another's. The city was reduced to a series of nodes: the first being the gate, the second the forum and the third another gate. The gate was designed to impress the traveller, whether

---

[62] Laurence (2007), pp. 102–16.

6.5 Rimini: the Arch set up in front of the city walls to commemorate Augustus'
restoration of the Via Flaminia from Rome to Rimini in 27 BC.

he was a loyal servant or a soldier marching on Rome.[63] It announced
arrival at a town, as can particularly be seen in the case of the arch of
Augustus set up at Rimini. The arch marked one end of the Via Flaminia,
just as the other was marked by a similar arch as the traveller entered Rome
over the Mulvian bridge.[64] The arch at Rimini was constructed in 27 BC to
celebrate the systematisation of the Via Flaminia (fig. 6.5).[65] It was viewed
after crossing the River Aprusa and its outwards-facing exterior contained
images of the gods Jupiter and Apollo, while that facing inwards contained

---

[63] Todd (1978), p. 72.   [64] Dio Cass. 53.22.   [65] *CIL* 11.365.

images of Neptune and Roma. The travertine used in this arch, which was placed in front of the gateways, enhanced the entry of travellers into the city and amplified the transition from moving along the Via Flaminia to arriving in Rimini. On the other side of the city, arrival from the north was marked by another imperial project: the bridge constructed by Tiberius over the River Ariminus. Within the city, entry into the forum was also marked by an arch. This sequence of arches, walls and bridges articulated urban space. The arch marked a permeable boundary and invited people to cross its threshold and enter a different type of space. Such arches, close to the points of entry into cities and into their fora, are a common feature of the surviving remains of the Roman cities of Italy and the West. They tended to be sited on the major roads leading through the city rather than being distributed across the grid of streets.

CITY WALLS AND URBAN LAYOUT 2: GAUL

In the Three Gauls, beyond Narbonensis with its Augustan colonies, we find a rather different urban pattern characterised by the presence of street-grids but without defences. Many of the plans of towns in Gaul are reconstructed from fragmentary excavated evidence and a level of conjecture, but there are a number of sites that have produced evidence both of the size and of the stratigraphic sequences that allow us to date the appearance of a grid of streets and also account either for the interaction between the layout of the grid and other extant urban features, or for the absence of such interaction. What we find is the utilisation of orthogonal planning to lay out new sites adjacent to existing features, or with respect to topographical features such as rivers (e.g. Amiens, Bordeaux, Limoges, Trier). It is at these sites in Gaul, mostly from the first century AD, that we can see the application of the knowledge of the Roman land-surveyors in action. The grids of streets that are created are far from even and are often bisected by roads at odd angles or aligned with respect to topographical features, or demonstrate the possibility for the original grid to expand to include a larger area.

A series of cities can demonstrate different approaches to urban planning. The town of Amiens was constructed on a green-field site at the point where the road to Boulogne laid out by Agrippa crossed the river Somme (fig. 6.6).[66] The original twenty *insulae* were constructed on an alignment

---

[66] Bedon (2001), pp. 67–76.

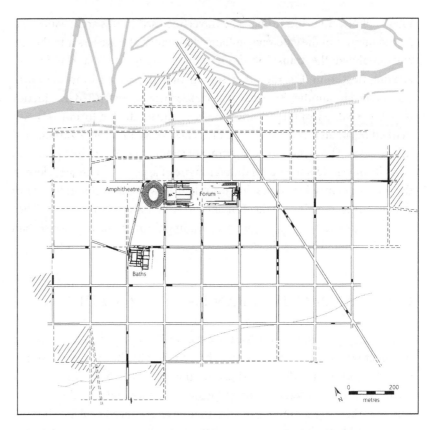

6.6 Amiens: a city without walls, featuring an extensive street grid at the centre of which lay its forum and amphitheatre, but the major road through the city cuts through this grid of streets at an angle of 45 degrees to the orientation of the grid.

parallel with the river and with no reference to the Agrippan road. There is a contrast here with Silchester, where the grid of streets was realigned so as to be orientated on the major road to London (see Chapter 4 for discussion). The initial grid of streets at Amiens can be dated to the early to mid-first century AD and was later expanded under the Flavian emperors to include a further forty, much larger, *insula* blocks, which increased its area to 140 hectares, nearly double that of Pompeii. At its centre lay a forum with a basilica and, by the end of the first century, an amphitheatre. The site as a whole displays a systematic division of space intended to create a large city, which seems indeed to have developed to some extent throughout our period. We should not, however, view this Gallo-Roman site in isolation from developments elsewhere. To the east at Ribemont-sur-Ancre a major 'rural sanctuary' was laid out down the slope of the side of the Ancre valley (fig. 6.7). It consisted of a large 'Romano-Celtic' temple at the summit

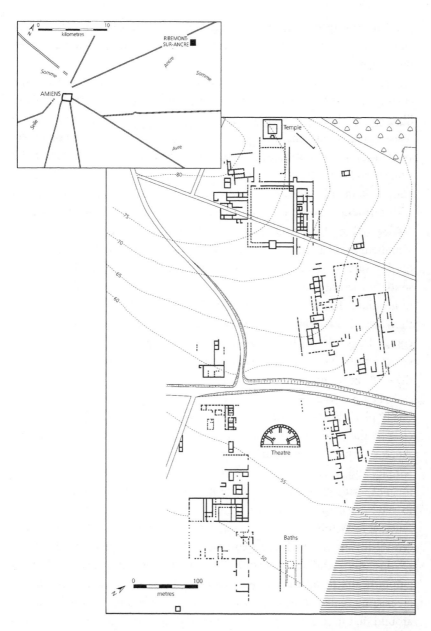

6.7 Ribemont-sur-Ancre: showing the monumental development of the sanctuary and (inset) its relationship with Amiens.

(overlying major cult deposits of the later Iron Age) with two ranges of buildings running down the slope to either side, leaving a central space, wider at the bottom than at the top, within which were a theatre and a large bathhouse on the same axis as the temple. The overall plan with its focal point and divergent ranges of buildings strongly resembles that of local villas, and was itself probably heavily influenced by indigenous pre-Roman settlement plans.[67]

Nevertheless, the monumental building types, the architecture and the epigraphy all echo practice in the urban centres. Arguably, the Ambiani, like several other *civitas*-capitals, had a bi-polar form of urbanism, with the new foundation and main city (*Samarobriva*, Amiens) expressing the Gallic version of Roman urbanism; whereas Ribemont-sur-Ancre, for all its Roman-style architecture, perpetuated a much more local form of central place. Several other towns in Gaul from the early first century can be found with this combination of a rural sanctuary and a green-field site with an orthogonal grid of streets; well-known examples include Sanxay and Vendoeuvre-du-Poitou or Chassenon. It is worth noting that these sanctuaries were not a pan-Gallic feature; they are, for instance, absent to the south of the Garonne, the area Caesar and others ascribed to the Aquitani rather than the Celts/Gauls, and provide another demonstration of how Roman-style urbanism was manipulated to suit regional or ethnic preferences. Thus, although Roman-style cities were an innovative form of settlement for Gaul, the new street-based settlements were integrated into the existing religious landscape of the province.

The connection between sanctuary sites and the development of orthogonally planned streets was not uncommon in Roman Gaul and is made clear by the example of Jublains (fig. 6.8). The town included an Iron Age sanctuary that was developed in the mid-first century into an octastyle temple, and where fifty or more votive offerings have been found in the form of terracotta statues of a maternal Venus. The grid of streets appears to have developed on a slightly different alignment from that of the sanctuary. Within the town (twenty-five hectares in area), there was a central forum, a set of baths constructed in the first century AD at the south-eastern end and, beyond the grid to the south-east, a theatre-amphitheatre from the late first century. This was a place constructed at an existing centre of religious worship which can be seen to have expanded around that function to include elements of Roman-style urbanism: a grid of streets, with monuments distributed across those streets to create an axis from the temple/sanctuary in the north-west to the theatre-amphitheatre in the south-east. The entire construction was undertaken within a century, but was short-lived. By the third century AD the baths may have been

[67] See Agache (1978).

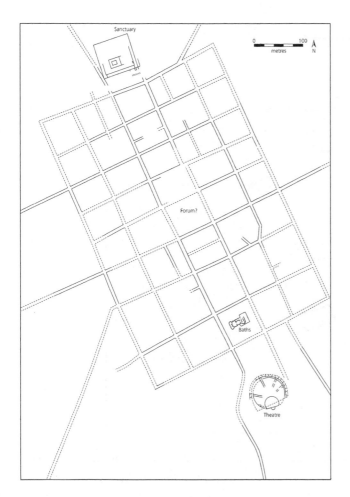

6.8 Jublains: plan showing the extent of urban development focussed on the sanctuary, that included a grid of streets linking the sanctuary to the theatre.

functioning but the city had been abandoned and replaced by a fortified store-building on the south-west edge of the former street-grid.[68]

The city of Paris (ancient Lutetia) was formed around the crossing point of the River Seine (fig. 6.9). The forum provided the focus for major roads from the south and an irregular grid of streets, but was orientated with reference to both the river and the major south-north route through the city.[69] Sanctuary sites may have been located at the Ile de la Cité and on the hill of Montmartre. A theatre and a theatre-amphitheatre were cut into the slopes of the site and integrated into the grid plan. The result, like that at Amiens, was a site that overlooked a river and featured religious foci

---

[68] Rebuffat (1985).   [69] Busson (2003), pp. 36–46, 64–79.

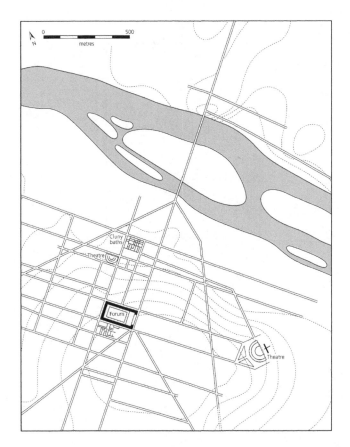

6.9 Paris: plan showing the relationship between the through-route and bridging-point of the river Seine and monumental development within the city.

at a distance from the city. Thus the grid did not contain all the features of urbanism but was instead integrated into a wider landscape of religious significance. This is not, however, to suggest that the grid of streets and monuments was not a major innovation, nor that the central authorities, local or provincial, did not regard the street grid as a fundamental device for the development of urbanism in the first century AD.

Another city constructed from an extant Iron Age nucleus was Bordeaux (fig. 6.10). There the grid of streets, of between twelve and fifteen hectares, dated to the period AD 5–10 and created a small city with its alignment orientated with reference to the River Garonne. The development of a religious focus at the site is attested epigraphically with dedications to members of the imperial family, Drusus and Claudius.[70] There was an

---

[70] *CIL* 13.589–91.

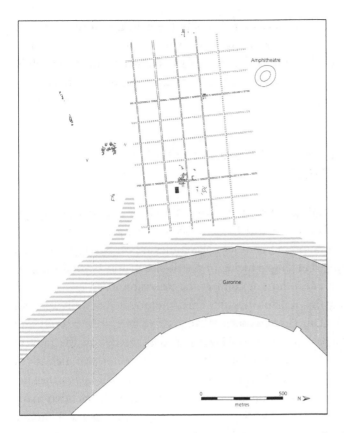

6.10 Bordeaux: plan showing the layout of the city in relation to the ancient line of the river Garonne (shaded area).

indigenous religious sanctuary 55 km to the north at Saint-Germain-d'Esteuil that was further developed in the Roman period; it falls into the pattern observed at other sites, although it was a day's travel away. The phenomenon of an urban grid, a river and an external sanctuary site needs further discussion in order to place it within the context of Roman urbanism. The presence of a sanctuary outside the city is not a phenomenon unique to Roman Gaul, but can also be found in the Italian peninsula and Africa, and should not be seen as indicative of a form of resistance to the presence of Roman urbanism or the persistence of more rural habits (see Chapter 9 for further discussion of such sanctuary sites). Instead the town with its grid was integrated into the existing cultural landscape associated with the rituals found in the sanctuaries. For those behind the project to create a city with a grid of streets, choices had to be made to identify which features were desirable and in what location they should be constructed. In the case of Jublains, the choice was made either to place the town next to the sanctuary or to amplify the existing sanctuary by the addition of a grid of streets (fig. 6.8). This contrasts with our other examples where a location next to a river was chosen for the town, whilst at the same time the populace used monumental development to enhance the importance of the sanctuary.

CITY WALLS AND URBAN LAYOUT 3: NORTH AFRICA

In Africa Proconsularis, most cities seem not to have had walls during the Roman period. This may partly be explained by the legal hurdles imposed on the construction of walls, but several colonies appear never to have built them, suggesting that the financing of a wall-circuit was beyond them or that the African elites did not connect the provision of an *enceinte* with status in the way that Italian cities did. This is not to say that walls were not a mark of status at all. Colonies such as Timgad and Djemila were built with them, while large cities such as Tipasa that had acceded to the rank of colony paid for their construction.[71] What they were not, was a clear-cut indicator of status with all *coloniae* having walls and all *oppida* lacking them. Analysis of the situation is made more difficult by the fact that many pre-Roman sites had their own walls before they were incorporated into the Empire – both Punic cities along the coast and native *castella* in the interior. Some cities were later awarded the rank of honorary colony, but this was not caused by the presence of walls themselves. For instance, Utica, the residence of the governor of Africa before the refounding of Carthage, possessed a set of city walls in the first century BC, but did not gain the rank of colony until the reign of Hadrian;[72] while Haïdra, a Flavian colony, appears not to have had a circuit of walls, which is somewhat surprising given that it had been the base of the *Legio III Augusta*.

When we do find evidence of wall-circuits being built under the early Empire, it is generally at a very specific group of cities which might be described as being on the periphery of 'civilised' or even 'Romanised' Africa. Very few wall-circuits were constructed prior to the second century AD (see Table 6.1). The only examples from Numidia – Timgad and Djemila – received their walls on their foundation under the Emperor Trajan, but, as we shall see below, the fortifications were not a particularly

---

[71] *AE* 1954, 130 for Tipasa's status under Hadrian or Antoninus.
[72] Caes. *B Civ.* 2.25.1; *CIL* 8.1181.

Table 6.1 The construction of walled circuits in North
Africa in the second and third centuries AD

City	Date of construction	Province
Djemila	Trajan	Numidia
Timgad	100	Numidia
Iomnium	mid-2nd C.	Mauretania C
Rapidum	167	Mauretania C
Tipasa	146–7	Mauretania C
Banasa	end 2nd C.	Mauretania T
Sala	pre-144	Mauretania T
Thamusida	end 2nd C.	Mauretania T
Tocolosida	2nd C.	Mauretania T
Volubilis	168–9	Mauretania T
Rusazus	201	Mauretania C
Castellum Perdicense	227	Mauretania C
Castellum Citofactense	227	Mauretania C
Ain el Hadjar	227	Mauretania C
Castellum Dianense	234	Mauretania C
Sertei	222–35	Mauretania C
Castellum Thib...	222–35	Mauretania C
Castellum Vanarzanense	238–44	Mauretania C
Lemellef	238–44	Mauretania C
Cellae	243	Mauretania C

useful feature since both towns extended beyond them. All other walls with
epigraphic documentation were constructed during the second and third
centuries in the provinces of Mauretania Caesarensis and Mauretania
Tingitana, and can be explained with reference to their context in time
and space. There were two principal phases of wall-construction in the
region. The first, second-century phase saw walled circuits constructed in
the major cities of Tingitana, such as Volubilis and Banasa, and in large
cities on or near the coast of Caesarensis, such as Tipasa or Iomnium. These
were all in cities that could be subject to raiding, and so the building of walls
could be seen as an attempt to create a feeling of security in the inhabitants,
as well as a place of refuge; they also made a statement to any would-be
enemies about the permanence of the Empire. The places in which walls
were constructed thus happen to have been *coloniae* or the larger cities, so
that walls signified that there was something worth defending in this phase
of urban development in the two provinces of Mauretania. The second
phase of wall construction came in the third century in Mauretania

Caesarensis, under Severus Alexander and Gordian III, and appears to have been imperially inspired; moreover, these walls had a purely defensive function. The cities that had defences constructed around them were all in the border region to the south-west of Djemila and were very different from those of the first phase of wall-building – native *castella* or *pagi* rather than *coloniae* or major cities.[73] It is therefore clear that the building of a circuit of walls was never an essential feature of Roman urbanism in North Africa.

The North African cities demonstrate a range of approaches to the layout of the street-grid with similar types of cities reacting to growth and expansion in very different ways. First, there was a large group of towns, many of which were pre-Roman centres, which never had a unified regular street-grid. Second, there were those new, or refounded, cities that were created with street-plans which they maintained throughout the Roman period. Third, there were Roman implantations on to fresh or cleared sites such as the first- and early second-century colonial settlements, which started with regular grids but often rapidly abandoned the plan as they expanded beyond their original area. Finally there was a group of older, pre-Roman cities such as Lepcis that had regular street-grids before the Roman period which they continued to use and expand.

Native settlements such as Thuburbo Maius, Tiddis and Bulla Regia opted not to impose uniformity on to their road network even in those parts of the cities that were developed in the Roman period. A regular street-plan was obviously not a priority for the inhabitants of the towns, even if they otherwise professed their allegiance to Roman culture through the provision of baths, the construction of temples and the erection of Latin inscriptions. Instead, roads followed the contours of the sites upon which the cities lay. The absence of such a grid was clearly not an impediment to a town's growing status. Thugga's lack of a street-grid did not stop it becoming a *municipium* in 205 or a *colonia* in 261.

Cities constructed *ex nihilo* and colonies were obviously rather different in the circumstances of their creation, and unsurprisingly, had a street-grid imposed upon them by their Roman planners at their formation. As such, they were Roman rather than African in their layout, but this was often not the case in their development. Carthage, Timgad, Sbeitla, Haïdra and Djemila were all built with planned grids (figs. 6.11, 6.12, 6.13, 6.14 and 5.6). Carthage respected its street-grid as it expanded in all directions, but the maintenance of such an expression of uniformity and civility could be

---

[73] Jouffroy (1986), p. 241.

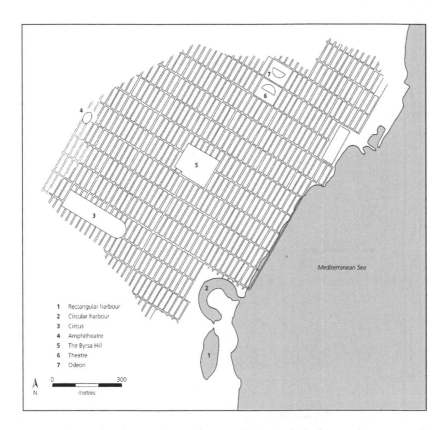

6.11 Carthage: plan showing layout of city in relation to the harbour and monumental developments and the extensive grid of streets.

expected at the residence of the proconsul of Africa and other important imperial officials (fig. 6.11). As the highest-profile Julian/Augustan colony and eventually the largest city in Africa, Carthage was perhaps always going to be thoroughly 'Roman' in the conception and maintenance of its layout.

Not all Roman colonies treated their street-grid in the same way as Carthage. Sbeitla, Djemila and Timgad all outgrew their planned state, and in doing so abandoned the regular gridiron plan that their founders had created to a greater or lesser degree (compare fig. 6.12 with 5.6 and 6.13). Timgad rapidly expanded beyond its original bounds without simply extending its original plan outwards. Indeed, the earlier plan was undermined by the destruction of the wall-circuit and the construction of housing over it.[74] Some structures, such as the Large Northern Baths and the Baths of the

---

[74] Ballu (1903), pp. 5–8.

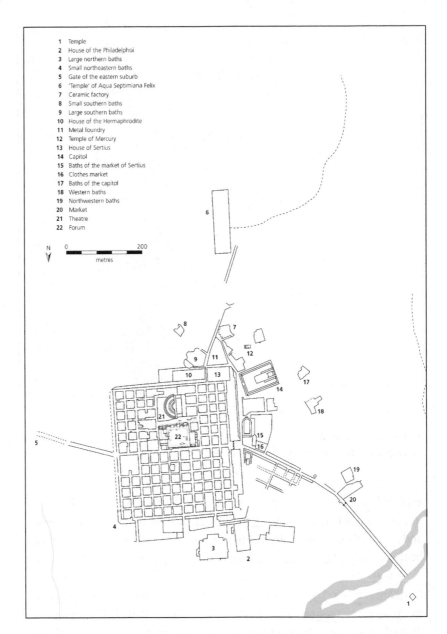

1   Temple
2   House of the Philadelphoi
3   Large northern baths
4   Small northeastern baths
5   Gate of the eastern suburb
6   'Temple' of Aqua Septimiana Felix
7   Ceramic factory
8   Small southern baths
9   Large southern baths
10 House of the Hermaphrodite
11 Metal foundry
12 Temple of Mercury
13 House of Sertius
14 Capitol
15 Baths of the market of Sertius
16 Clothes market
17 Baths of the capitol
18 Western baths
19 Northwestern baths
20 Market
21 Theatre
22 Forum

6.12 Timgad: plan showing development of the city within the original walled area and the expansion of the city, including monumental development, beyond the walls.

Philadelphi, were on the alignment of the old town, but many other monuments and houses built during the second century and later in the western suburbs were not on any system of alignment; indeed, many of the streets fluctuated in their size as well as their direction. Even the *capitolium*,

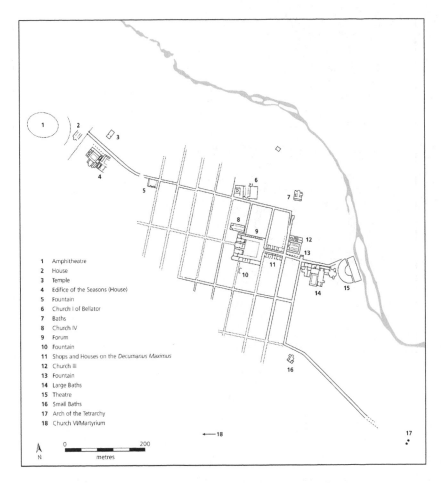

1 Amphitheatre
2 House
3 Temple
4 Edifice of the Seasons (House)
5 Fountain
6 Church I of Bellator
7 Baths
8 Church IV
9 Forum
10 Fountain
11 Shops and Houses on the *Decumanus Maximus*
12 Church III
13 Fountain
14 Large Baths
15 Theatre
16 Small Baths
17 Arch of the Tetrarchy
18 Church VI/Martyrium

0　　　　200

metres

6.13 Sbeitla: plan of the street grid and monuments within the city.

built in AD 146 and situated just outside the old city, was not aligned to the old street-grid.[75] Towards the north-west and south-east it was the roads to Lambaesis and Mascula, rather than the street-grid, that provided the articulation for monuments and houses; but even in these areas, roads rarely ran perpendicular to, or parallel with, the main streets. This abandonment of such a Roman ideal at a colony is surprising given that Timgad's elite were making very definite statements about their 'Romanness' in other ways, such as the use of inscriptions and baths. It is tempting to attribute this shift to an adaptation by the people of the city to an African cultural context where a city plan was not regarded as important.

[75] Ballu (1903), pp. 193–206 and Barton (1982), pp. 308–10.

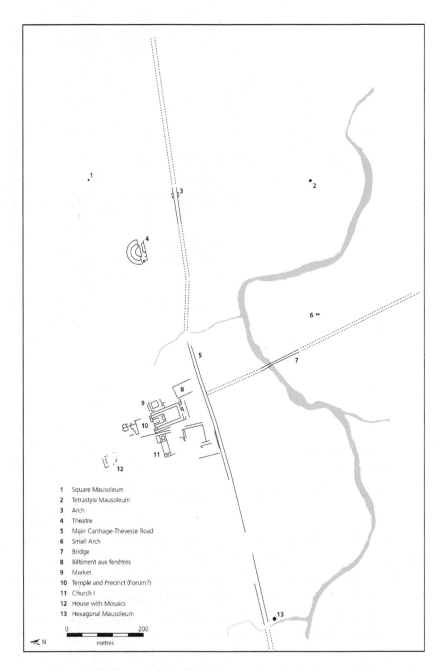

6.14 Haïdra: plan of the city showing the distribution of monuments in relation to the main routes through the city.

1   Square Mausoleum
2   Tetrastyle Mausoleum
3   Arch
4   Theatre
5   Main Carthage-Theveste Road
6   Small Arch
7   Bridge
8   Bâtiment aux fenêtres
9   Market
10   Temple and Precinct (Forum?)
11   Church I
12   House with Mosaics
13   Hexagonal Mausoleum

Other pre-Roman towns, and in particular some Punic communities, adopted, expanded or continued to maintain regular street-grids throughout the early Empire. Throughout all of the discussion on African cities, it is necessary to recognise a longer Punic tradition of urbanism that impacted on many 'Roman' African cities and their development. Punic and Numidian culture continued in various guises, not least in religion, throughout the period of study. The Tripolitanian cities started to make use of regular street-plans before the end of the Republic, as can be seen both in Lepcis (early first century BC) and in Sabratha (second half of the first century BC, fig. 6.15), the former on a considerable scale. The Punic cities were clearly engaging with wider Hellenistic theories of urbanism, but it is important to note that some areas of Carthage had been orthogonally planned as early as the eighth century BC (fig. 6.11).[76] These cities maintained these ideals into the Roman period, with Sabratha laying out a new street-grid to the east of the original one in the later second century AD.

Like city walls, a regular street-grid was not a key feature of many African cities and, as we saw in the previous chapter, many developed a form of connective architecture rather different from what can be found in the Italian peninsula. It is worth comparing the relative emphases within the surviving inscriptions from Africa and Italy (Tables 6.2–6.4), based on the findings of Hélène Jouffroy.[77]

The data from the first century AD show a relatively similar pattern, albeit with a greater emphasis in Africa on temple-building and a lesser emphasis on the construction of amphitheatres and theatres for the holding of games. The difference continued in the second century, with the prominence given in Africa to temple-building and honorific arches, a feature that carried on into the third century. As in Italian cities, monumental arches were used to mark transitions between the countryside and the city (e.g. at Thuburbo Maius and Haïdra).[78] Those cities that did not have walls, or had outgrown them, often used several arches on major roads to indicate to the traveller at what point he or she was leaving a rural landscape behind and was entering the city. The main road between Lambaesis and Mascula passed through Timgad; as it passed through the 'Lambaesis Gate', its direction, which was largely north-west to south-east, altered slightly towards east-west (fig. 6.12). Curving as it passed through the newer areas of the city, the road entered the original *colonia* at the misleadingly named 'Arch of Trajan'. There it became the *decumanus maximus* and

[76] Niemeyer (1992), pp. 39–41.   [77] Jouffroy (1986).   [78] Duval (1982), pp. 649–50.

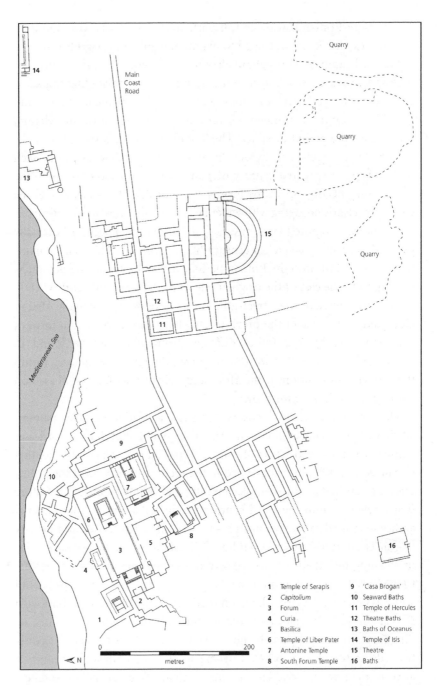

Main
Coast
Road

Quarry

Quarry

Quarry

Mediterranean Sea

1	Temple of Serapis	9	'Casa Brogan'
2	*Capitolium*	10	Seaward Baths
3	Forum	11	Temple of Hercules
4	Curia	12	Theatre Baths
5	Basilica	13	Baths of Oceanus
6	Temple of Liber Pater	14	Temple of Isis
7	Antonine Temple	15	Theatre
8	South Forum Temple	16	Baths

0   200

metres   N

6.15 Sabratha: showing two monumental zones each associated with a different orientation of the grid of streets.

Table 6.2 Comparison of building projects in the first century AD (data from Jouffroy 1986)

	Italy (%)	Africa (%)
Walls	5	4.1
Major projects	19.1	19.6
Temples	34	43.3
Honorific arches	4.2	6.2
Functional buildings	13.6	13.4
Monuments for spectacles	24.1	13.4

Table 6.3 Comparison of building projects in the second century AD (data from Jouffroy 1986)

	Italy (%)	Africa (%)
Walls	–	3.2
Major projects	17.7	13.4
Temples	32.8	44.5
Honorific arches	3	10.2
Functional buildings	27.3	19.1
Monuments for spectacles	19.2	9.6

Table 6.4 Comparison of building projects in the third century AD (data from Jouffroy 1986)

	Italy (%)	Africa (%)
Walls	8	3.9
Major projects	21.8	18.1
Temples	25	39.8
Honorific arches	1.5	12.9
Functional buildings	26.5	19.6
Monuments for spectacles	17.2	5.7

followed the almost east-west orientation of the original street grid (see above). Leaving the east gate of the original *colonia* it again shifted alignment to run east-south-east towards Mascula, and as it left the eastern suburbs another monumental arch marked the city's limits. As with the

Monumentalize
Monuments +
entrance to
city

Italian examples above, settlements across the African provinces, belonging to a range of types, demonstrate the importance attached to monumentalising the entrance to a city. This was clearly one element of the Italian vocabulary of monumentalisation that was incorporated enthusiastically by both veterans and non-Romans in Africa, continuing into the late Empire. The arches also accorded the possibility of honouring the reigning emperor for either his military victories or his generosity to the city (e.g. the Arch of Severus Alexander at Thugga); the Arch of the Severans at Lepcis, with its friezes of a triumph (fig. 5.4), the siege of a city and dynastic harmony, did both.[79]

THE LAYOUT OF THE ROMAN CITY IN THE WEST

summary

Just as the Roman land-surveyors found a variety of approaches to the layout of towns, from those of the past such as Terracina to those of the present such as Haïdra, so we can observe the results of urban formation or urban layout with respect to the grid, walls (if present) and the siting of temples. The world of the cities of Italy, seen from the perspective of, say, the second century AD, was one in which there was an expectation that they had walls, which had frequently been constructed in the past, and had been laid out with respect to a grid-plan of streets with temples located on the high points and in the forum. In contrast, in Gaul the cities were laid out symmetrically with a grid of streets without walls or defences, but with reference to earlier religious sites and often situated close to a river or some other natural feature of the landscape. Such a set of urban features can also be found at Trier in Germany, where the original Augustan street-grid was in need of resurfacing by the second century,[80] or in the *municipium* of Verulamium.[81] For the most part, the cities in our third area of study, the four African provinces, were without walls or had expanded beyond their walled enclosure, and might or might not feature a grid of streets depending on their origin and evolution. The most recent examples, at Timgad or Haïdra, displayed the patterns of symmetry found in the land-surveyors' manuals, but in other cases the expansion of the city had occurred without reference to a grid-pattern and instead was composed of linear developments that gradually created the patterns of armature that were discussed in the previous chapter.

[79] Haynes (1956), p. 74.   [80] Wightman (1970), p. 78.   [81] Creighton (2006); Niblett (2005).

The Roman state appears to have regarded the rectilinear grid of streets as a desirable formation for the production of urbanism. This is most clearly seen in the expansion of Italica in the second century AD (see Chapter 4), although something on a similar scale was seldom attempted at other sites. Perhaps Italica (fig. 4.5) represents the end of a process of urban development that had seen grids of streets adopted across Gaul and in Spain (e.g. at Córdoba) for over one hundred years, as a tried and tested formula for the layout of a town. The almost contemporary second-century developments at Timgad demonstrate the limitations of a grid as a means of organising a town that was expanding organically, with the result that the city extended beyond the grid and developed armature. The grids of streets were always subject to further development, whether by the addition of new public buildings to create new routes through the evenly divided grid or through the extension of the city beyond the grid. What we need to remember is that the grid was a means for organising space, both civilian and military, at green-field sites. That grid shaped the city but was subject to uneven development or the development of streets and routes of greater importance, as well as the formation of prominent loci that were preferable to those more isolated from the major routes: within the grid (to locations of ritual and government), through the grid (the routes to other places) or connecting with prominent locations within the countryside (sanctuaries).

7 | Assembling the city 1: forum and basilica

THE FORUM IN TEXTS

By the time Vitruvius came to write *De architectura* (*On Architecture*) in the early first century AD, the forum had become a central feature of every city in both Italy and Greece.[1] He explains the difference in form within these two distinct urban cultures: in Greek cities the forum was square with double colonnades, whereas in Italian cities it was rectangular because it was in this space that *spectacula* and gladiatorial games were held according to ancestral custom. The size of this rectangular space would have varied according to the size of the population, so that at the games the space did not appear half-empty or too crowded. Earlier examples from Italy demonstrate some variation – Alba Fucens: 142×44 metres; Cosa: 90×30 metres – and do not conform to Vitruvius' suggested 3:2 proportion of length:breadth. The forum, as Vitruvius shows in his text, was very much a place of *negotium*, or business, with provision for *tabernae* (shops/offices) to be let out to the *argentarii* (money changers/bankers) and the positioning of an adjacent basilica in a warm location for use by *negotiatores* (traders) during winter.[2] Another series of buildings adjacent to the forum were those of local government: the treasury, the *curia* and the prison.[3] Vitruvius' text concerns the meaning or use of a forum – as a place for traders and *negotium*, but also as a place for government. He makes no mention of a temple dominating the central piazza of the forum, and indeed the association need not have been central to the urban form that we understand as a space surrounded by public buildings. None of the early fora constructed in Latin colonies had a temple dominating the space, as can be seen at Paestum, Cosa and Alba Fucens.[4] Instead, what was included at these sites conformed to the emphases already highlighted – a basilica for trade and a *curia* or Senate house for government. The latter, for Vitruvius, should have reflected the *dignitas* of the *municipium* or *civitas* and its acoustics should have enabled the assembled parties to hear the

---

[1] Vitr. *De arch.* 5.1.1.   [2] Vitr. *De arch.* 5.1.4.   [3] Vitr. *De arch.* 5.2.1.
[4] Gros (1996), pp. 207–34.

discussion within its interior.[5] The whole forum was a place for public and private business controlled by the magistrates of the city.

THE DEVELOPMENT OF THE FORUM AND THE BASILICA IN ITALIAN TOWNS

The colony of Cosa demonstrates the rudimentary nature of a forum during the third century BC and the development of an architectural definition of the forum in the second century BC (figs. 2.2–2.5).[6] In its earliest incarnation from 273–197 BC, a forum was located on the flattest part of the site and was certainly laid out as a rectangular space, but its facilities were limited to the provision of an abundant water-supply from rock-hewn cisterns with a capacity of 1,738,000 litres and a circular building for meetings of the colonists.[7] In addition, trees were planted to delineate the space. No purpose-built religious structure can be located on the site prior to an altar constructed during the Punic Wars. Following the reinforcement of the colony in 197 BC, the area was redeveloped to contain a smaller piazza surrounded by houses that were substantially larger than those found elsewhere in the colony, with shops/offices facing on to the forum. The second century BC saw the replacement of the original *curia* with a larger structure (28×17 metres in dimension), which was again rebuilt later in the same century. Next to the *curia*, on the long south-west side, a temple was added – the first and only temple within the forum. A further addition on the south-west side, to the north of the *curia*, was a basilica (36×27 metres in dimension). The actual piazza was demarcated by colonnades and considerable work was undertaken to level the area. The whole area was marked as a separate space from the rest of the city by a triple arch situated on the approach to the forum from the north-east; such arches delimiting the forum were also constructed in Pisaurum, Potentia and Fundi in 174 BC.[8] What we find by the end of the second century is a defined, rectangular space, around which were the buildings of *negotium*: a *curia*, a place for assembly and a basilica. In addition there were shops as

---

[5] Vitr. *De arch.* 5.2.2.

[6] See Brown *et al.* (1993) for details of excavated data and interpretation, to be read with Fentress (2004) and Sewell (2005).

[7] Sewell (2005) presents a hypothesis for a much larger forum area than that which has been excavated on the site.

[8] Livy, 31.49.6, 32.2.6–7, 33.24.8–9, 41.27.13.

well as a temple (although this was dwarfed by the temples on the heights of the city). What is so striking about the absence of an architecturally defined forum with a basilica in the third century, and then its presence in the second century, is that a similar trajectory of development was followed in the Forum Romanum at Rome itself.[9] The influx of new colonists in 197 BC certainly marked a new beginning with greater definition of an architectural hierarchy across the site as a whole,[10] yet parallels, in terms of the second-century development of a forum-basilica-*curia* complex, can also be found at other Latin colonies, such as Alba Fucens,[11] Fregellae (fig. 1.3)[12] and Paestum (fig. 2.1).[13] Temples were built in the fora at two of these sites – Cosa and Paestum – but were not created to be focal points; rather they were among a number of buildings arranged around a space in such a way as to facilitate public and private business.

   The development of an architecturally defined forum was not confined to the Latin colonies across the peninsula. By the late second or early first century BC, L. Betilienus Varus was enhancing the appearance of his Hernician city of Alatri with the addition of streets (*semita*), an aqueduct, baths, a *porticus*, a *campus* (training ground) and, possibly in the forum if Zevi is correct about the exact structure of the area, a *horologium* (sundial), a basilica and a *macellum* (market-building).[14] The list is interesting for what is left out – walls, temples, a forum – and we can see it as a series of additions to urban features that already existed. Indeed we might even assume that the *horologium*, the basilica and the *macellum* were established to delineate the space of the forum. What had previously existed was a city with a formidable walled enclosure, sacred sites and a place for public meetings or a forum, to use the Latin terminology.

   In another Italian town, Pompeii, closer to the Greek cities of southern Italy, we can trace the development of the forum as a defined space. The city had existed with a walled circuit, a grid of streets and its sacred sites to Apollo and Hercules from the sixth century BC; on to this framework of urbanism was developed what has become a classic forum, dominated by its imposing temple. The date of the original forum was investigated by Maiuri through excavation in the late 1930s and early 1940s (fig. 1.2). He identified a votive deposit in the forum close to the Temple of Jupiter beneath the original altar, which he dated to the fourth or third centuries BC.[15] The actual definition of the piazza flanked with shops on its eastern side was

[9] See Welch (2003) for origin of the basilica in Roman culture.   [10] Fentress (2004).
[11] Mertens (1969).   [12] Coarelli (1998), pp. 56–61.
[13] Pedley (1990); Greco (1999); Greco and Theodorescu (1987).   [14] Zevi (1976).
[15] Maiuri (1942), p. 308.

dated by him to the fourth century at the earliest and the shops beneath the Eumachia building were developed in the late third to second centuries BC (fig. 7.1).[16] Hence, by the beginning of the second century BC, there was already a forum with a sacred focus, but not a temple, and commercial facilities in the form of shops, adjacent to the Temple of Apollo in its own precinct. His excavations also identified three phases of paving of the piazza surface, which he saw as stretching back to at least the third century BC. The entire space (with dimensions of 142×38 metres) was aligned towards Mount Vesuvius, and Coarelli has suggested that the focus of ritual was on the god Jupiter Vesuvius, with an altar located over the votive deposit discovered by Maiuri at the northern end of the forum.[17] The presence of this altar in the forum explains the decision on the part of the pre-Roman Pompeians to construct a temple at the northern end of their forum at the end of the second century BC.[18] The unique combination of the altar in the forum with Mount Vesuvius provided the opportunity for building a temple that would dominate the forum, a feature singularly absent from the forum of the city of Fregellae, which conforms to the model found in the Latin colonies at Alba Fucens, Cosa and Paestum with a *curia*.[19] At about the same time, a *macellum* and a basilica were added and further additions were made to the southern end of the forum with structures housing the administration of the city.[20] The southern end of the forum was subsequently enhanced with a portico constructed by Vibius Popidius in the 80s BC.[21] With the arrival of the Sullan colonists, the existing temple to Jupiter in the forum was torn down and replaced with a new structure dedicated to Jupiter, Juno and Minerva (fig. 1.2 for Sullan construction – note also the amphitheatre).[22] This action fused the local development of the forum with the Roman triad of deities to produce a colonial space, which is quite unlike the fora of earlier Latin colonies. The unique sequence or set of circumstances at Pompeii which led to the development of a forum dominated by a single temple demonstrates a need for care when considering the final form of the fora of Italy. It would appear that the forum was a defined space for public and private business, rather than a space dominated by a temple or *capitolium* (temple to Jupiter, Juno and Minerva).

---

[16] Maiuri (1941), p. 385.   [17] Coarelli (2002), p. 39.   [18] Maiuri (1942) for excavations.

[19] Coarelli (1998), pp. 56–62; contra Zanker (1998), p. 53.

[20] Maiuri (1942); De Ruyt (1983), pp. 137–49; Dobbins (1994) casts doubt on the dating of the *macellum*.

[21] *CIL* 10.794.

[22] Zanker (1998), pp. 62–4; Zevi (1996) and Lo Cascio (1996a or b) on the situation in Pompeii after the arrival of the colonists.

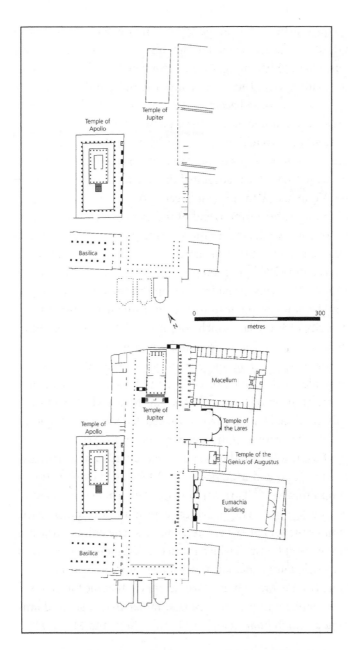

7.1 Pompeii: the forum in the first century BC (upper) and the forum in the first century AD (lower). The process of development from one stage to the next was gradual, but with the result that the layout of the forum became much more defined and resembled the fora developing in Rome.

What is not unique to Pompeii is the enclosure of the forum and a change from a relatively open space into a closed space over the course of the second century. This can be observed at numerous sites, not least Cosa, but is first encountered in the literary record when Livy records that the censors of 174 BC spent considerable sums on the enclosure of a forum (*forum ... claudendum*: 41.27.12). They also constructed walls around the towns of Calatia and Auximum and from the sale of public land were able to build shops or *tabernae* around the existing fora in both these towns.[23] The emphasis in Livy is on a fundamental change in the nature of urban space from open areas into defined and closed-off piazzas. In mentioning the addition of temples of Jupiter at Pisaurum and Fundi, no location is given so it may be right to assume that it was not in the forum itself.[24] Rather it is the new phenomenon of surrounding the existing rectangular space of the forum with shops and porticoes that we see in the archaeological record of Pompeii, Paestum and Cosa from the second century BC. These were facilities to enhance the utility of the forum, a space whose rectilinear origins date to before the second century in Italy – regardless of whether a city was a Roman colony or an Italian *municipium*. The culture of cities across the peninsula underwent a fundamental change during the second century BC to create the architectural space of the forum, which Vitruvius would later compare to that of the Greek *agora*.

THE IMPERIAL FORA IN ITALY: THE CREATION OF SACRED SPACE

The forum in Pompeii in its final form appears at first glance as a space that was designed as a totality with a clear focus on the *capitolium* (figure 7.1). This illusion is created by the first-century AD additions to the forum. First, arches flanked the *capitolium*, maybe in the same way as in the Forum of Augustus at Rome. The entire eastern side of the forum was developed as a series of public buildings: the Eumachia building; a *porticus* with a dedication to Augustan Concordia and Pietas; the Temple of the Genius of the Colony; and finally the so-called Temple of the Lares, which was aligned at ninety degrees to the *capitolium*. These created a unified façade that replaced the earlier shops on this side of the forum. The focus, as Zanker suggests, was firmly on the imperial cult.[25] The models for these buildings may have come from Rome itself. However, the effect of these individual

---

[23] Livy, 41.27.10.   [24] Livy, 41.27.13.   [25] Zanker (1998).

projects was to create a unified, defined, rectilinear space that was dominated by buildings associated with religious cults, with additional space for commerce provided by the Porticus of Eumachia. The result was that, by AD 79, the forum was a commercial and religious centre, although the shops themselves had disappeared (like those in the Forum Romanum some two hundred and fifty years earlier).[26] It is a pattern that can be identified in other cities across Italy.[27] For example, at Brescia the forum had been reorganised by the late first century AD (fig. 7.2). Originally the major village of Rome's allies, the Cenomani, it possessed a sanctuary in the location of what would become the forum.[28] The people of the city had gained Latin citizenship in 89 BC, with the option of becoming Roman citizens for those holding political office, and so had the status of a city.[29] An associated development was the construction of new cult-buildings for four deities at the northern end of the forum.[30] The piazza of the forum was laid out at a slightly later date to create a rectangular space measuring 139×40 metres bisected by the major route through the city;[31] this may have been linked with its new status as *Colonia Civica Augusta Brixia*.[32] By the Flavian period, a basilica had been added at the southern end and colonnades of shops had appeared on the longer sides of the space. Finally, at the northern end, a new *capitolium* was added in AD 73/4, with three *cellae* (aisles) and a *pronaos* (portico), which dominated the space.[33] The division of the forum by the road created two spaces: one dominated by commerce and the other by religion. Even after one hundred and fifty years the original sacred site of the Cenomani continued to exert its influence, a fact confirmed by the location of the city's theatre adjacent to the *capitolium*. These developments created a quite different architectural format from that of the early first century, but it involved a similar spatial configuration focussed on an Italian sanctuary (the place of the *capitolium*) and making provision for *negotium* or commerce.[34]

The model presented by the forum at Brescia, with space delineated by colonnades on the long axes, a basilica at one end and a temple at the other, and with the piazza divided by a road or street, can be found in numerous cities in the first century AD. The new colony at Aosta (founded in 25 BC,

---

[26] Dobbins (1994) for the dating of different elements.   [27] Gros (2000) for full survey.

[28] Livy, 32.30.6, 31.10.2, 21.25.14; Polyb. 2.17.4, Strabo 5.1.9.

[29] Pliny *HN* 138 suggests *municipium*; Asconius *Pis*.3.5 suggests *colonia*; see Mollo (2000) for epigraphy.

[30] The changes have been dated to 89–49 BC by AAVV (1979), pp. 26–45; Mansuelli (1971), p. 129.

[31] AAVV (1979), pp. 90–5.   [32] AAVV (1979), p. 161.   [33] AAVV (1979), pp. 47–87.

[34] Zanker (2000), pp. 33–6.

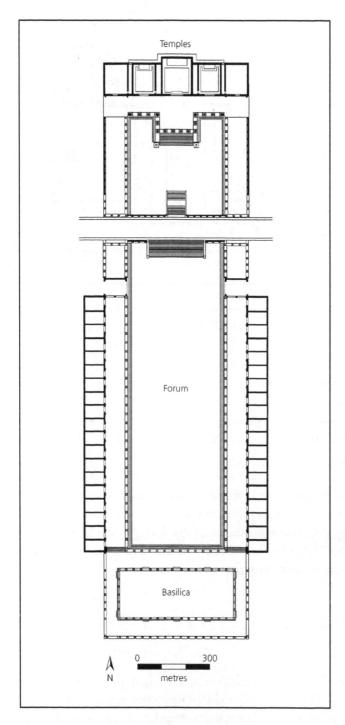

7.2 Brescia: the forum is bisected by a through-route creating a division of space; one area that is associated with the religious sphere and the temples, and another associated with *tabernae* (shops) and the basilica – locations of *negotium* (business).

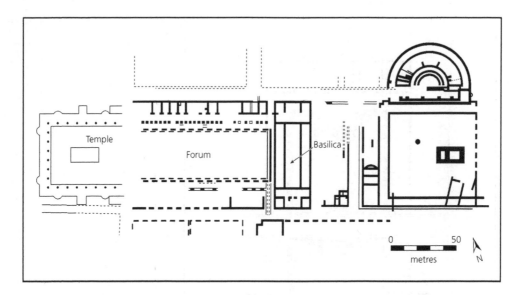

7.3 Augusta Bagiennorum (modern Benevagienna): the forum with its temple complex resembles the architectural space found at Brescia (cf. fig.7.2). The plan also shows the close proximity of the theatre and another temple complex.

fig. 2.6) had a very similar forum to that of Brescia, as did Luni, Augst and Augusta Bagiennorum or modern Benevagienna (fig. 7.3).[35] At Brescia, however, the existing focus provided by the temples was adapted to the needs of Roman urban life. In contrast, at Aosta the forum with its basilica, shops, porticoes and temples was constructed on a green-field site with no previous religious connections. The inclusion of a temple as well as a basilica shows that a new meaning had become attached to the forum by the time of Augustus so that it was seen as a space for religion as well as *negotium*. This dual role was marked by the fact that the street running through the forum divided the sacred space of the altars and temples from the space of business and *negotium*.

THE FORUM AND THE CITY IN BARBARIAN EUROPE

These new fora of the first century AD in northern Italy, dominated by one or more temples, may have been the model for new towns in Gaul and Spain. In towns as distant from one another as Augst and Paris we can identify this

---

[35] Dio Cass. 53.25.3–5; Corni (1989); see Ward-Perkins (1970), pp. 5–8 for further examples.

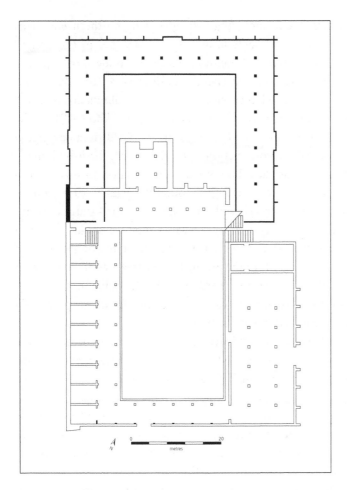

7.4 Conimbriga: two phases of the forum. In black is the later Flavian phase that was built around the existing temple when the *tabernae* (shops) and basilica were demolished. Note the placing of steps that mark changes in level on the earlier phase – dividing the forum into two sections.

architectural type appearing from the end of the first century AD. We must, however, be cautious in postulating the widespread adoption of this model. Few sites have the stratigraphic sequences required to identify the process of development. One site that does is Conimbriga in modern Portugal, ancient Lusitania.[36] The Iron Age settlement had a forum added to it in the Augustan period, which was located on a level area and built on the limestone bedrock, and measured just 50×50 metres (fig. 7.4). It formed a precinct with a central colonnaded space, *tabernae* (shops/offices), a

[36] Mierse (1999), pp. 85–91, 213–20.

[handwritten margin notes: Forum - religion commerce politics]

basilica and a sacred area including a temple at its northern end. This forum possessed all the elements found in Italy, whether in Pompeii or Brescia: religion, commerce and politics.[37] However, in the Flavian period the existing forum, the *tabernae* and the basilica were torn down and replaced with a single much larger temple set within a colonnaded piazza.[38] If this had been discovered without the benefit of our knowledge of the earlier Augustan phase, it would have been identified as a sanctuary, particularly if viewed in conjunction with the nearby bath-building.[39] However, there are signs that there was a civic function to this space – some twenty statue-bases were arranged around the piazza area in front of the temple and should be linked with the fragments of ten statues discovered within the Flavian forum.[40] At the same time we should not play down the religious function of the space as demonstrated by the finds of votive epigraphy located within the precinct.[41] What we see at Conimbriga is a move within the architecture towards a greater provision for the sacred and a reduction in the space dedicated to the civic functions previously associated with the *tabernae* and the basilica.

The balance between sacred and civic space was a common feature of the fora of Spain and Gaul. At Baelo, in the province of Baetica, the forum was closed off from the through traffic of the city's streets (fig. 7.5). Within the space were placed: three temples at the northern end, set at a higher level on a terrace; a basilica to define the southern edge of the lower piazza area; on the western side structures that may have been for the magistrates and decurions; and finally on the eastern flank a series of *tabernae*.[42] The division of the space into an upper part that included the temples and a lower part that formed the main piazza is familiar to us from the examination of Brescia. This spatial separation of the sacred from the business sections of the forum was maintained in the middle of the first century AD in Baelo when the Temple of Isis was constructed adjacent to the three existing temples.[43] Although we may suggest that the *macellum* to the south-west of the basilica was located so as to be close to the forum, its focus (and entrance) was on a street outside it.[44] It is possible that the *macellum*, which was built towards the end of the first century AD, removed the commercial functions from the *tabernae* within the forum itself.[45] For Bonneville and his

---

[37] Alarcão and Etienne (1977), p. 28.   [38] Alarcão and Etienne (1977), pp. 88–94.
[39] Alarcão and Etienne (1977).
[40] Alarcão and Etienne (1977), pp. 101–2; Etienne et al. (1976), pp. 236–47.
[41] Etienne et al. (1976), pp. 19–45.
[42] See Sillières (1995), pp. 85–128 for description and discussion.
[43] Bonneville et al. (2000).   [44] Didierjean, Ney and Paillet (1981).   [45] Sillières (1995), p. 120.

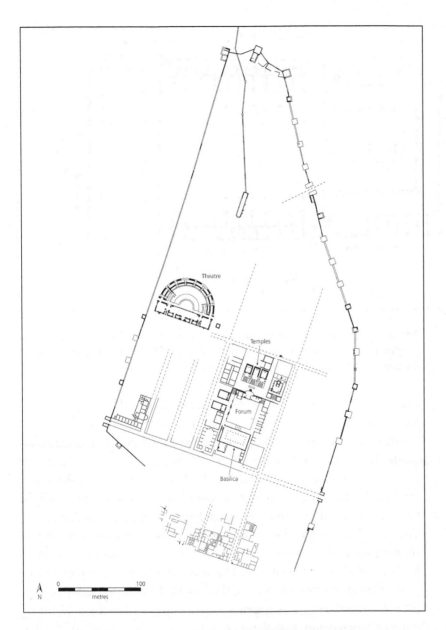

7.5 Baelo: plan of the city showing the development of the forum as an integral space through which no roads pass (cf. fig. 7.2), but nevertheless is at the intersection of the major roads through the city.

colleagues, the forum's temples should be related to the architecture of the Italian sanctuaries of the second century BC rather than to that of the forum and basilica found in Vitruvius.[46] What was different was that the

---

[46] Bonneville *et al.* (2000), pp. 196–8.

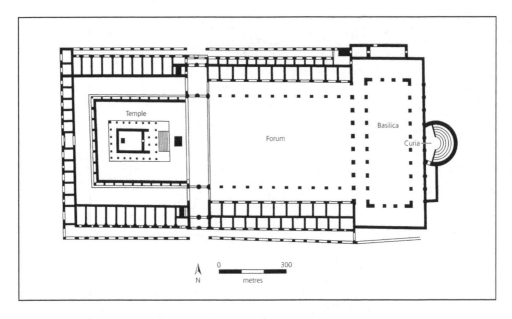

7.6 Augst: the double forum displays many of the characteristics of other fora in provincial cities, but with the addition of a circular *curia* built out from the basilica for meetings of the *ordo* and other public meetings.

religious focus of the sanctuary had been relocated within the forum itself and could include the deified emperors of the first century AD.[47]

The division of space seen at Baelo is also found in the 'double fora' of Gaul. The form is most clearly articulated at Augst, where the forum was bisected by a road running more or less north-south (fig. 7.6). To the west of the road lay the temple complex, surrounded by *tabernae* (shops/offices) that were accessed not from the piazza but from the surrounding streets. The part of the forum lying to the east of the road had a series of *tabernae* running along its northern and southern sides and the eastern end had a basilica and then a *curia* beyond. The orientation of the *tabernae* reveals a difference between the two parts of this 'double forum': one sacred and the other for *negotium*. It was a format that was repeated in Paris, Nyon (in modern Switzerland) and Bavai, to name just three other towns. The location of these fora was chosen with respect to the physical topography. For example, the forum at Paris was located at a central point within the street grid at the highest point overlooking the route across the river Seine and with a view across the river to the sanctuary at Montmartre (see fig. 6.9).

Not every forum needed a temple to provide its religious focus. The hillfort of Ruscino, near Perpignan in the eastern Pyrenees, developed a

[47] Bonneville et al. (2000), pp. 190–5.

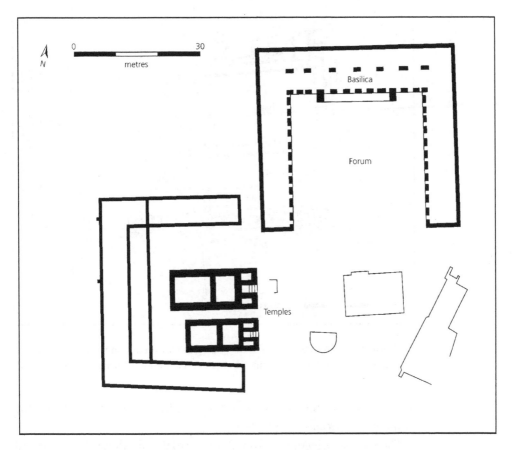

7.7 Glanum: the forum developed as a central space into which temples were added. This example shows an interpretation of Roman urbanism that could be described as a hybrid form, or involved a smaller investment of resources in the development of a rectilinear space for the forum.

forum with a basilica and an array of imperial statues (see below for discussion).[48] The phase of urban grandeur at Ruscino was short-lived with no further monuments constructed after the first century AD, and in the second century the town gradually disintegrated.[49] However, what this site shows is that the concept of a forum with a basilica and imperial statuary could penetrate to the remoter parts of the western provinces and was not confined to the Mediterranean coastal strip (compare Segobriga below). This pattern is confirmed by Glanum, twenty kilometres north-east of Arles. The town developed a forum at its centre in the last decade of the first century BC.[50] This was developed with two temples and a colonnaded space at right angles to them (fig. 7.7).

[48] Barruol (1978), pp. 430–1; Rosso (2000).   [49] Barruol (1982), p. 180.   [50] Congès (1992).

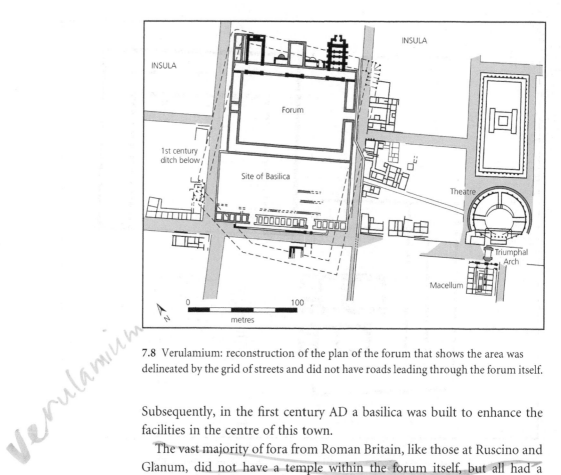

7.8 Verulamium: reconstruction of the plan of the forum that shows the area was delineated by the grid of streets and did not have roads leading through the forum itself.

Subsequently, in the first century AD a basilica was built to enhance the facilities in the centre of this town.

The vast majority of fora from Roman Britain, like those at Ruscino and Glanum, did not have a temple within the forum itself, but all had a basilica. Unlike the 'double fora' of Gaul, the British structures tended to be spaces set apart from the grid of streets and entered from a central point opposite the basilica. It is a format found at some sites in northern Italy, notably Velleia (see below). Verulamium in Britain does appear to have had at least one temple within the forum. Excavations suggest that the forum was built after the destruction of the town by Boudicca in AD 60/61 with a new grid of streets aligned on Watling Street, which passed through the centre of the town and connected it to London a day's journey to the south-east (fig. 7.8).[51] The forum with its basilica was established at the centre of the town with Watling Street running along its north-eastern side. The forum overlay an earlier 'central enclosure' on quite a different alignment, but this would indicate that there was some continuity of use or topographical significance, perhaps political/religious in nature, shared by these

---

[51] Niblett (2001) and (2005) has a full account of the evidence.

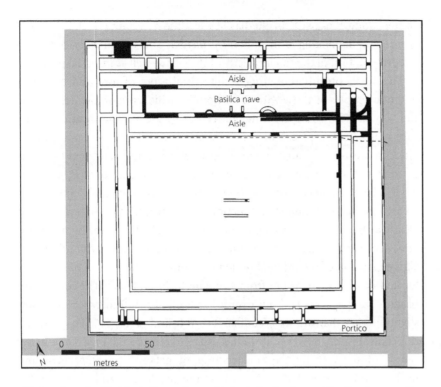

7.9 London: the Hadrianic forum is notable both for its size and for the absence of a temple – not a unique format by the second century AD, even in the Mediterranean and in Rome itself (for instance, the forum of Trajan).

two structures. There is evidence that inscriptions were set up in the forum, but only fragments remain.[52] Frustratingly, the archaeological evidence shows that there was a forum and basilica here, but because of the overlying structures the full plan, especially of the basilica, is virtually impossible to reconstruct (fig. 7.8). London, by contrast, saw the establishment of a Flavian forum-basilica complex that was replaced in the second century by a forum built in several phases on a much grander scale, resulting in a colossal forum-basilica measuring 166×167 metres (fig. 7.9).[53] Britain seems to have produced enclosed fora without temples, but it is uncertain whether this would have altered the fundamental use of the space, since it was always possible that permanent or temporary altars could have provided a religious focus. In any case, the basilica should not be seen as an entirely secular building, and the large, central chamber in the range of

[52] *RIB* 222, 226, 227, 228, 229.
[53] Brigham (1992a), (1992b); Brigham and Crowley (1992); Brigham (1990).

rooms along the 'back' of the basilica is almost certainly to be seen as a shrine, like its analogue in military *principia*, and presumably contained a representation of the tutelary deity of the city as well as imperial portraits.

This focus on differentiating architectural types of fora, those with or without temples or those with or without a basilica, might distract us from the very creation of a monumental centre to a city. The location of the forum as a central place, often on a higher if not the highest point in the city, is a feature that can be established at towns in quite different locations in time and space: for example London, Paris, Falerii Novi, Pompeii or Trier. The effort to construct a truly impressive monumental centre might have been the most important function of the forum. This can be seen most clearly at Bavai in Belgica (figs. 7.10 and 7.11). The town was by no means large – fifteen hectares at foundation, expanding to some forty hectares.[54] This expansion of the original settlement points to the success of this town located on the major route from Cologne to Boulogne.[55] The forum and basilica complex was laid out over an area of 240×110 metres, which was slightly larger than the very similar forum found at Trier.[56] To construct this central space, however, it was necessary to create a flat raised area at the centre of the city by the construction of galleries, *cryptoporticus* and terraces; this also had the effect of raising the forum and its associated monuments, as it were on a podium, so that they were a visual focus for those approaching the city. The chronological development of the forum remains a subject of debate. What is clear, however, from the epigraphy is that by the early years of the reign of the Emperor Tiberius, four imperial statues were set up at this location to commemorate the emperor's *adventus* (ceremonial progress), and the setting-up of imperial statues continued into the third century.[57] The basilica and forum were also reconstructed over this period, perhaps by order of the decurions.[58] The presence of an aqueduct, which fed water to the city, suggests that the forum was not the only impressive monument within this small settlement in Belgica and that the town was the central place in the region for the Nervii who worshipped the genius of their *'civitas Nerviorum Augusta'*– a feature of other central towns of *civitates* in Gaul and Germany.[59] These developments began in the

---

[54] Thollard (1996); Thollard (1997); Thollard and Groetembril (1999); Wightman (1985), p. 98.
[55] Corbiau (1985).   [56] Wightman (1985), p. 82.
[57] Thollard (1997); Hanoune and Muller (1999); *CIL* 13.3570; *CIL* 13.3571.
[58] Hanoune and Muller (1999); *CIL* 13.3572 for the existence of an *ordo*.
[59] Biévelet (1962); Adam (1979). The genius of *'civitas Nerviorum Augusta'* is attested in inscription *AE* 1969/1970.410, 1976.464; *CIL* 13.566 – Bordeaux; 13.6417 – Ladenburg; 13.6482 – Wimpfen.

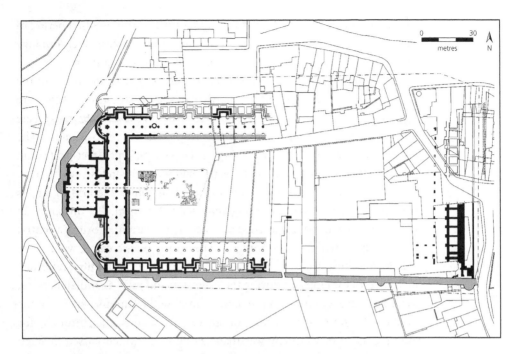

7.10 Bavai: a huge effort was made to construct a raised forum that would dominate the skyline with rooms and porticoes on concrete vaults (*cryptoporticus*) surrounding a central paved area.

7.11 Bavai: the west end of the *cryptoporticus* complex.

mid-first century AD and accelerated under the Flavians, whilst a period of major renovation followed in the second century;[60] a precise chronology might be achieved with further excavation at this important site.

These examples of fora from the north-west provinces and many of the cities of Italy and Spain had a particular spatial structure. They were rectangular spaces with major roads either passing through them to create the classic 'double fora', or skirting their edges. They were positioned at the centre and/or at a high point within a grid of streets. This street-grid could contain other public monuments, as we shall see in the following chapters. However, what we find is that the forum, as much as the grid of streets containing *insulae*, was the thing that defined a town. For instance, in Marsden's view London was created by the structure of the forum, a central space at the junction of two routes.[61] The forum, once created, was a place in which statues were set up to the emperor and his family and altars dedicated to the emperor during the Augustan and Julio-Claudian periods, as well as statues being set up to commemorate the famous persons of the locality. A governor's journey or an emperor's *adventus* through, for example, Gaul or Germany was made along roads which passed through fora that were surrounded by rectangular grids of streets.[62] This was the meaning of urbanism for the visual landscape in the north-west provinces. Perhaps it is no surprise that those towns with large or elaborate fora are also those places mentioned as starting points for journeys in the Antonine Itineraries, such as Silchester or Bavai.[63] The image of these places was created by their point within the road system, and the visual sense for travellers of arriving at a place manifesting an urban culture, including organised street systems, a central place which, in the case of Bavai, contained marble statues to commemorate Tiberius' *adventus*, and a basilica, a structure designed to protect the traveller or trader from the weather. The basilica and porticoes provided a further sense of grandeur or invited comparison with other fora and even those of Rome. After all, it was columns and statue-bases that were used to define a setting as being within the forum in the frescoes from the *insula* block known in antiquity as the *Praedia* (property) of Julia Felix in Pompeii. The forum not only provided for the traveller or dignitary with an entourage, but also created a space in which the local inhabitants could view the stranger and hear him speak, whether he was a governor with legal knowledge or a trader purchasing

---

[60] Thollard and Groetembril (1999).   [61] Marsden (1987).
[62] See Carroll (2001), pp. 41–61; Brigham (1992a).
[63] Silchester – Laurence (2001b); Fulford (2003); Bavai – Corbiau (1985).

goods or selling items not seen previously. The architectural space of the forum created a Roman locale, in which Romanness could be enhanced through buying and selling or the application of the governor's edicts and the legal apparatus of the state. The forum was the primary space in the city, within which Latin was used and seen in the form of monumental writing.[64] This factor should not be underestimated, for it was in the forum that social relationships were formally set out in writing, with the result that it became the place in which to view history and the memory of the past.[65] It was the place where Romanness was produced, as described by Tacitus' *Agricola*.[66] The fora of some of the major towns may also have been the place where tax was extracted from the provincials and where some of the more famous incidents of a Roman governor's tyranny over Rome's subjects and citizens occurred.[67]

FORUM AND BASILICA IN THE AFRICAN PROVINCES

The fora of the African cities do not follow the same trajectories of development as those of Gaul and Spain. They therefore need to be treated separately in order to evaluate what was happening.[68] The creation of fora in Africa was not limited to a single phase, unlike in Gaul where it was largely a first-century phenomenon. Unlike in Gaul, there seems to have been little development during the Flavian period but rather more under Claudius and Nero. The evidence for the construction of public monuments in the African provinces points to a different chronology of urban development from that of the other provinces in the West. Table 7.1 sets out the chronology of known construction across the period. Fora were created throughout the first three centuries AD, and when we also consider the building of basilicas, we find rather more evidence for urban development in the third century than elsewhere in the Empire. Indeed, this is a reversal of the situation in Gaul or Italy where few new fora appear to have been constructed after the early first century. What does this indicate about the nature of urbanism in Africa or the context for the development of urbanism there? The numbers alone appear to reveal a general pattern of urban expansion; but we need to remember that the conquest of the region was far from complete in the first century AD, and

[64] Woolf (1996).   [65] Woolf (1996), pp. 37–8.   [66] Tac. *Agr.* 21–2.   [67] See Cic. *Verr.*
[68] Balty (1994), p. 96.

Table 7.1 Construction of civic buildings in North African cities (adapted from Jouffroy 1986)

	Forum	Basilica	Curia
First Century BC	1	0	0
First Century AD	9	2	1
Second Century AD	10	3	5
Third Century AD	10	7	4

this factor might explain the uneven pattern of development, especially when compared with the Gallic provinces which had been pacified by the late first century BC.

The fora/basilica complexes of the North African cities display considerable diversity in their structure, layout and position within the city. Such differences also seem to imply that the function of the forum could differ from city to city. At Timgad, a Roman colony founded in AD 100, the city's forum was constructed and added to during the life of Trajan and his successors Hadrian and Antoninus Pius. Initially the complex was constructed with a paved area of around 50×42 metres and was surrounded by porticoes (fig. 7.12). To north and south a series of spaces, some sealed with metal grilles, may have been used as shops or meeting-places.[69] On the eastern side of the forum were the basilica and its dependent buildings.[70] On the west, municipal buildings, perhaps including a prison, but certainly a *curia* and a small courtyard, rounded off the complex.[71] Apart from a possible shrine in the southern portico the original space did not definitively include a temple.

During the second century the western side of the forum in particular was subjected to a series of developments that disrupted the portico and courtyard. The exact chronology of this is not clear. A rostrum for public speaking was constructed in the area in front of the portico. Presumably this predated the statues of victory consecrated to Trajan's Parthian victory of 116 that were placed on it as a result of a legacy of M. Annius Martialis, a soldier of *Legio III Augusta*.[72] Behind this rostrum, and connected to it by a flight of stairs, was a small tetrastyle temple (cella of 4.3×6.8 metres) that Ballu designated the 'Temple of Victory', although there is no known link to the gift of Martialis and the temple is not mentioned in the dedication of the statues.[73] It is likely that the temple and the rostrum were already in

[69] Ballu (1897), pp. 129–32.   [70] Ballu (1897), pp. 132–8.   [71] Ballu (1897), pp. 140–5.
[72] Ballu (1897), pp. 146; Zimmer (1989), pp. 45, 75; CIL 8.2354 + p. 1693.
[73] Ballu (1897), pp. 147–8 ; Jouffroy (1986), p. 215.

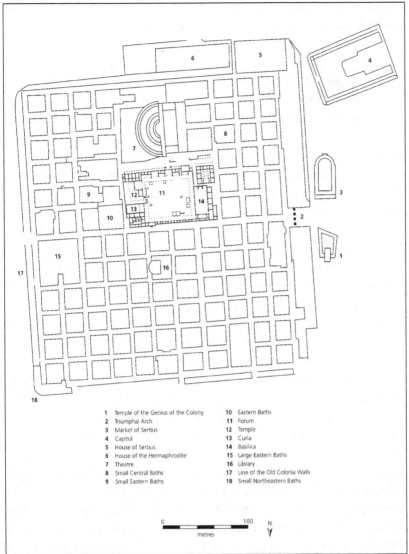

1	Temple of the Genius of the Colony	**10**	Eastern Baths
2	Triumphal Arch	**11**	Forum
3	Market of Sertius	**12**	Temple
4	Capitol	**13**	Curia
5	House of Sertius	**14**	Basilica
6	House of the Hermaphrodite	**15**	Large Eastern Baths
7	Theatre	**16**	Library
8	Small Central Baths	**17**	Line of the Old Colonia Walls
9	Small Eastern Baths	**18**	Small Northeastern Baths

7.12 Timgad: schematic plan of the original *colonia* with the forum presented in more detail. Note the small size of the temple; a *capitolium* was later built just outside the original *colonia*.

existence when the statues were erected and, notwithstanding their non-axial position within the forum and their interruption of the western portico, they may have been part of the original layout. Probably later, in the reign of Hadrian or Antoninus Pius, an aedicule (small shrine) of Fortuna Augusta was established next to the temple, which further disrupted movement along the western side of the forum. Further developments resulted in the blocking of the north-western entrance and encroachment on to the space behind the temple; again the date of these changes is unclear, but they must predate 238 because an inscription found there mentioning *Legio III Augusta* was mutilated following Gordian III's elevation to the throne.[74]

The forum of Timgad was primarily a location for public business associated with the *curia* and the basilica as well as being a place for the display of loyalty to Rome and for honouring the city's powerful and rich. The gods did appear in the forum to some extent but the whole area cannot be said to have been dominated by the small temple that occupied part of its western side or by the few peripheral statues to deities. A *capitolium* was not part of the complex, nor was one built at the time of the city's foundation; instead one was constructed outside the old town, at a considerable distance from the forum, in the second half of the second century.[75] The city's conception of the forum did not require a demonstration of loyalty to Rome in the form of the cult of the Capitoline Triad.

The forum complex at Thugga, with its surrounding piazzas and buildings, developed over the course of two hundred years and demonstrates an evolution in the way that the area was used over time (fig. 7.13). There was already an open space in the centre of the town bordered by monumental constructions, such as the monument of Masinissa, in the Numidian period; the structure of this site before the Imperial period is not, however, clear because of subsequent embellishment and the later creation of a Byzantine fortress over the forum which led to many monuments being despoiled for their masonry.[76] Thugga's form of administration is uncertain until the city became a *municipium* in 205. Prior to that a double community of a native *civitas* and a grouping of Roman citizens from Carthage (the *pagus*) lived side by side. The *civitas* had its own organisation and the citizens were governed from Carthage. Technically the citizens of Thugga should not have had their own *ordo* but one is mentioned as early as the reign of Claudius and there is some debate as to whether this is a later restoration. Notwithstanding their status the rich *pagani* of Thugga still paid for considerable construction at the city during the first and second centuries AD.[77] In the reign of Tiberius a 38.5×24-metre space was paved at

---

[74] *CIL* 8.2354. Ballu (1897), p. 149. *Legio III Augusta* was disbanded in 238 when Gordian III came to the throne in punishment for its role in suppressing the rebellion of Gordian I and Gordian II against Maximinus Thrax.

[75] Jouffroy (1986), p. 215.   [76] Saint-Amans (2004), pp. 44–9.

[77] See *AE* 1969–70, 653 ; Rives (1995), p. 105; Poinssot (1958), p. 10 ; Poinssot (1969), pp. 215–58.

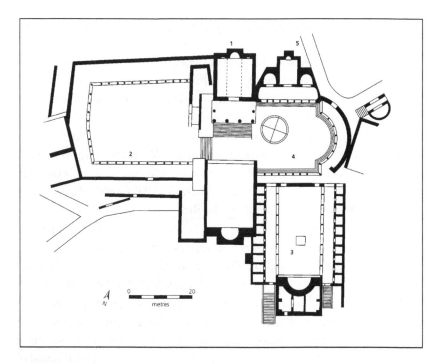

7.13 Thugga: plan of the forum: 1 = *capitolium*, 2 = forum, 3 = market/*exedra*, 4 = Place of the Wind-Rose and 5 = Temple of Mercury. At Thugga a series of interconnected plazas made up for the relatively small forum area. Other structures on the forum's west and north were dismantled when the area was incorporated into a Byzantine fortress and are therefore poorly understood.

the instigation of a citizen of Carthage who also erected religious structures including a shrine to Saturn.[78] In Claudius' reign a *macellum* was built close by, providing further space for business to take place. Almost one hundred years later, during the reign of Antoninus Pius, the porticoes of the forum were ornamented with columns and pools.[79] In the following reign the *capitolium* was constructed and Antoninus Pius' apotheosis was pictured on the pediment of the temple.[80] Although there was a clear desire to construct the *capitolium* next to the forum, it was not the priority of the community to have the temple open on to the plaza. Instead the side of the podium and *cella* dominated the eastern side of the forum. Access to the temple from the forum was via a staircase that turned through ninety degrees.

[78] *ILAfr.*, 558; see Rives (1995), p. 106.   [79] *ILAfr.*, 521.
[80] *CIL* 8.15513 and 26527; Barton (1982), pp. 316–17.

Capitolium not urgent in Africa

The forum itself was relatively small (38.5×24 metres) but the open space was supplemented, probably during the reign of Commodus, by the Place of the Wind-Rose, built to the east of the *capitolium* and contemporaneously with the construction of the Temple of Mercury to its immediate north.[81] The Place of the Wind-Rose provided a paved area in front of the *macellum* to the south and was a further venue for meetings. In doing so it enabled *tabernae* (shops/offices) to be set alongside the temples that surrounded the group of squares in the city centre. What the complex did not possess was a basilica, but, while it cannot be ruled out that one existed in the city, its absence chimes with the situation at Thuburbo Maius, which had a *curia* but again, apparently no basilica.

The forum and associated structures at Thugga did not offer a unified approach to the matrix of religious, business and judicial functions that characterised the 'ideal' forum. The shape of the central spaces was an *ad hoc*, non-uniform product of euergetism. During the Antonine period, when many other cities throughout Africa undertook large-scale work on their fora, the elite of Thugga created a series of interconnecting spaces that fulfilled the functions of more regular fora; but this was the culmination of a process that had taken over one hundred and fifty years.[82] This method of construction had the benefits of not over-taxing the finances of the city and the wealthy at any one time and of allowing the elite to demonstrate its wealth and status by gradually providing space for the community to meet, worship and conduct their business.

The evolution of the fora in the African provinces continued well into the third century, if anything on a larger scale than before. In certain cases the complexes that resulted dwarfed the old civic centres of the first and second centuries AD. This was obviously the case for the Severan forum at Lepcis Magna, but this was a special case of imperial sponsorship and should not be taken as indicative of the African conception of the forum/basilica complex in the Severan era (fig. 5.4). Nonetheless, the absence of a *capitolium* in either the city's old forum or in the new Severan forum underlines the fact that we should not necessarily expect to find a *capitolium* in the forum, or indeed at all. Instead, the new piazza at Lepcis was dominated by a huge temple, possibly connected with the cult of the emperors and often referred to as the Temple of the Severans, a constant reminder of the city's most famous family.[83] The Temple of the Severans could be thought of as taking the place of the *capitolium* at other cities; the *gens Septimiana*,

---

[81] *CIL* 8.26842 = *ILAfr.*, 516; Saint-Amans (2004), pp. 329–36.
[82] Duncan-Jones (1990), pp. 178–82.   [83] Ward-Perkins (1993), pp. 52–4; Wilson (2007), p. 299.

euergetistic providers of largesse to the city, were occupying the place of the Capitoline Triad. Perhaps it was the existence of a major temple linking a god or gods to the city that was the key aspect of forum construction in Africa; the exact nature of the deities involved was not crucial. Alternatively Lepcis may have been a special case; the old forum predated the city's incorporation into the Empire and its Temple of Rome and Augustus was sufficient to demonstrate loyalty.[84] The Severan Forum was also a special case, and a dynastic project need not have been constrained by the usual conceptions of the proper articulation of the relationship between religion and the city as expressed through the forum.

A series of other cities across the African provinces expanded or improved their fora under the Severans, and major works are attested from Thuburbo Maius, Iol Caesarea, Sbeitla and Uchi Maius.[85] Apart from the imperially sponsored creation at Lepcis, perhaps Djemila dem-onstrates the biggest transformation in its civic space. Djemila, founded under Trajan, had a forum by the reign of Hadrian (fig. 7.14).[86] It gained a *capitolium* by the middle of the second century, a market under Antoninus Pius, a basilica after 169 and a *curia* under the Antonines.[87] Clearly the old forum was unable to provide for all of the population's needs. The early third century saw a new, irregular but porticoed space created immediately outside the city walls (known as the Severan Forum even though it is unknown whether it was officially conceived as a forum).[88] In the third century this space did not usurp all the functions of the old forum, as a judicial basilica was not built there until the mid-fourth century. Considerable work was done, though, with the area being paved and porticoes erected. An arch was added in 216 and, as at Lepcis, a Temple of the Severans was constructed in 229.[89] In effect this became a transitional space between the old, walled, town and the expanding urban area along the city's spur to the south and the area of the theatre to the east. Increasingly it also became an arena for the display of the elite and the provision of facilities for the city's population.

The evolution of fora and their associated structures was a complex process in the cities of North Africa and occurred over three centuries, with the Antonine and Severan periods seeing the greatest expenditure on

---

[84] Di Vita (1982b), pp. 551–3.

[85] Thuburbo Maius – *ILAfr.*, 271; Iol Caesarea – Potter (1985), Potter (1995), pp. 32–4; Sbeitla – Duval (1982), pp. 612–13; Uchi Maius – *CIL* 8.26528.

[86] Février (1982), p. 353.

[87] Février (1982), p. 353; Février (1968), p. 40; *AE* 1916, 36; *CIL* 8.8318; Février (1968), p. 40.

[88] Février (1964), pp. 10–11.   [89] *AE* 1913, 120.

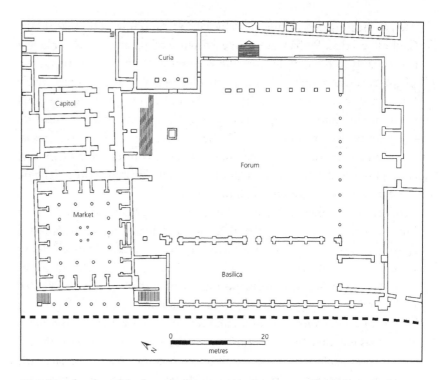

7.14 Djemila: plan of the forum and its associated structures. The laying out of the forum, the construction of the *capitolium* and the 'market of Cosinius' are all mid-second century, the *basilica Iulia* was built prior to AD 169.

and development of these complexes. In some cities the incorporation of earlier structures or open spaces could lead to irregular layouts (Thugga) or new plazas were formed to satisfy the inhabitants' desire for more impressive monumental spaces (Thugga, Lepcis, Bulla Regia). Even some purpose-built sites such as Djemila required a new space at a later date in order to improve the facilities. The basilica was a common factor in many, if not most, of these fora, and its absence in places may in fact be due to the failure of archaeologists to recover the structure or to transformations in urban topography in the Byzantine period. Although apparently not a constant, the *capitolium* was also common to most fora, with notably more being constructed in the Antonine and Severan periods than any other temple type. The developed African forum of the third century AD consisted of an open space surrounded by buildings that usually included a basilica, *curia* and *capitolium* and discharging the functions of justice, government, religion and the demonstration of loyalty to the Empire.

AN IMPERIAL SPACE

The origins of the forum as an architecturally defined, separate space can be traced back to the end of the second century BC, and it became a phenomenon that was to characterise all the cities of the Roman Empire. Into this space were placed the statues of magistrates, the elite or *euergetai* (benefactors) of the city who had held office and managed its affairs and even enhanced its urban life by holding banquets and games or constructing new buildings. Inscriptions and statues in the fora of Italy focussed on the elite and excluded foreigners, slaves and the ex-slaves who had become citizens, as well as the ordinary citizen.[90] We might conjecture that in the provinces the same process would have included the magistrates and ex-magistrates who had become Roman citizens and excluded all others as non-citizens. Statues were often placed in front of the columns of the colonnades to face on to the piazza area.[91] The internal space of the colonnades could have been used in a similar fashion as it suited the standing figure. Not surprisingly, the forum was the most desirable place for the erection of a statue of the emperor or other members of the imperial house and such statues gradually came to dominate it.[92] Indeed, statues of the emperors comprised up to sixty per cent of all statues known from the forum at Djemila and thirty-nine per cent of the statuary from the forum at Timgad.[93] Not only did the number of statues of the imperial family increase but their size and complexity also caused them to dominate the forum. For example, at Timgad the eastern side of the forum piazza is dominated by seven statue groups of the victorious emperor in a chariot or on a horse, which contrast with the standing statues of Timgad's notables on the northern side of the piazza.[94] Other imperial statues were placed directly in front of the *curia* on the western side of the forum. Both the *curia* and the basilica contained more imperial statues (no statues were dedicated to local notables in the basilica or *curia*). Not only were the emperors very prominent through the sheer number of statues dedicated to them, but their statues were also of a different type and on a grander scale than those set up to the local elite and were positioned in places of greater prominence. The survival of

---

[90] Mouritsen (2006).

[91] Zimmer (1989), p. 18 on Djemila, although this is not really the case for Timgad, his other case study. See also Trifiló (2008); Condron (1998) on Lepcis Magna and Chapter 5.

[92] Højte (2005), pp. 111–14.

[93] See Zimmer (1989) for a full study of both cities; also Witschel (1995).

[94] Zimmer (1989), p. 50.

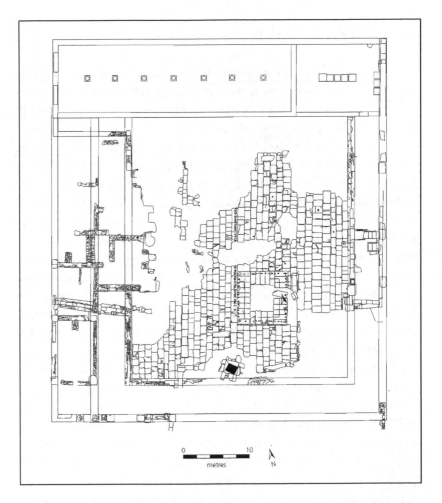

7.15 Segobriga: plan of excavated remains of the forum. The excavated pavement of the forum includes an inscription associated with a statue base at the centre of the paving. Note the statue bases in the room to the north-east of the paved area.

inscriptions in the fora of Lepcis, Djemila and Timgad is exceptional, but demonstrates the embellishment of these fora with statues of the rulers of the Empire.

The phenomenon was not unique to African cities. The forum at Segobriga, as it is currently known, displays traces of excavated inscriptions which offer an insight into the process of making a forum (fig. 7.15). The forum itself was paved by a Proculus Spantamicus, as recorded in an inscription set into the actual paving of the forum.[95] Parallels for this

[95] Abascal, Almagro-Gorbea and Cebrián (2002), pp. 158–9.

type of paving inscription can be found at Terracina and in the Forum Romanum in the capital. The paving of the forum points to the presence of a very large statue group at its centre, although the inscription and structure that lay immediately behind it are now lost.[96] Statues are known to have been set up to the imperial family, and specifically to Drusus and Germanicus, Tiberius' heirs.[97] However, it is the recent excavations from the eastern end of the northern colonnade that reveal the process of placing commemorative statuary within the colonnades during the first century AD.[98] The focus of the statue-group at the end of the colonnade was the altar dedicated to Augustus sometime between 2 BC and his death in AD 14, and around this altar fourteen honorific statues were established, with four others located at a greater distance. All the statues were set up by the *ordo* of the decurions and included three senators (of whom we know the names of two, Gaius Calvisius Sabinus, a legate and patron of the city, and M. Licinius Crassus Frugi, another patron) and an imperial scribe who was a patron of the city. Local officials were also commemorated, including magistrates who were also *flamines* (priests) of Augustus and a magistrate of the Lares Augustorum of Segobriga (there are also other statue bases, the details of which are difficult to determine). What is clear, however, is that the *ordo* of the decurions set out to provide an altar to a living emperor and to embellish the area around it with statues to local dignitaries and governors and other imperial officials who were designated patrons of the city. This patronage relationship connecting a city with a governor or legate of the province seems to have had its origins in the second century BC, but in Segobriga we find evidence for it as a continuing practice in the first century AD (see Chapter 11 for further discussion of this phenomenon).

There are further parallels elsewhere. The triumvirs settled the Seventh Legion in the colony of Béziers in 36–35 BC on what was an Iron Age *oppidum* located adjacent to the Via Domitia in Gallia Narbonensis. The statuary found in the forum reflects the town's triumviral/imperial origins.[99] Statues of Octavian/Augustus, Agrippa, Livia (wife of Augustus), Julia (the daughter of Augustus), Tiberius (adopted son of Augustus), Agrippa Postumus (the grandson of Augustus), Antonia (the sister-in-law of Tiberius), Drusus (the son of Tiberius) and Germanicus (the adopted son of Tiberius) were all found there. There is then a break in commemoration until the second century when we find a statue of

---

[96] Alföldy, Abascal and Cebrián (2003a) and (2003b).   [97] *CIL* 2.3103, 3104.

[98] The inscriptions are published in Alföldy, Abascal and Cebrián (2003a) and (2003b).

[99] Balty and Cazes (1995).

Antoninus Pius. The pattern suggests a short period of interest in the family of Augustus at the beginning of the first century AD which was not sustained. Unlike at Segobriga the focus was clearly upon the imperial family; inscriptions from the site commemorate decurions, magistrates, *augustales* and veterans, but the focus of the sculpture is on the imperial family descended from Augustus and Agrippa down to the Emperor Tiberius' two heirs who did not survive him, Drusus and Germanicus.[100] Gaius Caesar (grandson of Augustus) was also commemorated at Béziers as *princeps iuventutis* (prince of youth, *CIL* 12.4227). The statuary points to an enthusiasm for the family of Augustus and perhaps some form of imperial cult. Given the circumstances of the demise of Agrippa Postumus, it is notable that his statue at Béziers was simply not removed in response to political machinations at Rome. This indicates an intersection between the population at Béziers and the imperial court, but a relationship that was tenuous or only maintained at certain moments (manifested in erecting statues) during the early Imperial period. Some sixty-two Julio-Claudian statue groups can be found across the cities of the Roman West and were not confined to the towns that had a close relationship with Rome through their military origins. Ruscino (Perpignan), for example, in the Pyrenees boasted a forum with at least twenty statues dedicated to the imperial family. Nor was the forum the only place for the display of imperial statuary; Rose's 1997 catalogue reveals forty examples in the Roman West: seventeen in theatres, sixteen in the forum and basilica and seven in other locations. In particular the theatre, especially the *porticus post scaenam*, was an important location for commemorating the imperial family through statuary.[101]

The formal space found in the architecturally defined fora of northern Italy and Gaul did not influence the development of the cities of central Italy. Here the established fora might develop additional religious sites, such as at Pompeii, but for many cities the forum remained unaltered (e.g. at Alba Fucens). The pattern found at Pompeii is repeated in the newly founded Augustan city of Carsulae; the forum was composed of a central piazza around which were clustered temples, a basilica and other public buildings to create a unified space entered through arches by those travelling along the Via Flaminia.[102] In contrast, at Velleia a forum was built with

---

[100] *CIL* 12.4227–47; *AE* 1971. 246, 1977. 532, 1995.1076.

[101] Rose (1997), Rosso (2000). For a study of the distribution of statuary between public monuments at Sabratha and Lepcis Magna, see Condron (1998).

[102] Morigi (1997).

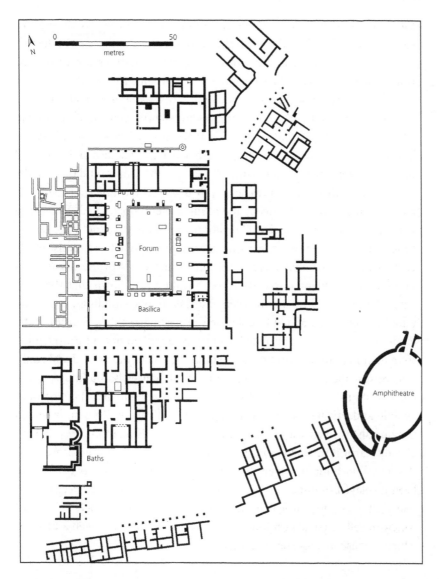

7.16 Velleia: plan of the excavated remains including the forum that has no temple and a relatively small paved area at its centre.

colonnades, shops and a basilica (fig. 7.16).[103] The entire structure seems to have been constructed around the need for a place for *negotium*. What is interesting about the example of Velleia and numerous other sites is that these spaces were marked off and had defined entrances, just as the final

[103] Criniti (2006), pp. 107–17.

forum at Pompeii could be entered by only six streets instead of the original eight and was closed to wheeled traffic. Like the new architecture of the fora in Gaul or northern Italy, the closure of space or marking it off from the rest of the city seems to have been the final stage in a process that began in the second century BC in the early colonies of Cosa and Alba Fucens.

The forum (and basilica complex) was an essential element of the Roman city and this is borne out by the fact that some towns are simply called 'Forum X or Y'. It was seen as the place in which the business of the city and its inhabitants took place and where the laws of the Empire and those of the city were on display for all to see, even if they could not read them. To facilitate this, covered porticoes and basilicas were constructed. The forum tended to be located in a central position within the street network, sometimes where there was an existing sacred place. What was consistently created was a space that was marked off from the rest of the city, so that on entering it inhabitants and visitors would have known that they had entered the core area of *negotium*. Further public buildings, including temples, were often added to enhance the existing facilities. Statues of the emperors gradually accumulated over time. Once laid out, a forum tended to remain in a similar form or shape until the end of our period and could only be reshaped through the enclosure of the space with buildings, porticoes or shops. The combination of architecture, statuary and *negotium* (public and private) created a space that was distinctly Roman, in which provincials as magistrates quite literally became Roman citizens, having already learnt Romanness in this arena of *negotium* as children. It was also the central location in which the majesty or *dignitas* of the city could have been displayed to outsiders (whether emperors, governors or beggars). In many cities the forum was located at a point through which or around which travellers passed on longer journeys, and may have been a place in which a pause in a journey was made.

> Within these premises of Aurelia Faustiniana is a bath; you can bathe here
> in the manner of the capital and every refinement (*humanitas*) is
> available.
>
> (Ficulea, Italy *CIL* 14.4015)

Bath-buildings are one of the commonest types of building in Roman cities,
more common indeed than all other classes of urban building apart from
houses. Furthermore, across the western provinces and North Africa they
are to be found in all sorts of settlements, be they forts, villas or lesser
towns; with the result that they are one of the most recognisable of Roman
building types and could be said to be as characteristic of Roman-style
living as any of the more famous markers of the Roman presence such as
forts, towns or villas. Their ubiquity and their presence at such a wide range
of places should make it clear that baths and bathing were intimately linked
to becoming and being Roman; by the same token, not to have baths or not
to have ready access to them suggests a level of disengagement from
Roman-style practices. Yet despite the importance of bathing proclaimed
by this ubiquity, bathhouses have until recently been rather the poor
relations of other building-types in the attention paid to them by modern
scholars. In part, this is probably because, at a very simple level bath-
buildings seem self-explanatory. From the simplest to the grandest, they
all display the same essential features. There was a suite of three rooms of
varying temperatures: the *frigidarium* (cold room), *tepidarium* (warm
room) and *caldarium* (hot room), the last two heated by underfloor
hypocausts and provided with basins for water to humidify the air. In
these the bather got progressively hotter so that the pores opened and the
sweat carried away dirt, and cleaning was aided by scraping the skin with a
curved *strigil* and by rubbing in oils. This would be all that the simplest type
of bath-suite – what the German tradition calls *Reihentyp* (row type) –
would provide for. Architecturally, baths could become more elaborate by
the addition of features such as a *laconicum* (hot, dry room), or separate
facilities for women (who otherwise would bathe at separate times), or
ancillary features such as latrines or a *palaestra* (exercise area). As we shall

see, however, investment in bath-buildings (and their associated features such as a water-supply and sewerage systems) could pass far beyond the relatively modest levels required simply for discharging the function of cleanliness. Some cities, such as Pompeii, had several sets of public baths (quite apart from the private ones attached to the residences of the grandest citizens). Imperial bath-buildings at Rome were amongst the largest structures in the Roman world and some leading western cities such as Carthage and Trier emulated these huge complexes; even lesser cities such as Paris possessed baths on a considerable scale.[1] Clearly bathhouses and what went on in them were much more important than simply their evident function of getting clean. It is recent research on why they were so important to citizens of the Roman Empire that has restored baths to their rightful place as carriers and expressions of Roman civilisation.[2] In order to understand the centrality of bathing to Roman lifestyles, we will trace the development of bath-buildings from the second century BC through to the middle of the third century AD. The trajectory of bathing and of the construction of bath-buildings is mapped first in Italy, with reference to epigraphy and the developments at a single site – Pompeii. The incorporation of bathing into the fledgling cities of Gaul, Spain, Britain and Germany is discussed before the focus shifts to the African provinces and a very different trajectory of development. What we shall see is that the bathhouse was produced as a new cultural form in the cities of Italy in the second century BC and became the hallmark of Roman urbanism at locations across Italy and the western Empire until, by the second century AD, it was impossible to imagine that anyone in the Empire did not bathe in a bathhouse.

By the middle of the second century AD, the Roman city was a place in which access to a bath-building and cleanliness was an essential feature. This was a defining feature of what it was to be Roman and had considerable importance for the definition of a place as a location of urban living. Even a small town or village near Rome would have its own bath-building; Pliny could point out that, if he did not wish to heat up the baths in his villa at Laurentum, he could always visit a neighbouring *vicus*.[3] The provision of baths for use by the owner's *familia* and dependents was a feature of many villas, although there were concerns that frequent bathing might sap the strength of the workforce. Baths are often found in auxiliary forts at the edge of Empire and some of the most substantial documentation of the workings of a bathhouse comes from the mining community in Vipasca.[4] If

---

[1] Nielsen (1990); DeLaine (1999b).　　[2] Yegül (1992); Fagan (1999).
[3] Plin. *Ep.* 2.17.　　[4] *CIL* 2.5.181.

we move back in time, this seemingly ubiquitous feature of Roman culture was rather less common. Aulus Gellius, writing in the second century AD, could recall a time in the second century BC when a consul had to requisition the men's baths at Teanum Sidicinum for his wife's bath;[5] Marcus Marius, the city's quaestor, had the baths cleared of male bathers, but the consul's wife complained of a delay and reported that the baths were dirty. There would not appear to have been suitable women's baths in which the consul's wife could bathe. The tale ends with the consul having Marcus Marius bound to a stake placed in the centre of the forum and then stripped naked and beaten with rods. The story highlights an expectation of suitable bathing facilities in cities and demonstrates that in the distant past not all cities in Italy possessed lavish bathing facilities that could be requisitioned for the exclusive use of a dignitary and his entourage.

There was a pride in the facilities on display in these structures. Advertisements for baths link the activity of bathing at Bologna or Ficulea in Italy or Lecourbe in Numidia with the culture or *humanitas* of the city of Rome. The text from Bologna states that: 'In the property of C. Legianus Verus is the bath; you can bathe there in the manner of the capital and every convenience is available', whereas that of Lecourbe in Numidia runs as follows: 'In the property of the Cominii, Monatanus, Felicianus Junior and their father Felicianus is the bath and all the *humanitas* of the capital is available'.[6] There is a degree of emulation that seeks to reproduce the bathing experience and culture of Rome. The advertisements were presumably aimed at those who had not experienced the facilities, including travellers – even from Rome – attracted to the familiar culture of bathing and the *humanitas* of Rome. To bathe in the advertised establishments was to engage in an activity, real or imagined, that was not only Roman but was to be found in Rome itself. Simply entering the building led you into a Roman space and moved your body into a new locale that was architecturally confined and was regarded as being closer to the heart of the Empire. However small a city or uninspiring an army camp might be, within the baths was an imagined world or community that linked an individual to others in bathhouses in the capital. In the fourth century, the exclusion of Christians from the act of bathing was regarded as an extreme or effective means of persecution; by not bathing the Christians were excluded from the civilised world.[7] The activity of bathing was a

---

[5] Gell. *NA* 10.3.3.
[6] *CIL* 11.721; *AE* 1933.49; for texts and literal translations see Fagan (1999), pp. 317–19.
[7] Libanius, *Orations* 2.305; see Robert (1943), p. 115.

communal one in which the status indicators of dress were shed; it took place in a specific space in which the body was shaped and groomed and from which stepped provincials whose appearance in terms of grooming, and also dress, identified them as fundamentally Roman.

THE TRAJECTORY OF BATH-DEVELOPMENT IN ITALY

Although it would appear that the baths were a defining feature of Roman urbanism by the second century AD, we need to remember that the oldest bath-buildings are to be located not in Rome but in Campania: the Stabian Baths in Pompeii dating back to the fourth or fifth century BC (fig. 8.1). Capua certainly had a *balneum* in the third century BC and Jouffroy can list evidence for baths at Aletrium, Cales, Capua, Cosa, Fondi, Pompeii and

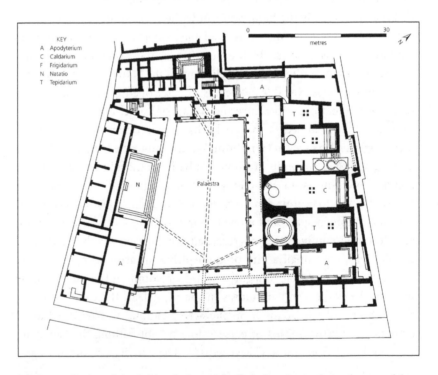

8.1 Pompeii: plan of the Stabian Baths; originally built prior to the settlement of the Roman colonists under Sulla, these were subject to adaptation and rebuilding prior to the destruction of Pompeii in AD 79. (The key also applies to all the following baths plans.)

Teanum Sidicinum in the second century BC.[8] The use of the men's baths at Teanum Sidicinum by a consul's wife illustrates the utility of the baths but may suggest that they were restricted to men at the settlement, or possibly that the women's baths of Teanum Sidicinum were insufficiently elaborate for the tastes of the consul's wife.[9] There is in fact something distinctively Italian as much as Roman about the origins of the baths and, unlike in the case of other buildings in the Roman city, there are four important chronological factors to bear in mind when examining baths:

(1) The action of bathing and its associated rituals became ever more elaborate and demanded buildings of greater utility, a consideration elaborated by Seneca in making a comparison between the baths of the second century BC and those of his own time in the first century AD.[10]

(2) There was a massive increase in the availability of the location of bathing in the cities of the Empire. This can be most graphically seen in relation to the city of Rome: in 33 BC there were 170 *balnea*, whereas in late antiquity there is a listing of 856 alongside ten or eleven *thermae*.[11]

(3) The style of bath-buildings was fundamentally altered by the development of hypocaust systems from about 100 BC, causing a change from individual bathing in tubs to the heating of larger pools and communal bathing.

(4) The style of bath-buildings was dramatically affected by the development and mass adoption of the use of glass during the first century AD.[12]

The city of Pompeii provides us with evidence for the chronological development of baths and bathing in a single urban context through to the destruction of the city in AD 79. What we see is the survival of some of the older establishments and their duplication by similar facilities throughout the first centuries BC and AD, which was perhaps indicative of an increase in the popularity of bathing or of a desire to create new baths that had different features – for example, that were lighter through the use of window-glass. Discussion will concentrate upon the larger structures in order to identify the changes that occurred across buildings of a similar size offering very similar facilities.

---

[8] Livy, 33.7.3; Jouffroy (1986), pp. 52–3; see also DeLaine (1999a).
[9] Gell. *NA* 10.3.3.   [10] Sen. *Ep.* 86.   [11] Yegül (1992), p. 30.
[12] See Broise (1991) on the glass revolution.

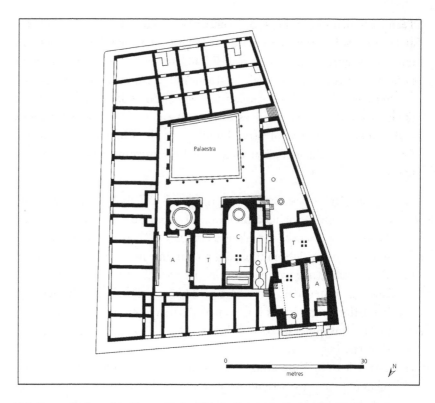

8.2 Pompeii: plan of the Forum Baths. This facility was built shortly after the settlement of the Sullan veterans.

Our earliest and best-preserved bath-building is that of the Stabian Baths, which originated in a series of hip-baths of the fourth or even fifth century BC (fig. 8.1). It is in the second century BC that we begin to see the classic pattern of a *palaestra* for exercise, a changing room, and heated rooms (*tepidarium* and *caldarium*). The building was substantially altered with the arrival of the Roman colonists and saw the addition of a *laconicum* (sweat room) and a *destrictarium* (a room for rubbing the body down after immersion or exercise). At about the same time the Forum Baths were constructed (fig. 8.2). Both these sets of baths had separate facilities for men and women. In terms of size, the buildings were comparable, but the size of the peristyle was considerably larger in the case of the earlier Stabian Baths (Table 8.1). Why the Forum Baths had a smaller peristyle has not to date been satisfactorily explained; we could simply argue that the size of the available plot to the north of the new *capitolium* limited the space available for a peristyle. Alternatively, we might wish to suggest that the person responsible for the construction of these new baths did not see a need for a larger

Table 8.1 Size of bath-buildings in Pompeii

Bath-building	Area of structures	Area including peristyle
Stabian baths	1050 sq. m.	3000 sq. m.
Forum baths	1000 sq. m.	1700 sq. m.
Central baths	1700 sq. m.	3500 sq. m.

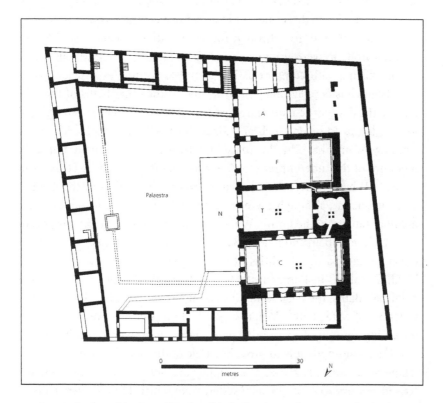

8.3 Pompeii: plan of the Central Baths. This facility was under construction at the time of the eruption of Vesuvius (AD 79).

peristyle, and this might reflect a less Hellenised view of how bathing should occur than that which produced the larger space for exercise in the Stabian Baths. The size of these structures was similar to that of other excavated bath-buildings found in Italy at Cales, Paestum, Velia, Teate Marrucinorum, Forum Sempronii, Faesulae, Ferentum and Florentia. They were, however, much larger than those found at Herculaneum and some other cities in Italy.

The third major baths, the Central Baths, were constructed with a large *palaestra* after the earthquake of AD 62 (fig. 8.3). The scale, size and design of these baths were new. The bath-block made no provision for segregated bathing and could be used for mixed bathing, or by men or women only at specific times. The complex was far from complete by AD 79, but exemplified the new technology of brick-faced concrete and large expanses of window glass facing the south and west. The presence of windows facing in this direction suggests that the main time of use was the afternoon, which may imply that the structure could not operate optimally in the morning. The structure was fitted into a single *insula*-block with some expansion into a side street (Vicolo di Tesmo) and located in a central position in the city at the intersection of two through-routes (Via di Stabia and Via di Nola); the Stabian Baths were also positioned on an intersection. It was also close to the existing bath complexes. The complete bathing experience would have been considerably different from that in the other baths of the city. During the day, particularly the afternoon, there would have been no need for the lamps found in such abundance in the Forum Baths. The large windows would have lit the spaces for bathers, in a manner found in literature of the time in praise of the lavish baths of Claudius Etruscus in Rome.[13] Whether there was the same level of decoration in the Central Baths is unclear, although there were certainly numerous niches built for holding statuary in the future. When compared to the ill-lit and lower roof spaces of the Stabian and Forum Baths, this new bath-complex would have outshone the existing facilities of the city. There were of course smaller bathing facilities in Pompeii: the Sarno Baths, the Republican Baths, the Suburban Baths, the Palaestra Baths and the Baths of Julia Felix, as well as Crassus' saltwater baths. What we see in Pompeii, however, is an ever-increasing amount of space in the city given over to bathing-facilities.

It is almost impossible to provide a scale of the costs involved in undertaking these works. However, the building of a *balneum* at Corfinum in the second century AD cost 352,000 sesterces, of which 152,000 were paid by the city.[14] Aulus Gellius records a scene in which Cornelius Fronto lay on his sick-bed surrounded by builders displaying plans of baths to him; he chose one and enquired about the cost, which was reported to be 300,000 sesterces, and a friend suggested adding a further 50,000 sesterces to the price.[15] This would have been in line with other figures for costs for the construction of baths found from Italy in the second century, although there is evidence for much higher costs of 2 million sesterces in one case, and much lower costs of 60,000 sesterces in another.[16] Whether repairs to

---

[13] Mart. *Ep.* 6.42; Stat. *Silv.* 1.5.   [14] *CIL* 9.3152.   [15] Gell. *NA* 19.10.
[16] Duncan-Jones (1982), p. 157 for the prices of these structures; Nielsen (1990), p. 121 argues that little can be concluded from these few examples.

older structures were less or more expensive is uncertain. The Baths of Clodius at Teanum Sidicinum were sold for the relatively low price of 60,000 sesterces.[17] These may have been rather dated or in a state of dereliction at the time of sale.

The building of new bathhouses within the cities of Italy appears to have been a feature of urban development. Seneca identified the novelties of such new establishments, which caused existing bath-buildings to be deserted.[18] Even given Seneca's moral tone, there seems to have been some truth behind this. We have already seen the revolutionary nature of the Pompeian Central Baths compared to the Stabian Baths. The light, airy spaces created would have provided a marked contrast to the low ceilings of the Stabian or Forum Baths. There was no provision for segregated bathing so that these new baths, although not dwarfing existing facilities, offered a very different bathing experience. If the baths were for men only or for segregated bathing according to a temporal arrangement, a much larger space was available to the communal bathers. Because the Central Baths were not completed prior to the eruption of Mount Vesuvius in AD 79, it is impossible to say whether the opening of the Baths would have caused some or all of the others to close. Contemporaries pointed to an almost insatiable demand for new facilities, and Pompeii's baths were mostly old.[19] Prior to this, there would not appear to have been any development of bathing facilities in the city that would have threatened the role of the Stabian and Forum Baths. Fagan has suggested that the Augustan develop-ment of the Stabian Baths put an end to the much smaller Republican Baths, in order to illustrate how the adaptation of existing facilities could prevent obsolescence.[20] However, the decision to replace the Republican Baths with an expanded area of housing may have resulted from other desires on the part of the owner. The bringing of water by aqueduct to the city may have enhanced existing facilities, but did not result in new bath-buildings being constructed. Competing with the Central Baths were those in the complex of Julia Felix named in the famous rental notice *Balneum Venerium et Nongentum.* Their location far from other competing facilities and close to the amphitheatre and *palaestra* may explain their success, rather than our having to assume a degree of luxuriousness on the part of the facilities themselves.[21] In short, if completed, the Central Baths would have changed the nature of bathing and it seems logical to suppose that some of the other major bathing facilities would have had to close or be redeveloped. It

---

[17] *CIL* 10.4792.   [18] Sen. *Ep.* 86.8–9.   [19] Plin. *HN* 33.153, 36.121, 36.189.
[20] Fagan (1999), p. 60.   [21] Cf. Fagan (1999), pp. 65–6.

is difficult to explain the proliferation of bathing facilities and the desire to build the monumental Central Baths in a town stricken by a recent earthquake. Over time bathing facilities were clearly provided in greater number and were more elaborate. This cannot be explained in terms of population growth, and we should resist explanations solely based on increased wealth and ostentation.[22] The cultural trend towards greater bathing facilities in the cities of Italy is just that, a fashion driving a change in the way urban life was experienced and expressed via the grooming of the body. What we see in Pompeii is the full development of this practice with its facilities over time.

By the end of the first century AD, bath-buildings were a facility expected to be found in any Roman city in Italy. It was, however, in the second century that the epigraphic record points to there being an increase in the construction of bath-buildings over all other urban types, and there was an increasing use of the term *thermae* in imitation of the magnificent bathing facilities provided in Rome by emperors from Titus through to Diocletian.[23] The cost of such structures was enormous. Pliny left 300,000 sesterces for the decoration of a set of baths at Como, but added a further 200,000 for running them;[24] whilst at Altinum a benefactor specifically made provision not just for their running costs – 400,000 sesterces – but also for their maintenance – 200,000 sesterces, having also provided 800,000 sesterces for their repair. However, there was a demand for bathing and also a desire to construct baths on the part of the elite. As we saw at Pompeii, bath-buildings were welcome additions at new locations across the city even if they duplicated existing features.

Looking beyond Pompeii, it is difficult to establish the overall trajectory of bath-building in Italy over a longer period or across numerous different cities. The erratic nature of the survival of inscriptions and the limits of excavation prevent a full account being given for every city. Hélène Jouffroy's tabulation derived from archaeological evidence, literary sources and epigraphy from Italy permits a comparison of the number of towns involved in the construction or repair of bath-buildings as opposed to amphitheatres (Table 8.2).[25] The latter were chosen because the games have been seen by historians as a location in which Romanness was displayed and defined.

The figures for amphitheatres give us a point of comparison. In no way should we see the numbers of either baths or amphitheatres as an exact

---

[22] Cf. Fagan (1999), pp. 78–84.   [23] Fagan (1999), pp. 134–5; Patterson (2006), pp. 151–4.
[24] *CIL* 5.5262; Brusin (1928), pp. 283–5; for other examples see Patterson (2006), pp. 156–8.
[25] Jouffroy (1986).

Table 8.2 Number of Italian towns involved in
building baths: amphitheatres

Period	Baths	Amphitheatres
Republic	18	8
First century AD	23	38
Second century AD	30	24
Third century AD	13	2
Fourth century AD	23	2

reflection of the numbers of baths or amphitheatres actually built. What we can adduce from the figures, however, is a marked decline in the construction or repair of amphitheatres. What is striking from these figures is the much higher emphasis on the building and maintenance of bath-buildings over time. Even in the third century, when relatively few building inscriptions survive from Italy, there are inscriptions referring to the maintenance and building of baths. The importance of amphitheatres for the definition of Romanness in the cities of Italy seems to decline or even disappear in the third and fourth centuries. In contrast, towns continued to maintain and even build bathing establishments throughout the third century AD. The language of the third-century inscriptions is that of restoration in most cases, but there are four examples of new bath-buildings at Verona, Paestum, Albenga and Lanuvium.[26] The increase in elaboration is also acknowledged in Septimius Severus' replacement of a *balneum* at Lanuvium with *thermae*.[27] The other acts of renewal were not undertaken by the emperor but were associated with patrons or curators of cities. The strength of the desire for new facilities may be ascribed to their function and use. Patterson argues that this was social, according to which the baths were seen as an environment for the demonstration of the local population's greatness and ability to dominate the environment by means of architecture.[28] At the same time, the shedding of clothes and bathing together emphasised a sense of community and provided a sensual environment, in which the body could be cleaned, groomed and massaged. Unlike other types of monument, the bath-building was not only used during the games or at festivals, but was a regular part of the temporal structure of urbanism.[29] The devotion of time to bathing was a sign of

---

[26] See Jouffroy (1986), pp. 149 and 165–7 for the relevant texts.
[27] *CIL* 14.2101.   [28] Patterson (2006), p. 160.   [29] See Laurence (2007), pp. 154–66.

civilisation and the more time spent the better. In addition, bathing was a feature of any health regimen and the heat of the baths was regarded as beneficial for adults.[30]

BATHS AND URBAN DEVELOPMENT IN SPAIN, GAUL, GERMANY AND BRITAIN

In the cities of the western provinces there seems to have been a direct link between urbanism or Romanness and bathing, and we might even say that bathing defined a person as Roman and urban. What is surprising is that Tacitus, in what we have already seen has become the classic passage for understanding the promotion of urbanism, does not include bath-buildings alongside the urban features promoted by Agricola – temples, fora and *domus* (houses), and reference is made to bath-buildings only at a subsequent stage in the Britons' adoption of Roman culture, when they are presented as an aspect of the process of their enslavement and of their indulgence in vices associated with these and other buildings and activities in the Roman city: *porticus et balnea et convivorum elegantiam* ('promenades, baths and elegant dining').[31] The logic of the passage is conventional in literature in associating temples, forum and houses with virtue but denouncing baths, *porticus* and extravagant dining as vice. We would argue that the elements presented in the passage should be treated as two sides of urban development that occurred at the same time, and would not follow Tacitus' reductive account of how the Britons were led into vice. The effect for Tacitus, however, was the creation of cities in Britain that held all the elements of Romanness, including vice. The sons of the British elite were made Roman not just by wearing the toga and learning rhetoric, but also by using the baths. Bathing transformed the body of the barbarian into one that was recognisably Roman, which could be dressed in a toga and speak Latin correctly – moreover its smell would have been transformed.[32] Access to baths in the cities of the Empire helped to establish a difference between the inhabitants of cities and the dirty rustics, who may have bathed irregularly. Galen evokes the ubiquity of bath-buildings across the Empire in his discussion of the bathing of infants written in the second century AD.[33] He cannot conceive of a person reading his work who did not have

---

[30] Bradley (2005); Harlow and Laurence (2008).   [31] Tac. *Agr.* 21; Plut. *Pyrrh.* 16.
[32] DeLaine (1999b), p. 13.   [33] Gal. *De Sanitate Tuenda* 1.9.

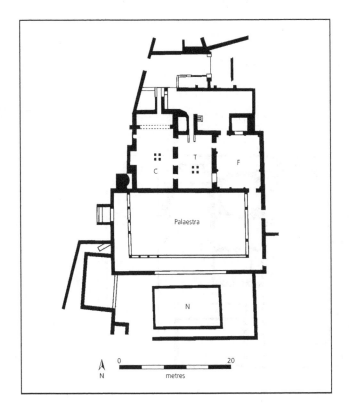

8.4 Glanum, a simple bath-building whose location next to the forum shows the importance of adopting Roman-style bathing even at an existing minor town of mixed Gallic and Greek antecedents and population.

access to a bath, for, as he says, he is 'writing not for Germans but for Greeks or for those who, though born barbarians by nature, yet emulate the culture of the Greeks'. The German barbarian bathed in a river, whereas the barbarian emulating the civilisation of the Mediterranean went to the baths; as Galen points out: 'ponds and rivers are to them as the bath is to us'.[34] Access to bathing was a distinguishing mark of civilisation and the Romans had caused the availability of bathing facilities to proliferate so that they were available to all Greeks, Romans and provincials residing in the Latin West.

Bath-buildings in the West display the familiar row of rooms of varying heat and would have been an increasingly familiar feature of the towns of the provinces. The earliest baths found to date are those at Glanum dated to about 40 BC (fig. 8.4).[35] The final form of the North Baths that succeeded

[34] Gal. *De Sanitate Tuenda* 1.9.   [35] Yegül (1992), p. 68; Congès (1992).

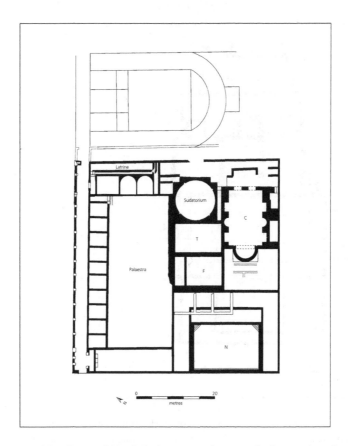

8.5 Saint-Bertrand North Baths: a second-century bath-complex of more ambitious plan and architectural forms supplementing the simpler, first-century Forum Baths, thus augmenting the number, scale and lavishness of the city's facilities.

an earlier set of baths at Saint-Bertrand-de-Comminges in the second century AD covered an area of 3240 square metres and may be seen as the provincial equivalent of the baths found at Pompeii (fig. 8.5). The basic pattern of a *frigidarium*, a *tepidarium*, a *caldarium* and a *natatio* within a *palaestra* appeared in the cities of the former barbarian provinces. Much effort has been spent in attempting to classify these buildings as architectural types, but most authors find that their architectural variation in plan form defeats the attempt to establish a typology.[36] Whatever their layout, however, bath-buildings in the provinces have a uniformity of function and spatial experience. A bath-building provided a Roman space in which to become clean. It was an expectation that every city or stopping-point on a

[36] Yegül (1992), pp. 68–78; Nielsen (1990), pp. 66–7.

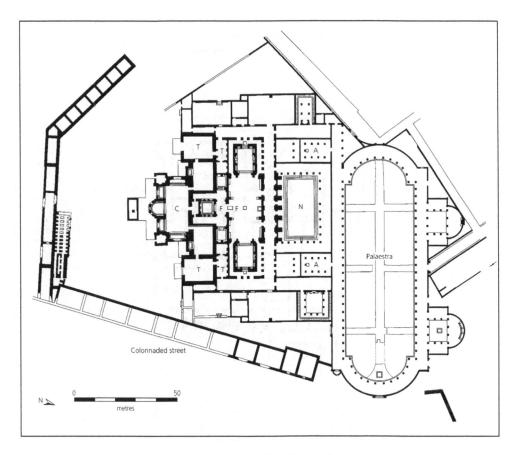

8.6 Lepcis Magna: the Hadrianic Baths. Inaugurated in AD 137, they were restored in AD 198–9 (*IRT* 396). A large *palaestra* surrounded by a colonnade lies to the north of the bath building, the *frigidarium* is at the centre with mirrored pools to east and west, to the south of the *frigidarium* is the *tepidarium* and then *caldarium*.

journey would make provision for the rituals of exercise, cleaning and massage that were characteristic of Roman culture. What varied was the size and splendour of the building. The largest by far were the vast *thermae* built in the major cities of the provinces: the Hadrianic Baths at Lepcis Magna (fig. 8.6; 5750 square metres excluding the *palaestra*) and the considerably larger Barbarathermen at Trier (fig. 8.7; 41,280 square metres including the *palaestra*) in the second century AD, which model themselves on the recently completed Baths of Trajan in Rome.[37] Other bath-buildings were ten times smaller than the North Baths at Saint-Bertrand, such

[37] Yegül (1992), pp. 186–92; Nielsen (1990), C79, C213.

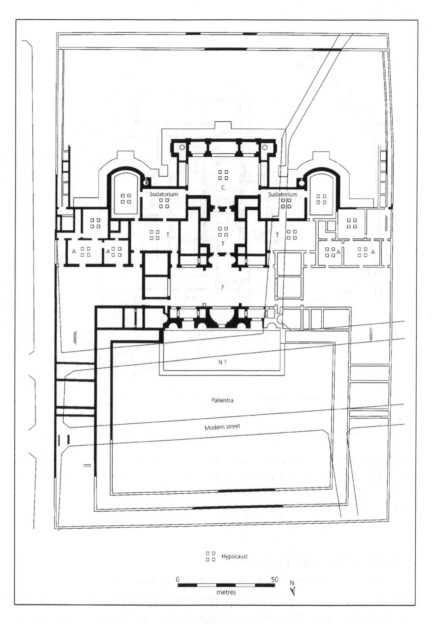

8.7 Trier 'Barbarathermen': a complex of 'imperial-plan' baths dating to the early second century, on a scale emulating those at Rome itself or at other major centres such as Carthage and thus expressive of the civic ambition of the Treveri.

as those found at Alesia or Iuliobona. Most bath-buildings were self-contained and covered a built area of less than 1500 square metres; what dramatically increased the size of the area encompassed by the structure was the addition of a *palaestra*. In the case of the North Baths at

Saint-Bertrand this increases the area covered by ninety per cent from 1700 to 3240 square metres.[38]

The evidence from these provinces indicates an increase in the avail-ability of bathing facilities and a demand for more elaborate facilities. The Augustan aqueduct at Conimbriga provided a regular water-supply for drinking, bathing and display at that centralised city.[39] Just as the forum displayed considerable change (see previous chapter), so too did the baths (fig. 8.8). The original Augustan bath-building with *caldarium, tepidarium, frigidarium, piscina, natatio* and *palaestra*, and covering an area of 1400 square metres, was replaced in the late first century or early second century with a much grander structure covering an area of 3500 square metres, which possessed facilities for indoor and outdoor bathing, a sweat room and a considerably larger *palaestra*. It was not only the scale of the building that was different. The structure followed or aped the design of the much larger imperial *thermae* in Rome (the Baths of Titus had an area of 14,000 square metres) or cities in northern Italy.[40] What is also clear is that property around the original Augustan baths was purchased for the expan-sion of bathing facilities, which permitted the construction of a larger symmetrical building on the original site. This suggests considerable cen-tralised control of the urban environment and the ability to gain access to the private property around the baths for the purpose of redevelopment. A structure on a similar scale to the later baths at Conimbriga is the Cluny Baths in Paris, firmly dated to the second century AD, which cover an area of 4490 square metres and have much in common with the architecture of *thermae* in Rome, as well as the rather earlier Forum Baths in Paris (fig. 8.9).[41] These were not just structures for bathing, but a means of distinguishing a city as having grander facilities than its neighbours – a fact emphasised by their exceptional size when compared to the majority of baths in the provinces, which covered less than half their area and employed architecture that facilitated the action of bathing but limited the space for display.

Looking across these four provinces, the vast majority of bath-buildings that can be dated were built in the late first and early second centuries AD.[42] The archaeological evidence coincides with Galen's expectation that all peoples should have access to bathing facilities, otherwise they were simply barbarians bathing in rivers.[43] The transformation from barbarian to

---

[38] The figures are from Nielsen (1990), C76.   [39] Alarcão and Etienne (1977), pp. 51–64.
[40] Alarcão and Etienne (1977), pp. 131–2: Nielsen (1990), p. 70.
[41] Nielsen (1990), p. 70.   [42] Nielsen (1990), pp. 65, 80.   [43] Gal. *De Sanitate Tuenda* 1.9.

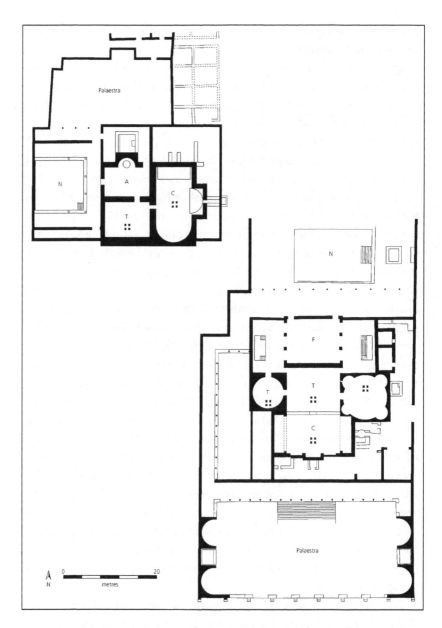

8.8 Conimbriga: upper figure shows the Augustan building; that was replaced by the much larger complex in the late first/early second century (lower figure).

Roman involved not just a change in lifestyle, but also considerable investment of resources in the building of the baths, the supply of water to them, ideally by an aqueduct, and the supply of wood for heating the building to a temperature that might be recognised by visitors as that of a *caldarium*. The

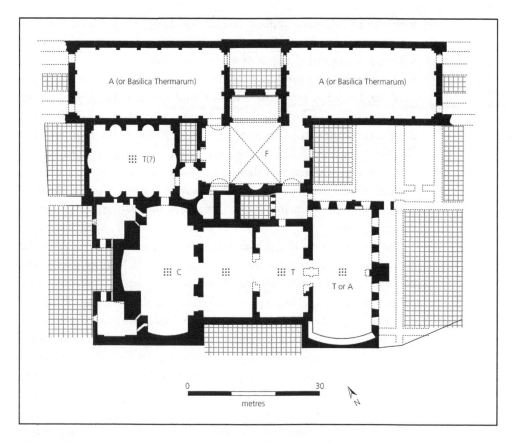

8.9 Paris Cluny baths: a large-scale baths of 'imperial' plan; one of at least three major bath-complexes at this otherwise unexceptional provincial city and, as at Trier, expressive of civic ambition (much of the fabric still stands).

latter is often given less attention than the actual process of construction, but its impact on the local economy and environment should not be underestimated.[44] The bathing process also involved an investment of time (a minimum of one hour),[45] and the presence of a *palaestra* points to the incorporation of exercise into the rituals of bathing. At the same time it may not be spurious to suggest that the presence of a *natatio* and *piscinae* looked back to a barbarian past of river-bathing (note that in Rome youths swam in the Tiber, so river-bathing was not a particularly un-Roman action).[46] Such continuity of tradition should not simply be rejected, since at Bath, for example, a temple and healing sanctuary were associated

[44] Blyth (1999) considers the costs.   [45] See Laurence (2007), pp. 158–9.
[46] See Arcellaschi (1996).

with warm water and a Roman-style bath-building. The iconography of the temple points to a continuing indigenous set of traditions being fused with a Roman architectural vision of space.[47] It would not be surprising if the adoption of bathing produced a similar hybrid of Roman and indigenous thinking. Indeed, some of the towns of Gaul appear to be little more than sanctuaries on to which have been added a grid of streets, baths and a theatre or theatre-amphitheatre, such as at Jublains discussed above in Chapter 6 (fig. 6.8).[48] The prominence of bath-buildings at sanctuaries in Gaul perhaps demonstrates the use of Roman architecture to accentuate traditional forms of worship.[49] At Sanxay, the conversion of a pair of temples into the principal baths underlines the association of bathing with the sacred.

The combination of sanctuaries and bathing appears alongside other architectural forms that we tend to associate with urbanism: for instance the *tabernae* and *porticus* dedicated by a *flamen* – priest – of Augustus at Néris.[50] Interestingly, some places referred to in the Peutinger Table with the prefix 'Aquae' display the epigraphy of religious worship and the use of Latin as a commemorative language, such as Aquae Neri or Aquae Sulis.[51] We should not just see bathing as a secular activity and Scheid argues forcefully for the role of bathing in rites of purification at Rome.[52] This reasoning runs counter to the assumption that baths in the Roman world were anything but religious, unless associated with a thermo-mineral spring.[53] On the whole, extra-mural sanctuary sites in Italy do not tend to be closely associated with bathing, even if few sanctuaries were located far from a city in which there was a bath-building.[54] Gaul, however, presents clear evidence for an association between bathing, as indicated by the construction of bath-buildings, and religion, as indicated by the presence of sanctuaries.[55] The link may be seen in the water sanctuary in Nîmes, dedicated to the spring god Nemausus, which was associated with baths and a theatre in its final form. Modern writers have been keen to see these associations as ones of medicine or healing, rather than religion *per se*; for instance, both Yegül and Nielsen are adamant in maintaining no

---

[47] Cunliffe and Davenport (1985); compare Van Andringa (2006) on Villards d'Héria.

[48] See Nielsen (1990), p. 14; Van Andringa (2002), p. 75; and papers in Naveau (1997) for Iron Age to Roman period continuities in the sanctuary.

[49] Van Andringa (2002), pp. 112–14; for other sites see Aupert (1991).   [50] *CIL* 13.1376–7.

[51] *CIL* 13.1370–88 compared to *RIB* 138–78.

[52] Scheid (1991); also Van Andringa (2002), pp. 113–14.   [53] Yegül (1992), p. 125.

[54] Coarelli (1987); papers in Quilici and Quilici Gigli (2003).

[55] Scheid (1991); see Perea Yébenas (1997) for soldiers and worship of Fortuna at the baths; see Sauer (1997) for the role of soldiers and civilians at sanctuaries.

connection with religion.[56] What the association with sanctuaries in the West suggests, however, is that the local population may have viewed the Roman practice of bathing rather differently from their rulers and could adapt Roman urbanism for their own purposes and uses.

BATHS AND URBAN DEVELOPMENT IN THE AFRICAN PROVINCES

By the fourth century AD, baths were one of the characteristic monuments of North African urbanism, with large-scale reconstruction and redecoration being one of the chief areas of public expenditure by the elite (Table 8.3). This was despite the relatively late beginnings of public bathing in the region. The main evidence for a pre-Roman bathing tradition comes from the frequently cited settlement at Kerkouane on the Cap Bon peninsula, where the courtyard-style houses of the third century BC contained hip baths in small rooms adjacent to the courtyards into which the used water could have been drained.[57] Punic private bathing does not really appear to have developed into a public bathing tradition before the Imperial period despite substantial trade with the Campanian region from the end of third century BC and strong connections with the rest of the Hellenistic world.[58] The epigraphic evidence collated by Jouffroy demonstrates that it was not until the first century AD that African baths began to appear; only three sets of baths are known to have been constructed by the end of that century.[59]

Given the wealth of the province of Africa in the Republican period and the early connections with Campania, the absence of baths in the epigraphic and archaeological record is surprising. This can partly be attributed to the fact that large stretches of North Africa were not occupied until late in the first century BC, following the defeat of Pompey, or during the first century AD, with the gradual push south-westwards into the Aurès mountains and the annexation of Mauretania; but within Africa Proconsularis it could partly be attributed to issues of preservation.

---

[56] Yegül (1992), pp. 92–127; Nielsen (1990), p. 146; Fagan does not refer to religion in his book on bathing (1999).

[57] Fantar (1987), pp. 100–1. One house seems to have two of these baths. There is also evidence of washrooms in buildings at Carthage during the second century BC – Thébert (2003), pp. 62–5.

[58] Lancel (1995), p. 283. There is some evidence for 'public baths' at Kerkouane, or at least buildings with hydraulic features, but evidence for their use and nature is fairly slim – Thébert (2003), pp. 57–8.

[59] Jouffroy (1986), pp. 193–5, 227–9, 272–6, 305–9.

Those regions of North Africa that came earliest under Roman sway are precisely those areas that have been continuously occupied since antiquity and where earlier baths are also more likely to have been replaced by later, more fashionable constructions. However, the tiny number of constructions up until the end of the first century AD is striking, and preservation is unlikely to be the key factor; rather the lack of first-century construction can be associated with the relative dearth of North African amphitheatres in the period. The African elite and populace appear not to have fully bought into the idea of expressing loyalty to Rome, or their cultural sophistication, through such buildings until the second century.

Nevertheless, once North Africans started to build baths they quickly became one of the key monuments of the Roman African urban landscape. While most of the largest North African baths, including the massive Antonine Baths at Carthage,[60] were built by the mid-second century, more towns were involved with building baths in the third and fourth centuries than in the second. However, much of the work in the later Empire involved reconstruction or redecoration rather than new building; even then there were notable exceptions, as the large (3300 square metres) 'Unfinished' Baths at Lepcis demonstrate.[61] Baths had an enduring popularity with the populace of North Africa throughout the Roman period in a way that was apparently not the case for other 'Roman' constructions. The importance of the bath complexes is also demonstrated by the way in which many were repeatedly redeveloped, rebuilt and redecorated throughout their extensive histories. For instance at Thuburbo Maius, the Baths of the Labyrinth, the Summer Baths and the Winter Baths, which were constructed around the beginning of the third century, were repeatedly reconstructed and redecorated into the late fourth/early fifth century (fig. 8.10).[62] The multiple phases of redecoration in the African examples reveal a continuing and ongoing concern among the elite to keep the structures up-to-date and fashionable. Some civic pride, even into the late fourth century, was obviously tied up in the maintenance and improvement of bathhouses.

The comparison of amphitheatres and baths (Table 8.3) is again revealing about attitudes to these two expressions of Roman culture in North Africa. Initially the amphitheatre appears to have been regarded as a more important indicator of a city's 'Roman' character than baths, despite the

---

[60] *CIL* 8.12513; Lézine (1968), pp. 1–78; Thébert (2003), pp. 141–3.   [61] Goodchild (1965).
[62] *ILAfr.* 273b; *ILAfr.* 285; *ILAfr.* 276. Ben Abed-Ben Khader et al. (1985), pp. 4–7, 61, 66; Alexander et al. (1980), p. 23.

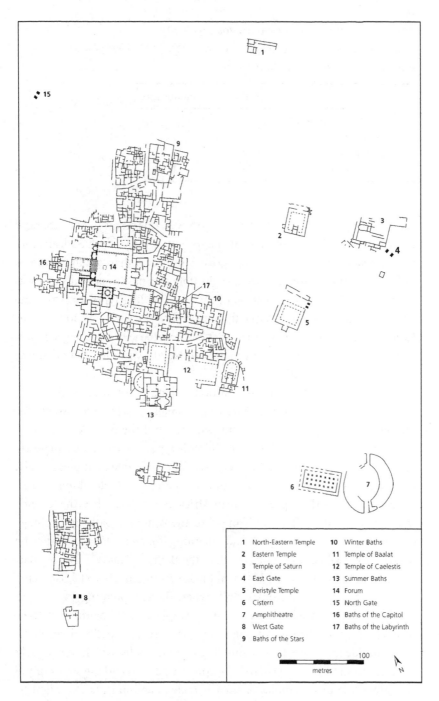

1	North-Eastern Temple	10	Winter Baths
2	Eastern Temple	11	Temple of Baalat
3	Temple of Saturn	12	Temple of Caelestis
4	East Gate	13	Summer Baths
5	Peristyle Temple	14	Forum
6	Cistern	15	North Gate
7	Amphitheatre	16	Baths of the Capitol
8	West Gate	17	Baths of the Labyrinth
9	Baths of the Stars		

8.10 Thuburbo Maius: plan of the city showing the position of baths in relation to other monuments within the excavated areas.

Table 8.3 Number of African towns involved in building baths:amphitheatres (Jouffroy's 1986 tabulation for North Africa patterns)

Period	Baths	Amphitheatres
To end of First century AD	3	7
Second century AD	22	9
Third century AD	27	5
Fourth century AD	24	2

relative inexpensiveness of the latter. However, this seems to have changed more dramatically than in Italy. By the second century North African cities were constructing baths in much greater numbers than amphitheatres – indeed the ratio is over 2:1, whereas in Italy during this period there was almost parity in the construction of the two building-types. In Africa the baths:amphitheatre ratio markedly increases in the third and fourth centuries. Over the long term it seems that baths were viewed as being a crucial expression of Romanness and urbanity in North Africa in a way that was not the case for amphitheatres.

There is some indication of evolution in bath-types in the region. The few baths of the first century AD were fairly small and simple constructions. However, from early in the second century until the fifth, African cities built and maintained the full range of bath-types. Given that by the early second century there were many very large and elaborate examples in Italy, it should not be a surprise that from this period, fully developed, large, 'Imperial'-type baths appear in North Africa. Examples such as the second-century Large North Baths at Timgad or the Antonine Baths in Carthage demonstrate an architectural and planning formula derived from the Roman Imperial bath-buildings such as the Baths of Trajan.[63] The regular, symmetrical layout of these baths and many of the smaller establishments in Africa clearly evoke Roman archetypes, thereby pointing to a desire among the African elites to echo the exemplars of Romanness in their own cities as statements of their high culture and political loyalties. Set alongside these very large symmetrical public baths, which were clearly designed to show off the generosity of private patrons and the status of the city, are numerous examples of smaller-scale establishments that attest to the burgeoning demand for bathing establishments by the population of

---

[63] Ballu (1903), pp. 38–48.

the cities. Whereas monumentality and status were key aspects of the other constructions, some baths could escape this pressure and concentrate on fulfilling practical and social needs.

The archetypal example of the North African passion for bath-building is Timgad. The city provides a considerable proportion of the known baths from Numidia because of the comprehensive nature of the clearance at the end of the nineteenth and beginning of the twentieth centuries of a site abandoned since antiquity. The veteran colony, *Colonia Marciana Traiana Thamugadi*, established by Trajan in AD 100, had at least thirteen sets of baths ranging in date from the second century (Large East Baths, Large South Baths) to a 'very late' period (Small North-Eastern Baths, Small Eastern Baths), whilst others are unlikely to predate the late third century (Small Central Baths, Baths of the Capitol, Small Southern Baths).[64] Given the size of the city this is a vast number and, although the state of the excavations makes it difficult to assess how many of these were operational at any one time, several large baths were in use in the city during the second and third centuries.

Why did Timgad in particular, and Africa more generally, have so many baths? Fentress has suggested that the vast number of inscriptions at Timgad is part of a demonstration of the Romanness of the veteran population and its descendants in the face of their position on the border of the Roman world.[65] The expression of a Latin, Roman culture may also have been emphasised by the repeated construction of an archetypal representation of Romanness by the Thamugadian population. As has been discussed above, bathing was a Roman, civilised form of behaviour and as such could be used to distinguish the inhabitants of a veteran colony from the tribes of the Aurès Mountains just to the south of the city. On the edge of the Empire the invocation of the concept of urban living could be seen as all the more powerful. This is unlikely to have been the motivation behind bath construction throughout North Africa. Cities on the Mediterranean coast cannot, in the second and third centuries at least, have been building baths to demonstrate the opposition and superiority of their society to that beyond the southern frontiers. The proximity of Italy, and the examples at Rome, showed the populace how to express their Romanness, while the wealth of Africa throughout the Roman period undoubtedly allowed them to indulge in this expression on a large scale.

---

[64] Ballu (1903), p. 53; Ballu (1911), p. 111; Germain (1973), pp. 54, 120, 137.
[65] Fentress (1984).

The vast amounts of water that were consumed by the baths and the expense required to provide it would also have been more impressive in the heat of a North African summer than in the midst of a winter on the Rhine where the provision of water could be assumed. The conspicuous consumption of water in the baths during the summer, while wadis dried up, was a potent demonstration of the wealth and power of those that constructed them, whether individuals or a community, and of the mastery of an expressly Roman civilisation over the vagaries of the natural world. In North Africa, with tribal communities to the south and harsh environmental conditions in summer, baths were a demonstration of the elites' determination to emphasise their Romanness and urbanity in the face of natural and human forces that were their antithesis.

CONCLUSION: URBAN LIFE AND BATHING

The construction or restoration of bath-buildings across the Empire was part of a continuous process of renewal of the urban infrastructure. Once a bath-building had been constructed, it needed to be maintained or embellished in line with contemporary bathing trends. This can be illustrated by Fagan's statistical study of Latin inscriptions from the West (excluding Britain) referring to the building, restoration or embellishment of bath-buildings (Table 8.4).[66] The chronological range of the 120 inscriptions referring to the construction of new bath-buildings makes for interesting reading. Given the general pattern of Latin inscriptions, the increase in the figure for the second century AD is remarkable and different to what one would expect (*c.* 15–16%).[67] This needs further explanation, which can only be provided once the figures are broken down regionally.

The inscriptions show that in the second century AD there was an expansion in benefactions within Italy and at the same time a peak in the recording of bath benefactions across the provinces of the West. This implies both growth in the number of bath-buildings within cities and an expansion of bathing facilities. The pattern derived from this relatively small number of inscriptions is of course distorted by differences in the ancients' regional taste for setting up inscriptions and their survival into modern times. However, there is a very distinctive shape to this evidence

---

[66] Fagan (1999), pp. 128–35.   [67] See Fagan (1999), p. 135 chart 2.

Table 8.4 Bathing benefactions in Latin
inscriptions (not including Rome) – figures from
Fagan 1999

Date range	Percentage
Second century BC – AD 14	9.2
AD 14–98	10.8
AD 98–192	26.7
AD 192–284	19.2
AD 284–392	30.8
AD 392–500	3.3

that can provide us with an understanding of the chronology of the proliferation of bathing facilities within Italy and across the West. These figures also confirm those referred to earlier, which were derived from Jouffroy's more comprehensive study of the total amount of evidence for the construction, restoration and embellishment of bath-buildings offered by the archaeological, epigraphic and literary sources within Italy and Africa. Interestingly, in Africa more bath-buildings are found in inscriptions in the third century than in the second century, whereas the reverse is the case for Italy. Looking at the admittedly limited data from Gaul, we can identify a distinct peak in the second century, the period in which monumentalisation attained its greatest extent in the cities of Gaul. The figures for Spain reflect a longer period of urbanisation at a select number of sites. For Germany and Britain, we simply do not have sufficient data from epigraphy to draw conclusions, although the archaeological dating would fit the picture from Gaul. The overall pattern, however, points to a continuing focus on the establishment of bathing facilities as the key feature of urban life across the cities in the West – a contrast to the general decline in the building of other monument-types over the third century.

Bathing was a feature of Roman urbanism and was an expectation of travellers to cities across the Empire. The prominence of bath-buildings in the urban landscape had not, however, always been as strong as it was in the second century AD. The factor of change needs to be remembered, and perhaps we should reframe the simplicity of an increasing number of bath buildings both within, and across, sites. Roman urbanism as a phenomenon produced a culture of bathing. The very presence or continued existence of a town led to the building of new or additional baths and/or the repair of existing bathhouses. Not only was the bathhouse an indicator of *civilitas*, it was the product of the Roman city. You could not have urbanism without the bathhouse, just as the bathhouse could not exist without urbanism. This chicken-and-egg situation points to the importance of bathing as a cultural phenomenon of urban societies across the Empire, and indeed one which was sustained into late antiquity. To have a city without a bathhouse was impossible whereas it was possible to have a city without a theatre or an amphitheatre – the subjects of the next two chapters.

9 | Assembling the city 3: theatres and sacred space

The theatre as an element of urbanism has its origins in the Greek cities of the fifth century BC and was to become an important feature of the cities of Campania and other parts of central Italy by the end of the second century BC. Combined with the fact that the first stone theatre, that of Pompey, was not built in Rome till the 50s BC and was followed by the construction of two further stone theatres, those of Marcellus and Balbus, by the close of the first century BC, this might suggest that the theatre was a building that was not characteristic of the Roman city. Indeed, the theatre does not seem to have become an essential urban element in the cities of Roman Spain or Britain. Yet, in Italy, North Africa and Gaul, the theatre was a feature of the urban landscape and one recognised by Vitruvius as a structure to be erected in the cities of the empire of Augustus. In Chapter 7 we examined the link between the forum and basilica complexes, which are prominent in Vitruvius' text, and their civic and religious functions in the political landscape of the Roman city. That space was shown to be part of the urban formation that created a sense of urbanness that was reproduced across the Roman Empire in the West. The forum was a sacred space, but there were others in the city too. Traditional approaches and ideas as to how to understand or approach theatres and their part in the creation of sacred space and the performance of the sacred in the Roman city have been subject to revision, with new viewpoints emerging.[1] Traditionally, the theatres of the Roman city have been treated separately from the temples. The reason for doing so was probably that today we see the events of the theatre as outside the realm of the sacred and located in what we might call leisure (source-books such as Cooley and Cooley's *Pompeii: A Sourcebook* maintain this division).[2] Vitruvius too separates the discussion of theatres from temples, although he does address the problem of how to locate the sacred space of the city built on a green-field site and links the theatres to religious festivals, but his view was probably only one of many discordant voices in antiquity and his apparent canonical authority may just be a result

---

[1] E.g. Derks (1998); Coarelli (2001).   [2] Cooley and Cooley (2004).   231

Vitruvius where gods should be located

of textual survival.[3] For Vitruvius the gods who protected the city, Jupiter, Juno and Minerva, were to be placed at a high point overlooking the walls. Mercury was to be placed in the forum or in the *emporium* with Isis and Serapis. Apollo and Bacchus were to be near the theatre and Hercules was to be located near the gymnasium, the amphitheatre or the circus. Mars was to be placed outside the walls in the *campus* (field of assembly) and Venus was to be close to the port. He then amends the list according to the thinking of the Etruscan *haruspices*, diviners without whom no Roman magistrate would have operated: Venus, Vulcan and Mars were to be outside the city, alongside Ceres, to free it from adultery, fire and conflict. Vitruvius does provide a connection between the space for the temples of Apollo, Bacchus and Hercules and the theatres and gymnasium of the city, but he does not address these buildings until much later in his treatise.[4] Moreover, the siting of the theatre is related only to the health of the person sitting in the *cavea* (auditorium), 'motionless with pleasure [they] have their pores opened' to every breath of wind from marshy areas.[5] Here we see again Vitruvius taking apart the city and leaving aside a sense of urban effect or composition which is achieved by considering the overall placement of structures in relation to one another.[6] The text conjures up a segmented city that does not have that overall conception of space that can be perceived when examining the archaeological evidence of Roman towns.[7] Recently, scholars have begun to view the theatre as a place in which 'a ritual projection' of the cult of neighbouring temples could be viewed or articulated in performance, and hence an effective discussion of sacred space needs to include both temples and theatres.[8] Other features of the city could be integrated with these structures; with Vitruvius we might add the *porticus* behind the theatre, which occurs in the Theatre of Pompey,[9] the *palaestra* and the baths.

In evaluating theatres and their role in the sacred space of the city we need to explore the relationship between performance in the theatres and worship at the temples. Moreover, we need to place the individual into this sacred space and to begin to understand how the use and meaning of the sacred was related to a sense of urbanness and was passed on from generation to generation. This chapter will examine how the temples, in conjunction with theatres and other public buildings, were used to hone citizens personifying the values of urbanness in a city. Some of these would

---

[3] Vitr. *De arch.* 1.7.1.   [4] Vitr. *De arch.* 5.10–11.   [5] Vitr. *De arch.* 5.3.1.
[6] Lefebvre (1991), pp. 271–2.   [7] Gargola (1995); Tilley (1994).   [8] Coarelli (2002), p. 84.
[9] Vitr. *De arch.* 5.9.

have been born into the urban environment of a city in Italy, after generations of urban life, others were migrants or veterans setting up a city and intending to create new citizens in the next generation, while yet others were first- or second-generation 'Romanised-barbarians' constructing urban life in recently conquered provinces.

THE ITALIAN TRADITION

Numerous rural sanctuaries with close relations to their neighbouring cities can be found across Italy.[10] The role of the sanctuary in the formation of cities is a subject that remains open to debate. The site of Pietrabbondante provides evidence for a sanctuary with a theatre that appears to have been the impetus for the formation of the city, or at least some form of proto-urbanism (fig. 9.1). The monumental structure that combines the sophistication of a theatre with an Ionic temple with places for three deities in the *cella* (the main room containing the statues of deity/deities) was constructed prior to the first century BC, but was short-lived and fell into disrepair in the Augustan period.[11] In its monumental centre, inscriptions in Oscan were found which refer to elected magistrates and other features that we tend to associate with a city. What seems to have happened in Pietrabbondante is that urbanism was not sustained, unlike at Iuvanum where an Augustan forum/basilica complex was added to an existing sanctuary.[12] This suggests that some sacred sites or sanctuaries, where urbanism appears to have been developing in the second or early first century BC, may not have been able to sustain that urban development over a longer period.[13] In any case, by far the largest sanctuaries with theatre complexes attached to them are found in cities: the famous sanctuary of Fortuna at Palestrina or the sanctuary of Hercules at Tivoli.[14] Strangely, at Rome the building of a permanent theatre was resisted even though a theatre was a required feature at the festivals of the gods.

The sanctuary of Juno at Gabii is a classic example of a temple with a theatre (fig. 9.2). It was located outside the town itself on an outcrop of tufa adjacent to the Via Praenestina. Like many sanctuaries it was situated close to water, Lake Gabinus. The temple was constructed in the second century BC on a site that was already apparently of great antiquity as a sacred place

[10] See for example: Coarelli (1987); Quilici and Quilici Gigli (2003).
[11] Coarelli and La Regina (1993), pp. 231–57.   [12] Coarelli and La Regina (1993), pp. 313–16.
[13] See Bradley (2000), pp. 171–8, 227–9.   [14] Coarelli (1987), (1989a), (1989b).

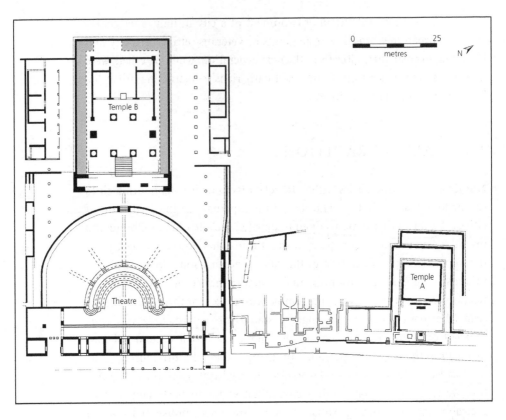

9.1 Pietrabbondante: plan of the sanctuary. Note the incorporation of a small theatre between the street and the temple itself.

and probably survived into late antiquity as a stopping-place for travellers. The arrangement and form of the temple is particularly telling. To the front of the rock-cut platform on which the temple itself is built, within a colonnade, there is a small theatre. We may assume that some form of retelling of myths was included within the worship of Juno. This relationship between the ritual performance of a place's myths within a theatre and the worship of gods in temples was a key feature of the Roman city, not just in Italy but also in the Three Gauls and other provinces of the Roman Empire. Moving on from the theatre towards the temple itself, visitors would have noted the trees to the side and rear of the structure that created an illusion that the massive architectural structure was set amongst a grove of trees. These had been deliberately planted in pits cut into the underlying rock. Towering above the grove and portico was the temple, raised on a podium and accessed via a set of steps.[15] By the Augustan period, however,

[15] Coarelli (1987), pp. 11–22.

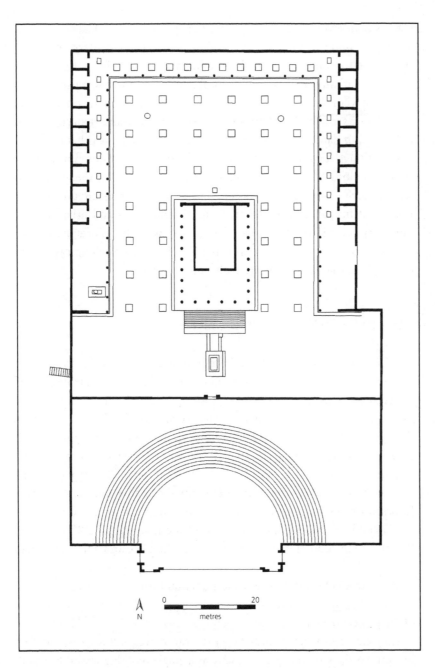

9.2 Gabii: plan of the sanctuary. Note the square pits cut into bedrock for planting of trees around the temple itself, causing the temple to be framed by trees and to create a wooded area to the sides and rear of the temple.

Gabii was in severe decline and referred to by Dionysius of Halicarnassus as a village as opposed to a *polis* (city) of the past.[16] The sanctuary set up over two centuries earlier continued to be maintained but did not manage to sustain an urban population in its locality because it was so close to Rome (nineteen kilometres) and consequently the population had looked to the capital for its urban life. It continued to exist within a suburban context. As at Pietrabbondante, the sanctuary alone did not sustain the urbanism of the past, although it continued to be a focus for travellers – Dionysius refers to inns being located close to the road alongside the ruins of the former city with its crumbling circuit walls.[17] The example of Gabii provides an important insight into the relationship of sanctuaries and urbanism: the sanctuary helped to sustain urbanism and was itself a focus of activity, but it did not alone constitute Roman urbanism. It is also a telling case of the effect of external factors on the evolution of a city.

THE BUILDING OF THEATRES

The Greek tradition of theatre building was present in southern Italy from the fifth century BC, but it was only in the second century BC that we begin to see the appearance of theatres in Campania and Samnium or in the sanctuaries of Tivoli and Palestrina. The explanation for theatre building in the towns of Campania and Samnium should not be sought in their proximity to Magna Graecia, since three centuries separated the appearance of the theatre in southern Italy and its adoption in Campania. Instead, we need to look at the connections between Campania and the Aegean, as focussed on the harbour of Puteoli. Roman imperial expansion into the Aegean and Asia Minor during the second and first centuries BC paralleled the gradual introduction of the stone theatre, first to Campania and then to Rome itself.[18]

The introduction of this new monumental form was far from straightforward. At Capua, contracts were let each year for the building of a section of the project over a period of sixteen years from 108–94 BC.[19] Each year a section was constructed and the next year it was followed by another section. So the structure we see today as a single building was in fact built in sections and construction of the building could be broken down into

---

[16] Dion. Hal. *Ant. Rom.* 4.53; Frayn (1993), p. 26.   [17] Dion. Hal. *Ant. Rom.* 4.53.
[18] Sear (2006), pp. 48–53.
[19] Frederiksen (1984), pp. 6, 8, 10, 11, 15, 16, 17; Sear (2006), pp. 11–12.

individual elements. At Pompeii, the Holconii specified that they had built a *cryptam* (substructure), *tribunalia* (privileged seating area) and *theatrum* – the last of these is considered by Sear to refer to the seating rather than the whole structure.[20] We can well imagine the construction site at Capua with money being spent on the *cavea* and more needed to erect the stage-building (*scaenae frons*) behind the *scaena* (stage). Once construction was complete, the theatre continued to require finance. Like the forum, it became a place where sculpture was added on a regular basis.[21] Moreover, a theatre once built did not simply last forever. Sear argues that the structure would need to have been rebuilt within one hundred and fifty to two hundred years of construction and a *cavea* built against a hillside would have been prone to slippage.[22] For example, by the Augustan period the second-century BC *cavea* of the large theatre in Pompeii had become unstable and needed rebuilding.[23] As Sear has shown, the theatre soaked up money not just in its construction costs, but also in repairs and the need for constant attention to the fabric of the building.[24] This may also have been true of other monuments in the city which have not been subject to Sear's delightful investigations into monumental collapse. Certainly there is plenty of epigraphic evidence for the need to repair structures in the Roman city, as already discussed in Chapter 8.[25]

What is clear from the chronology of constructing theatres in Italy in the second and first centuries BC is that by the time of the first emperors these innovative structures would have been in need of repair, or else risked falling out of use like the sanctuary at Pietrabbondante. An impetus to the provision of theatres was given by the construction of the first stone theatre in Rome by Pompey. With its shrine to Venus Victrix at the summit of the *cavea*, this was the largest theatre ever to have been built in the Roman world and cost some thirty million sesterces (compare the theatre at Lepcis Magna which cost about eight million sesterces or that at Herculaneum which cost one and a half million sesterces);[26] it contained sculpture, and was the venue for Pompey's greatest displays at the height of his power in 55 BC.[27] The shrine at the top of the *cavea* harks back to the sanctuaries of Palestrina, Tivoli and Pietrabbondante. It used to be seen as a means to deflect hostile criticism of the construction of a stone theatre in Rome, but we should rather regard it as confirmation that a theatre was a sacred

---

[20] *CIL* 10.833–5 = *ILS* 5638; Sear (2006), p. 1.   [21] Fuchs (1987); Sear (2006), pp. 15–16.
[22] Sear (2006), pp. 19, 51.   [23] *CIL* 10.833–5.   [24] Sear (2006).
[25] Thomas and Witschel (1991).   [26] See Sear (2006), pp. 11–23 for the calculations.
[27] Cic. *Pis.* 27.65; Dio Cass. 39.38; Plut. *Pomp.* 52.

space.[28] Not all theatres had temples; the Theatres of Marcellus and Balbus, both built in Rome under Augustus, did not have shrines incorporated into their structures. It is clear, however, that theatres were places for spectacles of a religious nature: whether the dedication of the building itself, a regular festival, the Secular Games held every one hundred and ten years, or the celebration of a victory over Rome's enemies. The building of these theatres in Rome may have led to a spate of emulation across Italy and the colonies of veterans in the western Mediterranean.

The majority of the 175 or so theatres known from Italy were constructed between the late Republic and the middle of the first century AD. Unlike in the early first century BC, when there were relatively few theatres in Italy, by the mid-first century AD the theatre had become almost a standard feature of the city in Italy. This is a major change and demonstrates the rarity of the theatre in the earlier period, and the impetus given to theatre-building by the construction of stone monuments in the capital.[29] Sear points out the utility of the theatre for display in the city; unlike in the amphitheatre, there was a focus to the audience's gaze – the elite seated at the front and the stage-building with its sculptural programme.[30] This was the place for the commemoration of individuals from the city and members of the imperial family, and constituted the second location in which such sculptural programmes could be set up, a fact often forgotten when so much of the literature focuses on the power of images in the forum.[31] In the provinces we find the emperor and his family building theatres in the veteran colonies which shared a sense of identity with the cities of Italy itself. For example, Agrippa constructed the theatre at Mérida between 16 and 15 BC and, not surprisingly, the building directly reflects developments in the capital and included within the *cavea* a shrine to the imperial cult.[32] Statues of Tiberius and Drusus the Younger, a veiled head of Augustus and some later sculpture point to the importance of this venue, alongside the forum, as a location for the display of images of imperial rule. The upper parts of the *cavea* were only completed later in the first century AD. One would expect the example of Mérida to have transmitted an ideal of theatre-building from the Augustan capital to the other cities of Lusitania, but this does not seem to have been the case. At Lisbon (Olisipo), during Nero's reign the Augustan theatre was enhanced by a *flamen* (priest) of Augustus, Gaius Heius Primus, with a new orchestra and *proscaenium* (stage) and some

---

[28] Tert. *De spect.* 10.5 description displays an unsurprising Christian hostility to paganism; Tac. *Ann.* 14.20 suggests criticism came from the older generation alone.

[29] Sear (2006), pp. 48–53.   [30] Sear (2006), p. 12; Rawson (1987) on seating.   [31] Rose (1997).

[32] *CIL* 2.474; Sear (2006), p. 264 for description and bibliography.

elaborate sculptural decoration, but this makes no reference to the imperial cult and includes the sleeping god Silenus.[33] In the Spanish provinces of Tarraconensis and Baetica, the theatres tended to be concentrated in colonies and to date from the first half of the first century AD.[34] What we do not see is a spread of this monument-type to cities across the provinces, nor do we see a long period of theatre-building. Indeed, we might conclude from the Spanish examples that theatre-building was an Augustan novelty that did not have a huge impact in this part of the Empire.

In contrast to the evidence from Spain, in Gallia Narbonensis we find that the Augustan model of the theatre, as found in Rome, was not only promoted in the veteran colonies, such as Arles and Orange, but also adopted in places without the presence of veterans, e.g. Toulouse and Vaison-la-Romaine, with the majority of the theatres built prior to the end of the first century AD.[35] There is an interesting discrepancy between the type of sculptural decoration found in the theatres of the colonies and that of Vaison-la-Romaine. In the colonies generic figures from mythology are found: the theatre at Orange has scenes from the life of Dionysus and an Amazonomachy; the theatre at Arles produced a famous statue of Venus, another of Apollo Citharoedus, others of three female dancers and a head of Augustus. In contrast, at Vaison-la-Romaine the figure of the emperor was more important, with statues of Claudius, Domitian, Hadrian and Sabina, alongside those of Apollo and Bacchus. The connection with the sacred is most clearly made at Orange, where the theatre was located next to a sanctuary.[36]

Leaving Gallia Narbonensis, the theatre constructed under Augustus at Lyon can be seen to have followed the Augustan pattern of theatre-building, with its decoration of female statues, a cuirassed figure, Apollo and a bearded Satyr within a theatre of a similar type to those of the Augustan colonies to the south. As the central place where the inhabitants of the Three Gauls displayed their loyalty to the emperor, and as the location of imperial officials in the mint, Lyon was integrated into the imperial conception of a city. It was also visited by numerous emperors over the course of the first century AD. The city and its monuments perhaps provided a model of civic architecture to be reproduced in other cities across the Gauls. We should note however, that the reception of the theatre

[33] *CIL* 2.183; Sear (2006), p. 265 for description and bibliography.
[34] Sear (2006), pp. 260–70 for relevant examples and dating.
[35] For a full listing of theatres in Gallia Narbonensis see Sear (2006), pp. 244–54.
[36] Bedon et al. (1988), p. 162.

into the Three Gauls has become a subject of considerable scholarly debate. Much ink has been spilt over the need to create a typology of the theatres of the Three Gauls, but all such attempts have failed, largely due to the sheer diversity of forms found.[37] We find throughout the literature the deployment of terms such as 'theatre' to signify a strong link with the theatres of Italy and 'theatre-amphitheatre' to denote a type apparently displaying a closer resemblance to an amphitheatre than to the Italic and Gallo-Roman theatres. These were not precise copies of the architecture found in Lugdunum or any of the other cities of Narbonensis. Instead, a conception of theatre architecture was borrowed and then adapted to furnish a community with a building that might be seen to resemble a Roman theatre. What all these structures had in common, though, is a provision for seating or a *cavea* from which the audience looked on to a stage or perhaps a religious shrine replacing the stage-building. Their dating, however, varies considerably from that of traditional theatres of the Italic type, built in the first century for the most part, and then the Gallo-Roman hybrids continuing throughout the second century. We do not wish to make a further futile attempt to classify these structures, but instead to discuss their location within or even outside the city, and their proximity to other monuments. In doing so, the discussion will focus on the reasons for erecting these structures that allowed the community to gather and watch a play or an explanation of matters of concern to them, be they religious or secular.

The town of Autun (Augustodunum) was constructed with a walled circuit in the Augustan period as a new town for the Aedui, replacing the hill-fort at Bibracte.[38] The town features an orthogonal grid within the walls, and in the first century AD, what was probably the largest theatre in Gaul was constructed within the enceinte in close proximity to an amphitheatre (fig. 9.3); a pattern also found in the Augustan colony at Mérida in Spain. The theatre at Autun was maintained in the second century AD and may have had a capacity for about eleven thousand spectators.[39] The new town did not, however, just acquire a theatre within the walls; to the northeast there was a sanctuary site with temples, to which a Gallo-Roman theatre was added in the second century AD.[40] What we are seeing here is the duplication of monument-types at a new town which was located in the landscape so that its sacred space was both contained within the town and

---

[37] Sear (2006), p. 99.   [38] Tac. *Ann.* 3.43–6.   [39] *CIL* 13.2658; Sear (2006), p. 225.
[40] Bedon (2001), p. 90.

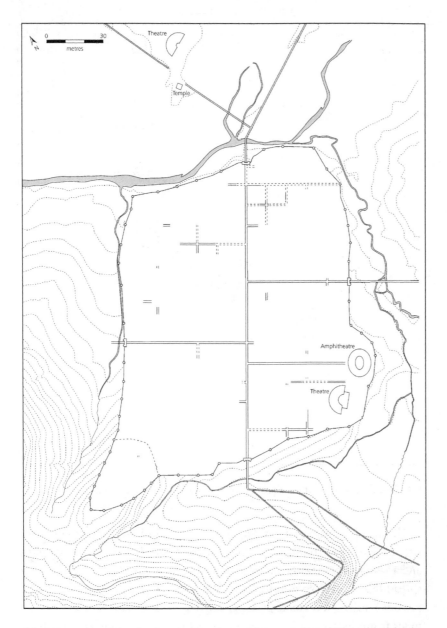

9.3 Autun: plan of the city showing locations of theatre and amphitheatre within the walls and the extra-mural theatre.

extended into the city's territory; there a theatre was constructed for the gathering of the community in a manner not facilitated by the existing temples.[41]

---

[41] Bedon (1999), pp. 175–83 on the relationship between sanctuaries and towns.

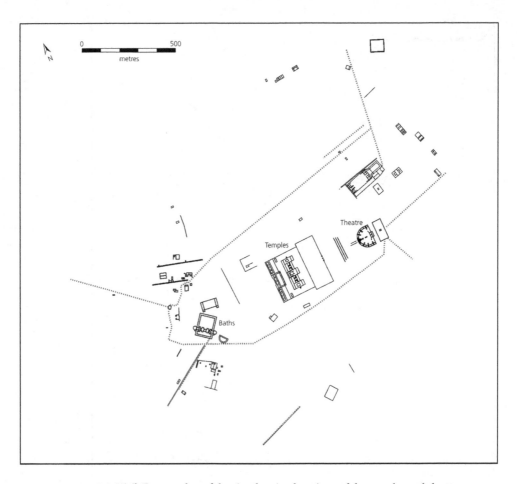

9.4 Vieil-Evreux: plan of the site showing locations of the temples and theatre.

The people known as the Aulerci Eburovices had a pre-Roman sanctuary site at Vieil-Evreux (Gisacum), which was duly monumentalised with baths and a wooden(?) theatre, as well as a sanctuary, and in the first century AD spread over some two hundred and fifty hectares (fig. 9.4). In the Roman period a town developed at Evreux (Mediolanum Aulercorum), seven miles from the sanctuary site, and its inhabited area contained a religious centre, baths and a theatre – perhaps a replication of the facilities available at the original sanctuary site.[42] This resulted in a bipolar community with the features of urban life being established in slightly different forms at each location. The sanctuary site at Vieil-Evreux gained a new stone theatre in the Italic style and a stage-building of the kind associated with Italic-style

[42] Bedon (2001), pp. 162–4.

temples.[43] Theatres, therefore, were constructed at sacred sites, whether in the city or at a 'rural' sanctuary some distance from the city. The sanctuaries, in fact, could develop the facilities of urbanism; for example, the sanctuary at Augine not only possessed a theatre but also baths fed by an aqueduct, while Grand in Normandy boasted a theatre, temple and bathing-establishments.[44] The theatre in Gaul was integrated into a conception of sacred space that also included the sites of springs, such as Champalement, which had much in common with the sanctuary sites of Italy monumentalised in the second century BC at locations with important natural phenomena such as springs or lakes.[45] What marks them out as so different is their dates. In Gaul theatres tended to achieve their final form in the second century AD and appear to have resulted from a desire to create a building or monument in which a community could gather together close to a religious site, often with the amenity of a bath-building (discussed in the previous chapter). The phenomenon of building a theatre both in a town and at a nearby sanctuary seems to have been essentially confined to Belgica, Lugdunensis and the northern part of Aquitania. We should note, however, that a similar pattern can be found at second-century Camulodunum, while we do find evidence of theatres being built in smaller communities, such as at the *vicus Petuariensis* (Brough-on-Humber), although it is unclear in the latter case what the nature of this settlement might have been.[46] In Aquitania, in the area south of the River Garonne, we do not find these large rural sanctuaries but can nevertheless identify a role for theatres both in the towns of the region, such as Saint-Bertrand-de-Comminges (fig.4.1), and in sanctuaries close to towns, such as at Thénac.[47] A similar relationship can be found in Belgica, such as that between the town of Amiens and its sanctuary at Ribemont-sur-Ancre (fig. 6.7), mirroring that at Evreux and Vieil-Evreux in Lugdunensis discussed above.[48] The sanctuary in this case displayed many of the features of Roman urbanism: baths, a theatre and a temple. The linear alignment had much in common with what we find in much earlier Italian sanctuaries that also feature baths, a theatre and a temple (e.g. Pompeii – fig. 1.2, or Gabii – fig. 9.2). What was missing, though, was a forum. That was located

---

[43] Sear (2006), pp. 231–2; Cliquet *et al.* (1998).   [44] Frézouls (1982).

[45] Such traditions are also obvious in Africa. For example the dedications at the spring of Aïn Drinn just outside Lambaesis, Janon (1973), p. 242, *CIL* 8.265; the monumentalisation of the spring at Zaghouan, the source of Carthage's aqueduct, Rakob (1974); or the massive complex of the Aqua Septimiana Felix at Timgad, Leschi (1947), pp. 87–99, Lassus (1981), p. 50.

[46] Sear (2006), pp. 196–7; *RIB* 707.   [47] See Sear (2006), pp. 198–206.

[48] Agache (1978), pp. 404–10; Sear (2006), pp. 207–14.

in Amiens together with an amphitheatre, which formed what might be described as an annex to the forum itself. Unlike the Italian examples of extra-mural sanctuaries (such as at Gabii), Ribemont-sur-Ancre is some twenty kilometres from Amiens – a distance not dissimilar to that of Rome to the sanctuary of Fortuna at Palestrina or to the sanctuary of Hercules at Tibur.

What is perhaps surprising is that one hundred and fifteen theatres have been located in Gallia Comata, compared to a mere twenty-three in the Spanish provinces, where it should be noted that relatively few amphitheatres are known (see Chapter 10). Only two certain examples, and one possible, have been found at towns in Britain, a province conquered at the end of the period of theatre-building in Italy and Gallia Narbonensis and in which the amphitheatre appears to have been of greater significance. Explanations of stone-robbing apart, there is a huge discrepancy in the distribution of this 'ubiquitous' structure which needs further explanation. Should we suggest that the form of urbanism adopted in Gaul was closer to that of Italy and embraced the theatre as an architectural form of some utility, whether located in a city or at a sanctuary? Interestingly, the Gallic examples adapted the Italian idea of the theatre in ways that defy typological classification, and some may have had little in common with the theatres with stage-buildings erected in Narbonensis, Spain and Italy during the first century AD. What was created was a hybrid architectural form, which was related to a Roman theatre but did not include many of its features. There was a very strong religious connection, as shown by the building of these Gallo-Roman theatres at sanctuary sites. Some of the earliest theatres in Italy were also found at sanctuary sites, but the similarity between Italian and Gallo-Roman sanctuaries should not be over-emphasised, for the reason that the Gallo-Roman theatre often allowed for a view of the temple from the seats in the *cavea*. At Augst, the stage-building has a gap in it to allow the contemporary temple, set on the same alignment, to become a distant part of it.[49] This was an architectural development that created a new, visual link between the theatre and the temple in its sanctuary. At the sanctuary at Champlieu, Sear highlights how the theatre was aligned with reference to the cult statue in the temple, and at Sanxay the alignment of the theatre was produced with reference to religious structures within the sanctuary.[50] What promoted theatre development in the second century AD within Gaul, Germany and, to a lesser extent, Britain, was a connection with religion that cannot be traced in

---

[49] Ward-Perkins (1974), fig.77.   [50] Sear (2006), pp. 204–5, 208–9 and fig. 34.

Spain or within Italy itself. Cultural difference can be identified here as having created new forms of architecture, normally categorised as Gallo-Roman theatres or theatre-amphitheatres. What sort of performances occurred, often within the orchestra rather than on a stage, is open to speculation.

THEATRE AND TEMPLE IN NORTH AFRICA

The Christian writer Tertullian, who wrote in the early third century, regarded theatrical shows as idolatrous and explicitly mentioned Pompey's theatre at Rome as being the progenitor of the link between religion and spectacles.[51] He pointed to processions leading from temples and altars to theatres and accompanied with incense and music. He linked aspects of stage performance to the gods Venus, Bacchus, the Muses, Apollo, Minerva and Mercury. For Tertullian the gods presided over the theatre and aspects of the shows were dedicated to them. He roundly criticised Christians who attended the theatre because of their exposure to immorality as well as to elements of pagan religion.[52] Spectacles and religion were inextricably linked in the mind of the arch-polemicist. That this link was not clear to all Christians can be seen from the effort that Tertullian put into convincing his Christian audience that the shows were idolatrous. Either some Christians did not see that there was an explicit link or they did not care. Tertullian may have believed in the close link between the theatres and religion and, importantly, processions, but in the physical remains of the city and the epigraphy of Roman Africa the connection between theatre and temple is less evident. Theatres are not, in the main, spatially linked to individual temples and there is considerable temporal dissonance between temple and theatre building, which may point to a level of disconnection for many communities between core religious practice and the use of theatres for ritual experience. There was constant temple building from the Augustan period onwards, with intensification during the second and early third centuries AD. Theatre construction on the other hand came in three distinct phases: a very limited Augustan phase, an Antonine expansion and a Severan continuation. The patterns of theatre construction in North Africa were similar to those of bath and amphitheatre provision. African populations did not build some types of Roman-style monument in large numbers until the later second/early third century.

[51] Tert. *De spect.* 10.   [52] Tert. *De spect.* 10.1.

Temple building began seriously under Augustus and, although a few prominent cities such as Carthage, Utica and Lepcis account for much of this work, smaller settlements such as Bir Derbal, Henchir El Hammam and Ghardimou attest to the beginnings of a tradition.[53] Some cities of Mauretania Caesarensis and Tingitana also attest to temple building under Juba II, a salutary reminder that Rome influenced building traditions and monumentalisation outside of its Empire.[54]

The proliferation of temple building in the first century was not matched by the construction of theatres. By the end of the first century AD only five cities had documented theatres. The old capital of Africa Vetus, Utica, had a theatre by the middle of the first century BC, as recorded in Caesar's *Bellum Civile* 2.25. The status of the city and the presence of the Roman governor there almost certainly played a part in its acquisition of a monumental set of buildings that may also have included the 'Republican' amphitheatre.[55] The importance of size, exposure to Roman ideas, and perceived status is clear in the other cities that built theatres in the first century AD. Only Cherchel (Iol Caesarea),[56] capital of Mauretania, and Lepcis Magna[57] are recorded as having constructed theatres in the Augustan period and by the end of the first century AD, only Hippo Regius is known to have joined this group.[58] These were all established Punic ports with important connections to Rome, or, in the case of Caesarea, the capital of the Mauretanian kingdom. The apparent lack of theatre construction at Carthage in the first century is surprising given its status, the fact that the bulk of the population were the descendants of Roman settlers and the work done on amphitheatres.[59] We may suspect that plays were performed in some other structure or that an earlier theatre has not been found; indeed, an opaque reference in the *Aeneid* may show that a theatre did in fact exist.[60] In general though, if African religious practice included the reenactment of a cult's myths, it took place somewhere other than in a purpose-built stone structure during the first century AD.

Of the cities that did construct theatres during this period, Lepcis in particular was engaged in a huge building programme at the beginning of the first century, and the theatre and temples fit in to this (fig. 9.5). The theatre can also be closely linked to some elements of temple building and be viewed as a monument for the display of civic virtue and generosity. Annobal Rufus, who was a priest and held the old Punic magistracy of

[53] Le Glay (1966), 1 pp. 287–9; 2 p. 11; *CIL* 8.14727.   [54] Jouffroy (1986), p. 185.
[55] Lézine (1968), p. 149.   [56] Picard (1976), pp. 386–97; Leveau (1984), pp. 34–5.
[57] *AE* 1968, 549.   [58] Marec (1954), pp. 79–87.   [59] Picard and Baillon (1992).
[60] Verg. *Aen.* 1.427–9; Ros (1996), p. 484; Sear (2006), p. 278.

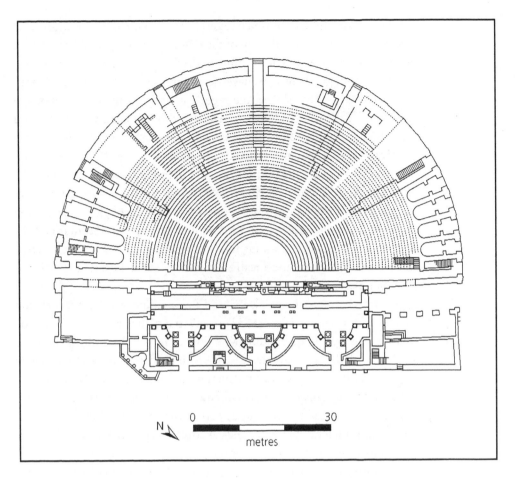

9.5 Lepcis Magna: plan of the theatre.

sufete, constructed the building at his own expense.[61] Further work was undertaken on the theatre later in the reign of Augustus.[62] Suphunibal, son of Annobal Ruso (Rufus?), constructed a temple to Ceres Augusta at the summit of the *cavea* on the central axis of the theatre in AD 35–6.[63] Clearly the shrine was an integral part of the theatre and may have been an expression of imperial cult linked with an important local deity.[64] The link between imperial cult and the theatre as a place for public performance and display was strengthened in AD 43 with the construction of a temple to the Augustan gods behind the theatre's stage-building. Unsurprisingly, given the benefactions of the Severan emperors, statues of Septimius Severus, Julia Domna and Caracalla were set up in the portico that

[61] *IRT* 321–3.   [62] *IRT* 521.   [63] *IRT* 269.   [64] Brouquier-Reddé (1992), pp. 164–6.

surrounded the temple, at which time a four-arched Janus was constructed and a mosaic was laid at the top of the *cavea*.[65] The stage-building and the temple's portico would have limited the view of the temple from the theatre, although there may have been glimpses of it from some seats. The proximity of the shrine, the regular establishment of dedications to emperors in the theatre and the presence of the temple to Ceres Augusta would have emphasised to those attending the *ludi* (entertainments) the involvement of imperial cult in the public life of the city.[66] The connection between religion and the theatre may have been reinforced at the end of the century when Tiberius Claudius Sestius paid for the construction of an altar and the orchestra's parapet (*proedria*), but, although the dedication for both is on one inscription, the relationship between the altar and the theatre is not clear.[67] Despite this imprecision, an explicit connection between religion and the theatre can be traced at Lepcis in the Julio-Claudian period and beyond.

Second-century Thugga also shows the conjunction between religion and theatre building (fig. 9.6). Thugga's main theatre was built in AD 168–9 as a stand-alone building with little to link it physically or in terms of views with the city's temples. Elsewhere in the city, however, there was an explicit link between theatre construction and religious cult. By the reign of Hadrian the city already had a small, cult theatre built by A. Gabinius Datus and his son M. Gabinius Bassus as part of the complex of the Temples of Concord, Frugifer, Liber Pater and Neptune.[68] The small cult auditorium was connected directly to the temples via a portal in the south-eastern wall of the complex. It did not possess a stage-building but had a large orchestra in which rituals or mythological plays connected to the deities could be enacted. Such a cult theatre, however, appears to be unique in Latin-speaking North Africa ('Latin-speaking' is important here, as there are examples in Greek-speaking Cyrenaica, e.g. at Balagrae).[69] At Bulla Regia the theatre was part of the very large monumental plaza complex that probably dates to the second century and which contained numerous shrines, fountains and statues.[70] It was therefore in close proximity to a wide variety of cult places, but the axiality and integrated temple-theatre complex of Lepcis or the cult theatre at Thugga was missing here. The decoration of theatres throughout North Africa is similar to that of Bulla, where statues of Dionysus, Mercury and Saturn sat beside colossal images

---

[65] Bandinelli *et al.* (1964), pp. 59, 83; Caputo (1987), p. 52; Sear (1990), p. 379.

[66] Condron (1998), pp. 42–52.   [67] *IRT* 347.

[68] *CIL* 8.26467 and 26470; Poinssot (1958), p. 29; Saint-Amans (2004), pp. 236, 287–98.

[69] Goodchild (1966–7).   [70] Beschaouch *et al.* (1977), pp. 40–5.

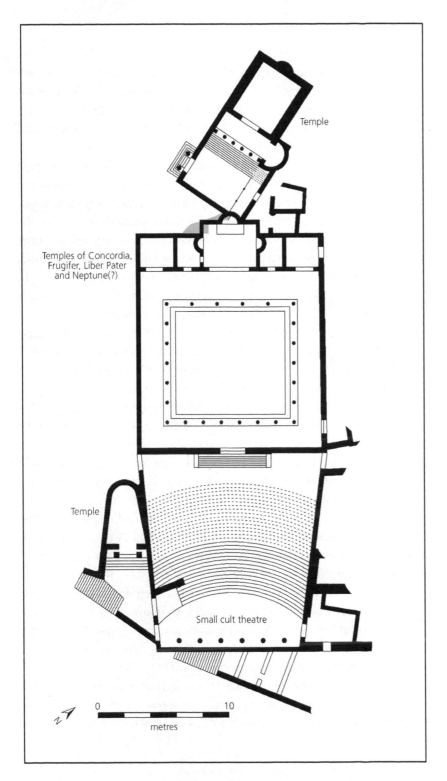

Temple

Temples of Concordia,
Frugifer, Liber Pater
and Neptune(?)

Temple

Small cult theatre

0   10

metres

9.6 Thugga: plan of the sanctuary that has elements in common with
the earlier Italian sanctuaries (see figs 9.1 and 9.2). The exact
relationship between the various temples and between the temples and
the theatre is disputed.

of Marcus Aurelius and Lucius Verus.[71] The deities and the emperors deserved to be honoured by the population of the city and their incorporation into the decoration of the theatre ensured their visibility. Again, as at Lepcis, the Bulla Regia theatre provided an important venue for the inculcation of loyalty to the imperial regime.

The spatial link between theatre and temple at Lepcis, Thugga and even Bulla Regia is absent in many African cities. Sabratha, Sbeitla, Timgad and Djemila all have theatres without any clear articulation with temples, although this does not preclude the possibility of processions between the theatre and the temples (moreover, their decoration incorporated statues of deities as well as imperial personages). At the end of the Roman period, Augustine recorded at least one and possibly two different festivals in honour of the goddess Caelestis at Carthage.[72] In both of these festivals actors (who allegedly performed lewd acts) took part, presumably acting out parts of the myth or demonstrating Caelestis' nature as a fertility deity. This latter aspect also appears to have been the reason for the procession of the prostitutes (the *meretricia pompa*) that appears in Augustine. Although there is debate about the extent to which Augustine's polemic can be trusted with regard to these aspects of the cult, there are enough parallels between elements in these pageants and other cults that they need not be tendentious statements.[73] Likewise, while there were over one hundred years between the end of our period and these events, and cults could change in their ritual over time, there is no real reason to believe that these elements were not also present in early imperial North Africa.

It was not until the Antonine period that the theatre became an integral part of the monumental vocabulary of North African towns. The reigns of Nerva, Trajan and Hadrian display an absence of building work on theatres, in marked contrast to the steady growth in the number of temples across the entire second century. A gap of around half a century between work on the Lepcis theatre and that of Hippo, and then of over sixty years between further work at Lepcis in 91–2 and the earliest accurately dated work in the second century in 157–8, again at Lepcis,[74] is truly striking.[75] Even if some of those theatres that archaeologists have dated to the 'second century' were actually constructed during the reigns of the early adopted emperors rather than later in the century – and, given the spread of the securely dated inscriptions, there is no reason to think that many of them were – a century

---

[71] Sear (2006), p. 276.   [72] August. *De civ. D.*, 2.4 and 26.
[73] Halsberghe (1984), pp. 2206–7.   [74] *IRT* 534 and 372.
[75] *IRT* 357–9 and 533; Sear (1990), pp. 376–82; Caputo (1987), pp. 109–10 and 77–9.

between the start of theatre construction and the Antonine expansion really does demonstrate that the elite of North Africa took some time to buy into this feature of Graeco-Roman culture, education and religious practice. The Severan period saw a continuation of the Antonine phase of construction and the last dated work on a theatre until the Tetrarchic period was undertaken in 225, at Skikda (Rusicade) in Numidia;[76] the refurbishments and new building that we see in the case of other monument types in the reigns of the Gordians and Gallienus did not happen (as Jouffroy notes, this could be due to the 'difficulties of the times' or to a gap in the epigraphic record).[77]

The high-point of the North African theatre was clearly in the mid-second to early third century, coincidentally at precisely the point when Apuleius writes about lecturing in the theatre at Carthage.[78] For Tertullian and Minucius Felix the entertainments within the theatre were considerably different from the activities for which Apuleius used it. As we might expect, their Christian polemic portrays a debauched, highly sexualised experience quite different from Apuleius' philosophical teaching.[79] Despite the violence of their rhetoric, their condemnation of the immorality of the theatre, the lasciviousness of the performances and the lust they provoked in the audience, and in particular the attendance of Christians at these spectacles, demonstrates the popularity of this form of entertainment for the Carthaginian population as a whole in the second century.[80] The shows are also an integral element in the epigraphy of the city. Inscriptions mentioning the *ludi scaenici* (theatrical shows) and *ludi scaenici cum missilibus* (theatrical shows with free gifts) are ubiquitous throughout North Africa (with the exception of the Tripolitanian theatres) in a way that is not true of Gaul or Germany. This may reflect the different epigraphic traditions of the region – North Africa is rich in inscriptions – but the frequency of *ludi scaenici* inscriptions demonstrates the importance of the *ludi* for the African elite. The lavishing of games and gifts on a community could last long in the memory but was ephemeral when compared to the construction of buildings; inscriptions commemorating generosity above and beyond the call of duty gave the gifts a longer life. So at Vallis in Africa Proconsularis, where a theatre remains to be discovered, an inscription

---

[76] Frézouls (1952), p. 175; *ILAlg.* II.37 and (possibly) II.5. The latest documented work on any entertainment building before the tetrarchic era was on the circus of Auzia, *CIL* 8.9065 = *ILS* 5661.

[77] Jouffroy (1986), p. 278.   [78] Apul. *Flor.* 17–18.   [79] Tert. *De spect.*; Min. Fel. *Oct.*37.11–12.

[80] Tert. *De spect.* 25.

records the giving of a more generous set of games and banquet than was required of the aediles.[81]

Temple building and theatre building did not run in tandem in Africa. While temple construction was clearly a priority for African cities, this was not true of theatres and clearly cities could make do without them. Obviously this also means that they were not a key feature of religious ritual in the first century AD, although plays may nevertheless have been so, and it may explain the focus on *ludi scaenici* in the epigraphy and the lack of theatre-sanctuaries and of spatial links between temples and theatres. The theatre would seem not to have been used for the same purposes in North Africa as it was in Gaul.

SACRED SPACE AND THE LEARNING OF URBANNESS

A key question at this point is how the city produced citizens and assured a continuity of culture at any given place. A city, after all, was a place where continuity of location into the distant future was presumed. For the city's reproduction in that future, it needed to transmit its identity and culture from the current generation to the next one, and so on. Prior to their conquest or assimilation by Rome, the cities of Italy developed an institution for this cultural reproduction. Its origins lie in the Greek institution of the *ephebeia*, which came to be translated into Latin as *iuventus*.[82] This social institution was for those adult males, mostly from the elite, who had just taken up the *toga virilis* but were not yet of an age to hold a magistracy. Its precursors were linked to the gymnasium and the need to build the body for battle, but they also involved the development of thinking skills and the ability to consider the actions to be taken. *Iuventus* denoted both the time of life and was also the name of the social institution that transformed *iuvenes* (young men) into adult citizens.[83] The institution is found in thirty-nine cities in Italy and seventeen in the western provinces.[84] It was an institution of some antiquity, and is mentioned by Livy in the context of the fourth century BC, whilst it continued to be present in Italy into the third century AD.[85] Youths were trained not only in aspects of the Greek gymnasium such as javelin-throwing, but also in beast-hunting or

---

[81] *CIL* 8.14783.   [82] Della Corte (1924), pp. 7–11; Jaczynowska (1970).
[83] Della Corte (1924), p. 11.   [84] Della Corte (1924), p. 11.
[85] Livy, 9.25; S. H. A. *Tres Gordiani* 4.6.

gladiatorial combat;[86] indeed, even the Emperor Titus seems to have had a detailed knowledge of gladiatorial combat.[87] These young men or *iuvenes* of the elite are attested standing for the aedileship in elections yet continued to be described as *iuvenes*;[88] in some cities the holding of the earlier post of *magister iuventutis* (master of youth) formed part of the magistrates' career structure known as the *cursus honorum*.[89] Once in office, they took care of the streets and sacred buildings of the city with a view to the future, and so needed to have had the identity and culture of the city inculcated into them. Across the western provinces, from North Africa through Baetica and Aquitania and on to Belgica and Germania, we can locate such institutions in the epigraphic record.[90] But it is Tacitus who articulates the process of their introduction.[91] The sons of chieftains (*principes*), not the chieftains themselves, were the means by which Latin was introduced as a language to Britain – alongside the toga. As we have seen, the result, for Tacitus, was a taste for the *porticus*, the baths and the dinner party. It has been suggested by Filippo Coarelli that at Pompeii, the provision of colonnaded porticoes close to the theatres was to enable the education of boys and young men (fig. 9.7). Tacitus therefore seems to be alluding to Agricola's transportation of the culture of the gymnasium to Britain, which can be set alongside the older generation's initiatives to build temples, fora and houses. He was writing only a generation later, yet could see that the process had been effective within this short period of cultural change. Agricola acted as if he were a patron of these new institutions, a phenomenon that only emerged in an epigraphic form in the western provinces during the second and third centuries.[92] What transformed the British elites' younger members at the end of the first century AD was the introduction of training for youths. The organisation of the institution varied from city to city. Sometimes it was regarded as a *corpus* (corporate group) or a *collegium* (a legal association) whilst elsewhere it was connected to specific divinities or locations, but we often find the presence of older men as procurators, curators, patrons or fathers, as well as the attachment of boys of a younger age. Such organisations of youths were led or incorporated into the culture of their city by other older men. Youths were even capable of articulating the identity of the city through a full-blown riotous attack on visitors watching the games in the local amphitheatre, but whether this behaviour was approved of by the older generation remains uncertain and unknowable.[93]

---

[86] Rostovtzeff (1900).   [87] Suet. *Tit.* 8.   [88] *CIL* 4.317.   [89] Jaczynowska (1970), p. 268.
[90] Della Corte (1924), p. 11; Jaczynowska (1970).   [91] Tac. *Agr.* 21.   [92] Jaczynowska (1970).
[93] See De Ruggiero (1948–58), 4.317–20 for the relevant evidence.

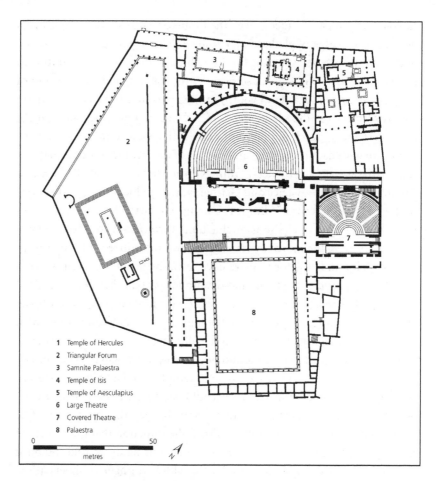

9.7 Pompeii: temples and theatres in this region of Pompeii alongside a running track and *palaestrae* provided a landscape for the education of *iuvenes* (young men) and the reproduction of local identity.

The role of transmitting an understanding of the city's cultural identity was not limited to the institution for youths. The festivals, processions and games associated with religious observation in each city, although varying across the western Empire, articulated its relationship with the supernatural, as well as its continued existence into the future. The setting for these events was often a combination of a temple and a theatre, but it is important to note that these combinations of theatre and temple were not just confined to the urban environment within the walls or street-grid. The link between the transmission of the culture of urbanness and a sanctuary has most clearly been articulated by Filippo Coarelli with reference to the series of public buildings surrounding the Triangular Forum at Pompeii: the Temples of Isis and Aesculapius, the theatre, the Odeon, the Samnite Palaestra and the 'barracks of the gladiators' (fig. 9.7).[94] The last of these and the theatre were linked to the Triangular Forum by a ramp or monumental staircase (later altered in the Sullan period). Within the confines of the Triangular Forum itself there was a running-track, a *Heroon*, or founder's tomb, and a Temple of Hercules and Minerva. There was also another public building located in Insula 7.6, just outside the main entrance to the Triangular Forum from the city, whilst a set of baths in Insula 7.5 is attested in the second century BC. The combination of features in this part of the city is rather overwhelming, but there is a logic to it. Coarelli suggests that the entire complex was based around the celebration of the mythic hero Hercules, who founded the city or at least named it.[95] He then proposes on the basis of Dionysius of Halicarnassus 7.72 that the youths of Pompeii processed up the ramp from the 'gladiator barracks' to the Temple of Hercules and Minerva within the Triangular Forum. The *palaestrae* point to the training of youth, as does the presence in the Samnite Palaestra of a copy of the statue of the *Doryphoros* by Polyclites and a statue base of Marcellus as *princeps iuventutis* (leader of youth). In short, this was the place in Pompeii where the youth of the city trained in the shadow of its founder, Hercules. It was where they developed physical strength and the ability to endure exercise, and where they recalled the deeds of Hercules at the temple and in the theatre. Additional features followed this theme – a set of baths in an adjacent *insula* block and the temple of Aesculapius to maintain the health of the youths, while votive deposits, including anatomical elements, have also been found within the Triangular Forum.[96] What Coarelli has shown in Pompeii[97] is that the elements of the city relating to the sacred were not confined to the temples but also included the rituals and performances of the games in the theatre, as well as the rituals of exercise associated with the stage of life known as *iuventus*, when boys were converted into men. This neatly configured landscape of the second century BC was altered by the arrival of the colonists in the first century BC and the construction of new bath-buildings, the Temple of Venus and the amphitheatre. Following this reconfiguration of the city, a palaestra was built adjacent

---

[94] Coarelli (2001).

[95] Coarelli (2001). Solin.2.5; Isid. *Etym.* 15.1.5; Mart. Cap. 6.642; Serv. *ad Virg. Aen.* 7.662.

[96] D'Alessio (2001).   [97] Compare Praeneste: Quilici (1980), (1989); Coarelli (1987), (2001).

to the amphitheatre.[98] This connection between elements within the city, which should also include the baths, creates what Mario Torelli sees in the context of the Roman city as a Le Corbusierian urban machine based around the sacred geography of the city and whose purpose is to generate citizens and the replication of a set of urban values over time and across generations.[99] But the question arises of whether the presence of a sanctuary of the type we have seen at Pompeii constituted a form of urbanism to be found across the cities of Italy and the western provinces, and of how it was incorporated into the structure of new city foundations.

The evidence for these institutions survives in inscriptions that frustratingly give little indication of what the *iuvenes* did as part of their membership of a *collegium*. The one place for which we do have some indication is Mactar in North Africa.[100] The surviving album listing the names of members, which is dated to AD 88, is scrupulous in giving the names of its members and their respective fathers. Three were freedmen rather than freeborn citizens of Mactar. This group, referred to as the *iuventus* of the *civitas Mactaritana*, provided at its expense a basilica constructed in a public space and two granaries. It is also described as worshipping Mars Augustus. Picard suggests that this body of seventy members had a military function and could be mobilised. This would therefore imply some form of military training, as proposed by Rostovtzeff and as was expected for young men in the cities of Italy.[101] The relationship of the seventy or so members listed to the rest of the population of Mactar (2000–3000) is open to discussion. The number of members is too great to represent the youth of the aristocracy alone and we need to look for a broader social definition. Indeed, perhaps we should imagine a relationship of status and that the group coincided with those eligible for recruitment into the legions, whether in the current or following generations. At Mactar individual males were introduced into the culture of urbanness through the institutions for youths and an association with the worship of Mars Augustus. Significantly for this discussion, the basilica was built close to a set of baths and next to the monumental stairway leading to the temple of Liber Pater. What the relationship was between these *iuvenes* and the nearby sanctuary of the god Hathor Miskar remains uncertain.[102] A problem for interpretation at Mactar is that we do not have evidence of a theatre at the site, but

[98] Welch (2007), pp. 95–7 suggests this *palaestra* might date to the early period of the colony, but the basis for this depends on a parallel with the Caesarian/Augustan colony at Emporiae and is open to other interpretations.

[99] Torelli (1989), p. 15.   [100] Picard (1957), pp. 77–95. Lézine (1968), pp. 169–76.

[101] Picard (1957), p. 82.   [102] Picard (1988).

whether that impeded the functions of the organisation of youths and the development of urban life remains unclear. Perhaps the absence of a theatre did not imply a lack of urbanness, since the institution known as *iuventus* or *collegium iuvenum* used the baths, sanctuaries and temples for developing citizens. A theatre would, however, have been a desirable addition and may have further enabled the development of urban life.

Rostovtzeff viewed the newly formed cities of the Roman West, and specifically the presence of *collegia iuvenum* from the time of the Flavians, as the basis for the shift in the recruitment of legionaries from Italy to the provinces.[103] He suggested that the provision of legionary recruits (i.e. Roman citizens) was the first duty of a newly formed city. Recruitment was from the youth of the city and, for Rostovtzeff, this implied the formation of *collegia iuvenum* in the cities and even in the villages of the West. For him, these were 'seminaries of the future soldiers'. We suggest instead that *collegia iuvenum* existed for the production not simply of soldiers, but also of Roman culture and urbanness, however patchy the evidence for them in the provinces. Equally, we can identify structures in provincial cities that may correspond to the facilities which were so essential to the training of young men in Pompeii. For example, the Coupéré building in Saint-Bertrand-de-Comminges can be interpreted as a place where young men trained their minds and bodies, but it does not appear to have been directly associated with a temple or other sacred site. Instead it seems to have much in common with the large *palaestra* at Pompeii.[104] Nevertheless, the date of the construction of provincial cities and the nature of their urban development meant that the traditional association, found in Italy, between a sanctuary and the theatrical performance of the myths surrounding a deity did not always translate into the language of urbanness as adopted or produced in the provincial setting in the late first century BC and first two centuries AD. This points to a difference in orientation of the cities of Italy compared to those of the provinces. The former used the theatrical performance of myth to create a distinct identity of place, whereas the new cities of the provinces bought into what they saw as a universal urban identity – an identity which necessarily replaced the 'barbarian' identity associated with what was unique to each particular place. The selection of elements of a perceived culture of urbanness produced a degree of hybridisation. Cultural elements from a 'barbarian' past could be embedded within the construction of sacred space, e.g. Sulis Minerva, but the performance of 'barbarian' myths in theatres associated with sacred

---

[103] Rostovtzeff (1900), p. 107.   [104] Esmonde Cleary (2007), pp. 49–51.

spaces was avoided. The learning of urbanness was facilitated by the social institution of *iuvenes*, or by *collegia iuvenum*. This institution engaged with the sacred and was the machine enabling urbanness to be reproduced over time. Religious sites were a location for learning urbanness, but this educative role was also performed by other urban institutions: the baths – the subject of the previous chapter – and amphitheatres – the subject of the following chapter.

10 | Assembling the city 4: amphitheatres

The games in the amphitheatre, whether beast hunts or gladiatorial contests or both, have become the iconic feature of Roman culture. This is true not just in popular culture, whether in film or on television, but also in academic scholarship. Keith Hopkins did much to elucidate a vision of Roman culture that was defined by means of the gladiatorial games in the amphitheatre (fig. 10.1).[1] However, we need to remember at the outset that at Rome there was no stone amphitheatre until 29 BC, when Statilius Taurus constructed one in the Campus Martius (later destroyed in the fire of AD 64), and it was only surpassed by the building of the Colosseum, which was opened by the Emperor Titus in AD 80 – a structure that would remain the largest amphitheatre in the Roman world.[2] It was not in Rome that the stone-built amphitheatre was developed, but in the cities of Italy that contained veterans. We need to look first at the cities of Italy to understand the presence of the amphitheatre in the Roman city, what this new structure meant and when it was adopted as a desirable addition to the fabric of these cities. From there we will examine the rather patchy adoption of the amphitheatre in the western provinces (fig. 10.2). It will also be important to consider the amphitheatre as an expression of Romanness. Did an amphitheatre make a city more Roman? Did the new monumental form developed in the cities of Italy give a distinctively Roman character to the cities of the West that was absent in the cities of the Greek world?

THE NEED FOR AN AMPHITHEATRE

In a groundbreaking article Kate Welch established a link between amphitheatres and the settlement of veteran colonists in the first century BC.[3] The amphitheatre had been recognised as one of a number of new public

---

[1] Dio Cass. 51.23.1; Hopkins (1983), pp. 1–30.
[2] See Welch (2007) for the chronology of the development of the amphitheatre in Italy to AD 80.
[3] Welch (1994); see now the book length study Welch (2007).

10.1 El Djem: the amphitheatre provides a model for the staging of Hollywood's conception of the Roman games.

buildings associated with the settlement of veterans at Pompeii from 80 BC. Welch demonstrated the origins of the amphitheatre in Italy lay not in the indigenous societies of Campania, but in the experience of these former soldiers, who had been trained in the manner of gladiators. She went on to suggest that this experience created a desire in the colonies of Sulla, Pompey, Caesar and Octavian to watch gladiators in a purpose-built arena. This linkage between the settlement of former soldiers and the presence of amphi- theatres in certain cities seems to have continued into the Empire, notably in Gallia Narbonensis and at other veteran colonies such as Mérida. The presence of amphitheatres in the cities of the province of Britain may also have had a military connection. This may not, however, have been the only factor. The finds of 'barbarian'-style weapons from Carmarthen suggest the possibility that a connection was maintained with ideas of warfare within the 'pacified' province, but in the case of Carmarthen the most likely link is with veteran soldiers.[4] This might suggest that the amphitheatre was a structure

---

[4] Scott and James (2003), pp. 326–9.

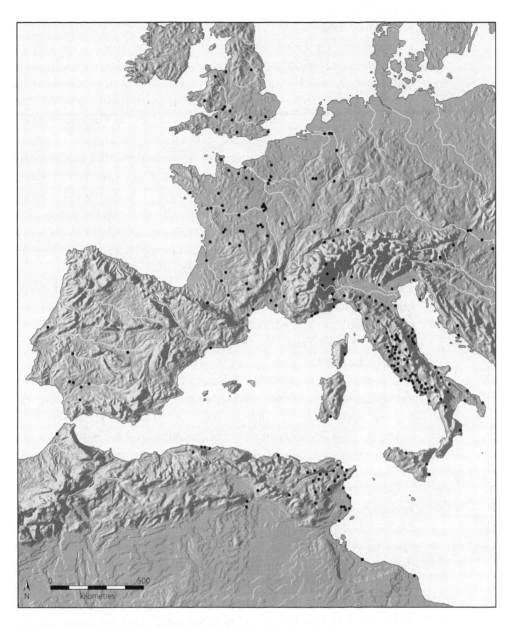

10.2 Distribution map of amphitheatres in the Roman West.

which could provide veteran soldiers or 'pacified' Britons with a link to their own violent histories. The presence of soldiers on the Rhine-Danube frontier could have been a catalyst for the construction of amphitheatres in the region. The original wooden amphitheatre at Vindonissa has been associated with the establishment of the legionary base of *Legio XIII Gemina* in the reign of Tiberius.[5] We should be wary, however, of positing this as a general theory applicable at all times and in all regions across the Empire, since there is no general pattern of amphitheatre building on the frontiers and we can frequently be certain of their absence in such locations.

Whatever the precise cultural origin of the amphitheatre, it seems clear that it was not a prerequisite for a gladiatorial show. Vitruvius, writing at the end of the first century BC, does not discuss the building of amphitheatres in his work on architecture.[6] Instead it was the forum which was the place for the games and the construction of the forum was to facilitate this. As we saw in Chapter 7, he suggests that the size of the forum was to vary according to the number of people attending the games.[7] It is difficult to imagine the construction of seating in the rather narrow forum at Pompeii (fig. 7.1). This space was laid out by the Oscan population prior to the Roman colony, so may not be of the dimensions Vitruvius had in mind. If we turn, instead, to the colony founded at Paestum in 273 BC, we find a colonnaded space well over fifty metres in width which could have encompassed the stone amphitheatre built at the site in the first century BC (fig. 2.1).[8] A similar attention to making the size of the seating area proportional to the number of spectators would have applied to any amphitheatre built in the first century AD; buildings on the scale of the Colosseum were appropriate for Rome, but not for Forum Novum (fig. 4.2). There was, however, a change in scale in the first century AD, which can be seen most clearly at Puteoli, where a functioning amphitheatre was replaced by a new Flavian structure. The original amphitheatre, in its final form by the 70s BC, had dimensions of 130×95 metres and had been used for the formal reception of King Tiridates of Parthia in AD 66; it was replaced by a larger structure with dimensions of some 149×116 metres and a system of structures below the arena floor as complex as those of the Colosseum at Rome.[9] These two structures appear to have become a feature of the topography of the city and are found on a series of glass vases where Puteoli's public monuments are represented with the two amphitheatres adjacent to each other.[10] The overall size of the new amphitheatre was not so different from that constructed at Pompeii, which measured 134×102 metres, or the original amphitheatre at Puteoli.[11] This highlights the limits to the amphitheatre's size: the human eye is only capable of seeing the action in the arena

[5] Golvin (1988), pp. 79–80.   [6] Vitr. *De arch.* 1.7.1.   [7] Vitr. *De arch.* 5.1.
[8] See Golvin (1988), p. 43 for the dimensions of the Republican amphitheatres; Tosi (2003), pp. 245–6; Russell (1968) for the Republican fora.
[9] Dio Cass. 63.3; Tosi (2003), pp. 173–6.   [10] Laurence (1996).
[11] Tosi (2003), pp. 162–4; Golvin (1988), p. 38.

at relatively close distances.[12] What was different in the new structures was the greater sophistication of the stage technology and the number of seats available. Bomgardner calculates that the capacity at Puteoli's new amphitheatre increased to some forty-seven per cent above the number of spectators capable of sitting in the arena at Pompeii, so that it could house in the region of 25–36,000 spectators.[13]

Many first-century AD Italian amphitheatres were considerably smaller than those of Pompeii and Puteoli, e.g. 86×62 metres at Carsulae in Umbria – reflecting the smaller scale of urbanism at this new town. When looking at the amphitheatre we need to realise that there was a difference in scale between the vast arenas of Rome, Milan, Tarragona or Carthage and those found in most of the towns of the Empire. The capacity of these amphitheatres varied considerably from a provincial example containing just over a thousand spectators all the way up to the Colosseum with its crowd of fifty thousand spectators. Golvin uses the architecture to estimate their variation in size and establishes the relative differential in terms of the number of spectators.[14] Her estimates may not be perfect, but they demonstrate the difference. Working with her figures for 148 amphitheatres, 53% could contain fewer than 10,000 people with only 17% being capable of holding more than 20,000 spectators. What was being built at all these sites, though, was a facility of a similar type, if not of a similar scale. Unlike the Colosseum, the amphitheatre at a city like Nîmes (fig. 10.3), might have been able to contain not just the entire male population of the city but also that of some of its neighbours. The viewing of violence either there or in the forum was clearly one of the key experiences of the Roman city, at least for those populations which committed resources to the construction of amphitheatres.

THE BUILDING OF AMPHITHEATRES

Amphitheatres are a relatively common find for archaeologists working on urban sites in Italy, and more than seventy have been identified across the possible four hundred and sixty Roman cities. What is striking from these finds, however, is the chronology of the construction of amphitheatres in Italy (see Table 10.1). Few cities would have had their own amphitheatre in

---

[12] Rose (2001).
[13] For relevant figures see Bomgardner (2000), pp. 47, 72; compare those of Golvin (1988), pp. 284–8.
[14] Golvin (1988), pp. 284–8.

10.3 Nîmes: the amphitheatre.

Table 10.1 Amphitheatre building in Italy (from Jouffroy 1988)

Period	Amphitheatres
Republic	8
First century AD	38
Second century AD	24
Third century AD	2
Fourth century AD	2

the period down to the Emperor Augustus. In the following century there was a glut of building across the cities of Italy, which continued into the second century AD. After that date virtually no amphitheatres were built. What we see in Italy is a very short-lived phase of construction. When we come to investigate the chronology of their abandonment there is little real evidence available. Giovanna Tosi has systematically pursued this issue, but in most cases has drawn a blank in the archaeological literature.[15] If anything, it would seem that the structures continued in existence into the fifth century AD in those cities that prospered.

What is clear from the chronology of the building of amphitheatres in Italy is that these buildings for spectacles were not a fundamental feature of Roman urbanism. A warning note has to be sounded, however; traditionally the presence of these buildings was established from standing remains, inscriptions or literary texts. It is only recently with the introduction of geophysical surveys at the sites of Roman cities that a greater depth of investigation has been achieved. There was no inkling that an amphitheatre had been built at Forum Novum until a full geophysical survey was conducted.[16] The structure was subsequently excavated to reveal a series of stone revetments, wooden post-holes and earthen banks that comprised a small wooden amphitheatre of dimensions 25×45 metres (fig. 4.2). How many other similar structures wait to be discovered cannot be estimated but their presence is clearly attested in the literary texts.[17] What is also clear from the excavations at Forum Novum is that the amphitheatre there fell out of use by the end of the second century AD or, at the latest, in the early third century.[18] Given these observations, we can still see validity in the chronological pattern of amphitheatre construction illustrated by Jouffroy; in Italy it was largely a phenomenon of the first and second centuries AD.

---

[15] Tosi (2003).   [16] Gaffney *et al.* (1997).   [17] Suet. *Tib.* 40.   [18] Gaffney *et al.* (2001).

AMPHITHEATRES AND THE CITY

The process of building an amphitheatre needs to be understood. A city did not simply purchase the plot of land and pay for the building (disappointingly, we have no information about costs). A city needed to gain access to the knowledge of how to build and use an amphitheatre, and find that knowledge desirable or useful, as well as affordable, and then employ it in the construction of the venue. Building inscriptions are fairly rare, but in Italy we have nineteen recording the status of those who paid for the work: seven had a military past, eight were local magistrates, two were former slaves and three were women, while the emperor paid in two cases.[19] There is a full range of benefactors in this list but the proportion of individuals having no link to the military is greater than that of people with experience in the legions; what evidence exists from Gaul, Germany and Britain points to a similar pattern.[20] Overall, the benefactors who had an interest in, and who paid for, the building of amphitheatres were as varied in terms of status as those of any other buildings. These were people who saw that to build a permanent amphitheatre was to create a different format for the games than simply to utilise banks of wooden seating in a forum or open space. We need to be aware that there were probably numerous locations employing wooden amphitheatres that have yet to be discovered so our distribution map is at best partial. Having said that, however, a stone amphitheatre was an additional amenity that, once built, reshaped the image of the city. It gave it a permanent capacity to hold games and these may have been of interest to neighbouring cities. Those neighbours visiting the amphitheatre may have gauged whether its size was appropriate to the city, i.e. not too cramped yet without the feeling of emptiness that pervades many of Europe's sporting arenas today. At the same time, the size of the stadium and the quality of the games may have been ranked against others in their region or even within their city. Such a tendency to comparison would have driven cities to assert their position by elaborating the architecture or the performances by gladiators and hunted beasts.

In Italy we can determine the location of seventy-eight amphitheatres in relation to the limits of their city.[21] Unlike theatres, which tended to be located within the walls of the city (84 per cent are attested as such), 58 per cent of known amphitheatres were located beyond the walls, with only 42 per cent actually inside the walls or within the street grid. The contrast

---

[19] Buonocore (1992), pp. 107–19; Gregori (1989), pp. 77–84; Fora (1996), pp. 85–9.
[20] Vismara and Caldelli (2000).
[21] See Tosi (2003) for the topographical position of each amphitheatre.

between the location of theatres and amphitheatres is striking, especially since both structures required considerable space. How can we explain it?

The construction of an amphitheatre involved the locating of a suitable available site within the fabric of the city. In a newly established city, such as the Augustan towns of Aosta or Carsulae, Autun or Mérida, the theatre and amphitheatre could be built in close proximity to one another within the grid of streets (figs. 2.6, 9.3, 2.7). Equally, in towns subject to colonisation by veterans, such as Pompeii or Nuceria under Sulla, parts of the grid of streets could be appropriated for these new buildings. In stabler times, however, it was more difficult for a city to find space. Minturnae expanded from being a Roman colony into a fully fledged city but, whilst its theatre was adjacent to the forum, its amphitheatre was located at a distance from it (fig. 6.4). This pattern can be identified right across Italy. The ability to build an amphitheatre in the centre of the city may have been limited by the possibilities for buying real estate close to the forum. In Pompeii during the Augustan and Julio-Claudian periods it was possible to acquire property close to the forum for the construction of new temples, but this pattern is not identified at other sites and may indeed be unique.[22] We do seem to find a preference for siting amphitheatres outside the city boundary. One possible reason is that this was where a temporary amphitheatre had been constructed but such an idea clearly cannot be proven, even if the information were available from excavations below the surviving structures that we see across Italy today. Gladiatorial games originally arose at Rome in association with funerals of the great men of the day, and there may have been a preference for locating an amphitheatre outside the city near the cemeteries that housed the dead. There may even have been a preference for keeping violence and killing outside the city. There were other factors at work, however. The amphitheatres at Alba Fucens, Ocriculum and Sutri were in part sculpted into hillsides formed from outcrops of the soft volcanic rock known to geologists as tuff (incorrectly called tufa by numerous archaeologists). These natural outcrops were shaped into the elliptical form of an amphitheatre with entrances cut and seating built up around the rock-cut arena. The availability of suitable outcrops may have been a factor in determining the position of the amphitheatre at these sites, but each was also built within view of the major roads running through its city. The result is that two of them were located outside the walls of the city. The availability of flat land for the construction of either the amphitheatre or a theatre in the hill-towns of the Apennines could cause both buildings to be located away from the centre of the city, as at Spello

---

[22] See Dobbins (1994) for evidence.

or Spoletum. It also needs to be borne in mind that people from neighbouring cities attended the games. It may not therefore be a coincidence that the amphitheatre at Pompeii was located in the district closest to its major neighbour Nuceria, just as in Nuceria the amphitheatre built in the first century AD was located in the district closest to Pompeii. The advertisements for gladiatorial games recovered from Pompeii refer to games in both cities.[23] The location of the newly built amphitheatre at Nuceria mirrored the position of the older structure built more than a hundred years earlier at Pompeii.

The pattern of location in the Gallic provinces is reasonably consistent and amphitheatres tended to be located on the edge of the street-grids or even outside them in close proximity to the *necropoleis* of the city (for example, at Agen, Bordeaux, Metz, Périgueux, Tours, Trier). It is possible that the designs of the street-grids did not leave space for the accommodation of new structures. We should not, however, see amphitheatres as directly connected to the dead but instead consider them as a part of the sanctuaries; for example, those respectively outside Toulouse or at Narbonne were in close proximity to a sacred site on the periphery of the city. The locations of amphitheatres across Gaul are not dissimilar to those of theatres, but this is not surprising given the similarities between the Gallic theatre and an amphitheatre.[24] Atttempts to disentangle those elements derived from amphitheatres and those derived from theatres could fill a whole book, but would reveal little about the meaning of these monuments as constructed in particular settings. They were hybrid structures which provided a setting for viewing gladiatorial combats in an orchestra/arena. At the same time it has to be noted that two of the cities that display the greatest development of Roman urbanism in Gaul, Lyon and Amiens (fig. 3.5, 6.6), have Italian-style amphitheatres rather than using the hybrid theatre-amphitheatre form. Often the theatre-amphitheatres of Gaul were set up close to sanctuaries (e.g. Ribemont-sur-Ancre, the sanctuary site associated with Amiens, fig. 10.4), and were even designed in some cases to create a view for the audience seated in the *cavea* not just of the gladiators slogging it out, but also of the temple associated with the sanctuary (see discussion in Chapter 9).

When looking at the distribution of known amphitheatres in Spain, we need to realise that we only have a partial picture; recently a new amphitheatre has been identified at Evora and others may be discovered in future.[25] The appearance of the amphitheatre in Spain does not, however,

---

[23] Sabbatini Tumolesi (1980).　　[24] Golvin (1988), pp. 226–36.

[25] Hipólito Correia (1994a), (1994b); Durán Cabello *et al.* (2009) for an update with 4 new amphitheatres discovered in the last decade at Bracara, Corduba, Sisapo and Legio.

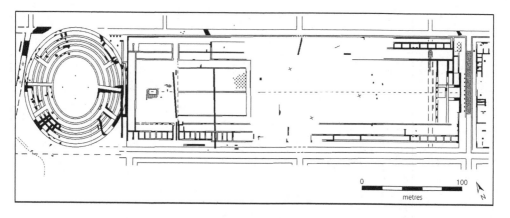

0   100

metres

10.4 Amiens: the amphitheatre was, exceptionally, built on a space adjacent to the forum; interestingly, the northern curve of seating encroaches on the space assigned to streets and disrupts the use of the street to the north of the forum.

seem to have spread in a similar manner to that found in Gaul or the African provinces. Instead, what we see is a dynamic of monumental construction closely related to developments in Rome. The earliest, built at Emporiae during the Republic, was a small arena that could hold about three thousand three hundred spectators (fig. 1.5).[26] The next to be constructed was at Mérida in 8 BC, with a dedicatory inscription to Augustus;[27] the surviving monument probably dates from the first century AD (fig. 2.7).[28] Interestingly, this rebuilding included a feature which in Rome would have been categorised as an imperial box, but which functioned as a site for the worship of the divine emperors, while the uppermost part of the arena wall was decorated with painted scenes of beast-hunting.[29] This was very much an imperial monument in a city rooted in the settlement of veteran soldiers during the Augustan period. The major centres of the provinces produced amphitheatres. Under the Flavians, Segobriga, the *'caput Celtiberiae'*,[30] had both an amphitheatre and a theatre constructed against the hillside outside the walls of the settlement, the amphitheatre having a maximum capacity of seven thousand five hundred spectators (fig. 10.5).[31] In the second century, as part of the reconstruction of the centre of Tarraco, an amphitheatre was built by the *flamen* of the province

[26] Sanmartí-Grego *et al.* (1994); all figures given here are based on those of Golvin (1988), pp. 284–8.
[27] Ramírez Sádaba (1994) for the epigraphy.
[28] Bendala Galán and Durán Cabello (1994) discuss dating of the surviving building; also Durán Cabello (2004); Nogales Basarrate (2000).
[29] Alvarez Martínez and Nogales Basarrate (1994).   [30] Plin. *HN* 3.25.
[31] Sánchez and Pérez (1994).

10.5 Segobriga: plan of the city showing the position of the amphitheatre and theatre located to exploit the existing slopes of the site, whilst being also in close proximity to the forum.

Spain

to seat some twenty-five thousand four hundred spectators and was later restored in the third century.[32] Not surprisingly, the largest amphitheatre was constructed at Italica and seated thirty-four thousand four hundred spectators on a site that was linked by a road directly to the Temple of Trajan at the centre of the grid. Interestingly, the main access to the new grid passed directly from the new Hadrianic road to the city via the site of the amphitheatre (fig. 4.5).[33] These structures were designed not just to hold games but also to display the magnificence of the city to travellers, and in Baetica we find that the preferred location of the amphitheatre was between the city and the Via Augusta, the principal highway of the province (for example, at Córdoba, Écija, Carmo, Seville and Cádiz).[34] They were large buildings in their own right and could be seen by travellers from a considerable distance, and indeed served almost as a badge of identity for a city as a result of their sheer rarity within the provinces of Spain. What we see at Italica is an idea of what a city should be if money were no object – a grid of streets with a temple and baths and just beyond it a very large amphitheatre (fig. 4.5), a view of urban space that was replicated at Tarragona, although with a smaller amphitheatre. By the end of the first century AD and certainly by the second century, there was a Roman conception of urban space that placed the amphitheatre at its edge rather than at its centre, although even at its edge it could occur within the walls as in Augustan Mérida a century earlier.

Britain

In the new province of Britain, we find a Flavian and early second-century phase of amphitheatre construction at sites predominantly situated in a small region of the south – Chichester;[35] Dorchester; Cirencester[36] and Silchester,[37] and at sites with a military presence, whether with soldiers or veterans – Carmarthen, Caerleon and Chester.[38] Significantly, the amphitheatres at both Caerleon and Chester were constructed adjacent to the military *campus* or parade-ground associated with the fortress, neatly highlighting the traditional association between military and gladiatorial training stretching back to the army reforms of Marius in 100 BC.[39] All the amphitheatres tend to be located beyond the walls of their city, often at sites convenient for their construction (for example, within abandoned stone quarries at Cirencester). At London, which had a developing infrastructure in the first century AD, a large amphitheatre was built during the Flavian period, but this may be better associated with the military fort at

w/ campus

---

[32] Dupré i Raventós (1994). [33] Corzo Sánchez (1994a).
[34] See Corzo Sánchez (1994b), p. 244. [35] White (1936); Golvin (1988), p. 87.
[36] Holbrook (1998). [37] Fulford (1989). [38] Wilmott, Garner and Ainsworth (2006).
[39] Mason (2001), pp. 105–6; Mason (2002), pp. 54–6.

Cripplegate rather than the civilian *emporium*;[40] in time the city would become the focus of both the province's administration and its road network.[41] Most amphitheatres in Britain show evidence of an initial timber phase which was later replaced with a stone structure, thereby demonstrating the success of, and desire to maintain, the amphitheatres through the second and even into the third century AD.[42] In contrast to the amphitheatres in the Iberian peninsula, those in Britain are at the bottom end of the size range, with Silchester housing some three thousand six hundred spectators; Cirencester about eight thousand and Chester, one of the larger amphitheatres in Britain, an audience of ten thousand.[43] The spread of amphitheatres in Britain requires a final comment. Compared to Italy or Africa Proconsularis, the amphitheatre was not widely adopted in the towns of the province and, where it did appear, unlike in Spain the structures were modest and designed for smaller audiences.[44] Yet, it was adopted as a monument-type within the very same period in which monuments of a similar nature were being constructed in other provinces.

The cities of North Africa need further explanation. In Africa Proconsularis, which mostly coincided with modern Tunisia, numerous examples of amphitheatres survive, of which only four were built prior to the second century AD: Carthage, El Djem (Thysdrus), Tébessa (Theveste) and Lepcis Magna (figs. 10.6–10.9). It is important to note that this building pattern is also seen with other structures; most first-century AD African cities did not record spending on temples, baths, etc. either, so this should not be seen as a repudiation of one element of Roman culture in favour of others. Those cities which constructed amphitheatres in the first century were special places. Carthage was not only a wealthy city with a large *territorium* (the *pertica Carthaginensium*), but also a Roman colony with Roman settlers and the residence of the governor of the province, who might have expected such a building. The Augustan/Julio-Claudian amphitheatre at Carthage, established within two generations of the refoundation of the city, issued a clear statement about the Romanness of the colonists as well as the relative importance attached to the amphitheatre in the creation of a major Roman colony.

Lepcis, although much smaller than Carthage, was wealthy with a large territory, but crucially had also been a loyal ally of Rome from the Jugurthine War onwards; its elite had started investing in Roman-style

[40] Hassall (2000), p. 53; Tac. *Ann.* 14.33; Amm. Marc. *Res Gestae*, 28.3.1.
[41] Bateman (2000).   [42] de la Bédoyère (1991), pp. 100–2.
[43] See Darvill and Gerrard (1994), p. 79 for discussion of size.
[44] Fulford (1989), p. 193; James (2003).

10.6 Lepcis Magna: standing remains of the amphitheatre.

buildings from the late first century BC.[45] This loyalty to Rome is spelled out in its Trajanic colonial name – *Colonia Ulpia Traiana Fidelis Lepcis Magna*. The Neronian amphitheatre made a clear statement about the importance of the city in regional terms (at least in the view of the governor) but also about its allegiance to the Roman state.[46] El Djem, another city to build an amphitheatre in the Flavian period, was periodically a residence of the proconsul.[47] Tébessa was the base of *Legio III Augusta* after about AD 75 until its move to Lambaesis under Trajan. The erection of the amphitheatre between 76 and 79 can be linked directly to the Flavian shift of the legion from Haïdra to Tébessa.[48] Given the significance of the games to groups such as the army, the importance of keeping the only legion in North Africa happy and the likely desire on the part of the Roman army to demonstrate its Romanness in what was still largely an alien land, it should not come as a surprise that the city also received an

[45] Mattingly (1995), pp. 140–1.   [46] *AE* 1968, 549.   [47] Jouffroy (1986), pp. 195–6.
[48] Lequément (1967), pp. 107–22.

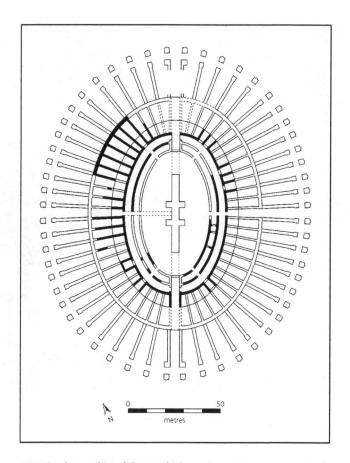

10.7 Carthage: plan of the amphitheatre.

amphitheatre early. There was, therefore, in the first century a group of important cities making a statement about their Romanness and their preeminence in Africa by constructing a special building in which to put on the archetypal Roman pastime of the games.

The amphitheatres in Africa Proconsularis varied considerably in size and we may wonder whether their size reflected a mental calculation of the size of the city population or the number of people expected to attend the games. Such a view would accord well with Vitruvius' consideration[49] of the need to fill the temporary structures built for gladiatorial games in the fora of Italy. We can compare the size of amphitheatres across the province of Africa Proconsularis (taking the largest measurements of length and width),[50] and produce a crude measure of the place of each

---

[49] Vitr. *De arch.* 5. 1–2.   [50] Data from Golvin (1988).

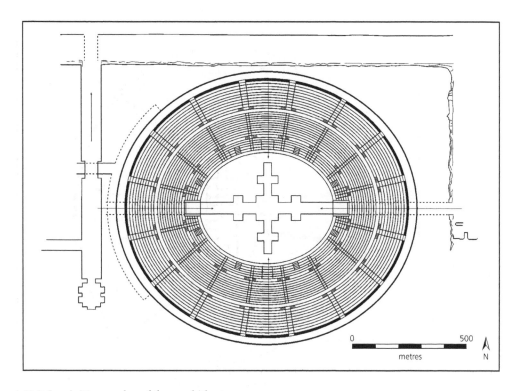

0 ▬▬▬▬▬ 500 ⋀
metres   N

10.8 Lepcis Magna: plan of the amphitheatre.

city within the hierarchy or network of cities within the province (Table 10.2). Carthage and Lepcis Magna head the list in the first century AD with amphitheatres to rival anything being built in Italy at the time. Tébessa also has a fairly large arena, whilst at El Djem a structure was cut into the rock to create an amphitheatre along the lines of that found at Sutri in Etruria (Italy). The rebuilding of this structure expanded the arena, but this was still not large enough, and in the third century a new amphitheatre was constructed which surpassed all those in neighbouring cities and was only eclipsed in size by that of Carthage. The redevelopment at El Djem, even if not completed, points to the city's growth over time, or at least a perception of its changing status. An alternative explanation is possible: as other cities developed amphitheatres, El Djem's arena looked increasingly small by comparison. This feeling of being left behind may have been implicit in the construction of larger arenas in this city. It was one of the residences of the proconsul and was in fact the location for the lynching of the imperial procurator and the proclamation of the proconsul Gordian as emperor in AD 238; the accounts of these events identify it

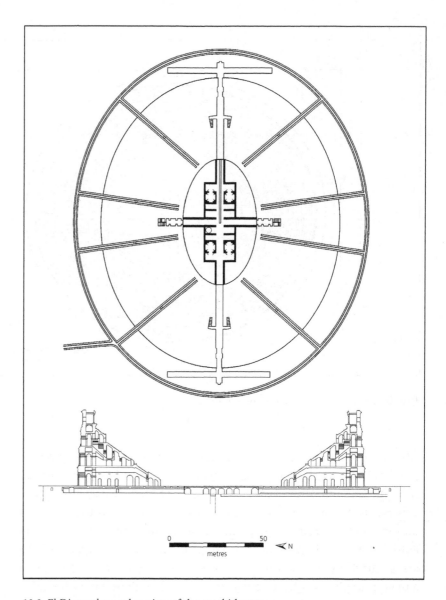

10.9 El Djem: plan and section of the amphitheatre.

as a significant city.[51] Hence the hierarchy of cities found in the texts is reflected in the sizes of their amphitheatres. El Djem was a city that had developed and expanded over a period of just under two hundred years and its development was mirrored in the redevelopment of its arena for beast-hunts and gladiatorial spectacles.

---

[51] Herodian, 7.4–6; S.H.A. *Tres Gordiani* 7–9, *Max.* 14–15. Herodian made the exaggerated claim that it was the Empire's second city. Herodian, 7.6.

Table 10.2 Africa Proconsularis: size of amphitheatres

Name of city	Size (in metres)	Date (AD)
Carthage 2	156×128	Second/third century
Thysdrus (El Djem) 3	148×122	Third century
Lepcis Magna	121×111	Neronian
Carthage 1	120×93	Augustan/Julio-Claudian
Utica (Utique)	118×98	Hadrianic
Sabratha	115×99	Second century
Sicca Veneria (Le Kef)	100×80	?
Uthina (Oudna)	96×81	Second century
Thysdrus (El Djem) 2	92×72	Second half of second century
Theveste (Tebessa)	83×70	74–79
Leptiminus (Lemta)	81×62	Second century
Thuburbo Maius (Henchir Qacbat)	77×62.5	Second century
Sufetela (Sbeitla)	71×59	Second century
Acholla (Bou Tria)	72×56	Second century
Seressi (Oum el Abouab)	69×54	?
Thaenae (Thina)	66×54	?
Thibari (Henchir Hammamet)	61×51.5	?
Mactaris (Mactar)	62×49	Second century
Thapsus (Ras Dimas)	67×43	Second century
Bararus (Rougga)	64×37.5	Third century
Ulisippira (Henchir Zembra)	60×50	?
Agbia (Henchir Ain Hedja)	60×?	?
Thignica (Ain Tounga)	56×46	Second century
Bulla Regia (Hammam Darradji)	60×40	Second century
Thysdrus (El Djem) 1	49×40	First century

Given the types of cities constructing amphitheatres in the first century AD, it could be asked whether these buildings really demonstrated the wider 'African' elite buying into this aspect of Roman culture at all. It is also noticeable that, while seven amphitheatres are attested for the whole of North Africa by the end of the first century, only three sets of baths are dated to that period.[52] Those few communities that were attempting to demonstrate their Romanness through construction in the first century AD prioritised the construction of an amphitheatre over the provision of baths.

What, then, could have provided the catalyst for the construction of other amphitheatres in the second century? After all, the regional capital Carthage had had an amphitheatre since the Augustan period and that

[52] Jouffroy (1986), pp. 193–7.

apparently had not influenced building trends. The presence of four amphitheatres scattered throughout the province provided a model, but the new
building could also have reflected the evolution of the region's relationship
with Rome, with the erection of such a Roman monument being the
physical manifestation of this process. The second century was also when
baths began to be built in some quantity (Table 8.3). The idea of Romanness
may therefore have taken hold and the amphitheatre, like the baths, formed
part of an ensemble that was adopted by cities in the province. Moreover,
the region had become wealthier by this period as a result of increased
exports to Rome and other parts of the Empire. The import patterns into
Rome and Ostia reveal that the Trajanic-Hadrianic period witnessed huge
growth in the number of amphorae being exported from Proconsularis to
the capital.[53] The profits which African exporters made from this trade may
well have helped to finance the second-century construction boom.

The construction of amphitheatres had largely ceased by the mid-third
century. This is not to say that they were all abandoned, and indeed several
cities repaired or rebuilt their amphitheatres during the fourth century,[54]
while literary works seem to attest to the Carthaginian population's continued mania for the games into the fifth century.[55] Some cities in
Proconsularis decided in the second century to follow Carthage, El Djem
and others and build amphitheatres, but this trend did not continue. The
expense of construction could have been a factor. Many cities, and especially the smaller ones, may not have been able to afford the vast amounts
necessary and so decided to concentrate on other physical manifestations of
Romanness such as the baths. Moreover, multiple examples in a single city
were extremely uncommon, El Djem and Carthage both clearly being
special cases. Other African cities without amphitheatres may have presented games by making use of alternative venues rather than erecting
purpose-built structures.

Amphitheatres were obviously important indicators of city status in
North Africa during the second and early third centuries and the major
cities competed to construct large buildings capable of servicing the
community but also demonstrating their perceived power, wealth and
status. For those cities that could afford them, they were also a way of

---

[53] MacMullen (1988), fig. 9–10.
[54] E.g. Thuburbo Maius: *CIL* 8.23894 = 12368 = 852; El Djem: Lequément (1967); Tipasa: Lancel
(1982), p. 775; Sétif: *AE* 1928 39, *CIL* 8.8482.
[55] August. *Conf.*, VII.6.13; August. *Enarratio in Psalmum*, 80, 102, 103, 146 and 147;
Quodvultdeus, *Sermo de tempore barbarico*, I.1; Canon 15 of the Council of Carthage demanded
that the sons of bishops should not attend spectacles.

demonstrating their Romanness. At the same time, possibly because of their expense and also because games could be staged elsewhere, it could be argued that an amphitheatre was not crucial to a city's image and everyday life in the way that baths were. Those cities that could not afford them demonstrated their cultural sophistication in other ways.

AMPHITHEATRES AND URBAN CULTURE

The distribution of known amphitheatres across the provinces of the Empire is utterly uneven (Table 10.3). In the eastern half there were very few of these uniquely Roman structures. When we look at the West, however, the figures show a strong presence of the amphitheatre in the cities of Gaul and Africa (fig. 10.2). Perhaps surprisingly, there are only as many in Spanish cities as in British, despite the fact that there were many more Spanish cities than British. Obviously the way in which sites have been preserved and the intensity of archaeological exploration can affect the nature of the raw data. This, however, does not account for the fact that amphitheatres have been found in twenty-seven cities in Gaul whereas in only fifteen in Spain, because the nature of preservation and investigation in the two regions is similar. A possible cause of this variation is the association between the amphitheatre and the military. Whereas a noticeable proportion of the population of Britain comprised soldiers or veterans (*c.* 5 per cent?), there were far fewer soldiers to be found in the Spanish provinces.

The large number of amphitheatres in Italy by the first century AD points to this feature of the city having enjoyed a greater cultural importance there in creating urban form. The absence of an amphitheatre from the majority of cities in Spain can be explained by its chronology of urban development. The Roman city as reproduced in Spain looked to and replicated an earlier model of urbanism in Italy than its counterparts in most other provinces. Spanish cities used a late Republican and early first-century model, which had not yet developed the full panoply of monuments that we find in Italy in the first and second centuries AD. Once established, however, Roman urbanism in Spain did not take up the amphitheatre, just as those areas in the East with a history of urban culture did not build amphitheatres (see below for further discussion of Spanish amphitheatres). This did not mean, of course, that gladiatorial contests were not held in the East.[56] During the

---

[56] Robert (1940); Golvin (1988), pp. 237–49.

Table 10.3 Regional distribution of known
amphitheatres (data from Golvin with additions)

Region	Number of amphitheatres known
Italy	77
Gaul	27
Africa Proconsularis	23
Britannia	16
Spain	15
Syria/Arabia/Palestine/Egypt	7
Pannonia	7
Germany	5
Numidia	4
Asia Minor	4
Sicily	3
Dacia	3
Noricum	2
Dalmatia	2
Mauretania	2
Macedonia	1
Greece	1

period when Roman urbanism was being developed for the first time in Gaul and Britain, the first and second centuries AD, we can see cities in both provinces focussing on this relatively novel item, and so the amphitheatre became a 'must have' feature. British cities were probably influenced by the large military garrisons to whom amphitheatres were evidently important; indeed, veterans may even have provided amphitheatres to create a more familiar urban world.[57]

The trajectory of Roman urbanism in Africa Proconsularis was similar and may have drawn on the examples of Roman Italy; indeed, the presence of so many amphitheatres across this senatorial province points to its close connection with the culture of cities in central Italy. The action of a single proconsul, emulating the Emperor Nero's enthusiasm for amphitheatre construction, caused Lepcis Magna's amphitheatre to be carved out of the rock. This Neronian edifice was a colossal 121×111 metres in dimensions and a lasting memorial to the governor of the province.

At an Empire-wide level, the fact that so many cities did not possess an amphitheatre makes it difficult to claim that it was an essential component

[57] Cf. Creighton (2006).

of the city (as Vitruvius recognised).[58] Within individual regions, however, and particularly Italy, Africa Proconsularis and Gaul, the presence of an amphitheatre marked out a city as being different from its neighbours who did not have the will to construct such a vast monument and sustain games that would fill the seats within it year after year. In Italy we find amphitheatres in almost as many cities as we can locate theatres. It must have been a key feature of urbanism across the Italian peninsula (apart perhaps from the south), but why was the example of Italy not taken up by other regions, apart from North Africa and to a limited extent the newly incorporated barbarians in the north-west provinces? There is no obvious epigraphic link with a single phase or with the actions of particular emperors in the promotion of these structures in the Empire. We cannot account for the pattern of their distribution with reference to the *adventus* or journeys of any particular emperor. Even though the charter of the Caesarian colony at Urso (44 BC)[59] stipulates that the *duumviri* should give gladiatorial games, we do not find a precise correlation between the Caesarian and Triumviral colonies and known sites of amphitheatres.[60] Clearly, as Welch demonstrates, gladiatorial shows were part of the way of life of these settlements, but this did not have to result in the construction of a stone amphitheatre.[61] Welch's conclusion of a correlation between stone amphitheatres and the settlement of veterans is attractive, but is driven by the evidence from Pompeii and just nine other cities.[62] There were plenty of colonies in which veterans were settled but where amphitheatres have not been located, although it must be borne in mind that we may not yet have detected the amphitheatres archaeologically. The empirical explanation of the link may not, however, be as important as the generic importance of gladiatorial games in the town charter from Urso. Gladiatorial games were part of the way of life of any city, and what enhanced that way of life was to have an amphitheatre or a range of seating (termed the *spectacula* in a building inscription from Pompeii).[63] The amphitheatre was also a new urban form, not appearing in the Latin language until the time of Augustus.[64] It therefore represented an addition to the range of buildings that constituted the urban nature of the city. It was not essential, but enhanced the standing of a place. This cultural value of building an amphitheatre was, however, relatively short-lived and was for the most part a phenomenon of the first

---

[58] Vitr. *De arch.* 1.7.1.   [59] Crawford (1996a) for text and translation.
[60] Welch (2007), pp. 88–90.   [61] Welch (1994), pp. 61–6.
[62] Welch (1994), p. 66; a thesis she follows through in her book published in (2007), pp. 74–9, 189–98.
[63] *CIL* 10.852, also 10.1074d; Welch (1994), p. 61.   [64] Etienne (1966).

and early second centuries AD. After this the financial outlay on such a structure was not seen to pay off in terms of the improvement to a city's way of life.[65]

At the local level of the city, the addition of an amphitheatre altered the existing structure of space. It provided a new venue for the expression of different elements of Roman society. The law, leisure and religion were all tied to the structure. The amphitheatre was a location for the punishment of those who contravened the law and, classically, for the punishment of those who denied the divinity of the gods. For instance, there are a few examples of martyrs executed for their Christian faith in African amphitheatres, although more were beheaded or died in prison.[66] Saints Perpetua and Felicitas and their companions were killed in the amphitheatre at Carthage in AD 202 and Saints Donatilla, Maxima and Secunda were martyred in 304 (the dating follows that of Tilley), probably at Thuburbo Maius; their bodies were interred in the burial ground attached to the amphitheatre for the disposal of executed criminals.[67] Through their function as venues for execution some amphitheatres (such as at Tarragona) became incorporated in the second and third centuries into a new religious history alongside their more traditional role.

AMPHITHEATRES AND SACRED SPACE

Already by the first century BC, amphitheatres had become part of the sacred landscape of the city, often located outside the central grid as defined (or not) by walls. At the games, often given by decurions, the forum would have been one location for processions and events, the theatres were the place for plays and/or music, but the place for athletics and gladiatorial combats was the amphitheatre.[68] It was connected to the other locations for games and entertainments, or to sanctuaries through the staging of processions (compare Chapter 9 on the role of *iuvenes*). At Tipasa in Mauretania, for example, the Antonine or Severan amphitheatre formed a nexus with two contemporary temples on the *decumanus maximus*.[69] The act of formally moving across the city during festivals created a structure to

---

[65] Patterson (2006b), pp. 179–82.

[66] Compare Euseb. *Hist. Eccl.* book 5 for the persecution of Christians in Lyon: many died in prison, some Roman citizens were beheaded, non-citizens thrown to the beasts in the amphitheatre.

[67] *Passio Sanctarum Perpetuae et Felicitatis* 18–21; *Passio Sanctae Maximae Donatillae et Secunda* 6; Tilley (1996), pp. 13–14.

[68] See for example *CIL* 10.1074d = Cooley and Cooley D8.   [69] Frézouls (1952), pp. 111–77.

urban space. The placement of the amphitheatre at a distance from the forum or other monumental centres expanded the distance travelled by the procession.[70] The addition of an amphitheatre, or specific place for the watching of gladiatorial events, altered the nature of the city and redefined the rituals associated with the annual games, as it gathered to it rituals that may have previously taken place in other venues or, through its particular placing within the urban topography and its specific type of contained space, allowed for the creation of new rites. The amphitheatre may also have given a community a chance to rearticulate their own past through the games and associated rituals conducted in the new structure. One of the most interesting elements of Perpetua's passion was that she and her companions were initially forced to dress in the garb of priests of Saturn and priestesses of Ceres before they rebelled and the guards relented; the Carthaginian community were using deaths within the amphitheatre to reaffirm their dedication to a particularly African pantheon that had dominated the region long before the Punic Wars.[71] It may also have been an opportunity for rearticulating the past.[72] The provision of amphi- theatres could certainly establish new urban armatures of the type identi- fied by MacDonald in the cities of North Africa.[73] The amphitheatre, like the theatre, was a place in which the order of society was confirmed: people seated in their correct place according to their status, the expression of a city's dislike of its neighbours (e.g. at Pompeii in AD 59) and the staged fighting and bloodshed by professional fighters. All these expressions of identity could have been articulated in cities which did not have an amphi- theatre, but possession of one allowed a person to watch them from a seat among fellow citizens and resident aliens, and thereby enhanced the expe- rience and permitted the demonstration of the urban culture of one's city to others.

For many cities, though, the amphitheatre had little purpose. The dis- tribution of the arenas across the Empire reveals that an urban culture could be achieved without this monument. Moreover, from the middle of the second century relatively few new amphitheatres were built. This did not mean that games featuring gladiators and beast hunts simply ceased to exist. Christianity certainly did not lead to their suppression.[74] Sculptural reliefs and figures featuring gladiators continue to be produced into the

---

[70] Rogers (1991), pp. 80–126; the best evidence for processions in texts is found at Ephesus.
[71] *Passio Sanctarum Perpetuae et Felicitatis* 6.1.
[72] Rogers (1991), pp. 140–4; at Ephesus (a city without an amphitheatre) we find a reinvention of the past by means of the institution of a new procession in AD 104.
[73] MacDonald (1986).   [74] Wiedemann (1992), pp. 128–64.

fourth century and we can also find mosaics and lamps that feature gladiators into late antiquity.[75] Gladiators may have enjoyed a greater longevity than many of the amphitheatres as a feature of the culture of the cities. What is clear, however, is that many cities attempted the building of an amphitheatre and benefited from the use of this amenity.

[75] E.g. La Regina (2001), p. 76.

11 | The Roman city in *c.* AD 250: an urban legacy of empire?

This book began with an account of the formation of Roman urbanism in the late third and early second centuries BC and the following chapters, as in other books on the Roman city, have focussed on the dates of the establishment of cities and monumental development. The latter could be regarded as having produced an urban culture across the Empire, but the previous chapters have shown a dramatic variation in the adoption, deployment and building of monument-types across the provinces of the Roman West.[1] We must now turn to the outcome of this process of urban formation and account for the variations within Roman urbanism across the western Empire.[2] More important, perhaps, is our intention to produce an understanding of the overall pattern of urbanism and to develop a macro-theory of Roman urban development that includes cities from right across the Roman West, rather than focussing on a single monument-type or province or the evidence from a single modern geographical region that coincides with a nation state. Unlike other accounts of the pattern of urbanism, we are less concerned here with the initial phase or adoption of the idea of having a town, and focus our discussion on the sustainability of Roman urbanism over the longer term or *longue durée*.[3]

Earlier chapters often began in Italy before moving outwards across the Mediterranean to Spain or Gallia Narbonensis and then across Gallia Comata and ultimately to Britain. This follows the pattern found in earlier books stretching back to the early twentieth century and the works of Francis Haverfield on both Romanisation and ancient town planning. In these the Roman conception of government by cities and the physical manifestation of the city spread inevitably across the landscape of Europe and the cities were gradually elaborated through the inclusion of monuments such as amphitheatres, theatres, etc.[4] For writers in the first half of the twentieth century, these were the benefits of civilisation brought to the barbarians of Europe.[5] The postcolonial generation of scholars (as seen in

---

[1] See Clarke and Robinson (1997) on differentiation between Roman cities.
[2] See Haussler (1999); Revell (1999), (2009) for alternative versions to our own thesis.
[3] Aitchison (1998).   [4] Haverfield (1913).   [5] Hingley (2000); Freeman (1997).

Martin Millett's *The Romanization of Roman Britiain*, and more recently in papers in Simon Keay and Nicola Terrenato (eds), *Romanization in the West*) saw things differently and understood the cultural changes that produced the city in terms of patronage and the acculturation of the Mediterranean *polis* to the social situation of the newly acquired provinces.[6] The patronage of the elite, often unstated, apparently spread the idea of the city and urban living to the rest of the population. Added on to this model of urban adoption or urban elaboration was a conception of agency (derived from the work of Anthony Giddens) by which the elite bought into the idea of the city, and Tacitus *Agricola* 20–2 has often been cited as evidence for this.[7] We need, however, to recognise that not all features of the city of Rome or the Roman city as reproduced by the local elites may have been acceptable to their followers. For example, Josephus notes that when King Herod introduced fights between beasts and criminals into Judaea, non-Jews were astonished at the expense and enjoyed the excitement and danger, while Jews viewed these games as a challenge to their ancient customs.[8] This example highlights how, in dealing with the Roman city, we need to extend the range of participants in it. An elite might present a novel form of Roman culture, but the creation of a town required the participation of a larger number of individuals, who might be attracted to a different structure of social and spatial organisation from what went before.

The new town or 'definite place' could empower individuals in new ways.[9] Part of the new structure of society was a conception of the city: an entity which was attractive not just for the elite, but for others who wished to live within grids of streets, in close proximity to monuments or a forum. The city became a *habitus* for many members of the non-elite across the Empire. During the second and third centuries AD, however, this ceased to be the case and in some regions we see an almost complete reversal in the building of monumental architecture which points not just to a shift in the expenditure of resources in the city, but also to a change in the *mentalité* of urbanism. It is these topics that form the subject of this final chapter, which examines these changes but also looks back to the impact of Rome on the formation of a culture of cities in the first two centuries AD. As readers will have noticed in earlier chapters, the cities of the African provinces do not follow the patterns of either Italy, Spain, Gallia Narbonensis or Sicily, nor those of Gallia Comata, Lusitania or Britain. Again the pattern of change is

---

[6] Millett (1990); Keay and Terrenato (2001).

[7] Giddens (1984); for discussion and some adjustment see: Millett (1990); Barrett (1997); Forcey (1997); Mattingly (1997); Grahame (1997); Revell (1999); Revell (2000); Mattingly (2004).

[8] Joseph. *AJ* 15.8.1.   [9] Barrett (1997); Forcey (1997).

rather different in North Africa from elsewhere and in this chapter we define among other things what it is that made the Roman city in Africa follow a different trajectory from its counterpart in Europe.

THE PATTERN OF URBANISM

The city, or urbanism, should not be considered in isolation from either its hinterland, or its relationship to other cities. The city was set within a world of cities that constituted an urban network, in part artificially woven into a pattern of Roman geography by means of the road system.[10] This wider geography of urbanism did not have a uniform pattern and in part helps to explain some of the regional differences apparent in the cities of the Roman Empire. The density of cities across the Empire varied considerably. For example, in Umbria in central Italy or Baetica in southern Spain the average distance between towns was thirteen kilometres, whereas in Britain or Gaul the next town was likely to be on average one hundred and five kilometres away.[11] These are the extreme cases, and the more usual pattern to the urban network of cities saw those in the Mediterranean located at an average distance of about thirty kilometres apart, while sixty kilometres was the average distance separating those in the western provinces.[12] What this implies is that the size of the rural hinterland of the Roman city was quite different according to its geographical location, so that the city of Carmarthen, for example, was built on the resources of a larger territory than that of Narni. There would of course have been differences in population density or in the ways in which the hinterlands of these cities were organised or developed to produce a surplus. Perhaps most importantly, Narni existed in close proximity to Rome, an urban market of one million people to which goods were supplied and from which profits may have returned to Narni. Rome as the ultimate 'consumer city' was also the ultimate market for goods and thus also the ultimate means for producing a surplus through the sale and redistribution of goods, which may have fuelled urban development within the towns of central Italy and across the Mediterranean.[13] What is clear from these examples is that the Roman

---

[10] Storey (2008) puts forward a model of the Roman world-economy that envisages economic behaviour to be embedded in its structure, but that individuals have the agency to deploy strategies of maximisation. For some the process transforms a principle of accumulation into a structure for ceaseless accumulation of goods.

[11] Bekker-Nielsen (1989), p. 28.   [12] Bekker-Nielsen (1989), p. 28.

[13] Morley (1996), pp. 55–82.

city's relationship with its hinterland and urban neighbours was at least partially dependent on its geographical location at the centre or the periphery of the Empire.

The density of towns or cities within a landscape is an important factor for understanding urbanism and its survival in the longer term. The rural populations of central Italy lived in close proximity to towns at maximum distances of eight to nineteen kilometres, and most rural inhabitants of the provinces lived within a day's journey of a town (i.e. within thirty-seven kilometres); it was only where urbanism was at best tenuous that we find the urban population dissociated by distance from the nearest city.[14] Rural dwelling at a distance from a city was not, however, an uncommon experience, characterising the geography of at least one third of the area of Gaul and the Germanies and existing to a similar degree in both the Spanish provinces and Britain.[15] There towns may not have had a hold over the landscape in the way that would be expected in areas where the urban network was of a greater density and the city was part of the *habitus* of rural living, as opposed to a distant place to which journeys were made infrequently. This variation could be described as the level of urbanisation of the countryside. Where the city network was denser the level of urbanisation of the countryside was greater and so facilitated a greater number of people to live within towns; where the network of cities was less dense, we can expect the countryside to have been less integrated with the city and so to have been less supportive of an urban population. Recent work on the archaeology of towns in Roman Britain demonstrates a general pattern according to which the town became the generator of an urbanised countryside.[16]

The density of cities, at least in Italy, was a product of settlement-formation processes that dated back to periods before the third century BC. The reconfiguration of the landscape of central Italy through the building of long-distance roads and the settlement of colonists altered the existing settlement geography to generate the conditions for the evolution of the densest urban network in the Empire.[17] The survival of a settlement as a city was not a simple matter of economics. It could also have been ideological, relating to a city's history and infusing it with a value that was an asset to be maintained. Nowhere do we see this more clearly than at Cosa, a Latin colony which by the first century AD, and certainly the second century, was simply a town in the wrong place; yet there were numerous

---

[14] See Bekker-Nielsen (1989), p. 29 for these figures.   [15] Bekker-Nielsen (1989), pp. 27, 10.
[16] Gaffney *et al.* (2007); Mattingly (2006), pp. 379–426 for a review of the landscapes of Britain; Pitts and Perring (2006), but the thesis is questioned by Woolf (1998).
[17] Laurence (1999).

attempts to maintain the city and its monuments.[18] Cosa is also interesting because it lay within the nautical hinterland of the city of Rome (as defined by Morley) but, unlike the towns of inland central Italy, did not flourish.[19] Nor do we find the urban density of towns characterising inland central Italy along the coastal strip of Etruria. One explanation for this may be endemic malaria, but that condition would also have applied to much of central Italy within reach of the Tiber Valley.[20] Both these areas within the hinterland of Rome, in theory at least, existed under similar geographical and economic conditions; yet the inland region sustained a greater density of towns compared to the coastal region.[21] This reminds us that the city is a social phenomenon, rather than an economic product or indicator of economic well-being. The demand to sustain cities as a social surplus in the inland region of central Italy was seemingly higher and more success-fully carried out than in the coastal region, even though that was well-connected by patronage to the capital.[22]

Reading the descriptions of Pliny the Elder, Pomponius Mela and Ptolemy or examining the Barrington Atlas, it is clear that throughout the provinces there were numerous towns and a series of urban networks underpinned by communications, whether by road, river or the sea.[23] Once places were included in the geography of Marcus Agrippa at the beginning of the Imperial period, they had a habit of becoming fixed in the landscape of geographers. For example, Ruscino in Narbonensis, near modern Perpignan, appears in Pliny as *Ruscino Latinorum* to indicate that the population were citizens with Latin rights. Archaeologically and epigraph-ically we can see the massive development of a forum (of dimensions 50×58 metres) with a basilica and imperial statuary in the first century AD.[24] By the end of that period, however, the public buildings lay abandoned. This did not stop the place from being included in Ptolemy's listing of *poleis* in the second century AD.[25] The rise and fall of cities as places is written into parts of the geographical section of Pliny's *Natural History*; for instance, Ruscino's neighbour, *oppidum Illiberis,* was a mere shadow of the great *urbs* or city it had been in the past.[26] Pliny includes cities that were worthy of mention or whose names could easily be rendered into Latin (*ex his digna*

---

[18] See Patterson (2006), pp. 92–101.   [19] Morley (1996), p. 64.   [20] Sallares (2002).
[21] See Witcher 2006 on rural settlement patterns and bibliography.
[22] Patterson (2006), pp. 99–100.
[23] Downs (1996); Keay (1996); Knapp (1996) for different approaches to these sources and Baetica.
[24] Plin. *HN* 3.32; inscriptions *ILN* 414–41; *RAN* Suppl.7: 67–80.
[25] Ptol. *Geog.* 2.10.6; cf. Mela 2.5.84.
[26] Plin. *HN* 3.32; compare the rise and fall of cities in Strabo and see Clarke (1999), pp. 274–6.

memoratu aut Latino sermone dictu facile 3.8), but his vision of the geography of cities in the provinces is that of a member of the Roman government, as can be seen in his enumeration of the cities and towns of Baetica, one hundred and seventy-five in total: nine colonies, ten *municipia* of Roman citizens, twenty-seven towns with Latin rights, six free towns, three allied towns and then the one hundred and twenty that paid tax.[27]

Some placenames in the provinces reflected the status of a city's citizens; for example, *Lucentum Latinorum* and *Dianum Stipendarium* indicated the presence in the former of citizens with Latin rights and in the latter of payers of tribute.[28] The relationship between cities and taxation seems to be a feature of the provincial sections of Pliny's text. For instance, the colony of Caesaraugusta, modern Zaragoza, is noted as paying no tax, and there is a sense that peoples incorporated into existing provinces came with their *oppidum*, from which the governor or procurator would extract tribute and taxation.[29] At the same time, we need to recognise that the ancient geographers were creating a vision of an empire that reflected well on Rome and its emperor. Listing a large number of cities or *poleis* not only showed off the geographer's knowledge, but was also part of the rhetoric of praise that created an empire full of cities.[30] The Empire needed cities as places from which to collect tax as well as in order to assert its claim to civilise barbarians and create a peace that was not 'a desolation'.[31]

A DESIRABLE URBAN *HABITUS*

The establishment of a town and the building of monuments and houses involved not only money but also human labour. This in itself should be viewed as an economic function of a town. Its building or rebuilding involved a large segment of the human population. To put a figure on it we might look at pre-Revolutionary Paris, where a third of the population was defined as builders.[32] Nevertheless, the building or rebuilding of a town or the building or restoration of a monument involved far more than just the labour of those involved in its construction on site. Materials needed to be extracted, processed and transported to the site, extending the impact of a building project across the landscape and into the hinterland of the city.[33]

---

[27] Plin. *HN* 3.7; a similar listing appears for Hispania Citerior – Plin. *HN* 3.18.   [28] Plin. *HN* 3.20.
[29] Plin. *HN* 3.24, 3.37.   [30] Compare Aelius Aristides, *Orationes* 26.   [31] Tac. *Agr.* 30, 38.
[32] Rudé (1959), p. 19, (1952), on the composition of pre-industrial city populations.
[33] DeLaine (1997), (2001) devises costs in terms of human labour for the construction of the Baths of Caracalla and for Ostian apartment blocks.

To realise a building project or the creation of a town, there had to be access to resources: building materials and the necessary production know-how, but also the desire to produce such a structure.[34] The last factor was an important dynamic within the urban economy, but was neither linear nor continuous, but rather subject to fluctuation and considerable variation even within a single region.[35] Building projects did kick-start urbanism, provide employment, and distribute economic resources from the elite to others within the community. These economic resources might have been utilised in new ways and to generate new services within the new settlement or to enhance the agricultural resources of the hinterland. Alternatively, the distributed economic resources could have been consumed in the purchase of goods supplied by outsiders. How the distributed economic resources were employed need not concern us too much, since the fact that such distribution occurred as a by-product of building projects is important in itself. Of course, when building projects ceased, only the sustainable activities resulting from the distributed economic resources derived from the projects could continue. Towns on major transport routes, whether seaports, river-ports or road-stations, could provide additional services to travellers who would continue to provide additional economic resources to the fledgling city.

Yet symptoms of urban regression can be identified in legal texts and government actions from the first century AD onwards. There appears to have been a consciousness that urbanism was fragile and that this fragility was increasing with time and required the attention of the authorities, who used legal opinion to legitimate interventions that extended from the public into the private realm. The town charters of the first centuries BC and AD were quite explicit that no one should unroof, demolish or dismantle a building, unless a guarantee was given to the *duoviri* that he would rebuild it.[36] These laws have been interpreted as measures to prevent a reduction in the number of homes in these cities.[37] The Senate's concern for the prevention of *ruinae* (ruins) can be seen in the *senatus consultum Hosidianum* of AD 45.[38] At the end of the second century AD the works of the Severan lawyers restate the need to enforce this law with a wider remit. The duties of a provincial governor included the problem of buildings in disrepair; his remit was to compel the owners

---

[34] See Rust (2006) for an extensive discussion on these issues.
[35] Rust (2006), pp. 145–59 for discussion.
[36] *Lex Tarentina* 32–5, Crawford (1996a), pp. 304, 307; Urso Charter 75, Crawford (1996a), pp. 404, 424.
[37] Phillips (1973), p. 89.   [38] *Senatus Consultum Hosidianum – ILS* 6043.

to make repairs and, where they refused, 'he should by the use of competent remedy against them patch up the unsightly appearance of buildings'.[39] As has been observed by Burton, a provincial governor was limited by time in the pursuit of such matters, unlike a *curator rei publicae*, who acted in effect as a surrogate governor and was appointed for a much longer period of time (up to ten years) specifically to set a city's affairs in order.[40] *Curatores* and provincial governors were senators with considerable experience and their roles were not seen as separate. [41] The *curator*, faced with a refusal to repair a building, could divert public funds for this purpose and charge the costs, plus interest, to the owner or sell the property.[42] These were measures intended to respond to a visible and growing crisis in the cities which led to some in the Roman West to become full of *ruinae* – an affront to Roman aesthetic sensibilities which expected to see a city maintained through time. A city's public funds, previously spent on monuments, might now be spent on restoring private structures for resale. Another abuse symptomatic of the collapse of urbanism is highlighted by an early third-century restatement of the law that a house or a part of a house should not be sold for salvage, with liability assigned to both vendor and purchaser.[43] *Curatores* also needed to ensure that public property was not encroached upon or subsumed into private property and could either repossess it or impose a rent upon it;[44] they were also directly involved in the management of restoration projects for public buildings as early as the mid-second century[45] and their presence in any city may be an indicator of temporary financial difficulties.[46] The instructions given to the *curatores* and governors were to preserve the finances of the cities by combining a diligence to duty with human benevolence that would prevent them from appearing arrogant to or humiliating the people of the cities in their care.[47] In the cities of Gaul, where the surplus to maintain the urban fabric had ceased to exist and what was left of the city was in many cases surrounded by ruins, this allowed them the possibility of benign neglect.

---

[39] *Dig.* 1.18.7, Ulpian; Jacques (1984), p. 295.   [40] Burton (1979), pp. 476–7.

[41] E.g. *CIL* 6.1448, 1507; see Liebenam (1897) and now Jacques (1983), (1984); *Dig.* 22.1.33, Ulpian; *Dig.* 50.10.5, Ulpian.

[42] *Dig.* 39.2.46, Paul; Burton (1979); Jacques (1984); Boatwright (2000), pp. 73–8; Liebenam (1897); see Lucas (1940) on the role of *curators*.

[43] *Dig.* 39.2.48, Marcian.

[44] *Dig.* 50.10.5.1; attested at Bettona in Umbria *CIL* 11.5182; also see *Dig.* 50.8.11, 50.9.4.

[45] *CIL* 12.1805 *curator* supervises work on the amphitheatre at Lyon; for other examples see Jacques (1984), p. 297; *Dig.* 50.12.1.

[46] Duthoy (1970); but see Whittaker (1994).   [47] *Dig.* 22.1.33, Ulpian.

This bleak picture of urban decline and a lack of monumental buildings has recently been countered by John Patterson with the suggestion that participation in and spending on urbanism changed in the second century, at least within Italy, to include a greater number of people.[48] In particular, there seems to have been a far greater role for the *collegia*, or guilds, within the cities. Inscriptions set up in both the East and the West record their presence, and what we know of their members gives us some insight into what sort of people inhabited the cities.[49] A *collegium* referred to a group of people who acted together, shared a common interest (trade, religion or simply the fact of being foreigners) and were an officially recognised group within the structure of cities.[50] Their members were regarded by the elite as rather more significant than the other inhabitants of the cities of the Empire. For example, at Puteoli we know of money distributions to decurions, *augustales, collegia* and then other *municipes* – a pattern repeated in other towns.[51] Special seats were assigned to members of *collegia* in the amphitheatres of Arles, Nîmes and Saintes.[52] The interpretation of the nature of these *collegia* attested in inscriptions is difficult and has been subject to numerous anachronistic readings of the evidence.[53] What is clear, though, is that the closer to Rome, the greater the number of professional *collegia* with magistrates – in fact three hundred and thirteen of the three hundred and forty-two magistrates belonging to professional *collegia* in Italy recorded in inscriptions came from Rome, Ostia and Portus.[54] The number of *collegia* and their major activity, the provision of banquets for members, was said to have had the effect of driving up food prices in the *macellum* at Rome in the late first century BC.[55] We can find evidence for *collegia* of builders, carpenters, sailors, shippers of oil, worshippers of Isis, and people associated with the forum (*forenses*) from right across the cities of the Roman West.[56]

It is possible that it was in towns which were important ports, with a substantial transient population, that *collegia* were of greatest significance. In the provinces, for example, Arles, Lyon, Vienne, Nîmes and Narbonne were all towns with a trading link from the Rhône valley to the

---

[48] Patterson (2006), pp. 125–83.   [49] Patterson (1994); Nijf (1997).
[50] See Diosono (2007) for a readable account.
[51] *CIL* 10.1881; *CIL* 5.7905, 7920, 11.4589, 6053, 6071, 6378.
[52] *CIL* 12. 697, 714, 3316–18; 13.1052, see Caldelli (2004), pp. 152–5.
[53] Perry (2006), provides a full account.
[54] Royden (1988), p. 238; by comparison the number of inscriptions referring to butchers is split more or less half and half between Rome and the rest of Italy, see Chioffi (1999).
[55] Varro, *Rust.* 3.2.16; Patterson (2006), p. 176.
[56] Waltzing (1899) for the fullest published listing.

Mediterranean and on to Rome as well as links northwards to the Saône and on to the legions in Germany.[57] Significantly, these were the routes used by the Roman state to supply the city of Rome and the troops on the Rhine, and it is logical to conclude from the evidence that these *collegia* were probably sponsored by the emperor or the state from the second century onwards.[58] People involved in trade and located along these access-routes of logistical interest to the government were able to divert money from their commercial activities for the maintenance of an urban presence. The density of inscriptions relating to these groups, and the number of groups named in them, increase along these major points in the communications network, which points to work or trade as a feature of identity formation and the gradual merging of the interests of these *collegia* with those of the state from the beginning of the second century.[59] We should not, however, stress unduly the uniqueness of these examples; sailors, according to the Severan lawyers' most ancient authority Solon, were seen to have a greater need for these associations than other less mobile professionals.[60] *Collegia* can be found as part of the epigraphic repertoire of any province,[61] which points to the universality of this form of group activity amongst the *plebs media* (the middling people, not the poorest of the plebs defined by the term *plebs sordida*),[62] and, according to an edict of Septimius Severus, they were expected to form part of the social landscape of Rome, Italy and the provinces.[63] Yet it has to be said that the pattern points to their enjoying a far greater prominence on the rivers of Gaul leading to the two provinces of Germany. Traders and craftsmen were the logical residents of any city, as well as those who derived an income from the markets held there. *Collegia* were also integrated into civic rituals at festivals and formed a prominent group at public banquets,[64] as well as having a strong connection with the elite through patronage and also with the workings of the Roman state.[65] Hence, we should see them and their activities as derived from the social and spatial structure that was so clearly focussed on the urban rather than the rural population.

---

[57] Sirks (1991), pp. 97–102; De Salvo (1993), pp. 396–412; Woolf (1998), p. 101; Waltzing (1899), pp. 524–32, 558–78, 536–40, 541–7, 548–52.

[58] Middleton (1979); De Salvo (1993), pp. 94–102; Sirks (1991), pp. 84–9, 313–22; on basis of Aur. Vict. *Caes.* 13.5 the origins are attributed to Trajan.

[59] Sirks (1991), pp. 313–22; De Salvo (1993), pp. 483–551 for the fourth century and *collegia*.

[60] *Dig.* 47.22.4, Gaius.   [61] E.g. Spain, Kulikowski (2004), pp. 53–6.

[62] Nijf (1997), pp. 243–4, Woolf (1990); Tran (2006) for status amongst the plebs and *collegia*.

[63] *Dig.* 47.22.1, Marcian; *Dig.* 3.4.1; Cotter (1996), pp. 84–6 on Hadrianic edicts; De Salvo (1993) for *collegia* of sailors, boatmen and bargemen.

[64] See Nijf (1997) for details of activities in the Roman East.   [65] Patterson (1998), pp. 160–1.

A NEW URBANISM?

In contrast to our earlier examination of the legal texts and the archaeological evidence from Gaul, Aelius Aristides, in a famous speech praising
Rome delivered and published in the second century AD, spoke of a world
of well-adorned cities spreading across the Roman Empire.[66] The substance
of this statement has been shown to be wanting from our earlier analysis of
the development and role of cities in the later second century AD. This
should not come as a surprise, since Aristides was praising Rome; yet
elsewhere in his *Orations* it is possible to identify a differentiation of the
places falling under the common title of *polis* or city: 'each of those cities – I
mean those which are of any account and have a great name'.[67] In other
words, there are cities and then there are cities that matter. It is in those
cities that matter where we can begin to see in the second century the
development of a new scale of urbanism. Italica may have set the trend with
its colossal baths emulating those of Rome, its huge *Traianeum*, new grid of
streets and vast amphitheatre (see Chapter 2).

It was in the second century, at a number of provincial cities, that
circuses were constructed in stone. The recent discovery of a circus at
Colchester constructed during the second century AD has sharpened our
understanding of the role of monuments in creating a name for a place.[68] In
many ways Colchester, although the first colony in the province, had
become overshadowed by London, and we should see the construction of
the circus, a structure one-tenth the size of the entire walled area of the
colony, as an attempt to keep it in the limelight as one of the preeminent
cities of the province.[69] The building of a circus linked Colchester to
developments in the capital where Trajan had rebuilt the Circus
Maximus on a new scale and created a new emblem of Roman urbanism
that surpassed the Colosseum.[70] Of course, circuses had existed earlier at
Rome and had been adopted in some cities with a strong connection to
Rome as part of the set of monuments that created well-adorned cities, such
as at Córdoba and Mérida in the first century AD, and we might agree with
Humphrey that the circus enjoyed a greater prominence in the Spanish

[66] Aelius Aristides, *Orationes*, 26.93.   [67] Aelius Aristides, *Orationes*, 30.2.

[68] Crummy (2005). The role of monuments as providing status is a feature identified by Lomas
(2003), p. 41 on the basis of *Dig*. 39.1.20.11; *CIL* 11.3614.

[69] Compare the role of the amphitheatre at Placentia, Tac. *Hist*. 2.21, Lomas (2003), pp. 40–1 or at
Carthage and Thysdrus. See Chapter 10.

[70] Ciancio Rossetto (2001).

provinces than theatres or amphitheatres.[71] What we see in the second century AD is the building of circuses in a larger number of cities located over a greater geographical area.[72] Few were built in Italian cities, however, and, where they do exist, they were constructed by the emperors.[73]

Five circuses had been securely identified in the north-west provinces at Arles, Vienne, Lyon, Saintes and Trier and we can now add Colchester to the list.[74] The importance of a circus for the development of a city as a prominent place can be seen at Arles. Its circus was constructed in the second century and we know that regular athletic and circus games were held there.[75] The city was to become a place for imperial celebration and in late antiquity was regarded as the most important city of Gaul.[76] Lyon, the provincial centre of the Three Gauls, also had a circus built in the second century, as did neighbouring Vienne. Further explanation is needed for Vienne's ability to undertake the construction of such a huge monument and we might look to its flourishing trade in lead and its numerous *collegia*.[77] Alternatively, this may be a classic example of peer-polity inter-action at work, with Vienne's decision influenced by the fact that Lyon had a circus. These cities could have put on chariot races without having to go to the trouble or expense of building a monumental structure in stone, but instead chose to construct what must be the largest and most expensive form of stone monument at the very time that other cities were ceasing to erect public buildings.[78] The cities that built circuses on the model of Trajan's Circus Maximus were breaking the mould of the stagnation and decline of urbanism that was so characteristic of Gaul and elsewhere in the second century AD. Significantly, the first circuses in the African provinces were built in this period at Carthage, Sousse, Lepcis Magna and perhaps Utica; as with other building-types it was the region's most important cities that erected circuses. The building of circuses continued in North Africa into the third century, fitting into the different chronology of city development there but also matching contemporary developments in some cities in Gaul and Britain.[79]

There is not enough information to be certain who paid for these monumental circuses, which were often sited outside the city itself.

---

[71] Murillo *et al.* (2001); Sánchez-Palencia *et al.* (2001); for other early circuses in Spain see papers in Nogales Basarrate and Sánchez-Palencia (2001); Humphrey (1986), p. 337.

[72] Humphrey (1986) for a survey.   [73] Humphrey (1986), pp. 576–8.

[74] Humphrey (1986), p. 389.   [75] *CIL* 12.670; Humphrey (1986), p. 396.

[76] Amm. Marc. *Res Gestae*,14.5.1, 15.11; Sid. Apoll. *Epist.* 1.11.10; Procop. *Goth.* 3.33.5; Bedon (2001), pp. 79–83.

[77] Bedon (2001), pp. 324–31.   [78] Humphrey (1986), p. 295.   [79] Humphrey (1986), p. 332.

Humphrey suggests that it was imperial patronage that made the main contribution to the building of a monumental circus (holding perhaps twenty to twenty-five thousand spectators).[80] We might therefore conclude that the presence of a monumental circus marked a place out as more prominent and more worthy than the other cities in the province that lacked one. Alternatively, if we regard the building of a circus as a local initiative, we should conclude that the presence of a circus occurred in cities that possessed the resources and the willingness to spend money on such an ambitious project. It is notable that a Severan senator, Cassius Dio, considered the latter a real possibility that needed to be discouraged to prevent a city's finances or landowners from becoming impoverished.[81] Either of the above scenarios highlights the distinctiveness of those cities which had the capacity to build and maintain a monumental circus and to put on games. Indeed, we should perhaps be less concerned with the details of who paid and more concerned with the fact that a monumental circus came to symbolise a city's status and to indicate a new form of urbanism involving a network of cities which, like Rome, had their amphitheatres, theatres and circuses and were capable of recreating the full range of urban experiences found in the capital of the Empire.

The other major development of the second and third centuries in some cities was the building of a defensive circuit of walls, which requires discussion in the context of the overall pattern of urbanism in the north-west provinces. Stone walls or defences were a feature of the towns of Italy of the Republic, and of the colonies founded by Augustus in both Italy and Gallia Narbonensis, but were not a feature of the cityscape of Rome until the time of Aurelian. The presence of stone walls tended to represent an assertion of its status by a *colonia*, a *municipium* or a *civitas*-capital.[82] Throughout the second century AD we find a few cities in the Germanies and Gallia Belgica constructing urban defences, whereas in the rest of Gaul none were built. In Britain, on the other hand, not only did London receive a new set of walls at the end of the second century, but thirty-two towns or cities constructed earthen ramparts with stone walls over the course of the second and third centuries. This could point to the stagnation or demise of urbanism but alternative explanations are possible. Many cities of Italy and Gallia Narbonensis had walls for the fundamental reason that, prior to the Julio-Claudian dynasty, the Roman world had been characterised by internal and external military conflict. In contrast, the cities of Gallia Comata did not

---

[80] Humphrey (1986), p. 333.   [81] Dio Cass. 52.30.
[82] For data and discussion of walls in the North-West provinces see Esmonde Cleary (2003).

develop walls, perhaps because they were not permitted to do so, or because the resources did not exist to fund such large, expensive and even 'unnecessary' physical boundaries – after all there is plentiful evidence of bathing facilities being built even in *agglomérations secondaires*, the equivalent of the Romano-British 'small town'.[83] Likewise there were successful cities in Gallia Narbonensis, such as Lyon, which did not build new walls to emulate Vienne or Arles.

The variation in the evidence for the second century across the northwest provinces suggests not so much fundamentally different approaches to Roman urbanism, but instead differences in the cycle of urban development. For example, in Britain the city developed at a different time from elsewhere and with an appreciation of urbanism which led to stone-facing urban ramparts and rectilinear street grids being prominent, factors which caused the towns of Britain to have more in common with the cities of Italy and Gallia Narbonensis than with the towns of Gallia Comata. The cycle of urban development in the early Roman Empire began and ceased at different times in different regions, but on the whole followed a similar trajectory, even though it was subject to different political, economic and social pressures according to its starting-point. The towns of Britain, like those of Africa, developed new features of urbanism throughout the second century, whereas such development had been distinctly patchy in the first century AD. In contrast, the cities of Italy, the Gauls and the Spains had by the second century come to the end of a cycle of urban development which had been characterised by the building of monuments, including temples, theatres, amphitheatres and circuses. Moving into the third century, we find that it is only in the African provinces that we can identify a continuing trend of development that added monuments to cities in a similar way to that of the previous century.[84] In the Gallic provinces and Spain, therefore, we can identify the development of preeminent cities (e.g. Arles or Mérida) and the collapse of a network of smaller cities,[85] whereas in Africa and Britain at the end of the second century a network of cities continued to exist alongside one or two much larger urban formations (notably London and Carthage). We are consequently seeing changes to the distribution of urbanism across a network of places, or to what we might consider to be the ways in which urbanism as a form of social surplus was distributed. By the third century, the social surplus was becoming

---

[83] Bouet (2003a) catalogues over 100 archaeological attestations; compare Bouet (2003b) for all baths in Narbonensis.

[84] Jouffroy (1986), p. 403.   [85] See Kulikowski (2004) for a discussion of this point.

concentrated in fewer places and disappearing in quite a number of provinces, although many places continued to be perceived as towns or a network of 'definite places'.[86]

PATTERNS OF URBAN DEVELOPMENT AND URBAN RECESSION

We have argued that the construction of Roman towns or cities, which were adorned with monuments, was sustained in different parts of the Empire at different times and in different ways; equally, there was variation in the point at which we might identify a stagnation or decline in urbanism. Throughout the period 250 BC to AD 250, however, cities were being developed and adorned with monuments somewhere in the Roman Empire. These observations indicate that the city as a surplus product of the presence of the Roman Empire appeared consistently over time, but not consistently in any one place over time. The pattern needs to be explained and related back to the economy that produced an increasing density of cities and an increasing number of monuments within them. The pattern of change should perhaps come as no surprise. It has long been observed from the study of shipwrecks in the western Mediterranean that the level of trade was higher in this period than in any other period of history down to the nineteenth century, and the study of pollution in the Greenland ice-cap and lake sediments of northern Europe has now made us aware that metal production was at its highest level prior to the Industrial Revolution.[87] This implies that information and ideas circulated with greater frequency and that a city could be placed in contact or even competition with cities further away than its local neighbours – a situation which may have increased the attractiveness of elements of urbanism to be found in Rome and other cities.[88] Within the overall pattern of wrecks and, less convincingly, in the pattern of metal production, we can identify a fall in the overall level of trade from AD 100, and we would expect to see a corresponding change in the amount and pace of city building and adornment.[89] At the heart of the economic cycle of city building and urban living lay an elite which disposed of its surplus wealth not only by means of patronage, but also by means of

---

[86] Horden and Purcell (2000), p. 77.
[87] Hopkins (1980), (2002); Parker (1992); de Callataÿ (2005).
[88] See papers in Andreau and Virlouvet (2002) on sea communication; such ideas should be extended to land travel, Laurence (1999), (2001b).
[89] De Callataÿ (2005), pp. 370–1.

loans. Thomas Wiedemann has demonstrated that, in the absence of secure banking facilities, the elite tended to put its surplus wealth to work by lending it to others.[90] A downturn in the trade-cycle therefore led to a decline in the amount of surplus wealth in the system, and consequently to a fall in the number of loans available and the amount of associated activity. The flow of money decreased for those living in cities and establishing new services, for example, resulting in an economic shortfall in what had been a mechanism for sustaining urbanism. Without the necessary finance, the means of producing or exchanging goods within cities was severely reduced and with it the social will to develop, adorn or even live in towns.

The model expressed above does not work, however. The presence of a growing and contracting economy does not explain the regional and temporal variation in the pattern of city development and monument building across the Roman West. We need to develop a model that will succeed in explaining this variation in the expenditure of the economic surplus in the construction of Roman urbanism. More than a quarter of a century ago, Keith Hopkins developed a model of the Roman Empire based on the fundamental observation that the low-tax economy of the state extracted an economic surplus from its provinces for expenditure on the army and within the city of Rome.[91] The model is not incompatible with Martin Millett's modelling of urban development in Britain led by the local elite.[92] The local elite needed to obtain the money for urban development from the central elite (comprising senatorial money-lenders), which was very active in the post-conquest periods in providing cash for city building (whether or not at interest); we might remember here that a major cause of the Boudiccan revolt in Britain was the calling-in of large loans by just such creditors, loans made fewer than twenty years after the invasion of the island and presumably destined for new, Roman-style displays of ostentation by the local elite.[93] Just as Hopkins' model of taxation emphasises expenditure and trade in the centre and at the periphery, so Millett's model of town formation portrays expenditure on towns developing in the frontier zones of the Empire occurring in relation to expenditure on the army or the organisation of the infrastructure of a frontier province.[94] It resulted in the development of an urban network with a variety of facilities,

---

[90] Wiedemann (2003).

[91] Hopkins (1980), restated in (2002) and in (1996) as seen over the long term. See Storey (2004) for a reappraisal of the issues underlying Hopkins' model and a shift towards a world economy based on world systems' theory that has much in common with the Hopkins model.

[92] Millett (1990), pp. 65–133.   [93] The basis for this argument is Cassius Dio 62.2.

[94] Compare the argument in Laurence (2001b).

but was different from the urbanism of the Mediterranean: 'an adequate, rather than excessive, provision of facilities'.[95] We could consider the pattern of urbanism in Gallia Comata in the first century AD to have been similar in nature; yet, as we have seen, the patterns of urbanism in Britain and Gaul were rather different in the late second or early third centuries. It is also difficult to use Millett's model to relate the development of urbanism in Britain during the late first and second centuries AD to the earlier development of urbanism and city adornment in Italy. The frame-work established by Millett has in any case been reconfigured during the last two decades to establish a conception whereby persons living under Rome consumed the idea of Romanness, including Roman urbanism, in quite different or even discrepant ways at both local and regional levels.[96] Such observations are, of course, true at a local level and we recognise a role for these agent-led choices that engaged individuals with a structure of empire based around cities to a greater or lesser extent. In fact, the pattern of urban development appears to have been related to the speed with which the idea of Roman urbanism was transmitted, replicated or adapted; and the regional/chronological variations that can be observed reflect the particular attraction and widespread communication of certain ideas about the nature of urbanism (e.g. the urban grid of streets) or the needs of a city in terms of facilities (e.g. baths or amphitheatres), as well as the economic realisation of such projects. Although the emphasis in recent scholarship has been on variation in Roman culture, of which urbanism forms a prominent part, we feel that we should still attempt to explain Roman urbanism as a macro-economic phenomenon (to echo Hopkins), according to which the city, as a product of surplus or a social phenomenon, enjoyed an increasing geographical distribution across western Europe and the western Mediterranean over the course of the first century AD, but then this network of cities and facilities contracted in the second and third centuries AD.[97]

As readers of earlier chapters will by now appreciate, there is one region in the Roman West which at least appears to have been an exception to this pattern – the African provinces. The dates of the development of monument-types reveals that in North Africa, unlike anywhere else in the Roman West, construction continued into the third and even the mid-fourth century, whether we are looking at the establishment of fora, the paving of streets or the building of temples, baths or honorific arches

---

[95] Millett (1990), p. 104.   [96] Millet (1990); Hingley (2005) reviews the bibliography.
[97] Hopkins (2002).

(although in line with patterns elsewhere there was a slowdown in the building of amphitheatres, theatres and circuses).[98] The cities of Africa appear to have adorned their cities to a much greater extent than the other provinces of the West in the third century. Richard Duncan-Jones' analysis of epigraphically dated public buildings in the African provinces by reign has, however, demonstrated that there was a steady increase in building activity throughout the second century which was sustained into the third, partly through the intervention of the Severan dynasty, but that later in the third century building activity, though continuing, was at a much lower rate than in the mid-second century.[99] There are some signs that even in the Severan period all was not well with the cities of North Africa, since we have surviving evidence of *curatores rei publicae* being sent to some of the major cities of the region, such as Sbeitla in 196, Timgad in 199 and Thugga and even Lepcis Magna prior to the middle of the third century.[100] The dispatch of a high-ranking senator to a city to undertake a similar role to that of Pliny the Younger in Bithynia is indicative of some form of disruption to the civic process and a need for intervention by the state, but it should be noted that these *curatores* were far more prominent in the cities of Italy and can be found in other provinces from the beginning rather than the end of the second century.[101]

The role of patronage by the Severan emperors extended beyond the financing of new monuments and included the privileging of North Africa in the supply of olive oil for the *annona*; this disrupted the supply from Baetica to Rome and to military sites, and may explain the prominence of ceramics of African origin at numerous sites including Ostia and Rome.[102] What we see here is the interplay of the political economy, represented by patronage, with the developing market economy of oil production and export, whereas in much of Gallia Comata the political economy, in the form either of patronage or of intervention by *curatores rei publicae*, was entirely absent. Instead we find the earlier market economy, which had been underwritten by the political economy and the desire for towns, moving towards a natural economy in which cities no longer had a vital

---

[98] Jouffroy (1986), p. 403.   [99] Duncan-Jones (2004), pp. 34–6.

[100] Lucas (1940) for the discussion of the data, to be read with Burton (1979) and Jacques (1984), pp. 221–49; Dore (1988), p. 84; Di Vita, Di Vita-Evrard and Bacchielli (1999), p. 158; individual cities encountered specific problems: for instance Utica faced difficulties caused by the silting of the harbour – Alexander and Ennaifer (1973), p. xix; Lepelley (1981), p. 941.

[101] Plin. *Ep.* 10; Jacques (1984), pp. 261–300 for the discussion of the role of *curator* in a city.

[102] Reynolds (2005); compare Le Roux (1999) for similar conclusions based on evidence of senators and equestrians from Spanish and African provinces.

role to play;[103] we should expect the ecological geography or natural economy to have reasserted itself over time (as argued by Horden and Purcell).[104] The example of the African provinces demonstrates that the production of well-adorned cities as a surplus was embedded in the political economy of the Empire. Urbanism was neither particularly an indicator of the economic health of a region nor, by itself, embedded into the market economy of any region or every locality. Regional variation in the distribution and sustainability of cities depended on the configuration of the relationship between the natural economy, the political economy and the market economy, and within this relationship or economic structure we need to place the individual, developing an identity, becoming Roman or consuming culture.[105] The survival of cities was also affected by time-space distanciation: where cities were within easy reach of the rural population, they enjoyed greater sustainability due to the inclusion of a greater percentage of the rural population within their markets, whilst it was those regions that had the lowest density of towns or cities that experienced the greatest urban regression in the second and third centuries AD (such as vast stretches of Gallia Lugdunensis). Equally, those cities which were on good communications routes, whether by sea, river or land, and were integrated into the space-time economy of the state had a better chance of survival over time (e.g. Arles, Trier, Tarragona, etc.), and undertook building projects on the new monumental scale attested from the city of Rome at this time (these factors are also reflected in the overall pattern of epigraphic commemoration).[106]

THE CITY AND THE CENTRE OF POWER

At the beginning of this book, we highlighted how the formation of Roman urbanism in Spain under the Republic depended on the interaction of the local elite with the senatorial aristocracy in Rome. The intersection between cities and individuals from or in the capital of the Empire had an important role to play in the Imperial period as well. What we wish to address here is how connections between the centre of the Empire and cities in the provinces may have shaped the pattern of urbanism in the Roman West. At the centre of the Empire was the Senate, which was not a hereditary

---

[103] Patterson (2001), pp. 369–71 develops the interrelationship of micro- and macro-economies; see now also Storey (2004).
[104] Horden and Purcell (2000).   [105] Mattingly (2004).   [106] Woolf (1996), (1998).

aristocracy, rather one which was constantly being replaced by new members drawn from the *equites* (knights). One of the most interesting phenomena of the Roman Empire was the gradual change in the composition of the Senate: Italian families were gradually replaced by members of other Italian families, who were in turn replaced by western and then eastern families drawn from the provinces.[107] Under the Flavians, between 17 and 23 per cent of known senators were from the provinces, whereas by the time of the Severans, more than 50 per cent of known senators came from the provinces.[108] This pattern of representation of provincials in the Senate is of interest for the simple reason that it shadows the overall pattern of urban development across the provinces. For example, just as there was strong representation of senators drawn from Gallia Narbonensis, the Three Gauls and the Spanish provinces in the first century AD, so there were also significant developments involving cities in those provinces during this period. Similarly, in the African provinces extensive urban development in the second half of the second century and into the third coincides with there being a greater number of senators whose origins were in cities across Africa (see Tables 11.1 and 11.2; note that the peak in the number of African senators predates the reign of Septimius Severus). By the end of our period, few senators were drawn from Gaul and Spain, whereas the eastern provinces and North Africa continued to feature strongly.

The linkage between urbanism and membership of the Senate might be traced back to a speech given by the Emperor Claudius in AD 48, which is preserved not only in the text of Tacitus but also on a bronze tablet from Lyon.[109] The speech formed part of a debate in response to a petition from the elite in Gallia Comata that they should be allowed to stand for office in Rome and hence gain membership of the Senate. Claudius cited the practice of both Augustus and then Tiberius of allowing that 'the flower of the colonies and *municipia* everywhere – that is, those who were worthier and wealthier – should sit in the Senate house' and argued that this practice should be extended to the Three Gauls, which had for a hundred years remained at peace with Rome. Opposition to the idea of 'Gallic' senators came from a Senate which was no longer purely Italian but had come to include senators from Spain and Gallia Narbonensis. The first senator from the Three Gauls came from Autun (Augustodunum), a city regarded with particular favour by Rome, whose people were described as 'brothers of the Roman people', and which, remarkably for Gaul, possessed a defensive

---

[107] Hopkins (1983), pp. 123–4.   [108] Hopkins (1983), p. 200; Hammond (1957), p. 77 for data.
[109] Tac. *Ann.* 11.23–5; *CIL* 13.1668.

Table 11.1 Origins of senators (data in % from Hopkins 1983: 200)

Region	69–79	81–96	98–117	117–138	138–161	161–180	180–192	193–212	218–235	Third c.
Italy	83	77	66	56	58	54	55	43	47	44
Provinces	17	23	34	44	42	46	45	57	53	56

Table 11.2 Origins of senators from the provinces (data in % from Hopkins 1983: 200)

	69–79	81–96	98–117	117–138	138–161	161–180	180–192	193–212	218–235	Third c.
Western origins	70	76	56	46	24	10	8	15	14	14
African origins	10	5	6	16	27	31	31	26	26	23
Eastern origins	17	16	35	37	47	54	61	57	58	58

circuit of walls by this date.[110] Nevertheless, a total of only sixteen senators is known from the Three Gauls, compared to some thirty-nine from Gallia Narbonensis,[111] and we must therefore conclude that Gallic senators were to be a rare phenomenon over the course of the following two hundred years.[112] Evidence from the province of Africa points to the existence of strong links between senators from that province and their families and the people of their native cities.[113] We need to imagine a network of connections running through the social structure of a senator's native city and the possible benefits to be gained from the knowledge and access to the centre of power that he could command (for instance, his patronage could have had a considerable effect on the peasantry).[114] The importance of having connections to Rome lay in the fact that one could avoid having to enter the crowded circle of power centred on the governor.[115]

Clearly members of the provincial elite wanted to become senators in Rome and we need to try to understand the motivations for this desire and the effect of having a local man in the Senate for the cities of the West. John Patterson considers the effect on the cities of Italy in financial terms.[116]

[110] Bedon (2001), pp. 88–92. Tac. *Ann.* 11.25; see Rodgers (1989) for the continuing prominence of Autun at the end of the third century.
[111] Burnand (1982), pp. 391–2.
[112] For the Spanish provinces see Le Roux (1982); Castillo (1982). [113] Corbier (1982).
[114] See for example Saller (1982), p. 167. [115] Apul. *Flor.* 168; Saller (1982), pp. 168–9.
[116] Patterson (2006), pp. 191–215.

He suggests that, if a wealthy local decurion gained entry into the Senate in Rome, that man's wealth and its expenditure would move to Rome and be spent on his new ostentatious lifestyle which was required to impress other members of the Senate and the emperor's court. The transfer of capital expenditure included the purchase of a house. For the towns of senators from the provinces, the effect was significantly increased in the second century when an imperial edict required all senators and those standing for office and entry into the Senate to have one third of their wealth invested in land located in Italy (later the proportion was reduced to a quarter).[117] The immediate effect was to increase the price of land in Italy and to reduce the value of provincial land. The grounds for the measure were a feeling that a senator's home should be in Italy and that Italy should not be a place for senators merely to visit. Hence, a city in the provinces with a senator in Rome faced the removal in the short term of a source of finance for civic projects and the development of its landscape. The senator may have been absent from the region for significant amounts of time and on his return would have been, as a senator (technically) resident in Rome, exempted from *munera* (obligatory financial gifts to the city).[118] Whether he brought back money into his home city is far from certain, although Corbier uses a study of the evidence from North Africa to suggest that no dislocation of resources occurred.[119] What he did bring, however, even if absent, was a new status for his city as a place that could be recognised by a governor or procurator as having a citizen of a similar status to them.[120] That status did not cease with the death of the senator and, as Hopkins has suggested on the basis of the Augustan marriage laws, the senator's descendants over the next three generations were regarded as having the same status as senators actively engaged in the politics of Rome.[121] The local senator may also have been important in the transmission to his hometown of cultural values found collectively amongst senators in the capital.[122] The symbolic value for the city may have been more important than the loss of resources now spent by its most affluent member in Rome.

Another way of viewing the relationship between the elite of the Empire and the development of cities is to examine the distribution of the *equites* (those with property worth over 400,000 sesterces); for the most part the data must be drawn from the tombstones of equestrian officers who had

---

[117] Plin. *Ep.* 6.19; S.H.A. *Marc.* 11.   [118] Hopkins (1983), p. 190.   [119] Corbier (1982).

[120] Saller (1982), pp. 185–6; Apul. *Flor.* 16 on an individual's status within their home city on retirement from the Senate.

[121] Hopkins (1983), p. 190.   [122] Eck (1997) for discussion.

Table 11.3 Origins of the *Equestrian Officers* (Caballos Rufino 1996 based on Devijver 1991)

Period	Italy	Spain	Narbonensis	African provinces	The East
Flavian	46%	17%	10%	2%	16%
Trajan-Antonines	37%	10%	6%	10%	23%
Marcus Aurelius to Septimius Severus	32%	4%	2%	23%	21%
Caracalla to Gallienus	21%	1%	1%	24%	23%

served in the army.[123] The pattern of this group's distribution across Italy and the provinces is rather different from that of the senators (Table 11.3). Whereas the majority of known senators were drawn from the cities of Italy right down to the Severan period, we find that Italy ceased to provide the majority of known members of the equestrian order before the end of the first century AD. This implies that the Senate maintained a degree of resistance to the inclusion of members from the provinces for ideological reasons, apart from in exceptional circumstances, rather than including a selection of members from the wealthiest class (i.e. the *equites*) representative of all parts of the Empire. The distribution of known equestrian officers across the provinces can provide us with a gauge by which to measure the geographical distribution of the wealth of the super-rich. The northern provinces (the Three Gauls, the Two Germanies and Britain) hardly feature in these data, indicating the concentration of this wealth in the south. The Spanish provinces and Narbonensis are fairly well represented down to the middle of the second century but then seem to have substantially fewer equestrians. By contrast, the African provinces demonstrate a marked increase over the second century and into the third – the very period in which euergetism in the cities of North Africa was at its most prominent.

The pattern of the origins of equestrian officers follows the overall pattern of urban development in the Roman Empire, unlike that of the origins of senators which is artificially skewed towards Italy and, later, the Greek world. What this plots is the pattern of available resources for urban development over time and it highlights the changes in the patterns of wealth which favoured Italy and the Gallic and Spanish provinces in the first century, but the African provinces by the third. The distribution of senators and equestrian officers had wider implications than the availability of finance for urban development. The wealthy, through patronage, were

---

[123] Duncan-Jones (1967), p. 159; Brunt (1983); Pflaum (1961), (1982).

also involved in the provision of banquets, feasts and perhaps most importantly banking facilities.[124] Even if they still owned land in their cities, run
by their agents, their absence from their hometowns could have affected the
supply of loans upon which the activities of the cities at a much lower level
might depend. Moreover, it could have brought building work within their
cities to a halt and thus removed a significant source of income for the
residents. Some senators may even have left their hometowns and returned
later in life to find many of the privately owned buildings in ruins. It needs
to be stressed that equestrian officers did tend to return home, hence the
changes in percentages of representation reflect not the dislocation of
resources but the economic stability or growth of a region, or perhaps
the ability of a region to engage with the higher levels of government in
the Empire.

The patterns that we have seen so far point to a structural difference in
the distribution of those with status and wealth across the provinces, which
continued to reflect the prejudices found in the debate in the Senate in AD
48 over the inclusion of provincials from Gallia Comata in its ranks. The
patterns seem to tie into our understanding of the trajectories of urban
development north of Gallia Narbonensis. Moreover, the fact that there
was only one procurator for the provinces of Lugdunensis and Aquitania
and only one for Belgica and the Two Germanies suggests that the state
regarded a great swathe of the Roman West as underdeveloped or lacking in
resources for the procurators to deal with.[125] The ability of a procurator to
deal with these vast geographical areas, when compared with the fact that
another of their number only had to deal with the island of Cyprus, is
slightly staggering and must suggest their greater detachment from the
activities of the Roman state.[126] Similarly, the great benefactor of cities,
the Emperor Hadrian, largely overlooked the developing cities of Gaul, the
Germanies and Britain, focussing instead on Italy, Spain, Africa and the
Greek East.[127] The pattern of appointment of *curatores rei publicae* to cities
across the Empire abruptly ceases north of Lyon, with only three examples
attested in the Three Gauls.[128] This represents the view from Rome, which
regarded the provinces of the north as different from those of the south and
so became less involved with the affairs of the cities of the former. If we accept
these patterns, created by distance from the Mediterranean, we might
compare the number of known *equites* coming from the province of

[124] Wiedemann (2003).
[125] Pflaum (1961), pp. 1053–5, 1056–8; Pflaum (1982), pp. 119, 121.
[126] Burton (1993), p. 25.   [127] Boatwright (2000), p. 207.
[128] Jacques (1984), p. 256; *CIL* 13.1697, 2950, 3258; for Lyon see Jacques (1983), pp. 220–4.

Table 11.4 Equestrian officers in epigraphy from the Spanish provinces (data from Caballos Rufino 1999)

Period	Tarraconensis	Lusitania	Baetica
Early Julio-Claudian	9	7	23
Later Julio-Claudian	18	8	23
Flavians	51	3	27
Trajan – Hadrian	87	3	24
Antoninus Pius – Marcus Aurelius	38	3	18
Commodus – the Severans	5	3	15
Total	208	27	130

Lusitania with the number drawn from the other two Spanish provinces (Table 11.4) and see what a difference proximity to Rome made; we should also note that a far higher number of known equestrians was produced by the larger cities of Tarragona, Córdoba and Mérida.[129] All these provinces had their governor and their procurator, but what created the difference was direct engagement with Rome, and, since the overall pattern of the number of equestrians in Tarraconensis and Baetica broadly follows the overall increase and decrease in the number of shipwrecks, we may suggest that the two phenomena were linked and that the presence of equestrians not only displayed an emblematic connection to Rome in terms of status but can also be seen as an indicator of wealth.

If this represented the view from Rome, is it also possible to construct the cities' view of the centre of power? There are, of course, no written sources with which to investigate this subject. Nevertheless, a feature of the cities of the Roman West was the setting up of statues of the emperor. The carving and erection of a statue of an emperor was an action that connected the person who paid for the statue, the decurions who permitted its public erection and the population which gazed upon the emperor's features and read or were read the inscription to the emperor, in Rome or with his armies. Some nine hundred and sixty-six dedications have been catalogued across Italy and the western provinces, and their distribution can be seen as a guide to the degree of connection of the cities of a particular province to the centre of power (Table 11.5). The northern provinces provide less than 3 per cent of the total, whereas Italy, Africa and Numidia provide more than 70 per cent. Even Narbonensis does not really share in this expression of connectivity to the capital. What these figures make clear is that not only

---

[129] See Caballos Rufino (1999) for details.

Table 11.5 Distribution of imperial statue bases in the Roman West
(Augustus to Commodus; data from Højte 2005)

Province	Number of statue bases	Percentage of statue bases
Italy (not City of Rome)	399	40
Africa Proconsularis	177	18
Numidia	153	15
Baetica	69	7
Tarraconensis	47	5
Mauretania Caesarensis	41	4
Lusitania	26	3
Narbonensis	20	2
Alpes	14	1
Aquitania	12	1
Mauretania Tingitana	11	1
Germania Superior	11	1
Lugdunensis	4	0.4
Belgica	3	0.3
Germania Inferior	2	0.2
Britannia	2	0.2

was the north distant from Rome's point of view, but the figure of the
emperor and the centre of power was regarded as distant by those in the
northern provinces.

The pattern seen in Table 11.4 should be seen as part of a wider picture of
the use of inscriptions on stone to commemorate, for the most part,
monumental buildings and the dead. The overall pattern of epigraphic
density across the Roman West has been analysed by Greg Woolf with a
view to examining the patterns of cultural change in Gaul.[130] The pattern
is an important one, however, and particularly for discussion of the city in
the late second and early third centuries, the period in which most inscriptions were set up.[131] The greatest density of inscriptions, not surprisingly,
appears in Italy within the areas with the greatest concentration of cities.
Africa Proconsularis has a similar epigraphic density to parts of central
Italy. Numidia, southern Italy and Gallia Narbonensis have relatively high
epigraphic densities. We then begin to find lower epigraphic densities in
Baetica, the Three Gauls and Mauretania Caesarensis, followed by even

---

[130] Woolf (1998), pp. 77–105 based on figures in Harris (1989), pp. 259–73. See also papers in
Humphrey (1991) discussing Harris (1989) and those in Cooley (2002) for some critique and
local studies of the phenomenon.
[131] Woolf (1998).

lower epigraphic densities in Tarraconensis, Lusitania, Mauretania Tingitana and Britain. The overall pattern, which is mostly derived from the second half of the second century, can be seen to coincide with the patterns of urban densities found in the work of Bekker-Nielsen discussed earlier in this chapter. The epigraphic habit was a very urban phenomenon and, when the overall patterns of epigraphic densities from the Gallic provinces were broken down by Woolf, he found that the recorded inscriptions clustered in the larger towns: Narbonne, Nîmes, Lyon, Mainz, Trier, Bordeaux, Arles, Cologne, Vienne and Langres.[132] Indeed, as we have already discussed in relation to the *collegia*, vast swathes of northern Gaul were virtually without inscriptions, and the concentrations of epigraphy were firmly located in cities on key communications routes, with a general shift towards the Rhine-Saône-Rhône axis of state activity. Fascinatingly, at a period when we suggest that many towns of Gaul were in urban recession, the population continued to produce inscriptions largely as a result of funerary practices. Clearly people were still using cities and the city was still relevant to the lives of those living in eastern as opposed to western Gaul. We need to be utterly clear, however, that the pattern of epigraphy does not represent the actions of the entire population, nor should it be used as an indicator of the way in which 'the natives had become Roman'; instead we need to remember the composition of that element of the population commemorated or those whose actions were producing inscriptions.[133] Migration and population change were also factors, given that the distribution was focussed on larger cities and communication routes. Cities with higher densities of epigraphy therefore enjoyed a closer connection to the wider Roman world and ultimately to the centres of Roman power, whether on the frontier or at the heart of the Empire in Rome itself, and may be described as 'economically privileged locales'.[134] The heartland of this epigraphic culture coincided with the regions of greater urban sustainability: Italy, and the provinces of Africa, Numidia, Narbonensis, Sardinia and Baetica, with an extension from this heartland of Roman urbanism along the major communications routes, whether from Tarragona, Lyon, Bordeaux or London, across the land masses of northern and western Europe towards the frontiers of Roman control.

---

[132] Woolf (1998), pp. 86–7.

[133] For example Woolf (1998), pp. 99–100 finds that two-thirds of inscriptions in Narbonne commemorated freed slaves and one third the freeborn population.

[134] Woolf (1996), p. 37.

BACK TO THE CITIES

The discussion of these Empire-wide trends has moved us away from the major issue of the city and its sustainability over time, and we need now to focus again on the city as a place within which Roman social relations could be reproduced over time. The establishment of a city or town with a charter created or reproduced a particular form of social relations, according to which an elite group, the decurions, was defined by its wealth and willingness to hold office and contribute funds for the collective well-being of the city – whether by giving games, constructing a building or providing meals for the plebs.[135] Our evidence for the composition of the elite of cities points to the existence of two groups: first, a stable core of families which continued to produce decurions through time, and second, a larger group from which a decurion was produced for a single generation.[136] Moreover, the existence of sons of freedmen within the aristocracy, and the representation of freedmen in many of the cities of the Roman West, are dynamics within Roman urbanism that cannot be ignored. Decurions, freed slaves, the members of *collegia*, the plebs and slaves living in cities all constituted status groups that were defined, yet integrated within a system that in the long term could feature social mobility and the possibility, however remote, of descendants becoming members of the *ordo* of decurions.[137] Hence in the longer term, the elite incorporated socially mobile members of other parts of society and, as with the senatorial elite, newcomers were a feature of its social composition and indeed may have been essential for the maintenance of the numbers in the *ordo* of decurions.[138] Within the context of the 'new' or 'Roman' towns of Gaul or Britain or Spain, the development of a stable *ordo* may have been fraught with difficulties. The limited human and financial resources available to a city may have undermined the ability of individuals to pay for the obligations placed on magistrates, or constrained geographical mobility between the city and its territory. Separation from migration within the Empire could have caused a city to lack the human resources and economic vitality with which to sustain itself; whereas those cities situated at integral points within the communications network could have drawn on a wider set of human resources and become centres for more than just their agricultural hinterland.[139]

---

[135] See Burton (2001) on this urban structure of empire's relationship with Rome.
[136] Mouritsen (1990), (1996), (1997), (2006) develops this conclusion.
[137] E.g. Optatus, *Contra Donatistae: Gesta Apud Zenophilum* 1.   [138] Mouritsen (1996), p. 144.
[139] Meyer (1990), pp. 90–1 develops a similar argument in connection with Lyon.

In any discussion of the development of the Roman city, which inevitably involves epigraphy, greater emphasis is placed on the male than on the
female inhabitants. We need to realise, however, that at numerous levels the
female section of the urban population was active in forming and sustaining the city. Elite strategies for, and conceptions of, family formation and
inheritance depended not just on male but also on female lineage, and
women of all statuses across the city were directly connected to the elite
through patronage, playing an active part in legitimising the role of the elite
and even in individual membership of the *ordo* of decurions.[140] At the other
end of the scale, we can identify women of senatorial rank acting as patrons
of cities and the connections with Rome outlined above could be attained
through female rather than male participants in activities in the capital.[141]
These prominent female members of the elite may have been drawn from
those women who were priestesses in the cities of the Latin West and who
appear in relatively large numbers in Africa, Gaul, Spain and Italy; indeed, a
peak in the representation of priestesses of the cult of the emperors occurs
in the second century – coinciding, as we have seen above, with other
patterns within urbanism.[142] Individual priestesses came from a wide
spectrum of society, from senatorial or equestrian families down to the
lower classes, but the majority were members of families of the decurial
class and held their position as priestess in their own right, rather than as an
ancillary to a husband who was also a priest.[143] This establishes the prob-
able existence of female agency within the cities of the Roman West, which
is further confirmed by the prominence of priestesses as benefactors to
individual cities. Emily Hemelrijk demonstrates their role not just as
benefactors, but as the providers of funds to cities which were considerable
and much higher than the benefactions granted by males, due to the female
patrons being drawn from the upper echelons of society.[144] Though less
prominent within the epigraphic record, we have good evidence for female
elites providing the funds for urban development and taking an active role
in the construction of an urban culture, whether in building public monuments, setting up statues, providing funds for games or giving banquets.[145]
Other epigraphic studies of the role of women in the Roman city highlight

---

[140] Corbier (1982); Savunen (1995); Savunen (1997).
[141] See Hemelrijk (2004); Raepsaet-Charlier (1987), pp. 692–5 for female members of senatorial
       families in the provinces.
[142] Hemelrijk (2005), pp. 140–1 for the relevant data.   [143] Hemelrijk (2005), p. 142.
[144] Hemelrijk (2004), (2006), pp. 88–9.
[145] See Hemelrijk (2006) for a full listing of the evidence and analysis, also Briand-Ponsart (2004);
       Spickermann (1994).

their significance and ability to alter the urban environment, in ways that are not so different from those of their male equivalents; what is different, however, is that the evidence is skewed to cause the actions of the male elite to be represented in a far greater number of inscriptions.[146] What we would suggest is that, even without the right to participate in male office-holding, the female population of the city played an active public role and that their existence should not be analysed in terms of a dichotomy between private and public.[147] Women acted in public within an engendered urban world biased towards men, but their generous actions could still be recognised as maintaining or developing the city.[148] In consequence, we would stress that any urban development which lacks a textual record for its construction cannot simply be assumed to have been the action of a man, and that female agency must be considered in every case.

The development and survival of a city depended not just on the development of urban monuments and facilities which both men and women found attractive, but also on a population continuously inhabiting the site. Forum Novum in the Tiber Valley appears to have developed a range of monuments and cemeteries without developing an urban population. Most other cities managed to attract a resident population, but the maintenance of residents within cities may have been more than a matter of economics or access to suitable facilities. Demographers studying antiquity have long argued on the basis of their reading of comparative evidence that urbanism, even in the smaller cities, was characterised by a more virulent set of diseases due to the concentration of population in one place and that the urban death-rate would have been higher than the urban birth-rate.[149] As a result, urbanism could only be sustained by almost continuous migration to maintain the city's population. When applied to the Roman West, this argument may explain how migrants were initially attracted to the new cities, but also how, in order to maintain the levels of population initially attained, further migration was required, with migrants more easily being attracted to those cities which they saw or heard possessed better facilities and opportunities. This demographic thesis suggests that, in the longer term, there were simply too many cities and that the development of major centres (e.g. Lyon or Trier) was an inevitable outcome. Recently, however, Elio Lo Cascio has challenged the entire thesis

---

[146] Navarro Caballero (2001) for Spain; MacMullen (1980) for the initial study.
[147] *contra* Frei-Stolba et al. (2003).
[148] See Forbis (1990) on the language of female civic honour.
[149] Scheidel (2003); Morley (1996); Scobie (1986); *contra* Laurence (1997).

that the urban death-rate must have been higher than the urban birth-rate and concluded that earlier scholars have misread the comparative evidence.[150] In doing so, he highlights an important demographic phenomenon: the difference between a variation within the normal rates of mortality and an increase in the rate of mortality associated with a crisis which could raise it by more than 50 per cent.[151] This is not to reject migration as a fundamental aspect of city formation, but to highlight how the fluctuation in mortality rates could have had a major effect on the sustainability of cities and therefore needed to be countered with migration.[152] More important for our understanding of the increasing number of cities and their sustainability is the fluctuation in the rates of population increase and decrease. For example, Lo Cascio uses the surviving census figures to propose a rate of population increase in the region of 4–6 per cent *per annum* in the first half of the first century AD, which can be related to an expansion of the resources available to the population as a whole. Indeed, the expansion of urbanism itself indicates a growth in available resources and resulted in the creation of new markets for goods within an expanding empire.[153] In contrast, the advent during the second century of the epidemic known to historians as the Antonine Plague – however we interpret the diverse source material indicating the occurrence of a pandemic[154] – led to a fall in population of around 20 per cent, which would have had a major effect on the stability of the urban populations; indeed, they could only have been replaced over a period of seventy-five years (assuming an overall increase in population of 3 per cent *per annum*),[155] by which time the pandemic of the third century was aggravating what could be seen as a demographic crisis. Scheidel regards these figures as the minimum rate of population decrease and posits a maximum decrease of 50 per cent with an overall average of 25 per cent.[156] Of course such calculations are speculative but the results of the work of demographers cannot be ignored. It should be stressed that there is a very varied regional pattern to every pandemic which could cause some cities to be devastated whilst others are passed by.[157] Modern demographers have, however, provided some substance to the

---

[150] Lo Cascio (2001).   [151] Lo Cascio (2001), pp. 61–2.

[152] Rathbone (1981) reveals the fragility of colonial foundations.

[153] Lo Cascio (1996b), pp. 292–3, (2006); compare Scheidel (2002), pp. 98–9.

[154] Duncan-Jones (1996).

[155] Lo Cascio (1994), pp. 124–5; (1996b), p. 296; Littman and Littman (1973); Duncan-Jones (1996), pp. 134–5.

[156] Scheidel (2002), p. 99.

[157] Scheidel (2002) interrogates the more modern evidence and draws out this conclusion.

observation of Orosius that 'everywhere farms, fields and cities, without cultivators and abandoned by their inhabitants, gave way to ruins and woodland'.[158]

The implications of these demographic fluctuations in the second and third centuries should not be underestimated and should be viewed as phenomena alongside the economic trade cycle and the information drawn from the regional distribution of inscriptions. Responses to the presence of a pandemic can be expected to have varied as much as the form of the city and the cultures that supported Roman urbanism. The relatively abundant texts, both contemporary and from later periods, report the Plague having a greater effect in the large centres of population such as Rome, Aquileia and the bases of the army.[159] How far it affected a particular city or region is, however, impossible to assess and the debate over its effects cannot be substantiated with reference to urban construction.

Nevertheless, its demographic effect would have had wide-ranging economic implications for all: wages would have increased, whilst rents would have decreased, thus effectively stripping elites of the means to maintain their cities through euergetism.[160] There had been plagues before, even in the periods of greatest urban development, but the Antonine Plague was different in its geographical spread across the Empire from Egypt in the East to the army camps on the frontiers in the West; it was referred to as the Great Plague and was followed by a further pandemic in the third century.[161] Its effects may explain why some cities in the Empire at the end of the second century did not follow the trends of other places. The unique phenomenon of wall-building in the towns of Roman Britain or the further development of monuments in the cities of North Africa points, in this period of pandemics, to the availability of manpower, economic resources and the social will to spend a surplus on the costly development of urbanism. We could suggest that neither of these regions was as scarred by the effects of plague, especially when we also consider the growing dominance of North African produce in the markets of Rome and the western Mediterranean.

---

[158] Oros. *Historia adversus paganos*, 7.15.5–6.

[159] See Duncan-Jones (1996) for details of source material and an interpretation.

[160] Scheidel (2002); for critiques of Scheidel's conclusions see Bagnall (2002); Bruun (2003); Greenberg (2003).

[161] See Duncan-Jones (1996), pp. 109–11 on the frequency of plague.

FROM STRUCTURE TO AGENCY

The discussion up to now has looked at factors, such as demography (including the density of cities), economics or regional connectivity to the centre, which can be described as the structure or conditions within which urbanism existed. The long-term trends in demography, economics and politics affected the ability at a local level to produce the elements or social relations which we have found to constitute the Roman city. Choices were made, however, and could be quite different according to the location of the city. The building of walls in Roman Britain is just one of those regional types that appeared desirable to the local elite, but either was not a choice available in other areas, through a lack of economic means or labour power, or was not seen as desirable. The problem of understanding the choices made by individuals in the past is that we often do not have the information to understand fully cultural changes in taste and lifestyle. For example, Mouritsen has demonstrated a shift in the commemoration of the urban elite after death from the city to the rural estate in the first century AD.[162] Whether this reflected a detachment from the city on the part of the elite is impossible to evaluate. Yet the Roman city as a phenomenon mobilised and concentrated the rural surplus, making it more mobile and subject to being exported to other cities or regions (note that the local aristocrat standing for the most junior magistracy at Rome was required to invest heavily in land in Italy).

One of the problems of urbanism in the Roman period is that the concentration of wealth necessary for its maintenance could be diverted to other locations than the established cities. Through its ability to concentrate a surplus, Roman urbanism also provided new opportunities, including those associated with citizenship and recruitment into the army, and the city was the place in which new products and new architecture could be viewed. A sense of novelty could be found in the cities of the early Empire, whether in terms of the new architecture promoted by the emperors in Rome or in terms of the grids of streets in Gallia Comata. Underlying this phenomenon was a spirit of competition between cities or peer-polity interaction – a dynamic that could cause the spread of specific urban monuments such as stone amphitheatres to a variety of locations across the Empire over a period of one hundred and fifty years. The sense of novelty did not stop at architecture, and the study of ceramics can show

---

[162] Mouritsen (2006).

that, even in Italy in the first century AD, there was a dramatic increase in the variety and quantity of new products available for consumption.[163] The city also created a point of intersection of the Roman state with its subject population, or at least segments of it, whether through the collection of taxes, the organisation of local administration, the recruitment of soldiers or the holding of markets. Roman cities can be seen as the means of production of the Roman state and were places within which a series of cultural values could be maintained, some of which would have enabled the cultural transmission of Romanness from one generation to the next. Part of that conception of Romanness, or even the reproduction of that conception, was the further development of urbanism. What we see in some cities from the middle of the second century is a failure to transmit or to realise the transmission of a concept of urban development. We may even say that, outside the major urban centres, the concept of city development and adornment could only be sustained for a matter of about one hundred and fifty to two hundred years. As fundraisers find today, enthusiasm can be aroused for constructing or discovering something new, but its long-term conservation is of less interest. This may have been what caused monuments and even individual cities simply to wear out, while the level of disintegration was so great that neither the social will nor the economic power was there to address the problem of the *ruinae*, or, alternatively, the necessary labour and skills may not have been available within the region. The weakness of Roman urbanism was that elites could choose to move their resources elsewhere and the city as a product of social surplus could be deemed unnecessary.

The discussion so far has looked at the city as a social institution that could and did fail, but there is another side to this. The Roman cities in the heartland of the central Mediterranean formed an urban network with a higher overall population than in any other period of European history before the Industrial Revolution. The city was integral to Romanness in ways that cannot be underestimated, as demonstrated by the survival of cities at similar locations to this day. They were places which by the early third century may not have enjoyed the vitality or experienced the growth characteristic of earlier times but which nevertheless would be sustained over time, perhaps due to the provision of good clean water via aqueducts and/or through their location within a communications network integrating cities with one another. This was the network of places that would be developed into the bishoprics of Christian Europe during the next two

---

[163] De Sena and Ikäheimo (2003), compare Witcher (2006) for evidence from field survey.

hundred years. These are signs of the geographical resilience of Roman urbanism, even though the set of cultural meanings which had originally brought a city into existence may have become irrelevant as it was appropriated to produce citizens of God rather than citizens who would defend Republican Rome.[164] There were, however, elements of continuity: amphitheatres, theatres, circuses and fora continued in use in most cities for a further two hundred and fifty years or more. Monuments of the past, built in concrete, were to survive and be recast as the works of the devil in the medieval period and then to be recast again as symbols of a civilisation to be admired and emulated from the Renaissance down to more recent times. There are two sides to Roman urbanism: its historical fragility and its physical longevity. By AD 250 both features can be found in the cities of the Roman West.

---

[164] Lefebvre (1991), p. 167 for the spatial concept.

Bibliography

Abbreviations

Abbreviations of ancient sources are as in the *Oxford Classical Dictionary*, 3rd edition (revised). Journals and collections are largely as in *L'Année Philologique*. For convenience the journal and inscription collection abbreviations are provided below.

AC	*L'Antiquité Classique*
AE	*L'Année Épigraphique*
AJA	*American Journal of Archaeology*
AJPh	*American Journal of Philology*
AncSoc	*Ancient Society*
ANRW	*Aufstieg und Niedergang der Römischen Welt*
AntAfr	*Antiquités africaines*
AntJ	*Antiquaries Journal*
BAA	*Bulletin d'Archéologie Algérienne*
BAR Int. Ser.	British Archaeological Reports International Series
BASO	*Bulletin of the American Schools of Oriental Research in Jerusalem and Baghdad*
BCTH	*Bulletin Archéologique du Comité des Travaux Historiques et Scientifiques*
BJ	*Bonner Jahrbücher*
C&M	*Classica et Mediaevalia*
CAH²	*Cambridge Ancient History*. Second edition.
CB	*The Classical Bulletin*
CIL	*Corpus Inscriptionum Latinarum*
CJ	*The Classical Journal*
CPh	*Classical Philology*
CRAI	*Comptes Rendus de l'Académie des Inscriptions et Belles-Lettres*
EJA	*European Journal of Archaeology*
EOS	*Commentarii Societatis Philologae Polonorum*
ILAlg	*Inscriptions Latines de l'Algérie*
ILLRP	*Inscriptiones Latinae Liberae Rei Publicae*
ILN	*Inscriptions Latines de Narbonnaise*
ILS	*Inscriptiones Latinae Selectae*
IPT	*Inscriptions of Punic Tripolitania*

IRT   *Inscriptions of Roman Tripolitania*
JRA   *Journal of Roman Archaeology*
JRS   *Journal of Roman Studies*
LCM   *Liverpool Classical Monthly*
LibStud   *Libyan Studies*
MDAI(R)   *Mitteilungen des Deutschen Archäologischen Instituts (Römische*
               Abteilung)
MEFR   *Mélanges de l'École Française de Rome*
MEFRA   *Mélanges d'Archéologie et d'Histoire de l'École Française de Rome,*
               Antiquité
NSA   *Notizie degli Scavi di Antichità*
P&P   *Past and Present*
PBA   *Proceedings of the British Academy*
PBSR   *Papers of the British School at Rome*
RA   *Revue Archéologique*
RAN   *Revue Archéologique de Narbonnaise*
RdN   *Revue du Nord*
REL   *Revue des Études Latines*
RIB   *The Roman Inscriptions of Britain*
SEG   *Supplementum Epigraphicum Graecum*
ZPE   *Zeitschrift für Papyrologie und Epigraphik*

AAVV (1979) *Brescia Romana. Materiali per un museo II*. Brescia.

Abascal, J. M., Almagro-Gorbea, M. and Cebrián, R. (2002) 'Segobriga 1989–2000. Topografía de la ciudad y trabajos en el foro', *Madrider Mitteilungen* 43: 123–61.

Adam, R. (1979) 'Une fontaine publique à Bavay', *RdN* 1979: 823–36.

Agache, R. (1978) *La Somme pré-romaine et romaine d'après les prospections aériennes à basse altitude*. Amiens.

Aitchison, K. (1998) 'Monumental architecture and becoming Roman in the first centuries BC and AD', in *TRAC 98. Proceedings of the Eighth Annual Theoretical Roman Archaeology Conference*, eds. P. Baker, C. Forcey, S. Jundi and R. Witcher. Oxford: 26–36.

Alarcão, J. and Etienne, R. (1977) *Fouilles de Conimbriga I: L'architecture*. Paris.

Alexander, M. A. and Ennaifer, M. (1973) *Corpus des mosaïques de Tunisie. 1.1. Utique, insulae I, II et III*. Tunis.

Alexander, M. A., Ben Abed-Ben Khader, A., Besrour, S., Mansour, B. and Soren, D. (1980) *Corpus des mosaïques de Tunisie. 2.1. Thuburbo Majus, Les mosaïques de la région du forum*. Tunis.

Alföldy, G., Abascal, J. M. and Cebrián, R. (2003a) 'Nuevos monumentos epigráficos del foro de Segobriga I', *ZPE* 143: 255–74.

(2003b) 'Nuevos monumentos epigráficos del foro de Segobriga II', *ZPE* 144: 217–34.

Allison, P. M. (1992) *The Distribution of Pompeian House Contents and Its Significance* (PhD thesis, Sydney).

Allison, P. M., Fairbairn, A. S., Ellis, S. J. R. and Blackall, C. W. (2005) 'Extracting the social relevance of artefact distribution in Roman military forts', *Internet Archaeology* 17 (http://intarch.ac.uk/journal/issue17/allison_toc.html).

Almagro-Gorbea, M. (1995) 'From hillforts to *oppida* in "Celtic" Iberia', in *Social Complexity and the Development of Towns in Iberia, PBA 86*, eds. B. Cunliffe and S. Keay. Oxford: 175-208.

Álvarez Martínez, J. M. and Nogales Basarrate, T. (1994) 'Las pinturas del anfiteatro romano de Mérida', in *El Anfiteatro en la Hispania Romana*, eds. J. M. Álvarez Martínez and J. J. Enríquez Navascués. Mérida: 265-84.

Anderson, J. C. (1997) *Roman Architecture and Society*. Baltimore.

Andreau, J. and Virlouvet, C. (2002) *L'Information et la mer dans le monde antique*. Rome.

Andreussi, M. (1999) 'Pomerium', in *Lexicon Topographicum Urbis Romae* Volume 4, ed. M. Steinby. Rome : 96–105.

Arcellaschi, A. (1996) 'Rome et la natation', in *Les loisirs et l'héritage de la culture classique*, eds. J.-M. André, J. Dangel, and P. Demont. Brussels: 330–9.

Ardevan, R. (1989) 'Veteranen und Städtische Dekurionen im römischen Dakien', *EOS* 77: 65–80.

Arthur, P. (2002) *Naples, from Roman Town to City-State: An Archaeological Perspective*. Archaeological Monographs of the British School at Rome 12. London.

Aupert, P. (1991) 'Les thermes comme lieux de culte', in *Les Thermes Romains. Actes de la table ronde organisée par l'École française de Rome (Rome, 11–12 novembre 1988)*. Rome: 185–92.

Aupert, P. and Monturet, R. (2001) *Saint-Bertrand-De-Comminges II: Les Thermes du Forum*. Bordeaux.

Bacchielli, L. (1992) 'L'Arco Severiano di Leptis Magna: storia e programma del restauro', *L'Africa Romana* 9: 763–70.

Badie, A., Sablayrolles, R. and Schenck, J.-L. (1994) *Saint-Bertrand-de-Comminges I: Le Temple du Forum et le Monument à Enceinte Circulaire*. Bordeaux.

Bagnall, R. S. (2002) 'The effects of plague: model and evidence', *JRA* 15: 114–20.

Ballu, A. (1897) *Les ruines de Timgad; Antique Thamugadi*. Paris.
  (1903) *Les ruines de Timgad; Antique Thamugadi. Nouvelles découvertes*. Paris.
  (1911) *Les ruines de Timgad; Sept années de découvertes*. Paris.

Balty, J. C. (1994) 'Le centre civique des villes romaines et ses espaces politiques et administratifs', in *La ciudad en el mundo romano I*: 91–108.

Balty, J. C. and Cazes, D. (1995) *Portraits Impériaux de Béziers*. Toulouse.

Bandinelli, R. B., Caffarelli, E. V. and Caputo, G. (1964) *Leptis Magna*. Rome.

Barocelli, P. (1932) *Inscriptiones Italiae XI.1 Augusta Praetoria*. Rome.

Barrett, J. C. (1997) 'Theorising Roman archaeology', in *TRAC 96. Proceedings of the Sixth Annual Theoretical Roman Archaeology Conference*, eds. K. Meadows, C. Lemke, J. Heron. Oxford: 1–7.

Barruol, G. (1978) 'Circonscription de Languedoc-Roussillon', *Gallia* 36: 431–59.

(1982) 'Ruscino/ Roussillon Perpignan (Pyrénées-Orientales)', *RA* 1982: 179–82.

Bartoccini, R. (1958) *Il porto Romano di Leptis Magna*. Rome.

Barton, I. M. (1977) 'The inscriptions of Septimius Severus and his family at Lepcis Magna', in *Mélanges offerts à Léopold Sédar Senghor*. Dakar: 3–12.

(1982) 'Capitoline temples in Italy and the provinces (especially Africa)', in *ANRW* II 12.1. Berlin: 259–342.

Bateman, N. (2000) *Gladiators at the Guildhall. The Story of London's Roman Amphitheatre and Medieval Guildhall*. London.

Bedon, R. (1999) *Les Villes des Trois Gaules de César à Néron*. Paris.

(2001) *Atlas des Villes, Bourgs, Villages de France au Passé Romain*. Paris.

Bedon, R., Chevallier, R. and Pinon, P. (1988) *Architecture et Urbanisme en Gaule Romaine*. Paris.

Bekker-Nielsen, T. (1989) *The Geography of Power. Studies in the Urbanisation of Roman North-West Europe*. BAR Int. Ser. 477. Oxford.

Ben Abed-Ben Khader, A., Ennaifer, M., Spiro, M., Alexander, M. A. and Soren, D. (1985) *Corpus des mosaïques de Tunisie. 2.2. Thuburbo Majus, Les mosaïques de la région des grands thermes*. Tunis.

Bénabou, M. (1976) *La résistance africaine à la Romanisation*. Paris.

Bendala Galán, M. and Durán Cabello, R. (1994) 'El anfiteatro de Augusta Emerita: Rasgos arquitectónicos y problemática urbanística y cronológica', in *El Anfiteatro en la Hispania Romana*, eds. J. M. Álvarez Martínez and J. J. Enríquez Navascués. Mérida: 247–64.

Bérard, F. (1992) 'Vie et mort et culture des vétérans d'après les inscriptions de Lyon', *REL* 70: 166–92.

Beschaouch, A., Hanoune, R. and Thébert, Y. (1977) *Les Ruines de Bulla Regia* (Coll. de L'Ecole Française de Rome 28). Rome.

Bewley, R. and Fulford, M. (1996) 'Aerial photography and the plan of Silchester', *Britannia* 27: 387–8.

Bidwell, P. T. (1979) *The Legionary Bath-house and Basilica and Forum at Exeter*. Exeter.

(1980) *Roman Exeter: Fortress and Town*. Exeter.

Biévelet, H. (1962) 'Le grand aqueduc de Bavay', *RdN* 1962: 366–73.

Bispham, E. (2006) '*Coloniam deducere*: how Roman was Roman colonization during the Middle Republic?', in *Greek and Roman Colonization: Origins, Ideologies and Interactions*, eds. G. Bradley and J.-P. Wilson. Swansea: 73–160.

Black, A. (1992) *Corporatism, Medieval and Modern*, University of Dundee Political Science and Social Policy Occasional Papers 7. Dundee.

Blázquez, J. M. (2003) 'Hispania en tiempos de Trajano', in *Trajano*, eds. J. Alvar and J. M. Blázquez. Madrid: 121–38.

Blyth, P. H. (1999) 'The consumption and cost of fuel in hypocaust baths', in *Roman Baths and Bathing*, eds. J. DeLaine and D. E. Johnston. JRA Suppl. 37. Portsmouth, RI: 87–98.

Boatwright, M. T. (1997) 'Italica and Hadrian's urban benefactions', in *Italica MMCC. Actas de las Jornadas del 2.200 Aniversario de la Fundación de Itálica*, eds. A. Caballos Rufino and P. León. Seville: 115–36.

(2000) *Hadrian and the Cities of the Roman Empire*. Princeton.

Bomgardner, D. L. (2000) *The Story of the Roman Amphitheatre*. London.

Bonneville, J.-N., Fincker, M., Sillières, P., Dardaine, S., and Laharthe, J.-M. (2000) *Belo VII: Le capitole*. Madrid.

Boon, G. C. (1972) *Isca: the Roman Legionary Fortress at Caerleon, Mon.* Cardiff.

Bouet, A. (2003a) *Thermae Gallicae: les thermes de Barzan (Charente-Maritime) et les thermes des provinces Gauloises*. Bordeaux.

(2003b) *Les Thermes Privés et Publics en Gaule Narbonnaise*. Rome.

Bowman, A. K. (1996) 'Provincial administration and taxation', in *CAH² 10: The Augustan Empire, 43 B.C. – A.D. 69*, eds. A. K. Bowman, E. Champlin and A. Lintott. Cambridge: 344–70.

Bradley, G. (2000) *Ancient Umbria. State, Culture, and Identity in Central Italy from the Iron Age to the Augustan Era*. Oxford.

(2006) 'Colonization and identity in Republican Italy', in *Greek and Roman Colonization: Origins, Ideologies and Interactions*, eds. G. Bradley and J.-P. Wilson. Swansea: 161–88.

Bradley, K. R. (2005) 'The Roman child in sickness and in health', in *The Roman Family in the Roman Empire: Rome, Italy and Beyond*, ed. M. George. Oxford.

Briand-Ponsart, C. (2004) 'Autocélébration des femmes dans les provinces d'Afrique: entre privé et public', in *Autocélébration des Élites Locales dans le Monde Romain*, ed. M. Cébeillac-Gervasoni, L. Lamoine, and F. Trément. Clermont-Ferrand: 171–86.

Brigham, T. (1990) 'A reassessment of the second basilica in London, A.D. 100–400: excavations at Leadenhall Court 1984–86', *Britannia* 21: 53–97.

(1992a) 'Basilica studies', in *From Roman Basilica to Medieval Market*, ed. G. Milne. London: 81–95.

(1992b) 'Civic centre redevelopment', in *From Roman Basilica to Medieval Market*, ed. G. Milne. London: 106–13.

Brigham, T. and Crowley, N. (1992) 'Reconstructing the basilica', in *From Roman Basilica to Medieval Market*, ed. G. Milne. London: 96–106.

Brodersen, K. (1995) *Terra Cognita: Studien zur Römischen Raumfassung*. Hildesheim.

(2001) 'The presentation of geographical knowledge for travel and geography in the Roman World', in *Travel and Geography in the Roman Empire*, eds. C. Adams and R. Laurence. London: 7–21.

Broise, H. (1991) 'Vitrages et volets des fenêtres thermales à l'époque impériale', in *Les Thermes Romains. Actes de la table ronde organisée par l'École française de Rome (Rome, 11–12 novembre 1988)*. Rome: 61–78.

Broughton, T. R. S. (1951) *The Magistrates of the Roman Republic*. New York.

Brouquier-Reddé, V. (1992) *Temples et cultes de Tripolitaine*. Paris.

Brown, F. E. (1960) *Cosa II: The Temples of the Arx*. Memoirs of the American Academy 26. Rome.

Brown, F. E., Richardson, E. H. and Richardson, L. (1993) *Cosa III: The Buildings of the Forum: Colony, Municipium and Village*. Rome.

Brunt, P. A. (1971) *Italian Manpower 225 BC – AD 14*. Oxford.

  (1974) 'Conscription and volunteering in the Roman imperial army', *Scripta Classica Israelica* 1: 90–115.

  (1983) 'Princeps and Equites', *JRS* 73: 42–75.

Brusin, G. (1928) 'Grado. Nuove epigrafi romane e cristiane', *NSA* 1928: 282–94.

Bruun, C. (2003) 'The Antonine Plague in Rome and Ostia', *JRA* 16: 426–34.

Buonocore, M. (1992) *Epigrafia anfiteatrale dell'Occidente Romano III. Regiones Italiae II–V, Sicilia, Sardinia, et Corsica*. Rome.

Burnand, Y. (1982) 'Senatores Romani ex provinciis Galliarum orti', *Tituli* 5: 387–437.

Burnett, A., Amandry, M. and Ripollès, P. P. (1992) *Roman Provincial Coinage. Volume 1. From the Death of Caesar to the Death of Vitellius*. London.

Burnham, B. C. and Wacher, J. (1990) *The 'Small Towns' of Roman Britain*. London.

Burton, G. P. (1975) 'Proconsuls, assizes, and the administration of justice under the Empire', *JRS* 65: 92–106.

  (1979) 'The *curator rei publicae*: towards a reappraisal', *Chiron* 9: 465–87.

  (1993) 'Provincial procurators and the public provinces', *Chiron* 23: 13–28.

  (2001) 'The imperial state and its impact on the role and status of local magistrates and councillors in the provinces of the Roman Empire', in *Administration, Prosopography and Appointment Policies in the Roman Empire*, ed. L. De Blois. Amsterdam: 202–14.

Busson, D. (2003) *Paris, A Roman City*. Paris.

Caballos Rufino, A. (1996) 'La Romanización de las Ciudades de la Bética y el Surgimento de Senadores Provinciales', *Revista de Estudios Andaluces* 6: 13–26.

  (1999) 'Los Caballeros Romanos Originarios de las Provincias de Hispania. Un avance', in *L'Ordre Équestre: Histoire d'une Aristocratie (IIe siècle av. J.-C. – IIIe siècle ap. J.-C.)*, eds. S. Demougin, H. Devijver and M. T. Raepsaet-Charlier. Rome: 463–512.

Caldelli, M. L. (2004) 'Le élites locali fanno spettacolo negli edifici di spettacolo', in *Autocélébration des Élites Locales dans le Monde Romain*, eds. M. Cébeillac-Gervasoni, L. Lamoine and F. Trément. Clermont-Ferrand: 129–56.

Camodeca, G. (1999) *Tabulae Pompeianae Sulpicorum (TPSulp.). Edizione critica dell'archivio puteolano dei Sulpicii*. Rome.

Campbell, B. (2000) *The Writings of the Roman Land Surveyors*. London.

Caputo, G. (1987) *Il teatro augusteo di Leptis Magna*, Monografie di Archeologia Libica 3. Rome.

Carreté, J.-M., Keay, S. and Millett, M. (1995) *A Roman Capital and Its Hinterland. The Survey of the Territory of Tarragona, Spain, 1985–1990.* JRA Suppl. 15. Portsmouth, RI.

Carroll, M. (2001) *Romans, Celts and Germans. The German Provinces of the Roman Empire.* Stroud.

Castells, M. (2003) 'The new historical relationship between space and society', in *Designing Cities. Critical Readings in Urban Design*, ed. A. R. Cuthbert. Oxford: 59–68.

Castillo, C. (1982) 'Los senadores beticos: relaciones familiares y sociales', *Tituli* 5: 465–519.

Cherry, D. (1998) *Frontier and Society in Roman North Africa.* Oxford.

Chioffi, L. (1999) *Caro: Il mercato della carne nell'occidente romano: reflessi epigrafici ed iconografici.* Rome.

Ciancio Rossetto, P. (2001) 'Il Circo Massimo: la creazione di un modello architettonico', in *El Circo en Hispania Romana*, eds. T. Nogales Basarrate and F. J. Sánchez-Palencia. Madrid: 13–26.

Clarke, A. and Fulford, M. (2002) 'The excavation of Insula IX, Silchester: the first five years of the 'Town Life' project, 1997–2001', *Britannia* 33: 129–66.

Clarke, K. (1999) *Between Geography and History: Hellenic Constructions of the Roman World.* Oxford.

Clarke, S. and Robinson, D. (1997) '"Roman" urban form and culture difference', in *TRAC 96. Proceedings of the Sixth Annual Theoretical Roman Archaeology Conference*, eds. K. Meadows, C. Lemke, J. Heron. Oxford: 163–72.

Cliquet, D., Eudier, P., and Étienne, A. (1998) *Le Vieil-Évreux: Un Vaste Site Gallo-Romain.* Évreux.

Coarelli, F. (1967) 'Su un monumento funerario romano nell'abbazia di San Gulielmo al Goleto', *Dialoghi di Archeologia* 1: 46–71.

    (1984) *Guide archeologiche Laterza: Lazio.* Bari.

    (1987) *I santuari del Lazio in età Repubblicana.* Rome.

    (1989a) *Fregellae II. Il santuario di Esculapio.* Rome.

    (1989b) 'Il Santuario della Fortuna Primigenia. Struttura Architettonica e Funzioni Cultuali', in *Urbanistica ed Architettura dell'Antica Praeneste*, ed. B. Coari. Palestrina: 115–35.

    (1998) *Fregellae I. Le fonti, la storia, il territorio.* Rome.

    (2001) 'Il Foro Triangolare: decorazione e funzione', in *Pompei: Scienza e Società*, ed. P. G. Guzzo. Milan: 97–107.

    (2002) *Pompeii.* New York.

    (2005) 'P. Faianus Plebeius, Forum Novum and Tacitus', *PBSR* 73: 85–94.

Coarelli, F. and La Regina, A. (1993) *Abruzzo Molise*, 2nd edn. Bari.

Colin, X. (2000) 'Commerçants itinérants et marchands sédentaires dans l'occident romain', in *Mercati permanenti e mercati periodici nel mondo romano*, ed. E. Lo Cascio. Bari: 149–60.

Condron, F. (1998) 'Ritual, space and politics; reflections in the archaeological record of social developments in Lepcis Magna, Tripolitania', *TRAC 97. Proceedings of the Seventh Annual Theoretical Roman Archaeological Conference*, eds. C. Forcey, J. Hawthorne, and R. Witcher. Oxford: 42–52.

Congès, A. R. (1992) 'Nouvelles fouilles à Glanum (1982–1990)', *JRA* 5: 39–55.

Cooley, A. E. (2002) *Becoming Roman, Writing Latin? Literacy and Epigraphy in the Roman West*. JRA Suppl. 48. Portsmouth, RI.

Cooley, A. E. and Cooley, M. G. L. (2004) *Pompeii: a Sourcebook*. London.

Corbiau M.-H. (1985) 'Réflexions à propos de la voie Boulogne-Bavay-Cologne: sources antiques et documentation archéologique', *Les Etudes Classiques* 53: 61–8.

Corbier, M. (1982) 'Les familles clarissimes d'Afrique proconsulaire (Ier-IIIe siècle)', *Tituli* 5: 685–754.

Cornell, T. J. (2000) 'The city state in Latium', in *A Comparative Study of Thirty City-State Cultures*, ed. M. H. Hansen. Copenhagen: 209–28.

Corni, F. (1989) *Aosta antica. La città romana*. Aosta.

Corzo Sánchez, R. (1994a) 'El anfiteatro de Italica', in *El Anfiteatro en la Hispania Romana*, eds. J. M. Álvarez Martínez and J. J. Enríquez Navascués. Mérida: 187–212.

   (1994b) 'Notas sobre el anfiteatro de Carmona y otros anfiteatros de la Betica', in *El Anfiteatro en la Hispania Romana*, eds. J. M. Álvarez Martínez and J. J. Enríquez Navascués. Mérida: 239–46.

Cotter, W. (1996) 'The *collegia* and Roman law: state restrictions on voluntary associations 64 BCE–200 CE', in *Voluntary Associations in the Graeco-Roman World*, eds. J. S. Kloppenborg and S. G. Wilson. London: 74–89.

Crawford, M. H. (1989) 'The Lex Iulia Agraria', *Athenaeum* 67: 179–90.

   (1995) 'Roman towns and their charters: legislation and experience', in *Social Complexity and the Development of Towns in Iberia*, PBA 86, eds. B. Cunliffe and S. Keay. Oxford: 421–30.

   (1996a) *Roman Statutes*. London.

   (1996b) 'Italy and Rome from Sulla to Augustus', in *CAH² 10: The Augustan Empire, 43 B.C. – A.D. 69*, eds. A. K. Bowman, E. Champlin and A. Lintott. Cambridge: 414–33.

   (2006) 'From Poseidonia to Paestum via the Lucanians', in *Greek and Roman Colonization: Origins, Ideologies and Interactions*, eds. G. Bradley and J.-P. Wilson. Swansea: 59–72.

Creighton, J. (2006) *Britannia: the Creation of a Roman Province*. London.

Criniti, N. (2006) *Res publicum veleiatium: Veleia, tra passato e futuro*. Parma.

Crummy, P. (1988) 'Colchester (Camulodunum/Colonia Victricensis)', in *Fortress into City. The Consolidation of Roman Britain First Century AD*, ed. G. Webster. London: 24–46.

   (2005) 'The circus at Colchester (*Colonia Victricensis*)', *JRA* 18: 267–77.

Cunliffe, B. (1995) *Roman Bath*. London.

Cunliffe, B. and Davenport, P. (1985) *The Temple of Sulis Minerva at Bath*, University Committee for Archaeology Monograph 7. Oxford.

Curchin, L. A. (1990) *The Local Magistrates of Roman Spain*. Toronto.

(1991) *Roman Spain: Conquest and Assimilation*. London.

D'Alessio, M. T. (2001) *Materiali votivi dal Foro Triangolare di Pompei*. Rome.

D'Arms, J. H. (1970) *Romans on the Bay of Naples*. Cambridge, Mass.

Darvill, T. and Gerrard, C. (1994) *Cirencester: Town and Landscape*. Cirencester.

Davies, H. E. (2002) *Roads in Roman Britain*. Stroud.

Davies, R. W. (1969) 'Joining the Roman army', *BJ* 169: 208–32.

(1989) *Service in the Roman Army*. Edinburgh.

de Callataÿ, F. (2005) 'The Graeco-Roman economy in the super long-run: lead, copper and shipwrecks', *JRA* 18: 361–72.

Degrassi, A. (1963) *Inscriptiones Latinae, Liberae Rei Publicae, Volume 2*. Rome.

De La Barrera, J. L. (2000) *La decoración arquitectónica de los foros de Augusta Emerita*. Rome.

De La Bédoyère, G. (1991) *The Buildings of Roman Britain*. London.

DeLaine, J. (1997) *The Baths of Caracalla. A Study in the Design, Construction and Economics of Large-Scale Building Projects in Imperial Rome*, JRA Suppl. 25. Portsmouth, RI.

(1999a) 'Benefactions and urban renewal: bath buildings in Italy', in *Roman Baths and Bathing*, eds. J. DeLaine and D. E. Johnston. JRA Suppl. 37. Portsmouth, RI: 67–74.

(1999b) 'Bathing and society', in *Roman Baths and Bathing*, eds. J. DeLaine and D. E. Johnston. JRA Suppl. 37. Portsmouth, RI: 7–16.

(2001) 'Bricks and mortar: exploring the economics of building techniques at Rome and Ostia', in *Economics beyond Agriculture in the Classical World*, ed. D. J. Mattingly. London: 230–68.

De Ligt, L. (1993) *Fairs and Markets in the Roman Empire. Economic and Social Aspects of Periodic Trade in a Pre-Industrial Society*. Amsterdam.

(2000) 'Government attitudes towards markets and *collegia*', in *Mercati permanenti e mercati periodici nel mondo romano*, ed. E. Lo Cascio. Bari: 237–52.

Della Corte, M. (1924) *Iuventus*. Arpinum.

De Miro, E. and Polito, A. (2005) *Leptis Magna. Dieci anni di scavi archeologici nell'area del Foro Vecchio. I livelli fenici, punici, e romani (Missione dell'Università di Messina)*, Quaderni di Archeologia della Libya 19. Rome.

Derks, T. (1998) *Gods, Temples and Ritual Practices: the Transformation of Religious Ideas in Roman Gaul*. Amsterdam.

De Ruggiero, E. (1948-58) *Dizionario epigrafico di antichità Romane*. Rome.

De Ruyt, C. (1983) *Macellum: marché alimentaire des Romains*. Louvain-La-Neuve.

De Salvo, L. (1993) *I Corpora Naviculariorum: Economia privata e pubblici servizi nell'impero romano*. Messina.

De Sena, E. C. and Ikäheimo, J. P. (2003) 'The supply of amphora-borne commodities and domestic pottery in Pompeii 150 BC – AD 79: preliminary evidence from the House of the Vestals', *EJA* 6: 301–21.

Devijver, H. (1989) 'The geographical origins of equestrian officers', *Bulletin of the Institute of Archaeology* 26: 107–26.

(1991) 'Equestrian officers from North Africa', *L'Africa Romana* 8: 127–201.

Devijver, H. and van Wooterghem, F. (1989) 'The funerary monuments of equestrian officers of the late Republic and early Empire in Italy', *Athenaeum* 20: 59–99.

Diaconescu, A. (2004) 'The towns of Roman Dacia: an overview of recent archaeological research', in *Roman Dacia: the Making of a Provincial Society*, JRA Suppl. 56, eds. W. S. Hanson and I. P. Haynes. Portsmouth, RI: 87–142.

Didierjean, F., Ney, C. and Paillet, J.-L. (1981) *Belo III: Le Macellum*. Madrid.

Diosono, F. (2007) *Collegia: Le associazioni professionali nel mondo romano*. Rome.

Di Vita, A. (1982a) 'Il progetto originario del forum novum Severianum a Leptis Magna', in *150-Jahr-Feier Deutsches archäologisches Institut Rom, MDAI(R)* Suppl. 25: 84–100.

(1982b) 'Gli 'emporia' di Tripolitania dall'età di Massinissa a Diocleziano: un profilo storico istituzionale', in *ANRW* II, 10.2. Berlin: 515–95.

(1995) 'Leptis Magna. La ville des Sévères', *Karthago* 23: 71–7.

(2005) *I tre templi del lato nord-ovest del foro vecchio a Leptis Magna*, Rome.

Di Vita, A., Di Vita-Evrard, G. and Bacchielli, L. (1999) *Libya, the Lost Cities of the Roman Empire*. Cologne.

Dobbins, J. J. (1994) 'Problems of chronology, decoration, and urban design in the forum of Pompeii', *AJA*: 629–94.

Dondin-Payre, M. and Raepsaet-Charlier, M.-T. (1999) *Cités, municipes, colonies: les processus de municipalisation en Gaule et en Germanie sous le Haut Empire Romain*. Paris.

Dore, J. (1988) 'Pottery and the history of Roman Tripolitania: evidence from Sabratha and the UNESCO Libyan Valleys Survey', *Libstud* 19: 61–85.

Downs, M. E. (1996) 'Spatial conception in the ancient geographers and the mapping of Hispania Baetica', *CB* 72: 37–50.

Duncan-Jones, R. P. (1967) 'Equestrian rank in the cities of the African provinces under the Principate: an epigraphic survey', *PBSR* 35: 148–86.

(1982) *The Economy of the Roman Empire: Quantitative Studies*. Cambridge.

(1990) *Structure and Scale of the Roman Economy*. Cambridge.

(1996) 'The impact of the Antonine Plague', *JRA* 9: 108–36.

(2004) 'Economic change and the transition to late antiquity', in *Approaching Late Antiquity: The Transformation from Early to Late Empire*, eds. S. Swain and M. Edwards. Oxford: 20–52.

Dupré i Raventós, X. (1994) 'El anfiteatro de Tarraco', in *El Anfiteatro en la Hispania Romana*, eds. J. M. Álvarez Martínez and J. J. Enríquez Navascués. Mérida: 79–90.

(1995) 'New evidence for the study of the urbanism of Tarraco', in *Social Complexity and the Development of Towns in Iberia, PBA* 86, eds. B. Cunliffe and S. Keay. Oxford: 355–69.

(2004) *Tarragona: Colonia Julia Urbs Triumphalis Tarraco*. Rome.

Dupuis, X. (1991) 'La participation des vétérans à la vie municipale en Numidie méridionale aux IIe et IIIe siècles', in *Histoire et archéologie de l'Afrique du Nord (Actes du IV colloque International, vol.2: L'armée et les affaires militaires)*. Paris: 343–54.

Durán Cabello, R. M. (2004) *El teatro y el anfiteatro de Augusta Emerita*, BAR Int. Ser. 1207. Oxford.

Durán Cabello, R. M., Fernández Ochoa, C., and Morillo Cerdán, Á. (2009) 'The amphitheatres in Hispania: recent investigations', in *Roman Amphitheatres and Spectacula: a 21st century Perspective* (BAR Int. Ser.1946), ed. T. Wilmot, Oxford: 15–28.

Duthoy, R. (1970) 'Notes onomastiques sur les Augustales. Cognomina et indication de statut', *L'Antiquité Classique* 39: 88–105.

(1979) 'Curatores rei publicae en occident durant le principat', *AncSoc* 10: 171–238.

Duval, N. (1982) 'Topographie et urbanisme d'Ammaedara (actuellement Haïdra, Tunisie)', *ANRW* II, 10.2. Berlin: 633–671.

Eck, W. (1997) 'Rome and the outside world: senatorial families and the world they lived in', in *The Roman Family in Italy: Status, Sentiment, Space*, eds. B. Rawson and P. Weaver. Oxford: 73–99.

Epstein, S. A. (1991) *Wage Labour and Guilds in Medieval Europe*. Chapel Hill, NC.

Erdkamp, P. (2008) 'Mobility and migration in Italy in the second century BC', in L. De Ligt and S. J. Northwood (eds), *People, Land and Politics. Demographic Developments and the Transformation of Roman Italy 300 BC – AD 14*. Leiden: 417–50.

Esmonde Cleary, S. (1998) 'The origins of towns in Roman Britain: the contribution of Romans and Britons', in *Los orígines de la ciudad en la noroeste Hispánico, Actas del Congreso Internacional Lugo 15–18 de Mayo 1996*, ed. A. R. Colmenero. Lugo: 35–54.

(2001) Review of Fulford and Timby 2000, *BJ* 201: 515–18.

(2003) 'Civil defences in the West under the High Empire', in *The Archaeology of Roman Towns*, ed. P. Wilson. Oxford: 72–85.

(2007) *Rome in the Pyrenees. Lugdunum and the Convenae from the First Century B.C. to the Seventh Century A.D.* London.

Etienne, R. (1966) 'La naissance de l'amphithéâtre: le mot et la chose', *REL* 43: 213–20.

Etienne, R., Fabre, G., Lévêque, M., and Lévêque, P. (1976) *Fouilles de Conimbriga II: Epigraphie et Sculpture*. Paris.

Evans, E. (2000) *The Caerleon Canabae*. London.

Evans, D. R. and Metcalf, V. M. (1992) *Roman Gates: Caerleon*. Oxford.

Fagan, G. G. (1999) *Bathing in Public in the Roman World*. Ann Arbor.

Fantar, M. H. (1987) *Kerkouane: une Cité Punique au Cap-Bon*. Tunis.

Fear, A. (1996) *Rome and Baetica. Urbanisation in Southern Spain c. 50 B.C. – A.D. 150*. Oxford.

Fentress, E. (1979) *Numidia and the Roman Army: Social, Military and Economic Aspects of the Frontier Zone*, BAR Int. Ser. 53. Oxford.

　(1983) 'Forever Berber?', *Opus* 2: 161–75.

　(1984) 'Frontier culture and politics at Timgad', *BCTH* n.s. 17 B: 399–407.

　(2000) 'Introduction: Frank Brown, Cosa and the idea of the Roman city', in *Romanization and the City: Creation, Transformations and Failures*, JRA Suppl. 38, ed. E. Fentress. Portsmouth, RI: 11–24.

　(2004) *Cosa V: An Intermittent Town. Excavations 1991–1997*. Ann Arbor.

Février, P-A. (1964) 'Notes sur le développement urbain en Afrique du Nord, les exemples comparés de Djemila et de Sétif', *Cahiers Archéologiques* 14 : 1–47.

　(1968) *Djemila*. Algiers.

　(1982) 'Urbanisation et urbanisme de l'Afrique Romaine', *ANRW* II, 10.2. Berlin: 321–97.

Filippi, G. (1989) *Supplementum Italica* 5. Rome.

Finley, M. I. (1973) *The Ancient Economy*. London.

　(1977) 'The ancient city: from Fustel de Coulanges to Max Weber and beyond', *Comparative Studies in Society and History* 19: 305–27.

Fishwick, D. (1987) *The Imperial Cult in the Latin West: Studies in the Ruler Cult of the Western Provinces of the Roman Empire, Volume 1.1*. Leiden.

　(2004) *The Imperial Cult in the Latin West Volume III: The Provincial Cult (Part 3: The Provincial Centre; The Provincial Cult)*. Leiden.

Fora, M. (1996) *Epigrafia anfiteatrale dell'Occidente Romano IV. Regio Italiae I: Latium*. Rome.

Forbis, E. P. (1990) 'Women's public image in Italian honorary inscriptions', *AJPh* 111: 493–507.

Forcey, C. (1997) 'Beyond "romanization": technologies of power in Roman Britain', in *TRAC 96. Proceedings of the Sixth Annual Theoretical Roman Archaeology Conference*, eds. K. Meadows, C. Lemke, J. Heron. Oxford: 15–21.

Forni, G. (1953) *Il reclutamento delle legioni da Augusto a Diocleziano*. Milan.

　(1992) *Esercito e marina di Roma Antica*. Stuttgart.

Frayn, J. (1993) *Markets and Fairs in Roman Italy*. Oxford.

Frederiksen, M. (1984) *Campania*. Oxford.

Freeman, P. (1997) 'Mommsen through to Haverfield: the origins of Romanization Studies in 19th-century Britain', in *Dialogues in Roman Imperialism*, JRA Suppl. 23, ed. D. J. Mattingly. Portsmouth, RI: 27–50.

　(2007) *The Best Training Ground for Archaeologists: Francis Haverfield and the Invention of Romano-British Archaeology*. Oxford.

Frei-Stolba, R., Bielman, A. and Bianchi, O. (2003) *Les femmes antiques entre sphère privée et sphère publique*. Bern.

Frere, S. and Fulford, M. (2002) 'The *Collegium Peregrinorum* at Silchester', *Britannia* 33: 167–75.

Frézouls, E. (1952) 'Le théâtre romain de Tipasa', *MEFR* 64: 111–77.

(1982) *Les villes antiques de la France: Belgique 1*. Strasbourg.

Frova, A. (1973) *Scavi di Luni. Relazione preliminare delle campagne di scavo 1970–1971*. Rome.

Fuchs, M. (1987) *Untersuchungen zur Ausstattung römischer Theater in Italien und den Westprovinzen des Imperium Romanum*. Mainz.

Fulford, M. (1989) *The Silchester Amphitheatre: Excavations of 1979–85*. Britannia Monograph Series 10. London.

(2003) 'Julio-Claudian and early Flavian Calleva', in *The Archaeology of Roman Towns*, ed. P. Wilson. Oxford: 95–104.

Fulford, M. and Timby, J. (2000) *Late Iron Age and Roman Silchester: Excavations on the Site of the Forum-Basilica 1977, 1980–86*, Britannia Monograph Series No. 15. London.

(2008) 'Nero and Britain: the palace of the client king at Calleva and imperial policy towards the province after Boudicca', *Britannia* XXXIX: 1–13.

Gabba, E. (1972) 'Urbanizzazione e rinnovamenti urbanistici nell'Italia centro-meridionale del I sec. a.C.' *Studi Classici e Orientali* 21: 73–112.

Gaffney, V., Patterson, H., and Roberts, P. (1997) 'L'anfiteatro di Forum Novum', *Archeo* 16: 10–11.

(2001) 'Forum Novum-Vescovio: studying urbanism in the Tiber Valley', *JRA* 14: 59–79.

(2003) 'Forum Novum-Vescovio: from Roman town to bishop's seat', in *Lazio e Sabina* 1: 119–26.

(2004a) 'Forum Novum-Vescovio: a new study of the town and bishopric', in *Bridging the Tiber: Approaches to Regional Archaeology in the Middle Tiber Valley*, ed. H. Patterson. London: 237–51.

(2004b) 'Forum Novum-Vescovio. The results of the 2003 field season', in *Lazio e Sabina* 3: 109–14.

Gaffney, V. L., White, R. H and Goodchild, H. (2007) *Wroxeter, the Cornovii and the Urban Process*, JRA Suppl. 68. Portsmouth, RI.

Gargola, D. J. (1995) *Lands, Laws, and Gods: Magistrates and Ceremony in the Regulation of Public Lands in Republican Rome*. Chapel Hill, NC.

Germain, S. (1973) *Les mosaïques de Timgad, étude descriptive et analytique*. Paris.

Giddens, A. (1984) *The Constitution of Society*. Oxford.

Gilliam, J. F. (1956) 'Enrolment in the Roman imperial army', *EOS* 48.2: 207–16.

Golvin, J.-C. (1988) *L'amphithéâtre romain. Essai sur la théorisation de sa forme et de ses fonctions*. Paris.

González, J. (1986) 'The Lex Irnitana: a new copy of the Flavian Municipal Law', *JRS* 76: 147–243.

Goodchild, R. G. (1965) 'The unfinished "Imperial" Baths of Lepcis Magna', *Libya Antiqua* 2: 15–27. repr. *Select Papers of the Late R. G. Goodchild*, ed. J. Reynolds. London: 118–32.

(1966-7) 'A coin-hoard from Balagrae and the earthquake of 365 AD', *Libya Antiqua* 3–4: 203–11.

Goodchild, R. G. and Ward-Perkins, J. B. (1953) 'The Roman and Byzantine defences of Lepcis Magna', *PBSR* 21: 42–73.

Grahame, M. (1997) 'Towards a theory of Roman urbanism: beyond economics and ideal types', in *TRAC 96. Proceedings of the Sixth Annual Theoretical Roman Archaeology Conference*, eds. K. Meadows, C. Lemake, and J. Heron. Oxford: 151–62.

(2000) *Reading Space: Social Interaction and Identity in the Houses of Roman Pompeii*, BAR Int.Ser. 886. Oxford.

Greco, E. (1999) *Poseidonia – Paestum IV: Forum ouest-sud-est*. Rome.

Greco, E. and Theodorescu, D. (1987) *Poseidonia – Paestum: Forum nord*. Rome.

Greenberg, J. (2003) 'Plagued by doubt: reconsidering the impact of a mortality crisis in the second c. A.D.', *JRA* 16: 413–25.

Gregori, G. L. (1989) *Epigrafia anfiteatrale dell'Occidente Romano II. Regiones Italiae VI-XI*. Rome.

Gros, P. (1987) *Storia dell'Urbanistica*. Rome.

(1996) *L'Architecture romaine du début du IIIe siècle av.J.-C. à la fin du Haut-Empire*. Paris.

(2000) 'L'évolution des centres monumentaux des cités italiennes en fonction de l'implantation du culte impériale', in *Les élites municipales de l'Italie péninsulaire de la mort de César à la mort de Domitien: classes sociales dirigeantes et pouvoir central*, ed. M. Cébeillac-Gervasoni. Rome: 307–26.

Gruen, E. S. (1992) *Culture and National Identity in Republican Rome*. Berkeley.

Haensch, R. (1997) *Capita Provinciarum: Statthaltersitze und Provincialverwaltung in der Römischen Kaiserzeit*. Mainz.

Halsberghe, G. H. (1984) 'La culte de Dea Caelestis', *ANRW* II, 17.4. Berlin: 2203–23.

Hammond, M. (1957) 'Composition of the Senate A.D. 68–235', *JRS* 47: 74–81.

Hanoune, R. and Muller, A. (1999) 'La basilique du forum de Bavay: Bilan des recherches 1987–1996', *RA* 1999: 167–78.

Harlow, M. and Laurence, R. (2008) 'The representation of age in the Roman Empire: towards a life course approach', in *New Perspectives on the Ancient World*, BAR Int.Ser. 1782, eds. P. P. Funari, R. S. Garraffoni and B. Letalien. Oxford: 205–12.

Harris, W. V. (1977) 'The era of Patavium', *ZPE* 27: 283–93.

(1989) *Ancient Literacy*. Cambridge, Mass.

Haselberger, L. (2007) *Urbem Adornare: Rome's Urban Metamorphosis under Augustus*, JRA Suppl. 64. Portsmouth, RI.

Hassall, M. (2000) 'London: the Roman city', in *London Underground: The Archaeology of a City*, eds. I. Haynes, H. Sheldon and L. Hannigan. Oxford: 52–61.

Haussler, R. (1999) 'Architecture, performance and ritual: the role of state architecture in the Roman empire', in *TRAC 98. Proceedings of the Eighth Annual Theoretical Roman Archaeology Conference*, eds. P. Baker, C. Forcy, S. Jundi and R. Witcher. Oxford: 1–13.

Haverfield, F. (1913) *Ancient Town Planning*. Oxford.

Haynes D. E. L. (1956) *The Antiquities of Tripolitania*. Tripoli.

Hemelrijk, E. A. (2004) 'Patronage of cities: the role of women', in *Roman Rule and Civic Life: Local and Regional Perspectives*, eds. L. De Ligt, E. A. Hemelrijk and H. W. Singor. Amsterdam: 415–28.

(2005) 'Priestesses of the imperial cult in the Latin West: titles and function', *AC* 74: 137–70.

(2006) 'Priestesses of the imperial cult in the Latin West: benefactions and public honour', *AC* 75: 85–118.

Hillier, B. (1996) *Space is the Machine: A Configurational Theory of Architecture*. Cambridge.

Hingley, R. (2000) *Roman Officers and English Gentlemen: The Imperial Origins of Roman Archaeology*. London.

(2005) *Globalizing Roman Culture: Unity, Diversity and Empire*. London.

Hipólito Correia, V. (1994a) 'O anfiteatro de Conimbriga: Nota Preliminar', in *El Anfiteatro en la Hispania Romana*, eds. J. M. Álvarez Martínez and J. J. Enríquez Navascués. Mérida: 327–43.

(1994b) 'O anfiteatro de Evora: noticia de sua identificação', in *El Anfiteatro en la Hispania Romana*, eds. J. M. Álvarez Martínez and J. J. Enríquez Navascués. Mérida: 345–7.

Højte, J. M. (2005) *Roman Imperial Statue Bases from Augustus to Commodus*. Aarhus.

Holbrook, N. (1998) 'The amphitheatre: excavations directed by J. S. Wacher 1962–3 and A. D. McWhirr 1966', in *Cirencester Excavations V: The Roman Town Defences, Public Buildings and Shops*, ed. N. Holbrook. Cirencester: 145–75.

Holbrook, N. and Bidwell, P. T. (1991) *Roman Finds from Exeter*. Exeter.

Hopkins, K. (1978) *Conquerors and Slaves. Sociological Studies in Roman History Volume 1*. Cambridge.

(1980) 'Taxes and trade in the Roman Empire (200 B.C. – A.D. 400), *JRS* 70: 101–25.

(1983) *Death and Renewal. Sociological Studies in Roman History Volume 2*. Cambridge.

(1996) 'Centro e periferia. L'economia politica dell'Impero Romano', in *Storia dell'economia mondiale 1. Permanenze e mutamenti dall'antichità al medioevo*, ed. V. Castronovo. Rome: 213–32.

(2002) 'Rome, taxes, rents and trade', in *The Ancient Economy*, eds. W. Scheidel and S. von Reden. Edinburgh: 190–230.

Horden, P. and Purcell, N. (2000) *The Corrupting Sea: a Study of Mediterranean History*. Oxford.

Howego, C. (2005) 'Coinage and identity in the Roman provinces', in *Coinage and Identity in the Roman Provinces*, eds. C. Howego, V. Heuchert and A. Burnett. Oxford: 1–17.

Humphrey, J. H. (1986) *Roman Circuses: Arenas for Chariot Racing*. London.

(1991) *Literacy in the Roman World*, JRA Suppl. 3. Ann Arbor.

Humphrey, J., Sear, F. and Vickers, M. (1973-4) 'Aspects of the Circus at Lepcis Magna', *LibStud* 5: 4–12.

Hurst, H. R. (1988) 'Gloucester (Glevum)', in *Fortress into City: The Consolidation of Roman Britain (First Century AD)*, ed. G. Webster. London: 48–73.

(1999) *The Coloniae of Roman Britain*. JRA Suppl. 36. Portsmouth, RI.

Jacques, F. (1983) *Les Curateurs des Cités dans l'Occident Romain de Trajan à Gallien*. Paris.

(1984) *Le Privilège de Liberté: Politique impériale et autonomie municipale dans les cités de l'Occident romain (161–244)*. Rome.

Jaczynowska, M. (1970) 'Les organisations des iuvenes et l'aristocratie munici-pale', in *Recherches sur les structures sociales dans l'antiquité classique*. Paris: 265–74.

James, H. (2003) *Roman Carmarthen: Excavations 1978–1993*. Britannia Monograph Series. London.

Janni, P. (1984) *La mappa e il periplo*. Rome.

Janon, M. (1973) 'Recherches à Lambèse. II *Aquae Lambaesitanae*', *AntAfr* 7: 222–54.

Johnson, J. (1933) *Excavations at Minturnae Volume II: Inscriptions*. Philadelphia.

(1935) *Excavations at Minturnae Volume I: Monuments of the Republican Forum*. Philadelphia.

Jongman, W. (2000) 'Wool and the textile industry of Roman Italy: a working hypothesis', in *Mercati permanenti e mercati periodici nel mondo romano*, ed. E. Lo Cascio. Bari: 187–97.

(2003) 'Slavery and the growth of Rome. The transformation of Italy in the second and first centuries BCE', in *Rome the Cosmopolis*, eds. C. Edwards and G. Woolf. Cambridge: 100–23.

Jouffroy, H. (1986) *La construction publique en Italie et dans l'Afrique romaine*. Strasbourg.

Kaiser, A. (2000) *The Urban Dialogue. An Analysis of the Use of Space in the Roman City of Empúries, Spain*, BAR Int. Ser. 901. Oxford.

Keay, S. (1988) *Roman Spain*. London.

(1995) 'Innovation and adaptation: the contribution of Rome to urbanism in Iberia', in *Social Complexity and the Development of Towns in Iberia*, PBA 86, eds. B. Cunliffe and S. Keay. Oxford: 291–337.

(1996) 'Ideology and the location of Roman towns in Baetica', *CB* 72: 51–8.

(1998) 'The development of towns in early Roman Baetica', in *The Archaeology of Early Roman Baetica*, ed. S. Keay. JRA Supplement No.29. Portsmouth RI: 55–86.

Keay, S., Millett, M., Poppy, S., Robinson, J., Taylor, J. and Terrenato, N. (2000) 'Falerii Novi: a new survey of the walled area', *PBSR* 68: 1–93.

Keay, S. and Terrenato, N. (2001) *Italy and the West. Comparative Issues in Romanization*. Oxford.

Keppie, L. (1983) *Colonisation and Veteran Settlement in Italy 47–14 BC*. London.

(1984) 'Colonisation and veteran settlement in Italy in the first century AD', *PBSR* 52: 77–114.

(2000) *Legions and Veterans: Roman Army Papers 1971–2000*. Stuttgart.

Knapp, R. C. (1977) *Aspects of the Roman Experience in Iberia, 206–100 BC*, Anejos de Hispania Antiqua 9. Valladolid.

(1996) 'Ptolemy mapping Baetica', *CB* 72: 29–36.

Koolhaas, R. (1994) *Delirious New York*. New York.

Kulikowski, M. (2004) *Late Roman Spain and its Cities*. Baltimore.

La Chica Cassinello, G. (1956–61) 'Inscripciones dedicada a Tiberio Sempronio Graco', *Noticiario Arqueológico Hispanico* V: 178–80.

Laffi, U. (1966) *Adtributio e contributio, problemi del sistema politico-amministrative dello stato romano*. Pisa.

Lancel, S. (1982) 'Tipasa de Maurétanie: histoire et archéologie I. État des questions des origines préromaines à la fin du IIIème siècle', *ANRW* II, 10.2. Berlin, 739–86.

(1995) *Carthage: A History*. Oxford.

La Regina, A. (1966) 'Le iscrizioni Osche di Pietrabbondante', *Rheinisches Museum für Philologie* 109: 260–72.

(1975) 'Stazio Sannita', *Parola del Passato* 30: 163–9.

(1976) 'Il Sannio', in *Hellenismus in Mittelitalien*, ed. P. Zanker. Göttingen: 219–54.

(2001) *Sangue e Arena*. Rome.

Lassus, J. (1981) *La Forteresse Byzantine de Thamugadi: Fouilles à Timgad 1938–1956*. Paris.

Laurence, R. (1994) 'Modern ideology and the creation of ancient town planning', *European Review of History* 1: 9–18.

(1996) 'Ritual, landscape and the destruction of place in the Roman imagination', in *Approaches to the Study of Ritual*, ed. J. Wilkins. London: 111–21.

(1997) 'Writing the Roman metropolis', in *Roman Urbanism: Beyond the Consumer City*, ed. H. Parkins. London: 1–20.

(1998) 'Territory, ethnonyms and geography: the construction of identity in Roman Italy', in *Cultural Identity in the Roman Empire*, eds. R. Laurence and J. Berry. London: 95–110.

(1999) *The Roads of Roman Italy: Mobility and Cultural Change*. London.

(2000) 'The image of the Roman city', *Cambridge Archaeological Journal* 10: 346–8.

(2001a) 'Roman narratives. The writing of archaeological discourse – a view from Britain', *Archaeological Dialogues* 8: 90–122.

(2001b) 'The creation of geography: an interpretation of Roman Britain', in *Travel and Geography in the Roman Empire*, ed. C. Adams and R. Laurence. London.

(2002) 'The Roman urban revolution', in *Modalità insediative e strutture agrarie nell'Italia meridionale in età romana*, ed. E. Lo Cascio. Bari: 591–609.

(2007) *Roman Pompeii: Space and Society*, 2nd edn. London.

(2008) 'City traffic and the archaeology of Roman streets', in *Stadtverkehr in der Antiken Welt/Traffico Urbano nel Mondo Antico (Palilia 13)*, ed. D. Mertens. Wiesbaden: 87–106.

Lefebvre, H. (1991) *The Production of Space*. Oxford.

(1996) *Writings on cities; selected, translated, and introduced by E. Kofman and E. Lebas*. Cambridge, Mass.

Le Glay, M. (1961-6) *Saturne Africain: monuments I et II*. Paris.

(1966) *Saturne Africain: histoire*. Paris.

Lepelley, C. (1981) *Les cités de l'Afrique romaine au Bas-Empire, Vol. 2: Notices d'histoire municipale*. Paris.

Lequément, R. (1967) 'Fouilles à l'amphithéâtre de Tébessa (1965–66)', in *BAA* 2: 107–122.

Le Roux, P. (1982) 'Les sénateurs originaires de la province d'Hispania Citerior au Haut-Empire Romain', *Tituli* 5: 439–64.

(1999) 'Vectigalia et revenues des cités en Hispanie au Haut-Empire', in *Il Capitolo delle Entrate nelle Finanze Municipali in Occidente ed in Oriente*. Rome: 155–73.

Leschi, L. (1947) 'Découvertes récentes à Timgad: Aqua Septimiana Felix', *CRAI* 87–99.

Leveau, P. (1984) *Caesarea de Maurétanie: une ville romaine et ses campagnes*, Collection de l'École Française de Rome 70. Rome.

Levi della Vida, G. (1942) 'The Phoenician god Satrapes', *BASO* 87: 29–32.

Lézine, A. (1968) *Carthage-Utique: Etudes d'Architecture et d'Urbanisme*. Paris.

Liebenam, W. (1897) 'Curator rei publicae', *Philologus* 56: 290–333.

Ling, R. (2005) *Pompeii: History, Life, Afterlife*. Stroud.

Littman, R. J. and Littman, M. L. (1973) 'Galen and the Antonine Plague', *AJPh* 94: 243–55.

Lo Cascio, E. (1994) 'La dinamica della popolazione in Italia da Augusto al III secolo', in *L'Italie d'Auguste à Dioclétien. Actes du colloque international organisé par l'École Française de Rome (Rome, 25–28 Mars 1992)*. Rome: 91–125.

(1996a) 'Pompei dalla città sannitica alla colonia sillana: le vicende istituzionali', in *Les élites municipales de l'Italie péninsulaire des Gracques à Néron*, ed. M. Cébeillac-Gervasoni. Actes de la table ronde de Clermont-Ferrand (28–30 novembre 1991), Naples-Rome: 111–23.

(1996b) 'Popolazione e risorse nel mondo antico', in *Storia dell'economia mondiale 1. Permanenze e mutamenti dall'antichità al medioevo*, ed. V. Castronovo. Rome: 275–300.

(2001) 'Condizioni igienico-sanitarie e dinamica della popolazione della città di Roma dall'età tardorepubblicana al tardoantico', in *Thérapies, Médicine et Démographie Antiques*, eds. J. N. Corvisier, C. Didier, and M. Valdher. Arras: 37–70.

(2006) 'Did the population of Rome reproduce itself?', in *Urbanism in the Preindustrial World: Cross-Cultural Approaches*, ed. G. R. Storey. Tuscaloosa: 52–68.

Lomas, K. (1993) *Rome and the Western Greeks 350 BC – AD 200*. London.

(2003) 'Public building, urban renewal, and euergetism in early imperial Italy', in *'Bread and Circuses': Euergetism and Municipal Patronage in Roman Italy*, eds. T. Cornell and K. Lomas. London: 28–45.

Lott, J. B. (2004) *The Neighbourhoods of Augustan Rome*. Cambridge.

Lucas, C. (1940) 'Notes on the *curatores rei publicae* of Roman Africa', *JRS* 30: 56–74.

Luni, M. (2000) *Studi su Fanum Fortunae*. Urbino.

Lynch, K. (1960) *The Image of the City*. Cambridge, Mass.

MacDonald, W. L. (1968) 'Severan design at Lepcis Magna and Cuicul (Djemila)', *AJA* 72: 168.

(1986) *The Architecture of the Roman Empire Volume II: An Urban Appraisal*. New Haven.

Mackie, N. (1983) *Local Administration in Roman Spain A.D. 14–212*, BAR Int. Ser.172. Oxford.

MacMullen, R. (1980) 'Women in public in the Roman Empire', *Historia* 29: 208–18.

(1988) *Corruption and the Decline of Rome*. New York.

Maiuri, A. (1941) 'Pompei. Saggi nell'area del Foro', *NSA* 67: 371–404.

(1942) 'Pompei. Saggi negli edifici del Foro', *NSA* 68: 253–320.

Mann, J. C. (1983) *Legionary Recruitment and Veteran Settlement during the Principate*. London.

Mansuelli, G. A. (1971) *Urbanistica e architettura della Cisalpina romana fino al III sec. e.n.* Brussels.

Mar, R. and Ruiz del Arbulo, J. (1993) *Ampurias Romana*. Sabadell.

Marec, E. (1954) *Hippone la Royale: Antique Hippo Regius*. Alger.

Marsden, P. (1987) *The Roman Forum Site in London*. London.

Mason, D. J. P. (2001) *Chester: City of the Eagles*. Stroud.

(2002) 'The town and port of Roman Chester', in *Deva Victrix: Roman Chester Re-assessed*, ed. P. Carrington. Chester: 53–74.

Masturzo, N. (2003) 'Le città della Tripolitania fra continuità ed innovazione: I fori di Leptis Magna e Sabratha', *MEFRA* 115: 705–53.

Mattingly, D. J. (1995) *Tripolitania*. London.

(1997) 'Dialogues of power and experience in the Roman Empire', in *Dialogues in Roman Imperialism*, JRA Suppl 23, ed. D. J. Mattingly. Portsmouth, RI: 1–16.

(2004) 'Being Roman: expressing identity in a provincial setting', *JRA* 17: 5–25.

(2006) *An Imperial Possession. Britain in the Roman Empire 54 BC – AD 409*. London.

McCann, A. M. (1987) *The Roman Port and Fishery at Cosa*. Princeton.

Mertens, J. (1969) *Alba Fucens: Rapports et Études*. Rome.

Meyer, E. A. (1990) 'Explaining the epigraphic habit in the Roman Empire: the evidence of epitaphs', *JRS* 80: 74–96.

Middleton, P. (1979) 'Army supply in Roman Gaul: a hypothesis for Roman Britain', in *Invasion and Response: The Case of Roman Britain*, eds. B. C. Burnham and H. B. Johnson. BAR Brit. ser. Oxford: 81–97.

Mierse, W. E. (1999) *Temples and Towns in Roman Iberia*. Berkeley.

Millett, M. (1990) *The Romanisation of Roman Britain*. Cambridge.

Mollo, S. (2000) *La mobilità sociale a Brescia romana*. Milan.

Morigi, A. (1997) *Carsulae: Topografia e Monumenti*. Rome.

Morley, N. (1996) *The City of Rome and the Italian Economy, 200 BC – AD 200*. Cambridge.

(2000) 'Markets, marketing and the Roman elite', in *Mercati permanenti e mercati periodici nel mondo romano*, ed. E. Lo Cascio. Bari: 211–21.

Mouritsen, H. (1990) 'A note on Pompeian epigraphy and social structure', *C&M* 61: 131–49.

(1996) 'Order and disorder in late Pompeian politics', in *Les Élites Municipales de l'Italie Péninsulaire des Gracques à Néron*, ed. M. Cébeillac-Gervasoni. Naples: 139–46.

(1997) 'Mobility and social change in Italian towns during the Principate', in *Roman Urbanism: Beyond the Consumer City*, ed. H. Parkins London: 59–82.

(1998) *Italian Unification: A Study in Ancient and Modern Historiography*. London.

(2006) 'Freedmen and decurions: epitaphs and social history in Imperial Italy', *JRS* 95: 38–63.

Mrozewicz, L. (1989) 'Die Veteranen in den Munizipalräten an Rhein und Donau zur hohen Kaiserzeit', *EOS* 77: 81–90.

Murillo, J. F., Ventura, A., Carmona, S., Carrillo, J. R., Hidalgo, R., Jiménez, J. L., Moreno, M., and Ruiz, D. (2001) 'El circo orientale de *Colonia Patricia*', in *El Circo en Hispania Romana*, eds. T. Nogales Basarrate and F. J. Sánchez-Palencia. Madrid: 57–74.

Navarro Caballero, M. (2001) 'Les femmes de l'élite Hispano-Romaine entre la famille et la vie publique', in *Élites Hispaniques*, eds. M. Navarro Caballero and S. Demougin. Bordeaux: 193–201.

Naveau, J. (1997) *Recherches sur Jublains (Mayenne) et sur la cité des Diablintes*. Rennes.

Niblett, R. (2001) *Verulamium. The Roman City of St Albans*. Stroud.

(2005) 'Roman Verulamium', in *Alban's Buried Towns: An Assessment of St Albans' Archaeology up to AD 1600*, ed. R. Niblett and I. Thompson. Oxford.

Nicolet, C. (1991) *Space, Geography and Politics in the Early Empire*. Ann Arbor.

Nielsen, I. (1990) *Thermae et Balnea: The Architecture and Cultural History of Roman Public Baths.* Aarhus.

Niemeyer, H. G. (1992) 'Chronologie et caractères de l'habitat primitif: premiers résultats: 1986–1988', in *Pour Sauver Carthage. Exploration et conservation de la cité punique, romaine et byzantine,* ed. A. Ennabli. Paris: 38–41.

Nijf, O. M. van (1997) *The Civic World of Professional Associations in the Roman East.* Amsterdam.

Nogales Basarrate, T. (2000) *Espectáculos en Augusta Emerita.* Madrid.

Nogales Basarrate, T. and Sánchez-Palencia F. J. (2001) *El Circo en Hispania Romana.* Madrid.

Owens, E. J. (1991) *The City in the Greek and Roman World.* London.

Paillet, J. L. and Petit, C. (1992) 'Nouvelles données sur l'urbanisme de Lugdunum des Convènes. Prospection aérienne et topographie urbaine', *Aquitania* 10: 109–44.

Parisi Presicce, C. (1994) 'L'architettura della via colonnata di Leptis Magna', *L'Africa romana* 10: 703–17.

Parker, A. J. (1992) *Ancient Shipwrecks of the Mediterranean and the Roman Provinces,* BAR Int. Ser. 580. Oxford.

Patterson, J. (1994) 'The collegia and the transformation of the towns of Italy in the second century AD', in *L'Italie d'Auguste à Dioclétien. Actes du colloque international organisé par l'École Française de Rome (Rome, 25–28 Mars 1992).* Rome: 227–38.

  (1998) 'Trade and traders in the Roman world: scale, structure and organisation', in *Trade, Traders and the Ancient City,* eds. H. Parkins and C. Smith. London: 129–48.

  (2001) 'Hellenistic economies: the case of Rome', in *Hellenistic Economies,* eds. Z. H. Archibald, J. Davies, V. Gabrielsen and G. J. Oliver. London: 367–78.

  (2006) *Landscapes and Cities. Rural Settlement and Civic Transformation in Early Imperial Italy.* Oxford.

Pedley, J. F. (1990) *Paestum: Greeks and Romans in Southern Italy.* London.

Penn, A. and Dalton, N. (1994) 'The architecture of society: stochastic simulation of urban movement', in *Simulating Societies: The Computer Simulation of Social Phenomena,* eds. N. Gilbert and J. Doran. London: 85–126.

Perea Yébenas, S. (1997) 'Bānos para soldados y el culto de Fortuna', in *Termalismo Antiguo,* ed. M. J. Peréx Agorreta. Madrid: 149–67.

Pérez Ballester, J., San Mártin Moro, P. A., and Berrocal Caparrós, C. (1994) 'El anfiteatro romano de Cartagena (1967–1992)', in *El Anfiteatro en la Hispania Romana,* ed. J. M. Álvarez Martínez and J. J. Enríquez Navascués. Mérida: 91–115.

Perring, D. (1991a) *Roman London.* London.

  (1991b) 'Spatial organisation and social change in Roman towns', in *City and Country in the Ancient World,* eds. J. Rich and A. Wallace-Hadrill. London: 241–72.

Perry, J. S. (2006) *The Roman Collegia: The Modern Evolution of an Ancient Concept*. Leiden.

Pflaum, H. G. (1961) *Les Carrières Procuratoriennes Équestres sous le Haut-Empire Romain*. Paris.

(1982) *Les Carrières Procuratoriennes Équestres sous le Haut-Empire Romain Supplément*. Paris.

Phang, S. E. (2001) *The Marriage of Roman Soldiers (13 BC – AD 235)*. Leiden.

Phillips, E. J. (1973) 'The Roman law on the demolition of buildings', *Latomus* 32: 86–95.

Picard, G. C. (1957) *Civitas Mactaritana*, Karthago 8. Paris.

(1976) 'La date du théâtre de Cherchel et les débuts de l'architecture théâtrale dans les provinces romaines d'Occident', *CRAI*: 386–97.

(1988) 'Essai d'interprétation du sanctuaire de Hoter Miskar à Mactar', *BCTH* n.s. 18: 17–20.

Picard, G. C. and Baillon, M. (1992) 'Le théâtre romain de Carthage', in *Afrique du nord antique et médiévale; spectacles, vie portuaire, religions*, Histoire et archéologie de l'Afrique du nord: actes du Ve colloque international. Paris: 11–27.

Pisani Sartorio, G. (1999) 'Septizonium, Septizodium, Septisolium', in *Lexicon Topographicum Urbis Romae* Vol. 4, ed. E. M. Steinby. Rome: 269–72.

Pitts, M. and Perring, D. (2006) 'The making of Britain's first urban landscapes: the case of late Iron Age and Roman Essex', *Britannia* 37: 189–212.

Poinssot, C. (1958) *Les ruines de Dougga*. Tunis.

(1969) 'M. Licinius Rufus, patronus pagi et civitatis Thuggensis', *BCTH* n.s. 5: 215–58.

Potter, T. W. (1985) 'Models of urban growth: the Cherchel excavations 1977–81', *BCTH* n.s. 19 B: 457–68.

(1995) *Towns in Late Antiquity: Iol Caesarea and its Context*. Sheffield.

Pringle, D. (1981) *The Defence of Byzantine Africa from Justinian to the Arab Conquest*, BAR Int.Ser. 99. Oxford.

Quilici, L. (1980) 'L'impianto urbanistico della Città Bassa di Palestrina', *Römische Mitteilungen* 87: 171–214.

(1989) 'La struttura della Città Inferiore di Praeneste' in *Urbanistica ed Architettura dell'Antica Praeneste*, ed. B. Coari. Palestrina: 49–67.

Quilici, L. and Quilici Gigli, S. (2001) 'Sulle mura di Norba', in *Fortificazioni antiche in Italia età repubblicane*, ed. L. Quilici and S. Quilici Gigli. Rome: 181–244.

(2003) *Santuari e Luoghi di Culto nell'Italia Antica*. Rome.

Quilici Gigli, S. (2003) 'Norba: l'acropoli minore e i suoi templi', in *Santuari e Luoghi di Culto nell'Italia Antica*, ed. L. Quilici and S. Quilici Gigli. Rome: 289–321.

Raepsaet-Charlier M.-T. (1987) *Prosopographie des Femmes de l'Ordre Sénatorial (Ier–IIe siècles)*. Louvain.

Rakob, F. (1974) 'Das Quellenheiligtum in Zaghouan und die römische Wasserleitung nach Karthago', *MDAI(R)* 81: 41–89.

Ramírez Sádaba, J. L. (1994) 'Epigrafía del anfiteatro romano de Mérida', in *El Anfiteatro en la Hispania Romana*, ed. J. M. Álvarez Martínez and J. J. Enríquez Navascués. Mérida: 285–99.

Rasbach, G. and Becker, A. (2003) 'Die spätaugusteische Stadtgründung in Lahnau-Waldgirmes', *Germania* 81: 147–99.

Rathbone, D. (1981) 'The development of agriculture in the "Ager Cosanus" during the Roman Republic: problems of evidence and interpretation', *JRS* 71: 10–23.

Rawson, B. (1966) 'Family life among the lower classes at Rome in the first two centuries of the Empire', *CPh* 61: 71–83.

Rawson, E. (1987) '*Discrimina ordinum*: The *Lex Julia Theatralis*', *PBSR* 55: 83–114.
  (1994) 'The aftermath of the Ides', in *CAH²* 9: *The Last Age of the Roman Republic 146–43 B.C.*, eds. J. Crook, A. Lintott and E. Rawson. Cambridge: 468–90.

Rebuffat, R. (1985) 'Jublains: un complexe fortifié dans l'ouest de Gaule', *RA* 1985: 237–56.

Reiter, W. (1988) *Aemilius Paullus: Conqueror of Greece*. London.

Renfrew, C. and Cherry, J. (1986) *Peer Polity Interaction and Socio-Political Change*. Cambridge.

Revell, L. (1999) 'Constructing *romanitas*: Roman public architecture and the archaeology of practice', in *TRAC 98: Proceedings of the Eighth Annual Theoretical Roman Archaeology Conference*, eds. P. Baker, C. Forcey, S. Jundi. Oxford: 52–8.
  (2000) 'The creation of multiple identities in Roman Italica', in *TRAC 1999: Proceedings of the Ninth Annual Theoretical Roman Archaeology Conference*, eds. G. Fincham, G. Harrison, R. Holland, and L. Revell. Oxford: 1–7.
  (2009) *Roman Imperialism and Local Identities*. Cambridge.

Reynolds, P. (2005) 'Hispania in the later Roman Mediterranean: ceramics and trade', in *Hispania in Late Antiquity: Current Perspectives*, eds. K. Bowes and M. Kulikowski. Leiden: 369–486.

Reynolds, J. M. and Ward-Perkins, J. B. (1952) *The Inscriptions of Roman Tripolitania*. London.

Richardson, J. S. (1986) *Hispaniae: Spain and the Development of Roman Imperialism, 218–82 BC*. Cambridge.
  (1995) '*Neque elegantem, ut arbitror, neque urbanum*: Reflections on Iberian urbanism', in *Social Complexity and the Development of Towns in Iberia. PBA* 86, eds. B. Cunliffe and S. Keay. Oxford: 339–54.

Richmond, I. A. (1933) 'Commemorative arches and city gates in the Augustan Age', *JRS* 23: 149–74.

Ripollès, P. P. (2005) 'Coinage and identity in the Roman provinces: Spain', in *Coinage and Identity in the Roman Provinces*, eds. C. Howego, V. Heuchert and A. Burnett. Oxford: 79–93.

Rives, J. (1995) *Religion and Authority in Roman Carthage from Augustus to Constantine*. Oxford.

Robert, L. (1940) *Les gladiateurs dans l'Orient grec*. Paris.

(1943) 'Sur un Papyrus de Bruxelles', *Revue de Philologie, de littérature et d'histoire anciennes* 18: 111–19.

Rodgers, B. S. (1989) 'Eumenius of Augustodunum', *AncSoc* 20: 249–66.

Rodríguez Hidalgo, J. M. (1997) 'La nueva imagen de la Itálica de Adriano', in *Italica MMCC. Actas de las Jornadas del 2.200 Aniversario de la Fundación de Itálica*, eds. A. Caballos Rufino and P. León. Seville: 87–113.

Rodríguez Hidalgo, J. M. and Keay, S. (1995) 'Recent work at Italica', in *Social Complexity and the Development of Towns in Iberia. PBA* 86, eds. B. Cunliffe and S. Keay. Oxford: 395–420.

Rogers, G. (1991) *The Sacred Identity of Ephesus*, London.

Ros, K. E. (1996) 'The Roman theater at Carthage', *AJA* 100.3: 449–89.

Rose, C. B. (1997) *Dynastic Commemoration and Imperial Portraiture in the Julio-Claudian Period*. Cambridge.

Rose, P. (2001) *Spectators and spectator comfort in Roman entertainment buildings*. MA dissertation, University of Reading.

Rosso, E. (2000) 'La série de dédicaces Julio-Claudiennes de Ruscino, Château-Roussillon (Perpignan, Pyrénées-Orientales)', *RAN* 33: 202–22.

Rostovtzeff, M. (1900) 'Pinnirapus iuvenum', *Römische Mitteilungen* 15: 223–8.

Royden, H. L. (1988) *The Magistrates of the Roman Professional Collegia in Italy from the First to the Third Century AD*. Pisa.

Rudé, G. (1952) *Paris and London in the 18th Century. Studies in Popular Protest*. London.

(1959) *The Crowd in the French Revolution*. London.

Ruoff-Väänänen, E. (1978) 'Studies in the Italian *fora*', *Historia Einzelschriften* 32.

Russell, J. (1968) 'The origin and development of the Republican forums', *Phoenix* 24: 304–36.

Rust, T. C. (2006) *Architecture, Economics, and Identity in Romano-British 'Small Towns'*, BAR Int. Ser. 1547. Oxford.

Rykwert, J. (1974) *The Idea of the Town. The Anthropology of Urban Form in Rome, Italy and the Ancient World*. Princeton.

(1978) 'The street: the use of its history', in *On Streets*, ed. S. Anderson. Cambridge, Mass.: 15–28.

Sabbatini Tumolesi, P. (1980) *Gladiatorum Paria. Annunci di spettacoli gladiatorii a Pompei*. Rome.

Saint-Amans, S. (2004) *Topographie religieuse de Thugga (Dougga): Ville romaine d'Afrique proconsulaire (Tunisie)*. Paris.

Salama, P. (2005) *Promenades d'Antiquités Africaines*. Paris.

Sallares, R. (2002) *Malaria and Rome. A History of Malaria in Ancient Italy*. Oxford.

Saller, R. (1982) *Personal Patronage in the Early Empire*. Cambridge.

Salmon, E. T. (1969) *Roman Colonization under the Republic*. London.

Salway, B. (2001) 'Travel, *Itineraria* and *Tabellaria*', in *Travel and Geography in the Roman Empire*, eds. C. Adams and R. Laurence. London: 22–109.

Sánchez, J. and Pérez, L. (1994) 'Algunos testimonios de uso y abandono de anfiteatros durante el bajo imperio en Hispania. El caso Segobricense', in *El Anfiteatro en la Hispania Romana*, eds. J. M. Álvarez Martínez and J. J. Enríquez Navascués. Mérida: 177–86.

Sánchez-Palencia, F. J., Montalvo, A. and Gijón, E. (2001) 'El Circo Romano de *Augusta Emerita*', in *El Circo en Hispania Romana*, eds. T. Nogales Basarrate and F. J. Sánchez-Palencia. Madrid: 75–95.

Sanmartí-Grego, E. (1987) 'El Foro Romano de Ampurias', in *Los Foros Romanos de las Provincias Occidentales*, ed. Ministerio de Cultura. Madrid: 55–60.

Sanmartí-Grego, E., Aquilué, X., Castanyer, P., Santos, M., and Tremoleda, J. (1994) 'El anfiteatro de Emporiae', in *El Anfiteatro en la Hispania Romana*, eds. J. M. Álvarez Martínez and J. J. Enríquez Navascués. Mérida: 119–37.

Sauer, E. (1997) 'The Augustan army spa at Bourbonne-les-Bains', in *The Roman Army as a Community*, JRA Suppl.34, eds. A. Goldsworthy and I. Haynes. Portsmouth, RI: 52–80.

Savunen, L. (1995) 'Women and elections in Pompeii', in *Women in Antiquity: New Assessments,* ed. R. Hawley and B. Levick. London: 194–206.

(1997) *Women in the Texture of Pompeii.* Helsinki.

Scheid, J. (1991) 'Sanctuaires et thermes sous l'Empire', in *Les thermes romaines. Actes de la table ronde organisée par l'École française de Rome (Rome, 11–12 Novembre 1988)*. Rome: 205–16.

Scheidel, W. (2002) 'A model of demographic change in Roman Egypt after the Antonine Plague', *JRA* 15: 97–113.

(2003) 'Germs for Rome', in *Rome the Cosmopolis*, eds. C. Edwards and G. Woolf. Cambridge: 158–77.

(2004) 'Human mobility in Roman Italy: the free population', *JRS* 94: 1–27.

Scobie, A. (1986) 'Slums, sanitation and mortality in the Roman world', *Klio* 68: 399–433.

Scott, I. and James, H. J. (2003) 'The iron objects', in *Roman Carmarthen: Excavations 1978–1993*, ed. H. James. London: 326–9.

Sear, F. (1990) 'A stranger in town: finding the way in an ancient city', *Greece and Rome* 37: 204–14.

Sear, F. (2006) *Roman Theatres: An Architectural Study*. Oxford.

Sewell, J. (2005) 'Trading places? A reappraisal of the fora at Cosa', *Ostraka* 14: 91–114.

Shaw, B. D. (1981) 'Rural markets in North Africa and the political economy', *AntAfr* 17: 37–83.

(1983) 'Soldiers and society: the army in Numidia', *Opus* II, 133–59.

Sherwin-White, A. N. (1973) *The Roman Citizenship*. Oxford.

Shirley, E. A. M. (2000) *The Construction of the Roman Legionary Fortress at Inchtuthil*. Oxford.

(2001) *Building a Roman Legionary Fortress*. Stroud.

Sillières, P. (1995) *Baelo Claudia: une cité romaine de Bétique*. Madrid.

Sirks, B. (1991) *Food for Rome. The Legal Structure of the Transportation and Processing of Supplies for the Imperial Distributions in Rome and Constantinople*. Amsterdam.

Sommella, P. (1988) *Italia Antica: L'urbanistica romana*. Rome.

Sommer, C. S. (1984) *The Military Vici of Roman Britain*. Oxford.

Speidel, M. P. (1986) 'The soldiers' homes', in *Heer und Integrationspolitik. Die Römischen Militärdiplome als Historische Quelle*, eds. W. Eck and H. Wolff. Cologne: 467–81.

Spickermann, W. (1994) 'Priesterinnen im Römischen Gallien, Germanien, und den Alpenprovinzen (1.-3. Jahrhundert n. Chr.), *Historia* 43: 189–240.

Squarciapino, M. F. (1974) *Sculture del Foro Severiano di Leptis Magna*. Rome.

Storchi Marino, A. (2000) 'Reti interregionali integrale e circuiti di mercato periodico negli indices nundinarii del Lazio e della Campana', in *Mercati permanenti e mercati periodici nel mondo romano*, ed. E. Lo Cascio. Bari: 93–130.

Storey G. R. (2004) 'Roman economies: a paradigm of their own', in *Archaeological Perspectives on Political Economies*, eds. G. M. Feinman and L. M. Nicholas. Salt Lake City: 105–28.

(2008) 'Modeling the macro-economics of the Roman Empire', in *New Perspectives on the Ancient World. Modern Perceptions, Ancient Perspectives* BAR Int. Ser. 1782, eds P. P. A. Funari, R. S. Garraffoni and B. Letalien (eds). Oxford: 93–116.

Syme, R. (1981) 'Rival cities, notably Tarraco and Barcino', *Ktema* 6: 271–85.

Thébert, Y. (2003) *Thermes romains d'Afrique du nord et leur contexte méditerranéen: études d'histoire et d'archéologie*. Rome.

Thollard, P. (1996) *Bavay Antique*. Paris.

(1997) 'Fouilles sur le forum de Bavay (1993–1997). Aire sacrée, cryptoportique et terrasse sud', *RdN* 323: 65–139.

Thollard, P. and Groetembril, S. (1999) 'Fouilles sur le forum de Bavay (1993–1998). III Habitat, voirie, et stratigraphie au sud du forum', *RdN* 333: 23–66.

Thomas, E. (2007) 'Metaphor and identity in Severan architecture: the Septizodium at Rome between "reality" and "fantasy"', in *Severan Culture*, eds. S. Swain, S. Harrison and J. Elsner. Cambridge: 327–67.

Thomas, E. and Witschel, C. (1991) 'Claim and reality in Roman building inscriptions', *PBSR* 60: 135–77.

Tilley, C. (1994) *The Phenomenology of Landscape*. London.

Tilley, M. (1996) *Donatist Martyr Stories; The Church in Conflict in Roman North Africa*. Liverpool.

Todd, M. (1978) *The Walls of Rome*, London.

Todisco, E. (1999) *I veterani in Italia in età imperiale.* Bari.

Torelli, M. (1989) 'Topografia Sacra di una Città Latina – Preneste', in *Urbanistica ed Architettura dell'Antica Praeneste,* ed. B. Coari. Palestrina: 15–30.

Tosi, G. (2003) *Gli edifici per spettacoli nell'Italia Romana.* Rome.

Tran, N. (2006) *Les Membres des Associations Romaines: Le Rang des Collegiati en Italie et en Gaules sous le Haut-Empire.* Rome.

Trifiló, S. (2008) 'Power, architecture and community in the distribution of honorary statues in Roman public space', in *TRAC 2007: Proceedings of the Seventeenth Annual Theoretical Roman Archaeology Conference London 2007,* eds. C. Fenwick, M. Wiggins, D. Wythe. Oxford: 109–20.

Van Andringa, W. (2002) *La religion en Gaule romaine: piété et politique (Ier-IIe siècle apr. J.-C.).* Paris.

(2006) 'Un grand sanctuaire de la cité des Séquanes: Villards d'Héria' in *Sanctuaires, Pratiques Cultuelles et Territoires Civiques dans l'Occident Romain,* eds. M. Dondin-Payre and M. T. Raepsaet-Charlier. Brussels: 121–34.

Ventura, A., León, P. and Márquez, C. (1998) 'Roman Córdoba in the light of recent archaeological research', in *The Archaeology of Early Roman Baetica,* JRA Suppl. 29, ed. S. Keay. Portsmouth, RI: 87–108.

Vetter, E. (1953) *Handbuch der italischen Dialekte.* Heidelberg.

Vismara, C. and Caldelli, M. L. (2000) *Epigrafia anfiteatrale dell'Occidente Romano V. Alpes Maritimae, Gallia Narbonensis, Tres Galliae, Germaniae, Brittania.* Rome.

Vittozzi, S. E. (1994) 'Forum Novum Severianum di Leptis Magna: la ricostruzione dell'area porticata e i clipei con protomi di Gorgoni e "Nereidi"', *L'Africa romana* 10: 719–51.

Walda, H. (1985) 'Provincial art in Roman Tripolitania', in *Town and Country in Roman Tripolitania,* eds. D. J. Buck and D. J. Mattingly. Oxford: 47–66.

Walda, H. and Walker, S. (1984) 'The art and architecture of Lepcis Magna: marble origins by isotropic analysis', *LibStud* 15: 81–92.

(1988) 'Isotropic analysis of marble from Lepcis Magna: revised interpretations', *LibStud* 19: 55–60.

Wallace-Hadrill, A. (2003) 'The streets of Rome as a representation of imperial power', in *The Representation and Perception of Imperial Power. Proceedings of the Third Workshop of the International Network Impact of Empire (Roman Empire, c. 200 B.C. – A.D. 476),* eds. L. De Blois, P. Erdkamp, O. Hekster, G. De Kleijn and S. Mols. Amsterdam: 189–208.

Waltzing, J. P. (1899) *Étude Historique sur les Corporations Professionelles chez les Romains vol. 3.* Louvain.

Ward-Perkins, J. B. (1948) 'Severan art and architecture at Lepcis Magna', *JRS* 38: 59–80.

(1951) 'Tripolitania and the marble trade', *JRS* 41: 89–104.

(1970) 'From Republic to Empire: reflections on the early provincial architecture of the Roman West', *JRS* 60: 1–19.

(1974) *Cities of Ancient Greece and Italy: Planning in Classical Antiquity*. London.

(1982) 'Town planning in North Africa during the first two centuries of the Empire, with special reference to Lepcis and Sabratha: character and sources', in *150-Jahr-Feier Deutsches Archäologisches Institut Rom, MDAI(R)* Suppl. 25: Berlin: 29–49.

(1993) *The Severan Buildings of Lepcis Magna*. London.

Welch, K. (1994) 'The Roman arena in Late Republican Italy: a new interpretation', *JRA* 7: 59–80.

(2003) 'A new view of the origins of the Basilica: the Atrium Regium, Graecostasis, and Roman diplomacy', *JRA* 16: 5–34.

(2007) *The Roman Amphitheatre from its Origins to the Colosseum*. Cambridge.

White, G. M. (1936) 'The Chichester amphitheatre: preliminary excavations', *AntJ* 16: 149–59.

White, R. and Barker, P. (1998) *Wroxeter: Life and Death of a Roman City*. Stroud.

Whittaker, C. R. (1990) 'The consumer city revisited: the *vicus* and the city', *JRA* 3: 110–18.

(1994) 'The politics of power: the cities of Italy', in *L'Italie d'Auguste à Dioclétien*, Rome: 127–43.

(1995) 'Do theories of the ancient city matter?', in *Urban Society in Roman Italy*, eds. T. Cornell and K. Lomas. London: 9–26.

(1996) 'Roman Africa: Augustus to Vespasian', in *CAH²* 10: *The Augustan Empire, 43 B.C. – A.D. 69*, eds. A. K. Bowman, E. Champlin and A. Lintott. Cambridge: 586–618.

Wiedemann, T. (1992) *Emperors and Gladiators*. London.

(2003) 'The patron as banker', in *'Bread and Circuses': Euergetism and Municipal Patronage in Roman Italy*, eds. T. Cornell and K. Lomas. London: 12–27.

Wightman, E. M. (1970) *Roman Trier and the Treveri*. London.

(1985) *Gallia Belgica*. London.

Williamson, G. (2005) 'Aspects of identity', in *Coinage and Identity in the Roman Provinces*, eds. C. Howego, V. Heuchert and A. Burnett. Oxford: 19–27.

Wilmott, T., Garner, D. and Ainsworth, S. (2006) 'The Roman amphitheatre at Chester: an interim account', *English Heritage Historical Review* 1: 7–23.

Wilson, A. (2007) 'Urban development in the Severan empire', in *Severan Culture*, eds. S. Swain, S. Harrison, J. Elsner. Cambridge: 290–326.

Wilson, R. and Creighton, J. D. (1999) 'Recent research on Roman Germany', in *Roman Germany: Studies in Cultural Interaction*, JRA Suppl. 32, eds. J. D. Creighton and R. Wilson. Portsmouth, RI: 9–34.

Wirth, L. (1938) 'Urbanism as a way of life', *American Journal of Sociology* 44: 1–24.

Wiseman, T. P. (1977) 'Cicero, *Pro Sulla* 60–1', *LCM* 2.2: 21–2.

(1987) *Roman Studies: Literary and Historical*. Liverpool.

(1995) *Remus: A Roman Myth*. Cambridge.

(1998) *Roman Drama and Roman History*. Exeter.

Witcher, R. (2006) 'Settlement and society in early imperial Etruria', *JRS* 96: 88–123.

Witschel, C. (1995) 'Statuen auf römischen Platzanlagen unter besonder Berücksichtigung von Timgad (Algerien)', in *Standorte: Kontext und Funktion antiker Skulptur*, ed. K. Stemmer. Berlin: 342–58.

Woolf, G. (1990) 'World-systems analysis and the Roman Empire', *JRA* 3: 44–58.

   (1996) 'Monumental writing and the expansion of Roman society in the early Empire', *JRS* 76: 22–39.

   (1998) *Becoming Roman: The Origins of Provincial Civilization in Gaul.* Cambridge.

Yegül, F. (1992) *Baths and Bathing in Classical Antiquity.* Cambridge, Mass.

Zanker, P. (1998) *Pompeii: Public and Private Life.* Cambridge, Mass.

   (2000) 'The City as symbol: Rome and the creation of an urban image', in *Romanization and the City: Creation, Transformations and Failures*, JRA Suppl. 38, ed. E. Fentress. Portsmouth, RI: 25–41.

Zevi, F. (1976) 'Alatri', in *Hellenismus in Mittelitalien*, ed. P. Zanker. Göttingen: 84–96.

   (1996) 'Pompeii della città sannitica alla colonia sillana: per un'interpretazione dei dati archeologici', in *Les élites municipales de l'Italie péninsulaire des Gracques à Néron*, ed. M. Cébeillac-Gervasoni. Naples-Rome: 125–38.

Ziccardi, A. (2000) 'Il ruolo dei circuiti di mercati periodici nell'ambito del sistema di scambio', in *Mercati permanenti e mercati periodici nel mondo romano*, ed. E. Lo Cascio. Bari: 131–48.

Zienkiewicz, J. D. (1986) *The Legionary Fortress Baths at Caerleon.* Cardiff.

Zimmer, G. (1989) *Locus datus decreto decurionum. Zur Statuenaufstellung zweier Forumsanlagen im römischen Afrika.* Munich.

Index